The Ancient Near East A HISTORY

The Ancient Near East

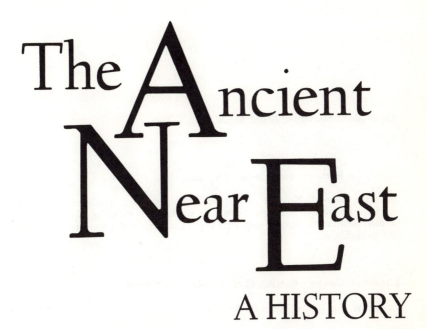

A HISTORY

William W. Hallo

William Kelly Simpson

YALE UNIVERSITY

Under the General Editorship of
John Morton Blum
YALE UNIVERSITY

 Harcourt Brace Jovanovich, Inc.

NEW YORK   CHICAGO   SAN FRANCISCO   ATLANTA

Cover photo courtesy of Standard Oil Co. (N. J.)

ISBN: 0-15-502755-7

Library of Congress Catalog Card Number: 71-155560

Printed in the United States of America

ACKNOWLEDGMENTS FOR TEXTUAL MATERIAL:

Chapter 5, Sections 2, 3, and 4, are adapted from William W. Hallo, "From Qarqar to Carchemish: Assyria and Israel in the Light of New Discoveries," *The Biblical Archaeologist Reader*, 2, edited by David Noel Freedman and Edward F. Campbell, Jr. Copyright © 1957, 1958, 1959, 1960, 1961, 1962, 1963, 1964, by American Schools of Oriental Research. Reprinted by permission of Doubleday & Company, Inc. Chapter 6, Sections 1, 2, 4, and 5, were first published in Hebrew in *Encyclopaedia Miqraith*, vol. 5 (Jerusalem: Hebrew Biblical Encyclopaedia, 1968), cols. 111–30; Chapter 6, Section 3, is an adaptation of material in the above publication. Chapter 6, Section 6, is to be published in English in *Encyclopaedia Judaica* (Jerusalem: Israel Program for Scientific Translations, forthcoming). Chapter 6, Section 7, was first published in Hebrew in *Encyclopaedia Hebraica*, Supplementary Volume (Jerusalem: Encyclopaedia Hebraica, 1967), cols. 604–08.

ACKNOWLEDGMENTS FOR ILLUSTRATIONS:

Figure 1, Ankara Arkeoloji Müzesi, Ankara; Figures 3 (left), 23, and 24, The British School of Archaeology in Iraq, London; Figures 3 (right), 4, and 15, The University Museum, Philadelphia; Figure 13, The Pierpont Morgan Library, New York; Figures 19 and 28, The Babylonian Collection, Yale University, New Haven; Figure 21, Edith Porada; Figure 25, *Atlas of Mesopotamia*, by M. A. Beek, Nelson/Elsevier, Amsterdam; Figure 27, Walter de Gruyter & Co., Berlin; Figures 30, 34, 37, 39, 40, and 44, Egyptian Museum, Cairo; Figures 32 and 36, Museum of Fine Arts, Boston; Figure 33, J.-Ph. Lauer; Figure 43, Metropolitan Museum of Art, Rogers Fund, 1934, New York.

PREFACE

This new history of the ancient Near East meets an insistent demand. Although many books are published annually in the general field of "Biblical archeology," the political and cultural development of preclassical antiquity has not been surveyed in English by specialists in the field since the days of Breasted and Olmstead. This omission is now being remedied by a number of collaborative efforts, among which pride of place unquestionably belongs to the revised edition of the *Cambridge Ancient History*. We urge the reader to refer to its fascicles as these are published; they supply a wealth of detail not attempted here. Such joint ventures, however, lack a unity of viewpoint that the material itself justifies and even requires. A measure of unity informs the grand themes underlying the vast panorama of ancient Near Eastern history; a common rhythm of successive crests and troughs punctuates historical development throughout western Asia and Egypt. The twin disciplines of Assyriology and Egyptology supply the essential tools for reconstructing such patterns. They have developed along very separate lines in the last several decades, but we have attempted to overcome their regrettable isolation from one another and to identify the major links between events and trends at both ends of the "Fertile Crescent."

An inherent limitation of our approach is its relative emphasis on Mesopotamia and Egypt at the expense of other parts of the Near East. This is not to deny the importance of those parts. Rather, it is here suggested that their historical development was not so fundamentally distinct from that of the high civilizations; the latter, abundantly attested in cuneiform and hieroglyphic, can thus serve as a paradigm for the more sporadically documented areas.

In relying heavily on the native textual sources—and, to a lesser extent, on the art and artifacts—as these have escaped destruction or survived interment over the ages, the historian faces a problem of communication. The ancient sources he confronts cry out to be heard, but their language differs from his, not just linguistically but in more profound ways. He must strive to understand not only their literal words but also the truths, often hidden in metaphors, that they have to convey. Thus he must approach them without condescension, treating their enigmas as symptoms of his own failure to grasp their true sense. Our essay, then, is an attempt to write ancient history by taking the ancient documents seriously without necessarily taking them literally. It is not only a history but a commentary on ancient history and historiography.

For older scholars, a project such as this might represent the summing up of a lifetime of reading and teaching. For us, it has meant the opening up of new vistas, insights, and relationships. Where new hypotheses seemed to require further testing, they have been left for treatment in the usual scholarly outlets. Where, however, they appeared self-evident or adequately demonstrated, they have been incorporated in the text. We have thus sought to approach a famous pedagogic ideal: to set forth matters so lucidly that the pupil may understand them, yet so profoundly that the scholar may learn from them.

Mr. Curtiss R. Hoffman was helpful in the preparation of the maps and charts for Part 1. Mrs. Susan Weeks was responsible for redrawing the line cuts in Part 2. We also wish to express our thanks to John A. Brinkman of the University of Chicago and to Richard A. Parker of Brown University, whose critical readings of the manuscript stimulated us to reconsider many debatable points. They are, of course, in no way responsible for the finished version.

WILLIAM W. HALLO

WILLIAM KELLY SIMPSON

CONTENTS

The Ancient Near East A HISTORY

[1] MESOPOTAMIA AND THE ASIATIC NEAR EAST

Stag inlaid with silver, with silver-plated antlers and head.

Bull plated and inlaid with silver.

Stag.

Bronze standard with geometric pattern and figure of a wild ass.

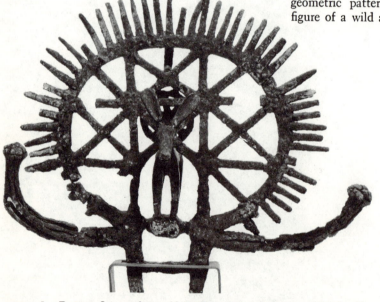

FIGURE 1   Bronze figures from Alaca Hüyük in Anatolia. (Third millennium B.C.)

THE NEAR EAST
TO THE END
OF THE STONE AGE

[1] INTRODUCTION: HALF OF HISTORY

"Beauty is truth, truth beauty," says the poet, and the claim may well be valid for beauty. But the same claim cannot be made for history. History is not truth, or at least not *the* truth. History is at best *a* truth, one among many ways of regarding the world. There are other ways with an equal claim to truth—physics, for example, or economics, or esthetics. History is distinguished from them, not by a greater universality or a lesser partiality, but simply by its own definition. Indeed, every intellectual discipline is thus delimited from every other. It is, however, easier for the individual historian to coin a definition of his field than to have all his colleagues agree to it. In fact, the problems of defining history, of establishing ground rules for the writing of history, and of tracing the history of history and its philosophy have generated a whole discipline of their own sometimes referred to as historiography.[1] The practicing historian (and the students whom he addresses) should thus be aware of the many difficult historiographic questions still to be resolved. Nevertheless, the historian must commit himself to a working definition of his trade, and the one proposed here is: *history is the temporal analysis of causality.* Thus defined, history takes its place among other modes of investigation into causation.

The premise that the cause, or origin, of a thing is a necessary and

---

[1] The progress of this discipline can be traced in journals such as *History and Theory: Studies in the Philosophy of History* and its bibliographical supplements.

sufficient explanation of it is widely accepted. In the exact sciences, for example, causation is empirically determined for variables that are not functions of time in the sense that an experiment involving given factors can be repeated next year under identical conditions and produce identical results. In the social sciences, where identical conditions never repeat, research is based on replication—that is, on utilizing the inevitable variables in order to isolate a hypothetical constant. Historical research similarly turns a seeming disability to account by relating phenomena in a temporal sequence, seeing in this chronological ordering of appropriate observations the first clue to their possible causal relationship.

This historical approach applies, of course, to many problems. Physical phenomena, for example, have their history, though till recently scientists rarely dealt with the historical factor in what they have long called "natural history." Medicine has its "case histories," and Shakespearean drama has accustomed us to seeing royal biographies called histories as well. Even theology recognizes a "history of salvation," albeit sandwiched between a beginning-time and an end-time that are beyond time and outside history. Thus broadly conceived, history or the historical method is a useful tool in many inquiries.

But we need a narrower definition, for our subject is only one kind of history, human history. Now the history of man could be treated like that of a zoological or even a botanical species. One could chronicle the emergence of the species in evolutionary terms, its differentiation into subspecies or races, and its interaction with the environment in various parts of the globe. But such a history is the province of the anthropologist. The historian's concern is with the conscious elements in mankind's long evolution, those elements, in other words, of which the subjects themselves were in some sense aware and of which they left some sort of record. Indeed, the historian's basic task is to organize that record into a meaningful causal sequence. He is not called upon to reconstruct a history antedating any such record or to speculate about the future beyond the documented present. For practical purposes, he is limited to that span of man's existence which is recorded in written documents, to which the contemporary historian may add oral evidence and such new mediums of communication as modern technology may devise. For all periods, material and artistic remains will add important dimensions to the evidence of the texts, but in the absence of texts they remain mute and enigmatic; they cannot constitute human history. We shall therefore further restrict our definition of human history as temporal analysis of causality *applied to the texts and other documentary remains of the past.*[2]

Strictly speaking, then, human history begins with writing. It begins

2 Compare Lee Benson, "Causation and the American Civil War: Two Appraisals," *History and Theory: Studies in the Philosophy of History* 1 (1961):163: "The historian's job is to explain human behavior over time."

when writing begins and *where* writing begins. It does not begin everywhere on earth at the same time, because texts do not begin to be written at the same time all over the earth. Writing began in the ancient Near East, specifically Sumer, and that is why, in a real sense, "history begins at Sumer." Writing spread quickly to Egypt and Elam, a little more slowly to the rest of the Near East. But it did not spread beyond the Near East for a very long time. Thus we can trace almost three thousand years of history in the Near East before we can speak of any real history in the rest of Asia, Africa, and Europe, let alone in the rest of the world. And the ancient Near East is, or should be, the province not only of the historian of the Near East but also of the historian of mankind in general. For half the recorded span of human history, it is the only part of the world that has a history. It is, in short, half of history.

It is the purpose of this volume to trace this half of history from its beginnings in prehistory to its convergence with the beginnings of the history of all Eurasia and Africa.

[2] AGES OF THE EARTH AND AGES OF MAN

Compared to the lifetime of an individual, or even of a nation or a culture, half of history may seem a long time. But it is only a small fraction of the total span of man's sojourn on earth to date. In turn, the human phase of earthly history occupies but a fraction of the present (Cenozoic) geological era, and this of the putative age of the earth itself (about 3,350 million years). It is as if every temporal dimension was a box contained inside another box that was not just larger but whole orders of magnitude larger. Such awesome proportions cannot be represented by a linear graph but can be expressed only in three-dimensional terms. We may, however, leave the earth and its geological eras out of our account. For purposes of perspective, it will suffice if we identify our present geological period. It is called the Quarternary Period by reason of being the fourth geological period during which some form of life has been present on earth, or the Pleistocene Period as being the most recent. The one million years of its existence thus far may also be designated as the Glacial Period, or Ice Age, for it underwent four great periods of glaciation during which the earth's temperature dropped so much that at higher altitudes and latitudes, much of the earth's surface, at least in the Northern Hemisphere, was covered by thick sheets of ice as is the polar ice cap today. Most geologists use the evidence of these successive glaciations to divide the period into three epochs: a Lower Pleistocene (including preglacial age, first glaciation, and first interglacial age), a Middle Pleistocene (second and third glaciations, with a second, or great, interglacial age in be-

tween), and an Upper Pleistocene (third interglacial and fourth glaciation). They differ as to whether the time since then marks a postglacial[3]
epoch or merely a fourth interglacial age, in which case the earth is headed
for still another ice age.[4]

Geology, however, is the study of the earth; the study of man, or
anthropology, prefers its own terminology for the same period, based on
the evidence of human culture. For man has been a part of the world
scene since the beginning of the Pleistocene Period. One of the principal
means[5] of distinguishing true man from his more apelike forebears in the
evolutionary scale is his mastery of tools, and the earliest tools he used
were made of stone—at least they are the first whose utilization can be
detected by modern anthropologists, unlike wood and other perishable
materials. Thus the anthropologist refers to the Pleistocene Period[6] as the
Stone Age or, more specifically, the Old Stone Age (Paleolithicum).
Subsequent periods of human development are similarly labeled by the
principal material or source of energy that served as the foundation of
human culture, so that the Stone Age is followed by the Bronze, the Iron,
and, most recently, the Atomic Age. In this usage, the historian is generally
in agreement with the anthropologist. There is ancient precedent, for as
early as the first century A.D., Lucretius coined the concept of Stone,
Copper, and Iron ages, while his Chinese contemporary, Yüan Kang, independently arrived at a similar concept. Before that, the human condition
was regarded as gradually declining. Hesiod began with the semidivine
Golden Age, passed through the Silver and Bronze ages, and considered the
immediate Homeric past the Heroic Age. By his logic, ours would represent
the basest age of all, a true stone age.[7] We will meet similar concepts of
history in ancient Near Eastern thought.

The anthropologist's finer subdivisions of the Paleolithic Age are
based on cultural assemblages[8] likewise derived from traces of human
existence and activity[9] and differ from those of geology. All of the great
sweep of the Lower and Middle Pleistocene is generally comprised in the

[3] In global terms, neo-thermal. Compare Grahame Clark, World Prehistory: A New
Outline, 2nd ed. (Cambridge: Cambridge University Press, 1969), pp. 21–23.
[4] A popular theme in contemporary apocalyptic literature. Compare Max Lerner,
Ideas for the Ice Age: Studies in a Revolutionary Era (New York: Viking Press, 1941).
[5] Perhaps the only one. Jacquetta Hawkes and Sir Leonard Woolley, Prehistory and
the Beginnings of Civilization, History of Mankind: Cultural and Scientific Development, vol. 1 (New York: Harper & Row, 1963), p. 37. Theoretically, one could con-
ceive of the existence of some tool-making animal that was not human or even ancestral to the human stock, but this possibility has never been seriously entertained.
[6] Or the first 99 percent of it; see the preceding paragraph.
[7] Robert F. Heizer, "The Background of Thomsen's Three-age System," Technology
and Culture 3 (1962):262.
[8] An assemblage is the repertory of tools, weapons, and other artifacts that characterize
a given culture.
[9] Compare Miles Burkitt, The Old Stone Age: A Study of Palaeolithic Times, 3rd ed.
(London: Bowes and Bowes, 1955).

so-called Lower Paleolithic Age. In turn, the Upper Pleistocene comprises two cultural periods, the Middle and Upper Paleolithic. But these designations are not used by all scholars in an absolute chronological sense; some prefer to use them to mark relative stages in the slow development of human culture. When such stages can be identified with complex assemblages at particular sites, they are given, in addition, the name of the type site, that is, the first site at which they were identified. For example, a typical Upper Paleolithic assemblage is the Acheulian. It is named for Acheul in France, where it was first identified. But it is also applied to finds from other sites in Europe as well as in Asia and Africa. Similarly, a particularly characteristic Middle and Upper Paleolithic assemblage is the Mousterian, or Levalloiso-Mousterian.

But the dating of these cultures remains highly problematic, as does their identification with a number of comparable assemblages in widely scattered areas. Therefore, the terminology of prehistoric anthropology of necessity uses a bewildering array of such provisional type site names. They illustrate the immense and perhaps insurmountable obstacle to proving larger interconnections solely by inference from skeletal and material remains—in short, to writing the "history of prehistory."

[3] THE NEAR EAST IN THE PALEOLITHIC AGE

The Lower Paleolithic witnessed the first three glaciations of the Pleistocene Ice Age, and the two great interglacial periods that separated them. In this uncertain environment, hominids (true men) of various species branched fully from the common ancestral stock of the higher primates. Their gradual assumption of an erect stature and the consequent freeing of their hands for the employment of stone tools were symptoms, and perhaps also causes, of the bifurcation. The tools were chiefly hand axes consisting of simple pebbles so primitively worked that it is often hard to distinguish them from pebbles worn smooth by water or chance; if wooden tools were used, they have left no trace. Other distinguishing human traits that may have begun to emerge this early were the ability to make (or at least preserve) fire and the rudiments of articulate speech. All these biological and cultural developments took place against a background of drastic climatic alterations and violent geological upheavals and in competition with subhuman species not only far more powerful but also in many cases more numerous. At any one time, the human population of the Lower Paleolithic cannot have numbered more than a few thousand, and large parts of the world, including northern Eurasia and all of America and Australia, were entirely uninhabited. It is now generally thought that the first hominids originated in sub-Saharan Africa and that they spread gradually from there into northern Africa and southern Eurasia. The Near East does not play a particularly conspicuous role in this development, except insofar as it happens already to constitute the approximate geographic midpoint of this first *oikumene*.[10]

The Middle Paleolithic embraces the last (third) interglacial phase and the beginnings of the last (fourth) glaciation. It is dominated by a skeletal type and a cultural assemblage that archeologists are tempted to associate with each other—in spite of the risk always involved in relating race and culture without documentary evidence. The biological type characteristic of the period is the so-called Neanderthal man, and it is associated with an industry called Mousterian (after the type site of Le Moustier in southern France) throughout the Mediterranean world and its hinterland. The stone tools characteristic of Mousterian sites had advanced beyond the simpler pebbles of Lower Paleolithic times to the so-called flake technique of detaching a usable fragment, thick and clumsy but already sharp, from a flint core. But the hominid types who apparently made and wielded these tools were not ancestral to ourselves; they were the last of several abortive offshoots from the hominid family tree destined for extinction.

The end of Neanderthal man marks the transition to the Upper Paleolithic and is in fact the first "historical" event (or, rather, process) that seems to rest on more than mere speculation. It took place during the inhospitable climax of the last glaciation and pitted the surviving Neanderthalers against the first true homo sapiens, who emerged, it is thought, from a center in the Near East. Equipped with such advantages as clothing and fully developed language, homo sapiens must have either exterminated the more primitive hominids outright or driven him to slow extinction on the northern borders of the habitable area.[11] In either case, the result was the occupation of the entire area from the Atlantic seaboard to Persia by the ancestors of modern man and their spread to East Asia and thence to the Western Hemisphere. Though some "paleoanthropic"[12] types survived somewhat longer in peripheral regions like East Asia, their numbers dwindled to insignificance, while homo sapiens experienced a first real population explosion in the Mediterranean heartland, whose total population probably passed the million mark during this period. At this time, too, the human species began to develop the unmistakable differentiations that we define as racial—that is, physical differences that, while not a barrier to fertile intermarriage, nevertheless rein-

---

[10] That is, "the inhabited world: used by the Greeks to designate their portion of the earth, as opposed to barbarian lands." *Greek-English Lexicon*, 6th ed., ed., H. G. Liddell and R. Scott (New York: Harper & Brothers, 1878), p. 1076.

[11] A third theory now finding favor is that Neanderthal man was simply an earlier subspecies of homo sapiens; that he coexisted for a time with a later subspecies called Cro-Magnon; and that the latter entered Europe only after the retreat of the ice sheet that had isolated and exterminated the Paleoanthropic species.

[12] A term sometimes used to describe the various early hominid types not ancestral to modern man.

forced, and were reinforced by, the emerging separation of homo sapiens into the three major and several minor races still distinguishable on earth today.

The pace of evolution was even greater in the cultural than in the biological realm during the Upper Paleolithic. Although much briefer than the two preceding stages, the end of the Old Stone Age and of the last glaciation witnessed much more dramatic cultural developments, for each development made others possible or necessary or both. The roles of clothing and language have already been mentioned as possible factors in the triumph of neoanthropic[13] man; by facilitating the transmission of new insights to succeeding generations, language must also have contributed to the relatively rapid emergence of his characteristic stone tool, the Aurignacian flint blade. Its slender profile meant an appreciable advantage in both sharpness and lightness over the earlier flake type—and over the hominids limited to them. Another characteristic stone tool of the period was the burin, or graver, which made it possible to work in bone. With bone, there emerged the needle, allowing not only improved clothing and shelter but also nets for fishing that, in turn, inspired the first rudimentary rafts and boats. Finally, stone began to be worked into crude vessels, including the first lamps; with these (and with torches) it was possible to penetrate the depths of the caves in which Upper Paleolithic men left their most remarkable achievements, the cave paintings of southern France and Spain. These paintings have been aptly termed "the most improbable event in human history,"[14] and they disclose a tantalizing glimpse not only of the physical appearance of the human habitat at the end of the Old Stone Age and man's esthetic response to it but also of the dim origins of mental processes, especially of religious impulses. The very inaccessibility of the paintings suggests that the esthetic impulse was not their primary motivation; it is more tempting to regard them as functional (for example, to assure the success of the hunt by magical means).[15] While it is still hazardous to speculate on the precise significance of such early expressions of the emerging human spirit, future research into some enduring traits of historical religions may yet enable us to discover some links between Upper Paleolithic concepts and, for example, Shamanistic survivals in Sumerian religion.[16]

[13] That is, the physical type of modern man.

[14] Hawkes and Woolley, *Prehistory and the Beginnings of Civilization*, p. 186.

[15] Gertrude Rachel Levy, *The Gate of Horn: A Study of the Religious Conceptions of the Stone Age, and Their Influence upon European Thought* (New York: Book Collectors Society, 1946), pp. 9–25.

[16] J. J. A. van Dijk, "Les contacts ethniques dans la Mésopotamie et les syncrétismes da la religion Sumérienne," in Sven S. Hartman, ed., *Syncretism, Scripta Instituti Donneriani Aboensis*, vol. 3 (Stockholm: Almqvist & Wiksell, 1969), pp. 171–206, esp. 174 ff. Beatrice Laura Goff, *Symbols of Prehistoric Mesopotamia* (New Haven: Yale University Press, 1963), pp. 212–64.

[4] THE NEOLITHIC REVOLUTION

Geologists and archeologists share a measure of uncertainty about the nature—and nomenclature—of the age that next ensued. The last great Pleistocene glaciation, and with it the Old Stone Age, came to an end about ten thousand years ago. The more temperate climate that has since prevailed may represent simply a new interglacial phase on the way to still another glaciation, or it may mark the beginning of a wholly new post-glacial period. The question can be evaded, if not resolved, by applying the rather noncommittal term Holocene (wholly recent) to the period since the Pleistocene and into the foreseeable future. For their part, archeologists have no trouble distinguishing the New Stone Age (Neolithic) from the Old Stone Age, but they disagree over what, if any, phase separates the two ages in any given part of the inhabited world. Here the term Mesolithic represents a convenient compromise to identify whatever cultural strata[17] and assemblages cannot be accommodated convincingly in either the Paleolithic or the Neolithic periods.

The uncertainty is to some extent aggravated by the fact that, with the increasing sophistication of material remains, it becomes progressively harder to treat the entire Mediterranean world, or even the Near East in particular, as a cultural unit. Whereas many widely scattered Paleolithic assemblages could be generally described as Acheulian or, later, as Levalloiso-Mousterian, before the end of the Old Stone Age Egypt and western Asia part ways. Some archeologists deny the existence of a distinct Mesolithic culture in Egypt except for intrusive elements from Palestine. Westernmost Asia, however, entered fully into the Mesolithic developments known from Europe. This is particularly well attested for Palestine, thanks especially to the important discoveries in the caves of Mt. Carmel and to so-called Natufian assemblages.

With their geographical and chronological extent limited, the principal Mesolithic finds may be quickly characterized. The stone tools of the period represent a further refinement of Paleolithic techniques, for the flint blades typical of Upper Paleolithic times were now successfully "miniaturized." The stone implements and weapons most characteristic of this period are therefore called microliths. They were well suited to the primary economic pattern of the period, which was as before the hunting of wild animals by the men and the gathering of chiefly wild plants by the women. Wherever man progressed beyond this essentially Paleolithic stage, he may be said to have entered the Neolithic Period. This did not happen everywhere at the same time. Thus, while the beginning of the Mesolithic is dated at about 10,000 B.C. by fairly universal geological considerations, the beginning of the Neolithic is defined by localized cultural develop-

---

[17] A stratum is a level of occupation, burial, or waste disposal at an archeological site that can be distinguished visually from those below (normally earlier) and from those above (normally later).

ments. And while the Mesolithic innovations grew organically from Paleolithic precedents, the Neolithic inventions implied a radical departure in the whole relationship of man to nature, with profound implications for all succeeding ages. They thus deserve the label first applied by Childe: the Neolithic Revolution.[18] We might also speak of them as the agricultural revolution, for what was involved was principally the domestication of plants and animals and the resulting emergence of the farming village as a new nexus of social organization.

Recent discoveries have tended to show that this revolution, by whatever name, took place first in the Near East about 7000, and spread gradually to the rest of the globe penetrating as far as China by about 4000.[19] Though some still look for the possibility of a later, independent duplication of the development in isolated areas like the New World, the concept of the monogenesis[20] of agriculture, if accepted, provides the second great prehistoric event that can be traced to the Near East when we recall that the origin of the neoanthropic race that triumphed over the Neanderthalers of the Upper Paleolithic has also been sought in this area. Then as now and for millennia subsequently, the Near East was the center of the oikumene, and its pivotal position may have contributed to its repeated, catalytic role. But a further factor now seems to have been operative. Two kinds of plant and four breeds of animal were involved in the beginnings of domestication. All six are present in the Near East, and only in the Near East. In fact, this is true not even of the entire Near East but only of one restricted part of it—the hilly flanks of the area watered by the Tigris and Euphrates rivers.

For some decades it was fashionable, following Breasted,[21] to designate the valleys of the Tigris-Euphrates and Nile and the intervening Mediterranean littoral as the Fertile Crescent. And, indeed, this was the site of several of the earliest high civilizations. But in fact the natural resources of these areas and their climatic conditions were not conducive to incipient agriculture. They required massive, sophisticated human effort to yield the abundance for which they later became famous, and the successful response to the challenge and opportunity that they posed for such efforts had no doubt much to do with the genesis of their high civilizations. For the Neolithic Revolution, however, a more hospitable environment was required. It is precisely the piedmont and upland areas beyond and above the "Fertile Crescent" (Figure 2) that provided the two necessary and sufficient conditions: adequate rainfall and the presence of the

---

[18] V. Gordon Childe, *Man Makes Himself* (London: Watts & Co., 1936), pp. 74–117.

[19] Hawkes and Woolley, *Prehistory and the Beginnings of Civilization*, p. 255.

[20] That is, the concept of a single origin for any given innovation.

[21] James Henry Breasted introduced the term in *Ancient Times: A History of the Early World* (Boston: Ginn and Co., 1916), pp. 100–07 and map between pp. 100 and 101. The term is still used in the posthumous edition of his textbook, *The Conquest of Civilization* (New York: Literary Guild of America, 1938), pp. 116–21.

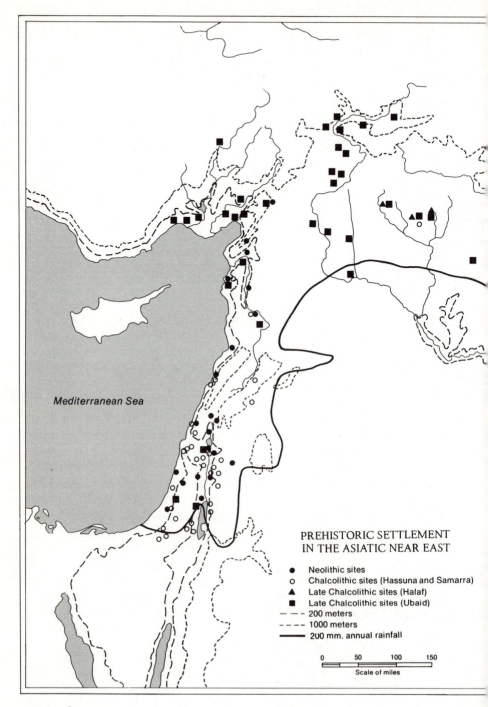

PREHISTORIC SETTLEMENT
IN THE ASIATIC NEAR EAST

● Neolithic sites
○ Chalcolithic sites (Hassuna and Samarra)
▲ Late Chalcolithic sites (Halaf)
■ Late Chalcolithic sites (Ubaid)
— — — 200 meters
- - - - - 1000 meters
——— 200 mm. annual rainfall

Mediterranean Sea

0   50   100   150
Scale of miles

FIGURE 2

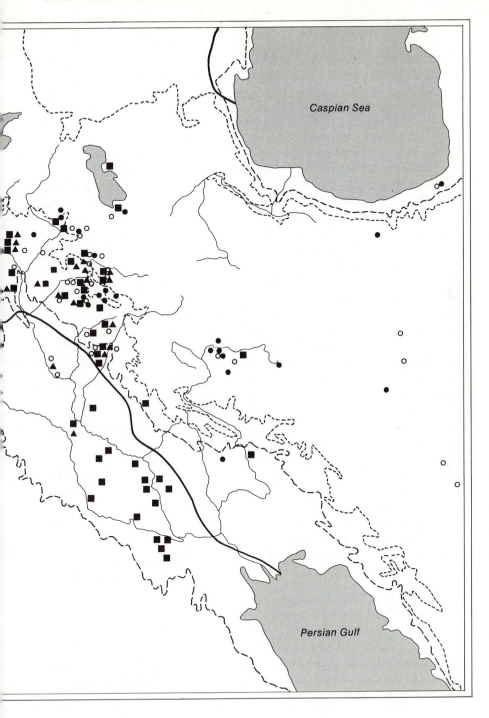

six wild plant and animal species that were to be domesticated—namely, emmer wheat, barley, goats, sheep, pigs, and the ancestor of the cow. It may be added that dogs had been domesticated, after a fashion, long before Neolithic times—not, like the other species, for the sake of their meat, milk,[22] hide, or wool, but as scavengers and particularly for the hunting needs of Paleolithic man.

What was the "cause" of the revolution of Neolithic times? If prehistoric events are hard to reconstruct, their causes are even more elusive. They are no more due to mere chance than are historical events, and we can no longer be satisfied with the kind of simplistic explanations once popular. If the chance discovery that discarded seeds subsequently sprouted led to intentional cultivation after 10,000, we still want to know why that discovery was not made in the preceding thirty thousand years when the same wild grains were being gathered or, as is much more probable, if the same discovery had been made long and often before, why it had not led earlier to intentional planting of the seed. Two proposed answers deserve serious consideration. One suggests that a dramatic change in climate, particularly a drop in temperature and rainfall, was a "shock stimulus" to new methods of ensuring adequate food supplies.[23] But like the old and now largely discredited theories of "climatic determinism,"[24] the newer ones do not seem to accord with the latest findings. Fluctuations in climate, where they can be detected at all in Neolithic times, are too slight and ambiguous to provide a convincing explanation for the revolutionary development at issue. The other answer looks rather to the human, or cultural, side of the ecological equation. Necessity, as usual, proves the mother of invention—but necessity not in the form of advancing desiccation but, it is suggested, of less tractable human relationships, or simply the effect of another major increase in the human population of the Near East.[25] Throughout the Upper Paleolithic, the wild game and vegetation of the region had sufficed to sustain the existing population because man was free to follow both from lowland to upland with each passing season. But an expanding population ruled out this possibility. Territorialism (a fundamental, biological characteristic) and tribal organization inherited from Paleolithic times, must have combined to urge Neolithic man to put an enforced stop to the untrammeled nomadism of his fellow man, though

[22] It is not certain that milking began with the beginning of domestication; when it did, it may well have started with the goat rather than the cow.

[23] On the assumption that as the soil dried out, it became progressively less fertile.

[24] See, for example, Elsworth Huntington, *Civilization and Climate* (New Haven: Yale University Press, 1915).

[25] Compare the massive effect that the contemporary population explosion is having and will yet have on our own culture. The possible causes of such population explosions were then, as now, complex. The notion that it is greater longevity is contradicted both by modern statistics (when due allowance is made for declining infant mortality) and by the ancient Near Eastern belief in a periodically decreasing life span.

as yet without demonstrable resort to much overt hostility. Once men were no longer free to follow the shifting food supplies to their seasonal source, they were forced to acclimatize the food supply to the fixed territory that they could defend. To this end, they now made use of what they doubtless knew all along—that grains grew where seeds were planted.

The domestication of animals must have evolved in response to the same challenge; indeed, on the western flanks of the Zagros and the southern shore of the Caspian, it preceded the domestication of plants, while at the other principal type sites of the Neolithic Revolution, that is, Jericho and other centers of the earlier Natufian assemblages in Palestine, the order was reversed. It is harder to reconstruct the actual technique by which animals may have been domesticated, but the *fact* of their domestication can be recognized clearly wherever the teeth and other remains of any one species can be identified as belonging predominantly to yearlings. At this age the meat is at its best, but the animal is in full vigor and hard to trap or hunt by Stone Age methods. Only a herd successfully penned or otherwise mastered by man could be slaughtered at this age. This discovery, made first at Jarmo,[26] has since been repeated at other sites.

If the domestication of plants and animals did not always follow the same order, the third element in the Neolithic Revolution, the evolution from temporary shelter to permanent settlement, was always the last step in the process. It has been traced in all three of the areas already mentioned—Caspian, Zagros, and Palestine—as well as at Catal Hüyük in Anatolia, with its startling clay and stone statuettes of deities and animals and its wall paintings and reliefs; but it is perhaps most dramatically illustrated at Jericho, where the transition can be traced all the way from open-air site to walled town, all of it falling within that phase of the Neolithic that is characterized by the use of stone for the manufacture of vessels—either exclusively or at least to the exclusion of clay—and is therefore called the prepottery (or aceramic) Neolithic. The introduction of pottery meant a change whose significance we must now explore.

[5] CERAMICS AND PREHISTORY: THE CHALCOLITHIC AGE

The invention of pottery can hardly be said to rival the epochal significance of the domestication of plants and animals, and archeologists do not date a new developmental or chronological epoch by it. It replaced

[26] Robert J. Braidwood, *The Near East and the Foundations for Civilization: An Essay in Appraisal of the General Evidence*, Condon Lecture Publications, vol. 7 (Eugene: Oregon State System of Higher Education, 1952), p. 30. For a first-hand account of life on this excavation, see Linda Braidwood, *Digging Beyond the Tigris: An American Woman Archeologist's Story of Life on a "Dig" in the Kurdish Hills of Iraq* (New York: Henry Schuman, 1953).

stone in the manufacture of vessels (except for votive or artistic purposes) but not of tools and hunting weapons; indeed stone axes and adzes remained characteristic for all of the Neolithic,[27] so that stone and pottery existed side by side in the later part of the period. It was only when metal began to replace stone in the production of tools and weapons that the New Stone Age can be said to end. But if the invention of pottery is not fundamental for history, it is nonetheless of supreme importance for the historian. For, once the basic ceramic techniques had been mastered, clay proved so much more workable than stone that it quickly became not only the most abundant source of objects in man's material repertory but also the readiest medium for reflecting every change in his artistic taste and expression. By virtue of both its great numbers and its variety, pottery serves as the archeologist's principal cultural and chronological determinant before the beginning of written records.

The massive addition of clay to the store of human resources is not likely to have taken place at the same altitudes as the Neolithic Revolution. The better clays used in modern times for the manufacture of porcelain are not found in the Near East at all, and even the secondary clays used for more primitive pottery are usually limited, in upland country, to lake and river beds.[28] Thus, while the first examples of pottery can be found at the early Neolithic sites of Jericho and Jarmo, the real flowering of ceramics had to wait until the "formative" stage of Near Eastern culture, when the "incipient agriculturists" began to move their permanent settlements from the high altitude and rainfall belts of the prepottery Neolithic down to a zone of more moderate altitude and rainfall—generally speaking to the 200–450 meter belt and the isohyetal belt of 200–400 millimeters (see Figure 2, page 12). This pattern of settlement emerged by the end of the seventh millennium and is attested in a great sweep of pottery-using sites from the Aegean in the west through Anatolia, Syria-Palestine, northern Mesopotamia, and Iran.

The second great step brought pottery cultures lower, into areas where rainfall was not adequate for agriculture without the sophisticated utilization of ground water (notably southern Mesopotamia and Egypt), and stimulated a "florescent"[29] period of cultural progress that laid the basis

[27] It is conceivable, though hardly susceptible to proof, that the later Sumerian veneration of the pickaxe goes back to some dim remembrance or recognition of its fundamental importance in the Neolithic economy.
[28] Hawkes and Woolley, *Prehistory and the Beginnings of Civilization*, p. 302. Unbaked clay vessels may, of course, have been made for millennia at all kinds of locations but would normally be preserved only by an accidental conflagration.
[29] "Formative," "incipient agriculturists," and "florescent" are the terms used by the University of Chicago archeologists to identify the successive stages of the last prehistoric periods identified in their excavations. See Robert M. Adams, "Developmental Stages in Ancient Mesopotamia," in Julian H. Steward, ed., *Irrigation Civilizations: A Comparative Study*, Social Science Monographs, vol. 1 (Washington: Pan American Union, Social Science Section, Department of Cultural Affairs, 1955), pp. 6–18.

of true civilization by the end of the fourth millennium. The last three millennia of the Stone Age, whose record can best be read from their ceramic remains, also form a crucial period in the transition from stone to metal technology. It may therefore properly be called the Chalcolithic Age. Although this term is often applied to specific areas, such as Anatolia, where actual metal objects began to turn up, it serves as a reminder that all the areas mentioned went through comparable cultural stages with more uniformity than the many separate designations of cultural assemblages currently employed in archeology might suggest.

Briefly, the most important of these assemblages can be identified here (at least for Mesopotamia, where they are best attested and serve as a kind of paradigm for adjacent areas). The earliest Mesopotamian pottery cultures (ca. 6000–4300) are named Hassuna, Samarra, and Halaf (after their type sites) in the north and Ubaid in the south.[30] The developed Ubaid style prevailed throughout Mesopotamia from about 4300 to 3500 according to one estimate. Thereafter the two halves of the country diverged again, with Uruk giving its name to the typical southern cultures and Tepe Gawra to those of the north.

In all the earlier assemblages, pottery was the outstanding element, achieving an artistic and technical perfection rarely surpassed in all subsequent history and worthy of serving to characterize the cultures as a whole (see Figure 3).

The later prehistoric cultures also included increasingly important architectural remains, but their other nonceramic components are generally less conspicuous than pottery in the excavations, being less durable, less numerous, or both. We are not, however, solely dependent on surviving material remains for the reconstruction of Neolithic and Chalcolithic culture and society. If we look at the records of the literate periods that follow, we find embedded in the later Sumerian, Akkadian, and (less often) Hittite vocabularies, a number of pre-Sumerian or substrate words that are a heritage from earlier periods. These can be used, with due reserve, to corroborate and complement the archeological record.[31]

Among the earliest substrate words are certain kinship terms, such as those roughly equivalent to our father-in-law, mother-in-law, son-in-law, daughter-in-law, brother-in-law, and perhaps clan. (Even earlier are the well-nigh universal words for father and mother, but their universality makes them of no use here.)[32] But Sumerian kinship terminology has not yet

[30] The first and second of the several stages that make up the Ubaid sequence are sometimes referred to as Eridu and Haji Mohammed respectively.

[31] Compare in detail Armas Salonen, *Zum Aufbau der Substrate im Sumerischen*, Studia Orientalia, vol. 37, part 3 (Helsinki: Societas Orientalis Fennica, 1968).

[32] Compare Maurice Lambert, "De quelques noms de parenté dans les langues mésopotamiennes," *Groupe Linguistique d'Etudes Chamito-Sémitiques* 9 (1962):52–54; and Maurice Lambert, "Les Noms du Père en Sumérien," in Zeki Velidi Togan, ed., *Proceedings of the Twenty-second Congress of Orientalists* [held in Istanbul, September, 1951] (Leiden: E. J. Brill, 1957), pp. 27–29.

FIGURE 3   Polychrome pottery of the Halaf style from Arpa-chiyah and Tepe Gawra.

been subjected to the rigorous methods of anthropology, and the precise functional significance of these early words still awaits evaluation.[33]

A somewhat more transparent survival of Neolithic (and perhaps even earlier) times is made up of a select group of words for stone weapons, notably various maces and the axe. But it should be noted that the pre-pottery Neolithic was a generally pacific time in human relations,[34] and

[33] Compare Åke W. Sjöberg, "Zu einigen Verwandtschaftsbezeichnungen im Sumeri-schen," in Dietz Otto Edzard, ed., *Heidelberger Studien zum Alten Orient Adam Falkenstein zum 17. September 1966* (Wiesbaden: Otto Harrassowitz, 1967), pp. 201–31.

[34] As indicated by the absence of fortifications in Neolithic settlements. The exception is Jericho, which, with its extraordinary wealth, may have excited the envy of her neighbors.

these words describe (and the comparable archeological finds of the period constitute) weapons not of war so much as of the hunt. It is thus not surprising to find the term for pitfall in this early vocabulary.

The domestication of plants and animals left linguistic traces in Sumerian, some of whose oldest identifiable professional names are those for plowman, miller, and shepherd-boy. An only slightly later stage supplied the more specialized terms for baker, fuller, and leatherworker, as well as for herdsman, yoke, sheaf, and sickle—the last being, next to the pickaxe, perhaps the most characteristic stone tool in the Neolithic repertory. This period also bequeathed to later Sumerian much of the terminology for beer-brewing, beginning with the grain from which it derived, the malt produced for germinating barley or emmer wheat, the mash produced by malting the cereal, and the end product, emmer-beer.

The complex brewing process virtually presupposes the existence of a diversified, watertight pottery, and here orthographic evidence is added to linguistic and archeological remains. For the earliest precursors of cuneiform writing show a variety of clay vessels in all possible clarity,[35] and in many cases these can be linked with the names of vessels attested in later texts or with actual surviving pottery forms.[36] The progress of ceramic techniques can be gauged by the similar emergence of signs, words, and actual finds of ovens, kilns, and, ultimately, of the potter's wheel. This last was not an unmixed blessing, however. The mass production it made possible also caused a decline in decorative style.[37]

Similar evidence points to gradual advances at this time in other activities directly related to the natural resources of southern Mesopotamia. The abundant clay lent itself not only to ceramics but to building in brick, the more so as the area was extremely poor in stone and lumber. The latter deficiency was compensated for however by a careful cultivation of fruit trees, aromatic woods, and, though it is harder to prove, grape-bearing vines. The abundant reed of the southern marshes encouraged basketry, while the ubiquitous flax of the ancient world probably inspired the first spinning and weaving before wool was discovered to be a superior source for thread. With these resources, the primary needs of Chalcolithic Mesopotamia were satisfied. Luxuries, however, had to come from abroad, and

[35] Armas Salonen, *Die Hausgeräte der Alten Mesopotamier nach Sumerisch-Akkadischen Quellen*, vol. 2, "Gefässe," Annales Academiae Scientiarum Fennicae Ser. B, Tom. 144 (1966):41–47.

[36] For a complete typology of ceramic forms, see Pinhas Delougaz, *Pottery from the Diyala Region*, Oriental Institute Publications, vol. 63 (Chicago: University of Chicago Press, 1952).

[37] Adams, "Developmental Stages in Ancient Mesopotamia," pp. 10 ff., dates this to the beginning of the Uruk period. Compare also Joan Oates, "Ur and Eridu, the Prehistory," M. E. L. Mallowan and D. J. Wiseman, eds., *Ur in Retrospect: In Memory of Sir C. Leonard Woolley* (London: British School of Archeology in Iraq, 1960), pp. 39 ff.

the first traders (like their successors in the Bronze Age) specialized in the importation of such relatively light but expensive nonessentials as precious and semiprecious stones, copper, and perhaps gold. These words and the associated professional and technical terms (smith, lapidary, craftsman, bronze, bellows) go back to a very early period. Of particular interest in this connection is the emergence of seals made of semiprecious stones and carved with designs and, later, inscriptions to identify their owners. These seals, in the form first of stamps and buttons[38] and later of cylinders, became characteristic of Mesopotamian culture. They probably owe their origin again to the prior prevalence of pottery, for they are readily impressed (or, in the case of cylinder seals, rolled) on the wet surface of vessels, bricks, or tablets before these are baked. They thus provide a convenient mark of ownership and attest to the emerging concept of private property; in the case of the later legal tablets, they may also serve to show that the seal-owner attested a court case, receipted a delivery, or obligated himself to abide by a contract. As such they are a principal, if indirect, testimony to the early emergence of legal and economic institutions in Mesopotamia. But beyond this, their decoration also serves as the single most abundant and continuous record of artistic development in Mesopotamia and in the countries under Mesopotamian influence.[39]

The art of the seals—and of the pottery—is also important for another reason, since it provides some of our best clues to the religious concepts of the Chalcolithic Age, as did the sculptures of Catal Hüyük for the pre-pottery Neolithic or the cave paintings for the Upper Paleolithic. Although this art is difficult to interpret, it occasionally bears comparison with religious concepts and motifs found more explicitly in later textual sources. It is sometimes geometric in character and sometimes representational, and at least one theory is that many of the human and animal figures were derived from the geometric designs (instead of vice versa).[40] Other evidence for religious expression is provided by the beginning of a recognizable temple architecture, but this development can best be traced at a more advanced level.

[6] ETHNOLOGY AND THE DAWN OF HISTORY

Physical, cultural and linguistic characteristics are the three classic traits that the individual shares with the group. (Advocates of the "collective unconscious" might add the psychological dimension but this has

[38] Briggs Buchanan, "The Prehistoric Stamp Seal: A Reconsideration of Some Old Excavations," *Journal of the American Oriental Society* 87 (1967):265–79 and 525–40.
[39] For a recent survey, see Briggs Buchanan, *Cylinder Seals*, Catalogue of Ancient Near Eastern Seals in the Ashmolean Museum, vol. 1 (Oxford: Clarendon Press, 1966).
[40] Goff, *Symbols of Prehistoric Mesopotamia*, passim.

no place in a work of history.) Potentially, they should also serve to differentiate one group from another, but they do so only when the groups are in total isolation from each other. As soon as two or more distinct groups intermingle, the resultant racial patterns are subject to laws very different from those governing the artifactual or linguistic results. The intermarriage of human races, let alone of subdivisions of human races, is fertile by definition; the same cannot be said of language or culture. To put it another way, physical characteristics are inherited, while cultural and linguistic ones are acquired. It is in the nature of inherited characteristics that, when they differ in the donors (parents), they will blend in the offspring in various combinations that are at least partially predictable. Acquired characteristics, by contrast, can be adopted by recipients not genetically related to the donor at all. There is no theory to account for the mechanics or to predict the proportions of the blend, nor, indeed, is there any evidence that such acquired characteristics blend at all. Thus, the symbiosis of two population groups differing in both race and language may produce a new stock that is mixed physically but not linguistically: the resulting generation may be wholly bilingual, that is, speak both languages equally well, or wholly unilingual, that is, opt for one language in preference to the other. Rarely does a truly mixed language result. Cultural traits likewise are notoriously independent of racial composition whenever the full light of history permits a controlled correlation. Thus elements such as kinship patterns, artistic styles, or industrial techniques of a smaller racial component may be imposed on or adopted by a larger one. In short, the end of human isolation produces a rapid blending and blurring of racial distinctions, but dominant cultural and linguistic traits continue to maintain their recognizable individuality for some time after initial contact between groups.

In spite of their best efforts, therefore, physical anthropologists have been unable to reconstruct a clear picture of racial differences in either time or space for the Near East in late prehistoric and ancient times. Datable finds have for the most part suggested minor variations on a generalized "Mediterranean" type—a mixture of long-headed (dolicho-cephalic) and round- or broad-headed (brachy-cephalic) skulls. But these differences have not formed consistent patterns that can be correlated even tentatively with specific movements or changes of population as attested by other lines of evidence. In attempting a classification of the population groups who are to play a part in the historical drama of the ancient Near East, we must therefore avoid a physical or racial taxonomy. We resort, instead, to an ethnic one, meaning by this a population grouping as distinguished in the first place by language, and secondarily by art, artifacts, and social organization. These ethnic factors, while independent of race, can be frequently correlated with one another and, perhaps more significantly, with the anthropological classifications preserved in the native nomenclatures. Ancient patterns of culture and language were observed and recognized by the ancients themselves, and much of the surviving documentation stresses the ethnic affiliations and designations that these patterns suggested. At the same time it must be admitted that, like physical differences before them, ethnic factors too became increasingly difficult to disentangle as the pace of interethnic communication and exchange quickened. An excessively ethnologic interpretation of historical events, such as has frequently been espoused in the past, is thus unwarranted for the more fully documented periods; it not only introduces distinctions not verifiable in the record but obscures more significant factors that did play a demonstrable role.[41] The attempt to assess the ethnic composition of the Near East is thus most appropriately made at the very beginning of its history.

We have already met one prehistoric ethnic entity whose traces survive in the written languages of later times as professional designations and technical terms from the substrate language of Mesopotamia. To this evidence can probably be added a large number of geographical names with no apparent etymologies in any of the known languages of the historical period. These geographical names recur, sometimes in identical form, over an area far wider than Mesopotamia alone. Some scholars regard them as evidence for the wide diffusion of a sparse, but linguistically homogeneous population during Neolithic times. If this evidence can be accepted, its archeological correlate is the Ubaid culture (above, Section 5) which, starting from a southern Mesopotamian base in the early fifth millennium, prevailed in much of the Near East by the middle of the fourth. This culture, once thought to have been derived from Iranian prototypes, is now held to be indigenous to Mesopotamia.[42] If so, then the presumed "Ubaidians" (as they are sometimes called)[43] represent the native substratum of the Mesopotamian amalgam, and its oldest identifiable ethnic component.

But the emergence of civilization in Mesopotamia awaited the infusion of ethnic elements that, from all available indications, were not native to the country. Indeed, if we may trust native concepts, (albeit late and Babylonian in orientation), they came from, or were linked to, the four corners of the compass, which bore ethnic labels in the traditional Mesopotamian view of the world as follows:[44]

---

[41] William W. Hallo, "Review of *Geschichte des Alten Vorderasien*, by Hartmut Schmökel," *Journal of the American Oriental Society* 78 (1958):305–08.

[42] Oates, "Ur and Eridu, the Prehistory," pp. 32–50, esp. p. 47. Discoveries of Ubaid assemblages in the Persian Gulf area have, however, reopened the question. Compare Geoffrey Bibby, *Looking for Dilmun* (New York: Alfred A. Knopf, 1969), pp. 375–81.

[43] For example, Samuel Noah Kramer, *The Sumerians: Their History, Culture, and Character* (Chicago: University of Chicago Press, 1963), pp. 41 ff.

[44] This schematic drawing attempts to render a variety of conflicting traditions not literally expressed in any single formulation.

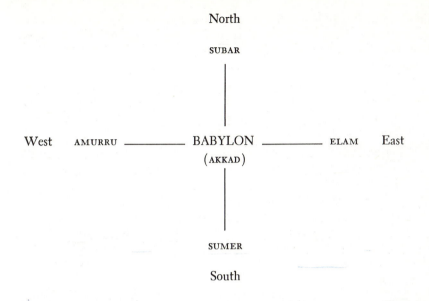

This scheme, while hardly doing justice to the complexity of the ethnic situation, may serve to outline it for most of western Asia.[45] In increasing detail, it is being vindicated by more recent discoveries.

The earliest intrusive stratum now appears to be the northern one which, following the native scheme, we may call the Subarian. In archeological terms it appears to correlate with the Gawra period in northern Mesopotamia (ca. 3500–ca. 2900) and the Uruk period in the south (ca. 3500–ca. 3100). The language of this stratum has hitherto been known only from a few geographical names and lexical entries in later texts and from the names of persons identified as Subarians. A recent discovery, however, promises to identify the first connected literary texts in the language.[46] It may even clinch the arguments in favor of regarding the Subarians as the inventors of writing. The longer survival of the Subarians as a cultural entity in the north than in the south (if the archeological correlation is granted) may reflect a firmer foothold in the areas where they first pene-

[45] Keeping in mind that ancient geographical terminology never coined terms for areas embracing more than "one underlying ethnic element and one underlying language" (Ignace J. Gelb, "New Light on Hurrians and Subarians," Studi Orientalistici in onore di Giorgio Levi Della Vida, vol. 1 (Rome: Istituto per l'Oriente, 1956), p. 390), we can see how, of necessity, such terms expanded to fill the geographical horizon. A comparable development may be seen in the name of Asia, which, beginning as the name of a city-state on the western coast of Asia Minor, gradually expanded in meaning to refer to all of Asia Minor and eventually to all of Asia.

[46] van Dijk, "Les contacts ethniques dans la Mésopotamie et les syncrétismes de la religion Sumérienne,"pp. 172–73, n. 2.

trated; in any case, it is reflected in a persistent tendency to refer to the north (Assyria from the point of view of Babylon, eastern Anatolia from that of Assyria) as Subar (Akkadian, Subartu).

In the south, however, the Subarians were confronted about 3100 by a new stratum which quickly surpassed them in cultural achievements. We may identify this stratum as the Sumerians, the inventors of true civilization. In their own tradition the Sumerians do in fact seem to regard themselves as having arrived in Mesopotamia from the south, probably via the Persian Gulf. Certainly their first settlements were close to the Gulf. They apparently subjugated any Subarians (and surviving "Ubaidians") still in the area, and the word Subarian became a synonym for slave in their language.[47] The earliest royal names of the Mesopotamian tradition have good Sumerian etymologies (see Chapter II, Section 1), and if the Sumerians did not actually invent writing, they quickly adapted it to their needs and developed it into a consummate medium for expression and communication. (Their further achievements will be detailed in Chapter II.)

The western component of the ethnic spectrum was predominantly Semitic. Its first manifestations are almost as early as those of the Sumerians, probably about 2900 (see Chapter II, Section 2). By 2300, they dominated Mesopotamia under the leadership of the city of Akkad, and thus their language is usually referred to as Akkadian or Old Akkadian, but Akkadian culture represents the accommodation of Semitic features to the Sumerian environment; the native sources refer to the unassimilated Semites as Amurrites (Amorites[48]), and to their western geographical base as Amurru.

It is less easy to date the first impact of the eastern component, but Elam was geographically linked so closely with Sumer that reciprocal influences were an almost constant factor from the beginning; Elam also served as the bridge for such influences between Mesopotamia and more distant parts of Iran.

---

[47] Compare the derivation of the word "slave" from "slav" in western languages.
[48] The latter form, familiar from "Biblical English," will be used here.

FIGURE 4   Portrait of Enheduanna, Sargon's daughter (disk partially restored).

II

THE EARLY BRONZE AGE
ca. 3100–2100 B.C.

[1] THE URBAN REVOLUTION: JEMDET NASR
ca. 3100–2900 B.C.

The year 4241 B.C. was once widely regarded as the oldest fixed date in history on the basis of calculations derived from the Egyptian calendar.[1] But this date has since been lowered by one Sothic cycle to about 2776,[2] and it is now generally agreed that the transition from prehistory to protohistory took place first in Mesopotamia, about 3100 B.C., and in short order also in much of the rest of the Near East. The transition can be defined by the invention of writing and the consequent ability to record contemporary events for posterity (see Chapter 1, Section 6). But the oldest written documents from Mesopotamia and each area to which the invention spread are still undeciphered,[3] and the first deciphered texts are not very informative. Our most reliable written evidence for the earliest historic (or protohistoric) period comes from later sources that recall or reflect earlier events and conditions. The term protoliterate has therefore sometimes been applied to this phase as well as, somewhat more arbitrarily, to the illiterate phase that immediately preceded it. This term will, however,

[1] James Henry Breasted, "The Oldest Fixed Date in History," *The Biblical World*, new series 28 (1906):108–12; and idem, *Ancident Records of Egypt*, vol. 1 (Chicago: University of Chicago Press, 1906), p. 30

[2] The beginning of a Sothic cycle is last recorded to have occurred in A.D. 139 and, counting backward by 1460 years at a time, should have fallen at 1320, 2780, and 4240 B.C.; minor adjustments in this theoretical scheme are, however, indicated in most modern reconstructions.

[3] For a proposed decipherment of the earliest Mesopotamian texts, see A. A. Vaiman, "Preliminary Report on the Decipherment of Proto-Sumerian Writing," *Pêrêdneaziatskïi Sbornik* 2 (1966):161–65.

be avoided here in order to emphasize the cultural break between the last prehistoric (that is, Protoliterate A and B)[4] and the first historic (that is, Protoliterate C and D)[5] phases. Moreover, writing was not the only component in the compound of innovations that marked the new era. Two others are also of fundamental importance: the accumulation of capital and the beginning of monumental architecture, including both public buildings (mostly temples) and fortifications. These combined to create the first cities and, together with some secondary innovations, the first civilizations. If the Neolithic Period witnessed the agricultural revolution, we may again follow Childe in describing the beginning of the Bronze Age at the turn of the fourth millennium as the urban revolution.[6]

Where did the first cities arise? A glance at the distribution of Early Bronze I sites (Figure 5) shows a decided change from those of prior periods (Figure 2, page 12). Specifically the sites are nearly all below an altitude of about 200 meters. This change of human settlement patterns implies that man had now mastered the various challenges posed by agriculture in areas of inadequate rainfall. In Egypt, this meant harnessing the waters of the Nile after the annual inundation; on the Mediterranean littoral, terracing; in Syria and across northern Mesopotamia, irrigation; in the water-logged valleys of the lower Tigris and Euphrates, a massive communal drainage effort in order to prevent the back-up of tidal salt water from the Persian Gulf and the capillary rising of saline ground water, which constantly threatened the valleys' soil with over-salinization.[7] The south Mesopotamian environment posed in a sense the gravest challenges, but by mastering it, the inhabitants of that area became the first to produce civilization in all its essentials. The area in question (the extreme south of Mesopotamia) may now be called Sumer, and its inhabitants Sumerians though these names are only English approximations of the Akkadian designations; the Sumerians themselves called their land *Kengir*, their language *Emegir*, and themselves *Sag-giga*, "black-headed ones."

Later, in part considerably later, Sumerian traditions reinforce the modern deduction that the first cities, and many of the other elements of civilization, originated in Sumer at the beginning of history or, in the native view, in antediluvian times. According to Sumerian traditions, more or less closely echoed by those in Akkadian, Hebrew, and Greek (Beros-

---

[4] That is, roughly what we have referred to as the Uruk Period in southern Mesopotamia (Chapter I, Section 5).

[5] Here, the Jemdet Nasr Period.

[6] V. Gordon Childe, "The Urban Revolution," *The Town Planning Review* 21 (1950):3–17; and idem, *Man Makes Himself* (London: Watts, 1936), pp. 157–201.

[7] Thorkild Jacobsen and Robert M. Adams, "Salt and Silt in Ancient Mesopotamian Agriculture," *Science* 128, no. 3334 (Nov. 21, 1958):1251–58. Reprinted in The Bobbs-Merrill Reprint Series in Geography, G-105. Compare also Robert M. Adams, *Land Behind Baghdad: A History of Settlement on the Diyala Plains* (Chicago: University of Chicago Press, 1965), pp. 17–18.

sos), the great flood was preceded by eight to ten long-lived generations of kings (variously: men)[8] who ruled in five cities, beginning with Eridu (Figure 6) on the shores of the great salt-water lagoon connecting to the Persian Gulf, and reaching as far north as Sippar in what later was called the land of Akkad.[9] The first seven antediluvians are linked with seven *apkallu*'s (semidivine sages), beginning with Uanna-Adapa, who passed into Greek sources as Oannes and into Genesis as Adam. (See Figure 6.) If we may believe a variety of different traditions, these sages were responsible for introducing the arts of civilization to Sumer. Among these, writing took first place, followed closely by such divinatory arts as astrology and, according to the Biblical version, music, metallurgy, and viticulture. Berossos adds that the first sages reached Sumer from the Persian Gulf, and some of their Sumerian names suggest as much. Also the Sumerian notions of a paradisiacal station on the Sumerians' way to Sumer center on Dilmun, probably to be located at or near the head of the Persian Gulf.[10] Modern opinion would tend to agree with this traditional view of the origins of civilization, if not with the form in which it was expressed.

What then were the ingredients of this first Sumerian civilization as revealed by the archeology of the Jemdet Nasr strata at various locations in southern Mesopotamia? Pride of place can be assigned to the invention of bronze, which has given its name to the two millennia now ushered in. In the outgoing Stone Age, copper had been used sporadically in its native form along with stone (hence the designation chalcolithic). But it was now discovered that copper could be alloyed with smaller quantities of rarer metals such as arsenic, antimony, and above all tin, usually in proportions of from 1:7 to 1:10, and that the resultant alloy, especially tin-bronze, was not only malleable, like native copper, but could also be cast from molds. These properties seem to have been discovered, or at least exploited, first in southern Mesopotamia, where the scarcity of stone may have hastened the end of the Stone Age. Although tin and copper also had to be imported, and from opposite directions at that, they were relatively lighter to transport and, when combined as bronze, much more economically worked into the desired shape. Thus, a tool and weapon industry

[8] For details, including variant traditions due (probably) to parochial prejudices, see J. J. Finkelstein, "The Antediluvian Kings: A University of California Tablet," *Journal of Cuneiform Studies* 17 (1963):39–51. Note that the antediluvian kings are sometimes inserted at the beginning of the Sumerian King List (for which see below, Section 2) but that they do not form a regular part of it.

[9] William W. Hallo, "Antediluvian Cities," *Journal of Cuneiform Studies* 23 (1970): 57–67.

[10] See William W. Hallo and Briggs Buchanan, "A 'Persian Gulf' Seal on an Old Babylonian Mercantile Agreement," *Studies in Honor of Benno Landsberger on his Seventy-fifth Birthday April 21, 1965*, ed. Hans G. Güterbock and Thorkild Jacobsen (Chicago: University of Chicago Press, 1965), pp. 207–08. Compare also Geoffrey Bibby, *Looking for Dilmun* (New York: Alfred A. Knopf, 1969), passim.

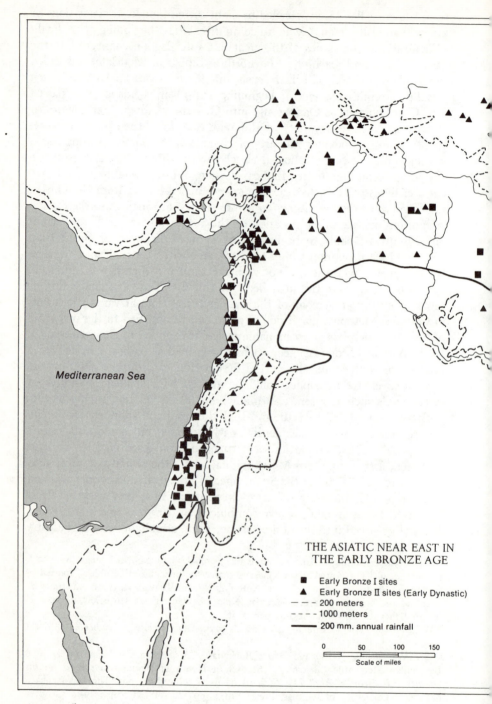

Mediterranean Sea

THE ASIATIC NEAR EAST IN
THE EARLY BRONZE AGE

■   Early Bronze I sites
▲   Early Bronze II sites (Early Dynastic)
— — — 200 meters
- - - - 1000 meters
—————— 200 mm. annual rainfall

0   50   100   150

Scale of miles

FIGURE 5

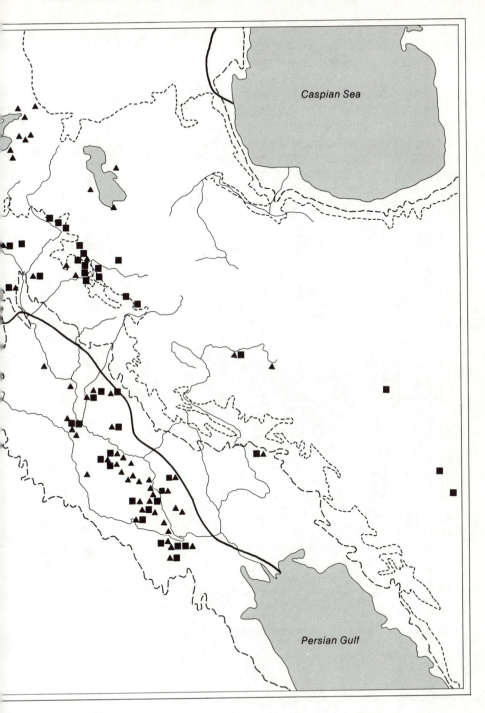

FIGURE 6 Antediluvian generations in Babylonian and Biblical traditions.

| Generation | BABYLONIAN TRADITIONS | | | BIBLICAL TRADITIONS | |
	Antediluvian Cities	Antediluvian Counselors ("Culture heroes")	Antediluvian Kings	Sethite Genealogy (Ancestors of mankind) (Genesis 5)	Cainite Genealogy ("Culture heroes") (Genesis 4)
1	Eridu	Uanna-Adapa (or Oannes)	Alulim "Stag"	Enosh "Man"	Adam "Man"
2	Patibira "Canal" or Badtibira "Fortress of the Smiths"	U'anduga	Alalgar "Drumstick"(?)	Kenan	Cain (farmer) Abel (shepherd) / Enoch (city-builder)
3		En-meduga	En-menluanna	Mahalalel	
4		En-megalamma	En-mengalanna	Jared	Irad
5	Sippar	An-Enlilda	Dumuzi the Shepherd	Enoch	Mehujael
6		Utu-abzu	En-menduranki	Methuselah	Methushael
7	Larak	En-mebuluga	En-sipazianna	Lamech	Lamech
8	Shuruppak		Ubar-Tutu, or Ziusudra	Noah	Jabal (pastoral nomad) / Jubal (musician) / Tubal-cain (smith)

"THE FLOOD"

quickly developed in southern Mesopotamia where the overland tin routes from the north converged with the overseas copper routes from the Persian Gulf.

But bronze in itself is neither a sufficient nor even a necessary ingredient of civilization. This word, derived from the Latin *civitas*, "city," or "city-state," implies the beginning of cities, and these in turn can be distinguished from the villages that preceded them by two principal factors: monumental buildings and fortifications. The former were probably made possible by the more efficient bronze tools now available; the latter were more than likely made necessary by the greater threat posed by the new bronze weapons. The former proved a magnet in time of peace, the latter in time of war. Both conspired to increase the density of population above anything possible in the earlier, purely agrarian economy. For the concentration of population in urban centers did not deplete the countryside; on the contrary, a corona of fertile land surrounded each city and, under the efficient management of the town-dwelling, absentee landlords, sustained a greater rural population at the same time.[11] And since population growth is the surest source of economic growth, it probably was the cause, almost at once, of the second essential ingredient of civilization, the accumulation of capital, and this in turn of the third, writing. It is generally held that the stimulus to the last invention (which we have already characterized as marking the transition from prehistory to history) was economic. Indeed, the first texts seem to be little more than records of such everyday matters as the number and nature of grazing animals entrusted by their owners to specified herdsmen. We are able to understand the general sense of some of these earliest texts even without being sure of their underlying language because their script is still almost pictographic in form and logographic in character—that is, each individual sign is an only slightly conventionalized drawing of a single referent, such as a cow. Numerals too are represented logographically in these early texts, as in most subsequent economic texts down to our own day, and they attest to some herds of considerable size. The texts indicate cattle as a characteristic form of individual wealth in this period, while the architectural remains point to temples as the typical form of collective capital.

The basic ingredients of civilization brought in their train certain derivative ones, which are present or presumed in some if not all of the assemblages of this period. The creation of the city implied a new form of

11 Compare: A. Leo Oppenheim, "Mesopotamia: Land of Many Cities," *Middle Eastern Cities: A Symposium on Ancient, Islamic, and Contemporary Middle Eastern Urbanism*, ed. Ira M. Lapidus (Berkeley and Los Angeles: University of California Press, 1969), pp. 3–18; and Robert M. Adams, "Conclusion," *Middle Eastern Cities*, ed. Lapidus, pp. 188–96. See in detail Robert M. Adams and Hans J. Nissen, *From the Ramparts of Uruk: The Natural Setting of Urban Societies in Southern Iraq* (Chicago: University of Chicago Press, forthcoming).

social organization in which tribal and kinship loyalties were replaced by political ones based on common dependence on a military machine headed by a king. The accumulation of capital surely involved the acceleration of craft and professional specialization, when inherited or acquired wealth freed at least some households from autarky (dependence on their own economic self-sufficiency). And the invention of writing required at most the further refinement of phonetization before it could be employed for noneconomic ends to create the first historical records and literary efforts. But all these developments can be traced more clearly in the succeeding periods.

While the basis for all these momentous innovations was being laid in southern Mesopotamia, the north of the country seems to have continued without noticeable interruption into the final phases of the Gawra period—not only at the type site, Tepe Gawra, but at others like Nineveh, Grai Resh, and Tell Brak. Elsewhere in western Asia, these two crucial centuries can best be correlated with the Early Bronze I period. The term should not be understood too literally as marking the sudden beginnings of bronze technology, for absolute dates are particularly hard to establish for metal objects. But the possibility cannot be ruled out that the new invention enjoyed a wide and even spectacular spread once its merits had been recognized. Nor did all the other components of civilization synchronize with it as in southern Mesopotamia. In Palestine, for example, Jericho had achieved urban status well before the end of the Neolithic Period, while in Syria and Anatolia, urbanization lagged behind the introduction of bronze, as did writing. On Cyprus, bronze itself made its appearance only a thousand years later, and the Early, Middle, and Late Bronze ages are therefore referred to rather as Early, Middle, and Late Cypriote; similarly, further west the various Bronze Ages go by the name of Minoan for Crete, Cycladic for the Aegean islands, and Helladic for the Greek mainland in order to avoid the ambiguities inherent in the corresponding Bronze Age labels. Only Egypt in its First Dynasty (ca. 3100–2900) witnessed all the principal elements of the urban revolution of southern Mesopotamia, probably under the direct stimulus of the latter area. Thus the history of the Early Bronze Age must, in very large measure, be told in terms of lower Mesopotamia and Egypt, with only a side-glance now and then at such illuminations as cuneiform and hieroglyphic sources, or archeological finds, may throw on the state of the intervening lands.

[2] THE GOLDEN AGE: ED (EARLY DYNASTIC) I
ca. 2900–2700 B.C.

Native Mesopotamian sources and their derivatives, including the Bible, are in impressive agreement that at about this time there ensued a natural catastrophe which threatened the extinction of all of mankind or at least of those elements of civilization that the previous eight generations (more or less) had painfully elaborated. Since these sources derived man and his attainments from divine inspiration, they generally regarded the catastrophe as evidence of divine displeasure with "what God had wrought"—a rueful case of second thoughts. And all agree that a "saving remnant" was found worthy to continue humanity, or civilization, in the nick of time, thanks to the intercession of a more benign deity. In their earliest form, these traditions centered around ancient Shuruppak (modern Fara in southern Iraq), whose king rode out the Flood in a boat and, in one version, ultimately achieved immortality. His names[12] in the various traditions are suggestive of his role and fate. In the earliest Sumerian version he appears as Ubar-Tutu, "Friend of the god Tutu," or as Ziusudra, "Life of long days." Later he is simply (and perhaps erroneously) called after his city, Shuruppak. The earliest Akkadian sources call him Atarhasis, "exceeding wise," while the later ones, incorporated in the canonical Gilgamesh epic, refer to him as Uta-napishtim, "he has found (everlasting) life." In the Bible his name is Noah, explained as "this one will cause us to repent from our [contemplated] deed and from the grief of our hands [which we meant to extract] from the earth, for the Lord had laid it under a curse"—although his name is related linguistically to a root meaning "to rest" and is semantically more nearly equivalent to his contemporary Na'amah, whose name means "pleasant."

The pervasiveness of the flood motif, which found its way into Greek mythology and recurs, perhaps independently, in much of the world's folklore, has led many to seek corroboration for it in the archeological record. For a time the excavations at Ur seemed to have crowned this quest with success, for here Sir Leonard Woolley found deep deposits of clay between the latest Ubaidian and the earliest Uruk-type deposits. But further analysis of this so-called flood pit has refuted any possible linkage of this evidence with the deluge of the literary tradition. Not only is the character of the deposit inconsistent with all of the literary descriptions of the deluge, but also the date of the Ur deposit is too early by centuries to fit the chronology of the Flood. The situation is more promising, however, at Shuruppak. Here the flood deposit, while more modest, is definitely of a fluvial character, and moreover it intervenes precisely between the Jemdet Nasr and Early Dynastic levels, that is, at the very point when the relative chronology of native sources places the Flood. On current estimates, the

12 In the transcription of royal and other personal names, hyphens are used to separate two or more words composing the name; theophoric elements (that is, components representing a divine name) are capitalized even when—as is often the case—they are not initial. See Henri Limet, "L'Anthroponymie Sumérienne dans les documents de la 3ᵉ dynastie d'Ur," fasc. 180, *Bibliothèque de la Faculté de Philosophie et Lettres de l'Université de Liège* (Paris: Société d'Edition "Les Belles Lettres," 1968).

absolute date involved is approximately 2900 B.C. The fact that neither Ur nor many of the other excavated sites of southern Mesopotamia reveal a comparable inundation at this time casts doubt on the universal character of the cataclysm depicted in the literature, but it should be remembered that the traces left by the Flood would vary at different sites with differing local conditions.[13]

There is, moreover, at least one other site where the Flood is represented by archeological evidence of this same date, and that is Kish. This is precisely the place where, according to the native chronographic traditions, kingship resumed, or began, when the Flood receded. We may thus conclude that the great deluge of the Mesopotamian sources was somewhat more localized than the texts picture it but that it was nonetheless a historical event associated with a specific point in time. Indeed in Akkadian usage "before the Flood" meant protohistoric time, and "after the Flood" meant fully historic time. The notion that Kish replaced Shuruppak as the seat of power in Mesopotamia after the Flood is also historically plausible: Kish lies considerably upstream from Shuruppak and the rest of the antediluvian cities, except for Sippar, and would thus have experienced an earlier end to the type of flood in question. As if in corroboration of the notion, the Sumerian word for flood, *amaru*, is virtually a homonym of the Sumerian word for Semite—(*a*)*marru* (Akkadian, *amurrû*)—and the Sumerians did not hesitate to make a play on words equating the Amorites with the Flood. They were, of course, victims of many Semitic irruptions from the west, Amurru, but they may well have applied the equation first to the original wave of Semites who, as we have suggested, entered the country in force about 2900 (Chapter I, Section 6).

It is worth noting that at least some of the first postdiluvian kings who ruled at Kish bore Semitic names. They inaugurated the first fully historical period in Mesopotamian history, called the Dynastic[14] or, more commonly, the Early Dynastic Period. This period permits a more secure correlation of archeological and historical data than is possible for earlier periods, especially on the basis of finds in the valley of the Diyala River (a tributary of the Tigris), where Early Dynastic development was first revealed. The period, divided into three subperiods of approximately equal duration, has a total span originally estimated at seven or eight hundred

[13] M. E. L. Mallowan, "Noah's Flood Reconsidered," *Iraq* 26 (1964):62–82 and plates 16–20; R. L. Raikes, "The Physical Evidence for Noah's Flood," *Iraq* 28 (1966):52–63; and Samuel Noah Kramer, "Reflections on the Mesopotamian Flood: The Cuneiform Data New and Old," *Expedition* 9 (Summer, 1967):12–18.

[14] Robert M. Adams, "Developmental Stages in Ancient Mesopotamia," in Julian H. Steward, ed., *Irrigation Civilizations: A Comparative Study*, Social Science Monographs, vol. 1 (Washington: Pan American Union, Social Science Section, Department of Cultural Affairs, 1955), pp. 13–17.

years.[15] It is here assessed at closer to six hundred years (ca. 2900–2300 B.C.), and even this figure may again have to be lowered. In western Asiatic archeology, it corresponds very roughly with the Early Bronze II period, although it should be remembered that there is as yet little unanimity among specialists in the field about the range of EB II.

The subdivisions of the Early Dynastic Period are also somewhat arbitrary,[16] but those adopted here will maintain the generational chronology already established as a working hypothesis for the protohistoric period (that is, about eight generations at approximately twenty-five years for an estimated total time span of two centuries per subperiod). Groups of seven to fourteen generations commonly recur in Near Eastern genealogies of much later periods,[17] and traces of the same kind of schematization are already apparent in the native dynastic lists. The oldest of these is generally known as the Sumerian King List, although the native name for it (taken, as commonly, from its opening words) was simply *nam-lugal,* "kingship." Since it is our basic tool for the reconstruction of early Mesopotamian chronology, it is well to consider briefly what it implied.

According to the Sumerian King List, at least in its canonical version as this was transmitted in the schools of Nippur, kingship was lowered from heaven after the Flood and was thereafter shared by eleven different cities, each of which enjoyed, at one time or another, one or more "turns" (*bala,* Akkadian *palû*)[18] at a real or spurious hegemony over all of Sumer

---

[15] Pinhas Delougaz and Seton Lloyd, *Pre-Sargonid Temples in the Diyala Region,* Oriental Institute Publications, vol. 58 (Chicago: University of Chicago Press, 1942), p. 134. The higher figure includes a century of the "Protoimperial" Period, which is here included in ED III.

[16] For a recent estimate of their absolute dates, compare Edith Porada, "The Relative Chronology of Mesopotamia. Part I: Seals and Trade (6000–1600 B.C.)," *Chronologies in Old World Archaeology,* ed. Robert W. Ehrich (Chicago: University of Chicago Press, 1965), pp. 133–200, esp. pp. 177–79. I have followed her chronological scheme in general, except for the third millennium, as follows (dates are approximate):

	Porada	Hallo
ED I	2900–2750	2900–2700
ED II	2750–2600	2700–2500
ED IIIa	2600–2500 ⎫	2500–2300
ED IIIb	2500–2370 ⎭	
Akkad	2370–2230 ⎫	2300–2100
Post-Akkad	2230–2100 ⎭	

[17] Abraham Malamat, "King Lists of the Old Babylonian Period and Biblical Genealogies," *Essays in Memory of E. A. Speiser,* ed. William W. Hallo, American Oriental Series, vol. 53 (New Haven: American Oriental Society, 1968), 163–73, esp. 165.

[18] J. J. Finkelstein, "The Genealogy of the Hammurapi Dynasty," *Journal of Cuneiform Studies* 20 (1966):105–06.

and Akkad until the accession of Hammurapi of Babylon.[19] The claim to such hegemony apparently depended on recognition by the priesthood and scribes of Nippur who, however, relied for their information on sources composed according to other principles, such as genealogical lists based on dynastic (family) relationships or local king lists based on lists of date formulas (see below, Section 6). The King List therefore includes not only those kings who may really have enjoyed a measure of national supremacy, but also as many of their predecessors and successors at their royal capitals as the sources may have contained, together with the lengths of their reigns and sometimes their filiation or other brief biographical notices. Then the total number of kings and regnal years for the city were given and, at the end of the entire list, the number of times each city ruled the land, the number of kings who constituted its successive turns (or dynasties), and the total number of years they ruled. A grand total of all regnal years was then arrived at by adding all the regnal years attributed to all the cities. This total has sometimes been interpreted as representing the Sumerian concept of the time span separating the Flood from Hammurapi. But, even discounting the legendary lengths of reign assigned to some of the earliest rulers, it is clear that this was not the intention of the King List. It has also been argued that the King List represented as successive many dynasties that were in fact contemporaneous, but again the text does not warrant this interpretation. On the contrary, other literary sources surely known to the same scribes show clearly that they knew of the contemporaneity of some of the royal names listed in successive cities in the King List. It is up to the modern historian to use these other literary sources, as well as contemporary monuments, to establish the synchronisms that the King List does not provide. Finally, the Sumerian King List has been accused of tendentiousness, specifically of propagating (perhaps in the interests of late Sumerian imperial experiments) an ideal of national unity in the face of a real disunity and particularism. This evaluation is also in need of modification. Early Mesopotamian political development[20] always existed in a kind of tension between centrifugal and centripetal forces, between petty-statism and imperialism, between the city-state as the traditional medium of political organization and the recurrent attempts to forge a greater unity. This tension was reflected in numerous institutional

---

[19] In its complete form, the list concludes with the last year of Damiqilishu of Isin (1794 B.C.), while Hammurapi ascended the throne of Babylon in 1793 B.C.

[20] Compare: Thorkild Jacobsen, "Early Political Development in Mesopotamia," *Zeitschrift für Assyriologie und Vorderasiatische Archäologie* 52 (1957):91–140; reprinted in idem, *Toward the Image of Tammuz and Other Essays on Mesopotamian History and Culture,* ed. William L. Moran, Harvard Semitic Series, vol. 21 (Cambridge: Harvard University Press, 1970), pp. 132–56 and 366–96; and Neils Bailkey, "Early Mesopotamian Constitutional Development," *American Historical Review* 72, no. 4 (1967):1211–36.

compromises:[21] an amphictyonic league[22] that united the separate city-states for cultic purposes, a high priestess at Ur who was the daughter of whatever king happened to lay claim to primacy among the various city-state rulers; a tradition of historical literature, royal names, royal titles, and royal hymns that was the common legacy of all the dynasties; and so on. The King List was thus simply one more expression, and one more resolution, of the same tension. It recognized the reality of different and even conflicting sovereignties among the separate city-states, while yet maintaining the ideal that, at any one time, one city and its king were recognized as first among equals.

There is, moreover, some evidence that at the very beginning of dynastic times, lower Mesopotamia did enjoy a measure of unity under the hegemony of Kish. The evidence must be gathered from a variety of sources. The King List itself records a long list of rulers at Kish before the first rival claimants appeared at any other city. The epic tradition of the succeeding period looks back on a "golden age" when the four quarters of the world[23] lived in harmony and, even, it seems, spoke a common language. As in the Biblical tale of the "confusion of tongues," this stage seems to be pictured as the immediate sequel to the Deluge.[24] Classical Sumerian mythology, which describes the gods as united in an assembly under the leadership of an elective executive, has been interpreted as reflecting an earthly form of "primitive democracy" in the earliest dynastic period, based on a loose league of equals, and it was a king of Kish who inaugurated the national shrine at the league's religious capital, Nippur (below, Section 3). Archeological evidence too suggests that Kish had the first, if not indeed the only, clear instance of a royal palace in the Early Dynastic Period.[25] Finally, the evidence of the royal inscriptions of all subsequent periods may be invoked to show the high esteem in which the title King of Kish was always held; long after Kish had ceased to be the seat of kingship, the title was employed to express hegemony over Sumer and Akkad and ultimately came to signify or symbolize imperial, even universal, dominion.

All these indications suggest that the memory of a united beginning

---

21 William W. Hallo, "Royal Hymns and Mesopotamian Unity," *Journal of Cuneiform Studies* 17 (1963):112–18.

22 Compare Chapter III, Section 2.

23 For these, see Chapter I, Section 6, but note that Elam's place appears to be taken by Hamazi.

24 Samuel Noah Kramer, "The 'Babel of Tongues': A Sumerian Version," *Essays in Memory of E. A. Speiser*, ed. Hallo, pp. 108–11; and J. J. A. van Dijk, "La 'Confusion des langues.' Note sur le lexique et sur la morphologie d'Enmerkar, 147–155," *Orientalia* 39 (1970):302–10.

25 P. R. S. Moorey, "The 'Plano-Convex Building' at Kish and Early Mesopotamian Palaces," *Iraq* 26 (1964):83–98 and plates 21–25.

under the uncontested leadership of Kish reflects a kernel of historical truth. If so, is it possible to account for this leadership of Kish, at the northern end of the first urban agglomeration, rather than one of the older centers at the southern end where the process of urbanization presumably started? A possible geological factor has already been mentioned in connection with the Flood. But beyond this it is important to note that Kish lies precisely within that circle, little more than fifty miles in diameter, which has seen "the most remarkable sequence of historic capitals in the world."[26] (See Figure 17, pages 90–91). Following the example of the earliest kings of Kish, later dynasties for much of the next four thousand years ruled Mesopotamia—and sometimes the whole known world— from successive sites in this small area, among them the Akkadians, Amorites, Kassites, Chaldaeans, Seleucids, Sassanians, and Abbasids. Such an unparalleled record cannot be wholly accidental and has plausibly been connected, whether as cause or effect, with another geographical coincidence: the convergence in this same "capital district" of many of the greatest traditional highways of the Near East.[27]

To precisely interpret the King List's sparse data for the first dynastic stage (ED I) is difficult. (For an attempted reconstruction see Figure 7.) According to this source, the first postdiluvian ruler was called "the Harrow." (The restoration of the signs is, however, uncertain, and it is not even clear whether they are to be read as Sumerian or Akkadian.)[28] He was followed by no less than twenty-two other kings of whom the first twenty, with one exception, are totally unknown from any other source. The exception is the thirteenth king, Etana, and this name immediately poses a problem, for outside the King List there is a clear tradition that Etana was the first ruler (after the Flood),[29] and even the King List records that he "consolidated all the lands [or many lands]." These conflicting versions can be reconciled only by breaking up the King List's sequence of twenty-three rulers into two or more parallel lines, one headed by "Harrow" and another by Etana. These parallel lines possibly continue

[26] David Oates, *Studies in the Ancient History of Northern Iraq* (London: The British Academy, 1968), p. 8.

[27] Ibid.

[28] The Akkadians took over the Sumerian system of writing and often used Sumerian words as logograms (words-signs) in preference to syllabic spellings of their Akkadian equivalents. This can result in ambiguity, especially where personal names are concerned. A comparable case would be the English usage of "etc.," which some readers would pronounce "et cetera" and others "and so forth."

[29] Compare the Legend of Etana and the Eagle, J. V. Kinnier Wilson, "Some Contributions to the Legend of Etana," *Iraq* 31 (1969):8–17 and plates 2–3. Other references to Etana occur in the "Pushkin Elegies" (line 97) and in the Akkadian Gilgamesh Epic (VII, iv, 49). See Samuel Noah Kramer, *The Sumerians: Their History, Culture, and Character* (Chicago: University of Chicago Press, 1963), p. 214.

		"THE FLOOD"		
Generation				
1			Etana [13]	
2			Balih [14]	
3	Mashkakatu [1] "Harrow"	Kalibum [7] "Dog"	Enmenunna (or Niminunna) [15] "Butterfly"	
4	Kullassina-ib'el [2] "He rules them all"	Qalumum [8] "Lamb"	Melam-Kish [16] Bar-sal-nunna [17]	
5	Nangish-lishma [3]	Zuqaqip [9] "Scorpion"		Samug [18]
6	En-dara-Anna [4]	Atab [10]		Tizkar [19]
7	Babum [5]	Ataba [11]		Ilku [20]
8	Pu-Annum [6]	Arwium, son of Sabitum [12] "Gazelle," son of "Hind"		Ilta-sadum [21]

NOTE: Bracketed numbers indicate the sequence in the Sumerian King List; variants are not noted. Single line (∣) denotes direct descent.

FIGURE 7   The First (legendary) Dynasty of Kish (Early Dynastic I).

that tradition of the association of each king with a learned vizier, as in the case of the antediluvians and of the later rulers of Uruk (below, Section 3).[30] At any rate, the proposed scheme has the merit of placing Etana and

[30] Thorkild Jacobsen, *The Sumerian King List*, Assyriological Studies, no. 11 (Chicago: University of Chicago Press, 1939), pp. 155–56, prefers to regard these kings as belonging to another city or to cities whose kings claimed the title King of Kish. But this seems unlikely as we now have at least ten such royal names from contemporaneous inscriptions (Albrecht Goetze, "Early Kings of Kish," *Journal of Cuneiform Studies* 15 (1961):105–11, esp. 109–11) and not one of them can be safely identified with the King List's first twelve names.

the beginning of kingship at the beginning of the Early Dynastic Period.[31] The scheme proposed here, adapted from another suggestion by Jacobsen,[32] thus reconciles the purely archeological nomenclature with the historiographic evidence.

Of the next seven generations in the Kish sequence nothing is known except the names, some of which have only recently come to light.[33] More are Akkadian than Sumerian, and (as far as their etymologies are clear) they are most often the names of animals or, less commonly, toponyms. More we cannot say because we have found neither contemporaneous monuments nor later literary allusions to a single one of these shadowy figures.

[3] THE HEROIC AGE: ED II
ca. 2700–2500 b.c.

The Golden Age of primitive democracy, as reconstructed in part from later mythology, was succeeded by an heroic age whose chief written reflection is found in epic literature but for which we enjoy for the first time the control of some contemporaneous, monumental texts. Several interrelated criteria distinguish the new phase from its predecessor. In archeological terms, the basic building material continued to be the "plano-convex" brick, flat on one side, rounded on the other, which was a distinguishing characteristic of the entire Early Dynastic Period. But its employment expanded, and with it the progress of urbanization, involving the twin factors of fortification and monumental architecture (more specifically, the building of temples). We can picture most of Mesopotamia at this time as organized in such a way that the entire population could, if the need arose, find shelter behind the safety of city walls. This did not

[31] In the reconstructions by Delougaz and Jacobsen, who with Frankfort introduced the nomenclature, the Early Dynastic Period began some 350 years before Etana, presumably the first dynast. The paradox was defended by Delougaz on purely archeological grounds: The term "Early Dynastic" having been assigned to the phase in which the first historical dynasties must be placed, it was found, on digging deeper, that there was no real archeological break until the levels now known as Protoliterate were reached. Thus what started as Early Dynastic a and b became Early Dynastic III, and the preceding periods became Early Dynastic II and I. Moreover, while in the tradition kingship may have begun with Etana at the end of ED II, in fact there were cities, and by implication rulers of cities, throughout the Early Dynastic Period. Therefore, the nomenclature in Delougaz's opinion is fully justified. (Oral communication to the author, 1953.)

[32] Jacobsen, *The Sumerian King List*, p. 152. Compare also Mallowan, "Noah's Flood Reconsidered," p. 69, n. 21a.

[33] William W. Hallo, "Beginning and End of the Sumerian King List in the Nippur Recension," *Journal of Cuneiform Studies* 17 (1963):52–57; and M. Civil, "Sur le nom d'un roi de Kiš," *Revue d'Assyriologie et d'Archéologie Orientale*, 63 (1969):179.

mean that everyone had to live permanently within walled cities, but rather that the rural population lived within a reasonable distance of one or another city; in fact, the settlement pattern of this period reveals that, in the principal centers of urban development, walled cities arose at a fairly constant distance from one another. There were at least four, and perhaps as many as six, of these centers (see Figure 5, page 30), and their prolif- eration at this time implied also the consolidation of the typical Early Dynastic political system—that is, the city-state under the leadership of a king. Such a system involved not only the protection but also the control of the surrounding countryside by each city and inevitably led first to con- flicts between neighboring cities for the terrain lying between them, then to increasing militarization, and finally to wars and attempted conquests farther afield. The literature of the Heroic Age thus preserves the memory of campaigns and sieges which, although small-scale in terms of the num- bers of men involved, covered considerable distances. And the contempo- raneous art reflects the tastes of an heroic age: contests between animals, warriors, or both characterize the seal cylinders, which by this time had become the most characteristic Mesopotamian art form.

The breakdown of the real unity of the Golden Age did not, how- ever, end the ideal of unity that it had engendered. All the city-states at that time shared a similar culture, including a common religion if not a single language, and appear to have given political expression to this bond by what has been termed the Kengir (Sumer) League.[34] This league is as yet not directly attested, but its existence can be persuasively argued from indirect evidence. Its center was no longer at Kish but at Nippur. This is significant because Nippur itself was never demonstrably the seat of a royal city-state. Rather it was a religious center, located at the geographical mid- point between Sumer in the south and Akkad in the north (from Kish northward along the Diyala), and sacred to the "chief executive" of the Sumerian pantheon, the god Enlil. It symbolizes the importance of the religious factor in the evolving pattern of Mesopotamian civilization.

Indeed, control of the countryside had not only military consequences for the various city-states but, by way of economic factors, religious ones as well. It accelerated the accumulation of capital and the specialization between urban and rural professions, or between technology and agricul- ture. And archeological evidence suggests that most of the resulting excess wealth and productivity went into building and furnishing temples. While many new temples arose on sites already sanctified by previous shrines, they were now much more elaborate, and many were totally new structures. Moreover, such was the significance of the temple within the cities of this

---

[34] Jacobsen ("Early Political Development in Mesopotamia," *Toward the Image of Tammuz and Other Essays on Mesopotamian History and Culture*, ed. Moran) dates the beginning of the league, and of Nippur's role in it, in the preceding period. For the Kengir League in later ED times, see pp. 147–48 of the above.

time that, outside of Kish, the earliest sources of kingship can be traced to religious, rather than military, leadership. Since no clear traces of royal palaces before ED III times have been found by excavations except at Kish (and possibly at Mari on the Middle Euphrates; the case of Eridu is still disputed), it would seem that the earliest city-state rulers resided in a part of the temple complex.[35] The myths list *en*-ship (that is, the high priesthood) first and well ahead of kingship among the norms of civilization.[36] In fact, the first inscriptionally attested royal title is not king (etymologically "big man" in Sumerian) but lord (etymologically "high priest" in Sumerian).

The development is clearest at Uruk, more precisely in its most ancient portion, which was called Eanna, "house of Heaven," after its principal sanctuary. This sanctuary was presumably sacred to An, the deified Heaven, but more particularly it was the seat of the worship of Inanna, "Lady of Heaven"(?), who later was exalted to equal rank with An and served as his consort. By a peculiarity of the Sumerian cult, female deities demanded male dignitaries as their chief ministrants (and vice versa), and at Eanna this appears to have led quickly to the consolidation of ecclesiastical and secular power in the person of the *en* (the high priest). Of these the first two were described as sons of the sun god, meaning perhaps sons of a priest of the sun god and possibly suggesting some kind of link with the antediluvian traditions of Sippar (or Larsa), where the worship of the sun god was most at home. The enigmatic note that the first was born in the sea and ascended to the mountains also recalls the hints of Persian Gulf origins associated with the antediluvians (above, Section 1). His son Emmerkar is credited with building Uruk, which presumably meant joining Eanna with Kulab, the settlement then lying on the opposite side of the Euphrates, for he and his successors were known in the literature as lords (or priests) of Kulab. In later traditions, Emmerkar, like the antediluvians, is again linked with a wise vizier, and he is, moreover, the hero of no less than four lengthy epics that no doubt were once meant to form a single cycle. Their order and historical details will be easier to reconstruct when all the relevant texts have been fully edited, but it is already clear that all deal with one grand theme: the relationship between Uruk and the city-state of Aratta, probably located somewhere in the interior of Iran.[37] The stories take place in the time "when Utu was king," that is, when the sun god was the overlord of Sumer, and begin with

[35] Moorey, "The 'Plano-Convex Building' at Kish and Early Mesopotamian Palaces," p. 83. According to Jacobsen ("Early Political Development in Mesopotamia," *Toward the Image of Tammuz and Other Essays on Mesopotamian History and Culture*, ed. Moran, pp. 375–76, n. 32), it was the *giparu* in which the earliest rulers resided.
[36] Compare Bailkey, "Early Mesopotamian Constitutional Development," p. 1215, n. 11, who notes other literary testimony to the sequence.
[37] See most recently Claus Wilcke, *Das Lugalbandaepos* (Wiesbaden: Otto Harrassowitz, 1969) and the review of this book by Jacob Klein, *Journal of the American Oriental Society* 91 (1971), 295–99.

Sumer, or at least Uruk, hard pressed by invaders from the west (Amurru). With Aratta's help, these are repulsed, and Emmerkar can turn to his religious duties, which he conceives as building and embellishing the temples of Inanna in Uruk and Enki in Eridu. For this purpose he needs raw materials that Sumer lacks: metals and semiprecious stones, above all lapis lazuli. Aratta abounds in these materials and, after lengthy negotiations including a challenge to single combat, seems to agree to an exchange for the grain Mesopotamia produces in excess. But the agreement breaks down, and Uruk resorts to arms, eventually, it appears, emerging victorious. The cycle so reconstructed would seem to preserve the memory of the beginning of organized trade in the key items of a Bronze-Age economy. Incidental light is also thrown on other aspects of the period, such as the role of the council of elders in the two city-states and the alleged beginnings of writing on clay tablets (a practice that we know actually goes further back).

In two of the epics, Emmerkar is associated with Lugal-banda, literally, "junior king," who figures in the King List as the next ruler of Uruk and is succeeded in turn by Dumuzi. This last is the hero of numerous compositions in which he appears in the company of deities and is himself in divine guise; these compositions therefore belong in the mythology and cannot be taken, at least for now, to yield any firm historical information. The epic cycle as such resumes with Gilgamesh, recalled in later sources as son of Lugal-banda and his divine wife Ninsun, grandson of Emmerkar, and certainly the most famous king of the First Dynasty of Uruk. Because of the copious legends that became associated with his name, the historicity of Gilgamesh used to be questioned. But recent discoveries have confirmed the existence of the contemporaneous rulers of Kish and Ur, and there now seems little reason to regard his reign as legendary. These three city-states—Kish, Uruk, and Ur—were preeminent in Mesopotamia throughout this period, as attested not only by the King List but also by the *Tummal Inscription*, a brief historiographic essay on the sanctuaries of Nippur. It credits Enmebaragesi with first building the temple of Enlil at Nippur. There is no reason to doubt that this indeed took place in ED II times. Although the city of Nippur had a long prior existence, and its Inanna temple can be traced back almost to the beginning of Uruk times (about 3400), there is no prior evidence of an Enlil sanctuary. Its foundation may well mark or symbolize the shift from Kish as political capital to Nippur as religious center of the rival city-states. If so, it is significant that its foundation is attributed to a king of Kish, for Enmebaragesi is known as King of Kish not only from the King List but also from two contemporary inscriptions, one found as far away as Tutub (modern Khafaje) in the Diyala region.

The *Tummal Inscription* goes on to credit Enmebaragesi's son Aka with the construction of the Tummal-building at Nippur. It is less clear about the rest of Nippur's benefactors.

Some sources name next a king of Ur, Mesannepadda (or Nanne), and his "son" Meskiagnunna, followed by Gilgamesh of Uruk and his son Ur-lugal (or Ur-nungal). Others reverse this order. Their very uncertainty about, or indifference to, the precise order seems to indicate that both groups of rulers were contemporaneous. But Gilgamesh was also contemporaneous with Enmebaragesi, according to a late royal hymn, and with Aka of Kish, according to *Gilgamesh and Aka*, an epic that tells in detail of an unsuccessful siege of Uruk by the army of Kish. Thus we can synchronize the end of the first dynasty of Kish,[38] the middle of the first dynasty of Uruk, and the beginning of the first dynasty of Ur. Of their various successors given by the King List, however, we know no more than the names. Conversely, the royal names known for this period from other sources do not appear in the King List, and they are therefore hard to place. (See Figure 8.)

A large number of these inscriptionally attested royal names bear the title King of Kish, apparently in the sense of overlord of the whole country. This is clearest in the case of Mesilim, whose name, title, and benefactions appear on votive inscriptions from the city-states of Adab and Lagash ahead of the names and more modest titles of the local rulers. Similarly, Mesannepadda, the king of Ur, claimed the Kish title in one of his inscriptions. But he, and others both before and after him, also claimed the title King of Ur. And the latter title begins to occur in the earliest archival texts from Ur, which belong to this period. It was, in sum, a time when the earlier preeminence of Kish and its sole kingship was still accorded respect but when the concept of kingship began to extend to other individual city-states too. As yet, the office of king appears to have been elective and rarely hereditary for more than a generation or two. Its duties were divided between the military and the religious sphere, possibly with different emphases in different cases, and trade was an important secondary responsibility. It remained for the succeeding period to institutionalize these elements into the patterns that became normative for Mesopotamia and much of the rest of the Near East.

[4] THE DYNASTIC AGE: ED III
2500–2300 B.C.

The end of the Early Dynastic Period did not loom as large as its beginning or middle in the memory of subsequent ages, and later literary

---

[38] As Jacobsen has pointed out (*The Sumerian King List*, pp. 168–69), Enmebaragesi originally began a second dynasty of Kish. My chronological reconstruction further assumes a gap between him and the end of the first dynasty. A new fragment of the Sumerian King List presumably begins a new dynasty of Kish with Enmebaragesi. Compare J. J. Nissen, "Eine neue Version der Sumerischen Königsliste," *Zeitschrift für Assyriologie und vorderasiatische Archäologie* 57 (1965):1–5.

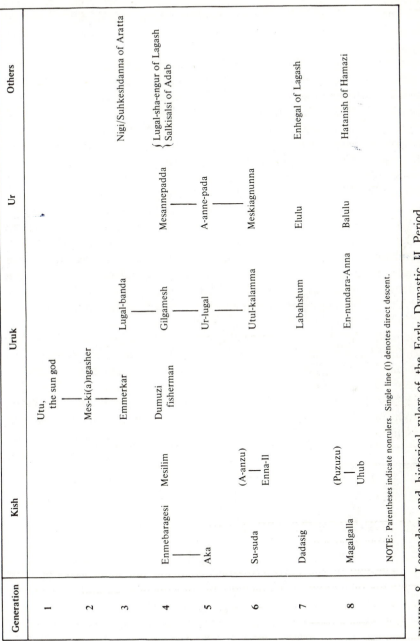

Generation	Kish	Uruk	Ur	Others
1		Utu, the sun god		
2		Mes-ki(a)ngasher		
3		Emmerkar		Nigi/Suhkeshdanna of Aratta
4	Enmebaragesi	Lugal-banda	Mesannepadda	Lugal-sha-engur of Lagash / Salkisalsi of Adab
		Dumuzi fisherman		
		Gilgamesh		
5	Aka	Ur-lugal	A-anne-pada	
6	Su-suda	Utul-kalamma	Meskiagnunna	
	(A-anzu) Enna-Il			
7	Dadasig	Labahshum	Elulu	Enhegal of Lagash
8	Magalgalla	En-nundara-Anna	Balulu	Hatanish of Hamazi
	(Puzuzu) Uhub			

NOTE: Parentheses indicate nonrulers. Single line (I) denotes direct descent.

FIGURE 8 Legendary and historical rulers of the Early Dynastic II Period.

reflections of it are extremely sparse. Earlier figures like Adapa, Ziusudra, Etana, and Gilgamesh were canonized in classical Sumerian texts; they became the heroes of new compositions in subsequent Akkadian literature and occasionally in Hurrian, Hittite, Hebrew, and even Greek derivatives. But outside the King List one finds no more than a scattered reference or two to a single ED III ruler in Sumerian literature, let alone in subsequent traditions. Even the King List has an unusually fluid text for this period, with the order of the dynasties transmitted in at least three variations.[39] For the historian, however, this deficiency is more than compensated for by increased contemporaneous documentation. Not only is there a new abundance of monuments (that is, royal or "historical" inscriptions, either on stone monuments and metal objects or on multiple clay bricks and cones), but also, for the first time, the archives of clay tablets begin to become sufficiently intelligible to play an important role in reconstructing the history of the period. These archives include two principal kinds of text, one economic (archival texts in the strict sense) and the other literary and lexical, the forerunners of the later canonical literature (and thus canonical texts in the wider sense). The canonical texts come chiefly from Fara (ancient Shuruppak) and Abu Salabikh (of which the ancient name is still unknown)[40] and already treat the first dynasty rulers of Uruk as divine figures; a minimum of a century must have intervened to account for the transformation, and other indications too place them in the early part of ED III. Here also belong the archival texts from Fara, while the latter half of the period has yielded even more numerous economic texts from Tel-loh (Arabic for "mound of tablets"), part of the ancient city-state of Lagash, as well as from other sites such as Bismya (ancient Adab). In between, the record is filled in by a small but significant group of contracts regarding real estate and other transactions generally inscribed on stone tablets or clay nails. Thus we are in a position to describe both the political and the social structure of the period from contemporaneous documents.

In the political realm, the principal change from the Heroic Age was the disappearance of elective kingship and its replacement by the dynastic

---

[39]

Nippur Recension	Larsa(?) Recension	Susa Recension
Ur II	Uruk II	Ur II
Uruk II	Ur II	Uruk II
Adab	Adab	Adab
Mari	Mari	Akshak
Kish III	Kish III	Mari
Akshak	Akshak	Kish III

(Compare F. R. Kraus, "Zur Liste der älteren Könige von Babylonien," *Zeitschrift für Assyriologie und vorderasiatische Archäologie* 50 (1952):29–60.)

[40] Robert D. Biggs, "The Abū Ṣālabīkh Tablets: A Preliminary Survey," *Journal of Cuneiform Studies* 20 (1966):73–88.

system of royal succession. At the same time, kingship was definitively institutionalized. It was no longer in any sense an *ad hoc* arrangement to provide leadership for occasional needs in the areas of warfare or monumental architecture, and the choice of the king was, therefore, no longer left to the judgment of his peers. Kings now claimed to rule by divine right, and this right remained in their family, passing to a brother or, more often, a son who was designated heir apparent in the lifetime of his predecessor. Achievement of this end required a firm alliance of royal and religious interests, including a whole new ideology, or theology, of kingship. It involved the proper designation, probably by means of divination, of one son as crown prince and of other children as high priests and high priestesses, even before birth. The crown prince, born of the sacred marriage between the king and the priestess of a given god, was considered the son of that god and subsequently invoked him as his personal patron. Other deities were regarded as endowing the prince with strength and wisdom, summoning him for kingship, and giving him his throne name—all prior to his birth. Once born he was said to have been suckled and reared by a goddess, and when old enough to take the field of battle, he was regarded as knight-errant for a god. Thus supernaturally endowed and legitimized, the king, on his accession, tended to lavish the same deities with temples and offerings. Although not itself directly involved with the day-to-day cult, the new kingship consequently benefited the priesthood, which now emerged as a separate profession of considerable numbers.

The alliance of the new, divinely sanctioned kingship with the royally endowed priesthood was not without its social and economic consequences. Throughout this period there was a gradual redistribution of wealth, especially in the form of agricultural land, leading to a sharp social stratification and, ultimately, to a class struggle and a new alignment of class alliances. At the beginning of the period, the city-state rulers were considered appointees of the deity (that is, priests), and shared their wealth, if not their power, with a "nobility" based presumably on the ability to render effective military assistance and with a larger class of commoners organized into clans based probably on kinship. But a continuous process of royal, priestly, and noble land purchases gradually reduced much of the class of commoners to the status of clients of palace, temple, and noble estates, where they subsisted on rations of cereals, oil, fish, milk, wool, and garments.[41] In addition, some free citizens were reduced to outright slavery, at least temporarily, through their inability to repay debts or their capture in war. It has been demonstrated that slavery never played a major role in Mesopotamia, probably because it was economically unfeasible, especially for industrial purposes, before Greco-Roman times; slaves were confined largely to domestic duties and repre-

[41] Ignace J. Gelb, "The Ancient Mesopotamian Ration System," *Journal of Near Eastern Studies* 24 (1965):230–43.

sented a luxury in any household.[42] But the proliferation of the client (or semi-free) class posed a more serious problem. At the end of the period in question, it led to the first recorded reform act, when Urukagina, last of the early Lagash rulers, attempted to restore an earlier balance of wealth by an alliance of temple and clients against palace and nobility. But the attempt failed, a victim of the prevailing international situation, whose background we may now sketch briefly.

While ED I had been characterized by the hegemony of Kish, and ED II by the contest between Kish in the Akkadian north and Ur and Uruk in the Sumerian south, a new factor now entered the picture. That factor was non-Mesopotamian according to the later traditions. Already Gilgamesh and Enkidu had campaigned ("walked proudly") along the Ulaia River,[43] the Sumerian gateway to Susa and all of Elam (compare Daniel 8:2, 16), and Enmebaragesi of Kish is reported by the King List to have defeated Elam ("carried off its weapons"). In the same source, the next (second) dynasty of Kish, which straddles the end of ED II (see Figure 8, page 47) and the beginning of ED III in our reconstruction (see Figure 9) is flanked by, that is, at least partly contemporaneous with, one each of Awan and Hamazi, with four rulers altogether. These city-states were located in western Iran, east of Sumer and Akkad respectively, and Awan, in particular, is known as the first capital of Elam and the seat of the first known native Elamite dynasty. (Their names are recorded for the entire ED III and Sargonic periods.) Elam had been open to the direct influence of Sumer and its cultural achievements since the beginning of the Bronze Age, for there was no geographical barrier between the two areas. But neither was there any natural barrier to Elamite invasions of Sumer, a recurrent feature in their millennial coexistence. The insertion of the two eastern dynasties at this point of the King List may thus reflect a brief Elamite hegemony over lower Mesopotamia at the end of the ED II period; it may even explain the end of that period.

The traditional centers of Sumero-Akkadian power apparently were not equal to the new challenge from the east when this was added to the perennial pressures from the west, where semi-nomadic, Semitic-speaking groups always threatened the Middle Euphrates. The names of the last Early Dynastic kings of Kish, Uruk, and Ur, as far as they are preserved in the extant portions of the King List, have not been identified convinc-

---

[42] Idem, "Approaches to the Study of Ancient Society," *Journal of the American Oriental Society* 87 (1967):1–8.

[43] W. G. Lambert, "Gilgameš in Religious, Historical, and Omen Texts and the Historicity of Gilgameš," *Gilgameš et sa légende*, ed. Paul Garelli, Cahiers du Groupe François-Thureau-Dangin, no. 1 (Paris: Imprimerie Nationale-Librarie C. Klincksieck, 1960), p. 47, n. 2.

ingly in contemporaneous inscriptions, whereas the royal names from new seats of power, like Akshak, near Kish, and Mari, on the Middle Euphrates, can be so identified. In particular it was the city of Adab that, according to later tradition, actually turned the tide. In two seventeenth century copies, allegedly made from an original royal inscription, Lugalanne-mundu of Adab is said to have "restored Sumer" and achieved universal dominion, becoming "king of the four quarters." This title is otherwise unknown before Naram-Sin of Akkad nearly two centuries later (below, Section 5), and the late tradition is not necessarily an accurate description of events eight centuries earlier. It does, however, reflect the general upheaval that marked the transition from the Heroic to the Dynastic Age.

It also indicates the source of the Sumerian counterattack. Just as Mari may owe its prominence to its role as defender of the northwestern frontier, so too on the eastern frontier of Sumerian hegemony, a little south of Adab, there arose two city-states, Lagash and Umma, whose function appears to have been to ward off further Elamite depredations and, when possible, to carry Sumerian arms, rule, and culture to Susa and Awan. Lagash and Umma, though not dignified with inclusion in the King List, left ample contemporaneous documentation of the success with which they discharged this task over the next five centuries, transforming Elam into a cultural, if not always a political, province of Sumer. But the new militarism required for the counterattack had its effect on the Sumerian city-states. Embassies, single combat, and, failing these, lightning campaigns or sieges with small bands of eager warriors tied by personal loyalty to their chosen leader no longer sufficed when the constantly rising standard of living in Sumer and Akkad awakened the envy of less favored neighbors. The breakdown of the "heroic style" and the evolution of the dynastic state were the inevitable result in international affairs.

It will be recalled that in the preceding period the ruler of Lagash still contented himself with a subordinate position vis-à-vis the King of Kish, Mesilim. By the end of the period, however, a certain Enhegal claimed the title King of Lagash as recorded on a monument noting the purchase of eight parcels of land. The title was assumed next by Ur-Nanshe, who, though of nonroyal parentage, established the dynastic principle at Lagash. He left numerous short inscriptions that reveal his ancestry, his progeny, his religious benefactions, and the fact that he exacted tribute from the mountains, presumably behind and beyond Elam, and brought it to Lagash by ship. He was succeeded by his son Akurgal, and his family maintained itself for three more generations. The greatest member of the dynasty was his grandson Eannatum, who not only subdued Elam, destroying Susa, its capital, and a number of other Iranian cities, but also extended his ambition to Sumer and Akkad. After his repulse of Akshak,

Generation	Kish	Adab	Mari	Lagash	
1	KALBUM		Ikun-Shamash	(Gunidu)	
2	Tuge	LUGALANNEMUNDU	Iblul-II	Ur-Nanshe	
3	Mennunna		ILSHU	Akurgal	
4	Lugalmu		....-zi (*Nin-metabarre*)	EANNATUM	Enannatum I
5	Inbi-Ishtar	Lugal-dalu	....-lugal		Entemena
6	*Ku-Bau*		....-lugal		Enannatum II
7	Puzur-Sin		....-bimushmash	En-entarzi	
8	Ur-Zababa	Meskigal	....-ni	Lugal-anda	Urukagina

NOTE: Rulers who claimed hegemony over all of Sumer are capitalized; females are italicized. Parentheses indicate nonrulers. Parallel lines (II) denotes marriage; single line (I) denotes direct descent.

FIGURE 9   Rulers of the Early Dynastic III Period (tentative reconstruction).

he claimed the title King of Kish as well as some kind of hegemony over the Sumerian south. But in moving west and north, he ran into the opposition of his nearest Sumerian neighbor, Umma. This city was so located as to share with Lagash its chief natural resources: the rich agricultural land called Edin, on which both bordered, and the principal watercourse, the Adab Canal, which tapped the waters of the Euphrates farther north. In earlier times, the inevitable disputes over these resources had been adjudicated by Mesilim, apparently in favor of Lagash, and Eannatum maintained the upper hand over Enakalle, the ruler of Umma, as he describes at length in the Stele of Vultures, which also preserves in relief a fine view of the battle-phalanx and other details of the Lagash military machine. But Umma too developed a powerful ruling dynasty under the challenge

Uruk and Ur	Umma	Akshak	Awan	Generation
Mes-gande			Peli	1
Melam-Anna	Enlil-gi		Tata	2
Lugal-Kitun	Ush	Unzi	Ukkutahesh	3
(Elilin)	Enakalle	Undalulu	Hishur	4
EN-SHAKUSHANNA	(Eandamu) Ur-Lumma	Urur	Shushuntarana	5
LUGAL-KINGINESHDUDU Il	(Bara-irnun) Gisha-kidu	Puzur-Nirah	Napilhush	6
LUGAL-TARSI/Lugal-kisalsi Ukush		Ishu-Il	Kikku-siwe-tempti	7
Lugal-ure/Argandea	LUGALZAGESI	Shu-Sin	Luh-ishan	8

of Lagash, and Enakalle's successors were more than a match for the successors of Eannatum. (See Figure 9 for the dynastic relationships.) Enannatum I was probably challenged by Ur-Lumma, but the latter was eventually defeated when Enannatum's successor, Entemena, concluded an alliance with Ur and Uruk, which had formed a condominium under Lugalkingeneshdudu. But Il rebelled against Enannatum II and brought an end to the dynasty of Ur-Nanshe.

The final chapter in the struggle was written by new dynasties in both cities. Urukagina, the reformer, was defeated and Lagash destroyed by Lugalzagesi. The numerous archival records from Lagash dating to Urukagina and his immediate predecessors give us a vivid picture of the declining fortunes of the city in these difficult years, and we must marvel at the almost blind dedication with which the scribes continued to record the day-to-day minutiae of a contracting economy.[44] After defeating Lagash, Lugalzagesi apparently moved his seat of power to Uruk and, whether by his military achievements or by his well-attested benefactions to the temple of Enlil at Nippur, achieved what had eluded Eannatum: recognition by the Nippur priesthood. He succeeded, not only to the condominium of Uruk and Ur, but to the hegemony of all of Sumer and Akkad, and is duly entered in the Sumerian King List, where he constitutes the Third Dynasty of Uruk. His triumphs were inscribed on vases which he dedicated at the religious capital of Nippur. Though his claim to have "straightened the roads from the Lower Sea [the Persian Gulf] to the Upper Sea [the Mediterranean]" may be questioned, he surely laid the basis for a combination of two discrete political principles—the dynastic and the imperial—which, fully realized under Sargon of Akkad, was to characterize the age that ensued.

[5] SARGON AND THE RISE OF AKKAD
ca. 2300–2230 B.C.

When Sargon of Akkad conquered Lugalzagesi of Uruk "together with [his] fifty governors,"[45] he laid the basis for a new departure in Mesopotamian political organization and ushered in a complex of social, religious, and artistic innovations that deserve to be regarded as a kind of cultural explosion. Its stimulus spread the norms of Sumer and Akkad far beyond their boundaries, and Mesopotamian influence of varying strength can be detected throughout the Asiatic Near East in what is generally regarded as its last Early Bronze phase (EB III or, in Albright's scheme, EB IV). Although Palestine, Syria, Anatolia, and large parts of Iran still lacked indigenous systems of writing, they entered the fringes of history as the Mesopotamian sources began to take serious notice of them. These sources, in ever-increasing abundance, illuminate matters both near and far. They include both contemporaneous sources, in the manner of the documentation for the preceding Dynastic Age, and later traditions, reminiscent of the traditions of the earlier Heroic Age. Indeed, the Sargonic Age captured the imagination of subsequent generations to such an extent that one of the real problems for the period is to extract the kernel of historical truth from the legendary accretions in which it became embedded.

---

[44] Compare Maurice Lambert, "La Guerre entre Urukagina et Lugalzaggesi," *Rivista degli Studi Orientali* 61 (1966):29–66.
[45] According to the copies of his inscriptions at Nippur.

Nowhere is this problem more acute than in connection with Sargon's origins and rise to power. One fact alone is clear, and it is negative: he could hardly have been born Sharru-ken(u), a name meaning "the king is legitimate, the legitimate king," which seems to be a veritable apology for the form of his accession.[46] Positive data are harder to come by. Sargon's father is variously identified as a certain La'ibum (in the older Sumerian sources), as an anonymous gardener (in the King List), and as unknown even to Sargon himself (in the late Akkadian tradition). At all events, Sargon seems to have been of humble birth. The late source identifies his mother as a high priestess, but not necessarily, like some priestesses, of royal parentage. Her marriage seems to have been illicit, for after bearing Sargon in secret, she exposed him to the Euphrates in a reed basket.[47] He was found by a water-drawer who raised him as a gardener, and as such he won the love and attention of the goddess Ishtar. The link with Ishtar, the Sumerian Inanna, which persists in all the traditions, may reflect another alliance with a priestess of the goddess;[48] but, whether by the help of a priestess or by some other means, the foundling suddenly appeared in the coveted role of cup-bearer[49] to Ur-Zababa of Kish. This king enjoyed a certain fame in later tradition and is assigned a legendary reign of four hundred years in some versions of the King List—but a more realistic one of six years in at least one. According to Sumerian traditions, the end of his reign, apparently at the height of its prosperity, was decreed by the god Enlil (or by Marduk according to a later Akkadian source), who transferred the divine legitimation from the older king to the young usurper in retribution for a cultic offense of the former.

In point of fact it is hard to believe that Sargon succeeded to the kingdom of Kish immediately upon the demise or deposition of Ur-Zababa. For that king was followed by four or five others in the King List before the last dynasty of Kish finally came to its end; and even if we accept only the lowest regnal figures given for them, these total fifty years. In other words, they were probably contemporaneous with most of Sargon's long reign of fifty-five years.[50] During these fifty years Sargon seems to have been busy establishing himself as an independent ruler at Akkad, the new

[46] It was assumed by an Assyrian usurper as late as 722 B.C. for much the same reason. (The latter's name in the Hebrew Bible is the basis for the English rendering, Sargon, and its derivatives, Sargonic and Sargonid. To avoid confusion, the Old Akkadian dynasty is conventionally referred to as Sargonic, the neo-Assyrian one as Sargonid.)
[47] Reminding us of the Biblical story of Moses; compare Brevard S. Childs, "The Birth of Moses," *Journal of Biblical Literature* 84 (1965):109–22.
[48] William W. Hallo and J. J. A. van Dijk, *The Exaltation of Inanna*, Yale Near Eastern Researches, vol. 3 (New Haven: Yale University Press, 1968), pp. 6–7.
[49] Or "freedman" or "captive(?)" according to later Akkadian sources.
[50] One variant has fifty-four years (the Birth Legend), and another fifty-six years, probably to match Naram-Sin's reign.

city he built somewhere on the Euphrates,[51] and campaigning far beyond the traditional borders of Sumer and Akkad. His first conquests may have been in the west, for Amurru felt his arms as early as his third or eleventh year, according to various later traditions.[52] In the northwest he penetrated as far as Purushkhanda, deep in Anatolia, to protect the rights of Akkadian(?) traders according to the later epic, called *King of Battle,* and a Hittite king of the seventeenth century recalled that he crossed the (Upper) Euphrates to receive the submission of only slightly less distant Hahhum.[53] In the northeast he campaigned against Simurrum (according to the evidence of a date formula from Nippur,[54] presumably belonging near the end of his reign) in the first recorded Mesopotamian penetration into Assyria. In the east he proceeded, perhaps after his conquest of Der, to Elam and Barakhshi (Markhashi), which he subdued totally, and thence, apparently by boat, as far as Dilmun at the head of the Persian Gulf. If this reconstruction of events is correct, it will be noted that he thus established his authority in a great ring around Sumer and Akkad (Figure 11, page 64) without as yet challenging any of the ancient seats of Mesopotamian power. The historical tradition insists, in fact, that when the challenge came, it came from them. After an initial uprising by the city of Kazallu, all the ancient city-states revolted in Sargon's old age (though there is no clear indication that he as yet ruled them). Even then he seems to have sought an accommodation with Lugalzagesi of Uruk, who was their leader. When that failed, however, he was in a position to move energetically and devastatingly. Uruk was defeated, its walls razed, and Lugalzagesi captured along with his "fifty governors"—that is, the petty kings of all the separate city-states. Both Uruk and Kish fell out of favor with Enlil, and, for the last five(?) years of his life, Sargon reigned as king

---

[51] The exact site of this famous capital has never been located, but it lay within the "capital district" (see Figure 17, page 90) and gave its name to the whole of that district. Together with Sumer in the south, it constituted the stage for early Mesopotamian history. In keeping with the native sources, we have identified the region as a whole as Sumer and Akkad, even though before the establishment of the dynasty of Akkad this involves a slight anachronism.

[52] Margaret S. Drower and J. Bottéro, "Syria Before 2200 B.C.," fasc. 55, *Cambridge Ancient History,* rev. ed., vol. 1 (Cambridge: Cambridge University Press, 1968), p. 7, n. 8, quoting C. J. Gadd, "The Dynasty of Agade and the Gutian Invasion," fasc. 17, *Cambridge Ancient History,* rev. ed., vol. 1 (1963), pp. 3–20. Drower and Bottéro hold that Sargon, "once he had united the whole of Mesopotamia under his sway, turned towards the west and marched out to conquer it." But Gadd's only basis for this chronology is that "two of Sargon's inscriptions place after the account of his victories in southern Babylonia a summary description of distant triumphs in a march up the Euphrates and widespread conquests in Syria" (p. 10). In fact, these inscriptions mention only thirty-four victorious campaigns and do not say specifically where or when they took place.

[53] Hans G. Güterbock, "Sargon of Akkad mentioned by Ḫattušili I of Ḫatti," *Journal of Cuneiform Studies* 18 (1964):1–6.

[54] Concerning date formulas, see below, Section 6.

of Kish, Uruk, and Ur and as overlord of all Sumer and Akkad. These triumphs were duly recorded in the temple of Enlil at the national religious capital, Nippur, together with the records of the king's Elamite victories, the spoils of which were donated to the temple.

These inscriptions, copied again and again by later generations, may have helped lay the foundations for the veneration in which some of the kings of Akkad were subsequently held. The enduring fascination with Sargon and Naram-Sin in particular was matched only by the interest shown in such later royal figures as Shulgi and Ibbi-Sin of Ur (Chapter III, Section 2), Hammurapi of Babylon (Chapter III, Section 5), Tukulti-Ninurta of Assur (Chapter V, Section 1), and Nebukadnezar or Nabonidus of the Chaldean Dynasty (Chapter V, Section 5). All these kings shared a common vision: to realize, no matter how briefly or ephemerally, the perennial ideal of Mesopotamian unity. Whether they succeeded or perished in the attempt, their memory apparently intrigued later generations beyond that of the more typical, but duller, periods of fragmentary petty-statism that intervened. In Sargon's case, the memory was enhanced by the fact that he was the first to graft onto the old doctrine of national hegemony the newer concept of dynastic succession and divine legitimation of a particular royal family. As a result, not only was all of Mesopotamia ruled by Sargonic kings for at least three more generations, but descendants and relatives of Sargon filled numerous high offices throughout the empire. (See Figure 10 for an attempted reconstruction of the interrelationships.) Since even the numerous royal progeny could not staff all the important posts, the king filled the balance with men who owed their appointments, and therefore their primary allegiance, to him rather than to the cities and populations entrusted to their care. In this way Sargon and his successors forged the first real empire out of a congeries of fiercely independent city-states and, for at least a brief period, succeeded in stemming their centrifugal tendency. In a few cases, Sargon seems to have felt strong enough to reconfirm the native dynasts in their old posts; thus under Sargon's first successor Meskigal is still found at Adab and under his second Urukagina is still, conceivably, at Lagash.[55] Even Lugalzagesi's life was spared, and he was allowed to return to his original base at Umma as a provincial governor.[56]

[55] For Meskigal, see Ferris J. Stephens, introduction to George Gottlob Hackman, *Sumerian and Akkadian Administrative Texts from Predynastic Times to the End of the Akkad Dynasty*, Babylonian Inscriptions in the Collection of James B. Nies, vol. 8 (New Haven: Yale University Press, 1958), p. 10. For Urukagina, see Jacobsen, "Early Political Development in Mesopotamia," *Toward the Image of Tammuz and Other Essays on Mesopotamian History and Culture*, ed. Moran, p. 395, n. 107.
[56] One source, however, seems to indicate that Sargon took Lugalzagesi's wife as a concubine in what became a classic feature of usurpation in the ancient Near East. Compare Stanley Gevirtz, "A Father's Curse," *Mosaic* 2 (1969):56–61, esp. 61; and George A. Barton, *The Royal Inscriptions of Sumer and Akkad*, Library of Ancient Semitic Inscriptions, vol. 1 (New Haven: Yale University Press, 1929), p. 117.

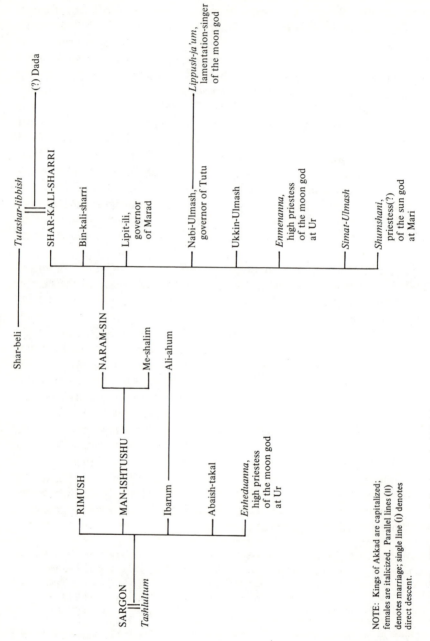

NOTE: Kings of Akkad are capitalized; females are italicized. Parallel lines (||) denotes marriage; single line (|) denotes direct descent.

FIGURE 10 The royal house of Akkad.

Sargon was not insensitive to the opposition that his new imperialism inevitably aroused, and particularly to the latent antagonism between the Akkadian-speaking north and the Sumerian-speaking south. He attacked these problems with characteristic vigor and originality by creating the double office of high priestess of the moongod Nanna at Ur and of the Heavengod An at Uruk, and investing his daughter Enheduanna with this double priesthood, parallelling his own assumption of the double kingship of Uruk and Ur, the ancient condominium of the principal Sumerian centers of the south. For the next five hundred years, his example was followed religiously: it became the right of the recognized ruler of all of Sumer and Akkad to appoint his daughter as high priestess to Nanna for life. Many of these princesses outlived their royal fathers and some even their dynasties and provided a unifying link even in periods of disunity. Enheduanna, however, was the greatest of this long line as well as the first. In addition to her portrait (Figure 4, page 26) and some brief inscriptions, she left two large cycles of hymns. One is in honor of the Sumerian goddess Inanna, justifying and commemmorating her exaltation to supreme rank in the pantheon as "Queen of Heaven" and consort of the deified heaven, An, king of the gods.[57] The other honors the temples of Sumer and Akkad, linking the cults of the two areas for the first time and completing the syncretism between the Sumerian Inanna, patroness of love and fertility, and the warlike Akkadian Ishtar, Sargon's personal deity.[58] The consummate literary style of Enheduanna suggests that she may have had a Sumerian mother;[59] in any case she represents the first known author in world literature and the artistic executor of the same purposes that her father sought to accomplish by military and political means.

Of Sargon's other children (Figure 10, page 58), two succeeded him as king. They reigned twenty-two (or, perhaps, twenty-four) years altogether and apparently continued in the footsteps of their more famous father, consolidating the empire that he had erected. Rimush, who beat down numerous insurrections by obstreperous governors of the Sumerian cities, was Sargon's first successor. The second, though the older of the two brothers, was Man-ishtushu, "who is with him?" whose name suggests that they may have been twins. His rule over distant Assur and Susa is attested by the monuments of native governors inscribed in his honor, the first of a millennial succession of such testimonials to Mesopotamian imperialism that ensue henceforth on all the frontiers of empire. In this case the inscriptions are of interest also for the local history of Assyria and Elam, as they provide a chronological anchor of sorts for the native historical tradi-

---

[57] Hallo and van Dijk, *The Exaltation of Inanna*.
[58] Ibid., p. 10. Compare also Åke W. Sjöberg and E. Bergmann S.J. (†), *The Collection of the Sumerian Temple Hymns, Texts from Cuneiform Sources*, vol. 3 (Locust Valley, N.Y.: J. J. Augustin, 1969).
[59] Compare Barton, *The Royal Inscriptions of Sumer and Akkad*, p. 117.

tions. Indeed, a later king of Assyria, Shamshi-Adad I, recalled Man-ish-tushu as the first builder of the Ishtar temple in Nineveh. Otherwise the memory of the two brothers was preserved only in the omen literature, a genre that began essentially with Sargon and became thereafter a characteristic vehicle of Mesopotamian historiography.[60] According to these omens, both brothers were killed by their own courtiers using, as specified in one case, their cylinder-seals (that is, the long spikes on which these seals were mounted before being attached to a chain worn around the neck).

[6] NARAM-SIN AND THE FALL OF AKKAD
ca. 2230–2100 B.C.

The assassination of Man-ishtushu paved the way for the accession of his son, Naram-Sin, and for the most brilliant period that the Sargonic empire—and perhaps any Mesopotamian empire—was to know. The new king enjoyed an almost unparalleled reign of fifty-six years. There is no convincing reason to doubt this figure,[61] even though it is not preserved in all copies of the King List, and it would be hard to accommodate in any shorter span of time all of the achievements and innovations that can be dated to this reign. Of these the most conspicuous may well be the transformation of the royal titulary,[62] which hitherto had been content to specify the political or cultic relationship between the ruler and his geographical domain—that is, "lord/high priest of Sumer, king of the nation" or "lord/high priest of the territory of Uruk, king of the territory of Ur." On what appear to be his earliest inscriptions, Naram-Sin claimed, or was accorded, the modest title of king of Akkad. But about halfway through his reign he introduced the title "king of the four quarters [of the world]" which was assumed after him by all those kings who proudly aspired to

---

[60] J. J. Finkelstein, "Mesopotamian Historiography," *Proceedings of the American Philosophical Society* 107 (1963):461–72. Long before Sargon, Gilgamesh of Uruk was already the subject of some omens, but these may be regarded as late or noncanonical. Compare ibid., p. 465, n. 13; and Lambert, "Gilgameš in Religious, Historical and Omen Texts and the Historicity of Gilgameš," *Gilgameš et sa légende*, ed. Garelli, pp. 43–46. Concerning canonicity, see Chapter VI, Section 2; concerning omens, see Chapter VI, Section 3.

[61] Jacobsen (*The Sumerian King List*, p. 112, n. 251), followed by many other scholars, reconstructs the reign at thirty-seven years, but there is no explicit textual evidence to support this figure.

[62] William W. Hallo, *Early Mesopotamian Royal Titles: A Philologic and Historical Analysis*, American Oriental Series, vol. 43 (New Haven: American Oriental Society, 1957), pp. 49–76.

universal dominion from a Mesopotamian base.[63] Not content with earthly honors, Naram-Sin presently also allowed himself to be entitled "god of Akkad," which at first may have implied only that he was the guiding "genius" or good fortune of his country.[64] The concept of a "divine Naram-Sin" quickly evolved, however, and with it a cult of the living ruler and of his deceased predecessors that was, for practical purposes, indistinguishable from the cult of the "real" gods and, like theirs, centered around the king's statue. Although it never reached Egyptian proportions, the apotheosis of the living Mesopotamian king was reasserted by Naram-Sin's first successor and was revived by various neo-Sumerian and Early Old Babylonian rulers, one of whom even had a number of temples built in his honor.[65] Late in his reign, Naram-Sin added still another title, that of "strong (male)," whose exact significance thus far eludes us. It may have been taken over by right of conquest from Naram-Sin's Elamite adversaries and signified something like "the great," an epithet much fancied by later rulers both ancient and more recent.

In matters of internal policy, Naram-Sin perpetuated and institutionalized the reforms that Sargon had only begun to experiment with. Like Enheduanna, his daughter Enmenanna became high priestess of the moon god at Ur, and he found equally high clerical or civil posts for the rest of his numerous progeny, including Shar-kali-sharri, who was destined to succeed his father and to rule for a quarter of a century. Of their combined regnal total of eighty-odd years, a fifth are so far known by "name," that is, by an official designation recalling some significant event of the preceding year.[66] This usage was introduced by Sargon, apparently at the end of his reign, in place of the older systems of dating by the names of local officials (so-called eponyms), known at Shuruppak, or by regnal years, attested for Urukagina and his immediate predecessors at Lagash. The eponym system was used subsequently in Assyria throughout its long history, and the regnal-year system was resumed in Babylonia beginning with the Kassites, as well as in most of the rest of the Asiatic Near East. It was replaced eventually by the simpler system of reckoning in eras, notably the Seleucid Era, which was gradually adopted throughout the Near East beginning in 312 B.C. And it was replaced in turn by denominational eras—

[63] Compare the surveys: ibid, p. 152; and M.-J. Seux, "Les Titres royaux šar kiššati et šar kibrāt arba'i," *Revue d'Assyriologie et d'Archéologie Orientale* 59 (1965):11–14.
[64] Jacobsen, "Early Political Development in Mesopotamia," *Toward the Image of Tammuz and Other Essays on Mesopotamian History and Culture,* ed. Moran, p. 395, n. 108.
[65] Compare Chapter III, Section 2, page 84; Henri Frankfort, *Kingship and the Gods: A Study of Ancient Near Eastern Religion as the Integration of Society and Nature* (Chicago: University of Chicago Press, 1948).
[66] Compare: Hans Hirsch, "Die Inschriften der Könige von Agade," *Archiv für Orientforschung* 20 (1963):22 and 28–29; and Albrecht Goetze, "Akkad Dynasty Inscriptions from Nippur," *Essays in Memory of E. A. Speiser,* ed. Hallo, pp. 54–59, esp. 56–59.

for example, the Jewish, reckoned from Creation (3760 B.C.); the Christian, from Christ's birth (A.D. 1);[67] and the Moslem, from Mohammed's flight from Mecca to Medina (A.D. 622). While it is true that these successive changes made for a more efficient chronology, the system of year names provided an invaluable record of the principal events and accomplishments of the various Babylonian dynasties, both contemporaneous and successive, for over five hundred years. Without their help, it would be hard to reconstruct the history of much of this period.

The increased need for and attestation of year names, or date formulas, under Naram-Sin and Shar-kali-sharri is part and parcel of the prosperity and economic growth of their time. In their reigns, legal and administrative documents appear not only at Lagash and Ur, where such texts were already well known in pre-Sargonic times, but also, for the first time in significant numbers, at sites such as Adab, Nippur, Susa, Gasur (the later Nuzi) and the Diyala Valley. Their language, like that of the contemporary royal inscriptions, is as often Akkadian as Sumerian, and such royal patronage of the once despised tongue may have inspired the beginnings of Akkadian belles-lettres, although only one or two literary scraps dating to Sargonic times have thus far been identified.[68] But if the literary evidence is circumstantial, artistic creativity is explicitly documented. Nearly all the surviving Sargonic works of art can be dated, if at all, to these two reigns. The visual arts enjoyed an ebullient, not to say explosive, new era, mirroring in visual form the confidence that world dominion must have inspired in the political sphere. Glyptic, relief, and sculpture display the individualized facial features, forceful modeling of rippling muscles, and confident rendering of background landscape that, while they owe something to Early Dynastic precedent, set the Sargonic style apart from all others. The bronze head of an unidentified Sargonic king found at Nineveh and the victory stele of Naram-Sin may be especially singled out in this connection.

In foreign affairs, too, Naram-Sin proved himself a worthy successor to Sargon, dominating a great portion of the Near East. From Purushkhanda in the northwest to Magan in the southeast, we can reconstruct a consistent pattern of military, diplomatic, and commercial activity on the basis of diverse lines of evidence (Figure 11). The most graphic kind consists of pictorial representations of the great conqueror himself, like the stele found near Diyar Bakr or the rock relief near Kara Dag. The latter, like its prototype, the famous victory stele mentioned above, commemmorates a great victory over the Lullubi, a mountain people whose king, Anu-banini, flaunted his power with a rock relief of his own, inscribed in Old Akkadian, near Saripul.[69] Equally explicit, if less graphic, evidence of Naram-Sin's activities is furnished by his building and votive inscriptions found at home (Nippur, Adab, Ur, Marada, Lagash) and abroad (Susa, Nineveh, Tell Brak). At Brak, moreover, the remains of the king's fortress or palace provide testimony that more than a momentary occupation of the area was intended. Inscriptions and date formulas furnish contemporary evidence for other conquests abroad (Magan, Simurrum, Mardaman, Arman, Ibla) and for building operations at home (Nippur, Zabalam). Dated economic texts also furnish direct evidence of economic activity at sites such as Tutub, Adab, and Nippur, and undated ones from as far away as Gasur (the later Nuzi) also appear to belong to this period. A long treaty with Elam not only is further evidence of Naram-Sin's influence in this area but also constitutes invaluable material for the study of Elamite and is the oldest major document in that language.[70] In light of all this contemporary documentation, it is hard to discredit Old Babylonian copies of lost originals that record additional conquests, especially in the north (Subartu) and northwest (Talhat, the Amanus, Lebanon and Taurus Mountains, and the Mediterranean coast as far as Ullisu). The so-called Cutha Legend even connects Naram-Sin, like Sargon before him, with distant Purushkhanda. But thereby hangs a tale.

The later traditions about Naram-Sin are as abundant as those about Sargon, but they are less unanimous. The lost ending of the Cutha Legend presumably recalled the empire's ultimate deliverance from the rampaging hordes of Anu-banini, and in another fragmentary text Naram-Sin seems similarly to have extricated himself from a rebellion by most of his native Akkadian and Sumerian subordinates under the leadership of Kish. But an equally persistent tradition depicts Naram-Sin as the very model of the hapless ruler who came to grief in the end. His fall is brought on by his own sacrilege, in the Sumerian version against Nippur and its god Enlil, in the Akkadian version against Babylon and Marduk. Both versions agree in identifying the instrument of divine retribution as the Gutians. Yet this ethnic group does not appear in contemporaneous texts until the time of Shar-kali-sharri, and he apparently maintained the empire through all, or most, of his quarter-century reign. We are therefore forced to conclude that later traditions telescoped the two reigns, assigning both their triumphs and their disasters to the more famous of the two kings. Such distortion is not unparalleled in late Near Eastern history (see below, page 149).

[69] Neilson C. Debevoise, "The Rock Reliefs of Ancient Iran," *Journal of Near Eastern Studies* 1 (1942):76–105, esp. 80–83, and plates 1–3. This article traces the entire history of Iranian rock carvings through Parthian times.
[70] Walther Hinz, "Elams Vertrag mit Naram-Sin von Akkade," *Zeitschrift für Assyriologie und Vorderasiatische Archäologie* 58 (1967):66–96.

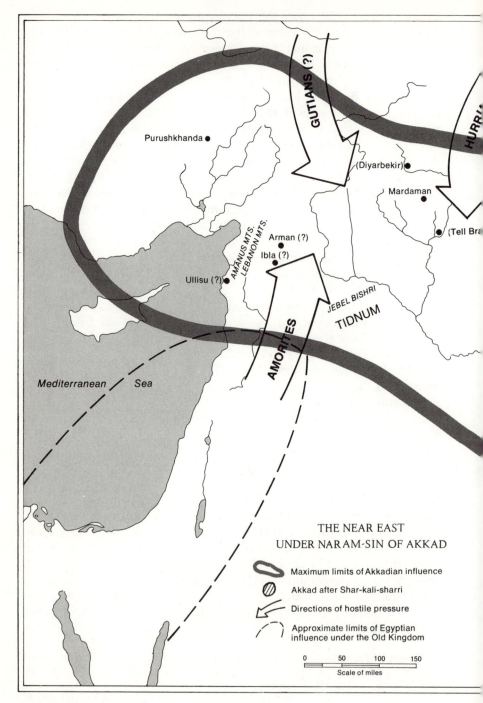

THE NEAR EAST
UNDER NARAM-SIN OF AKKAD

Maximum limits of Akkadian influence

Akkad after Shar-kali-sharri

Directions of hostile pressure

Approximate limits of Egyptian
influence under the Old Kingdom

```
0        50       100      150
Scale of miles
```

FIGURE 11

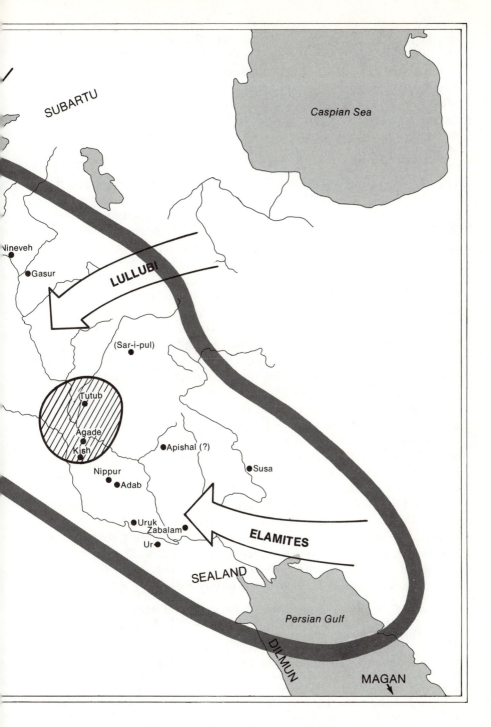

The actual course of events was considerably more complex. If we may believe the omens, Shar-kali-sharri met the same violent end as the sons of Sargon (see above, Section 5). In any case, his reign was followed by three years of anarchy, expressed tellingly by the phrase "who was king, who was not king," both in the omen literature[71] and in the King List. After this, in the King List's usual formula for the end of a dynasty, "Agade was smitten with weapons and its kingship carried to Uruk." Before this final demise, some versions of the text record two more kings of Akkad, Dudu and Shu-Durul, but they ruled only a small area from the city of Akkad northward along the Diyala River (in Sumerian: Durul). The staggering contrast between the empire at its greatest extent and this rump kingdom no doubt had much to do with the tradition of a catastrophic and sudden debacle and with the attempts to explain it by appeal to mortal (royal) delict and divine retribution through the agency of the Gutians. But were the Gutians in fact the crucial factor in the collapse of Akkad?[72] Recent research suggests a more modest role for them and a correspondingly more important one for internal dissension and domestic upheaval, as well as for such diverse foreign elements as the Elamites, the Lullubi, and the Hurrians. The last were emerging as a factor in and around Mesopotamia; already they ruled Urkish and Nawar in Upper Mesopotamia and Karkhar in the Iranian foothills,[73] and they were destined for far more important roles in the history of the second millennium. While all these assaults were being mounted against the empire along its long northeastern border, the opposite frontier was very probably under persistent Amorite pressure centered on Mt. Basar, where Shar-kali-sharri engaged them in battle (Figure 11, page 64). The "end of Akkad" was etched in later memory as a chronological turning-point, heralding the end of an age, much as the Deluge had echoed its beginning. But, given all the adverse circumstances, the wonder is less that it followed hard on the death of Shar-kali-sharri than that it did not take place earlier.

The forty or fifty years that ensued are variously known in modern scholarship as the Late Akkadian, Post-Akkadian, or Gutian Period. Hitherto the period was widely estimated at two, or even three, times as long as this, and its history has consequently been difficult to restore. It now seems clear that it was characterized by a brief relapse into petty-statism such as marked Mesopotamian history with every succeeding im-

[71] Compare E. A. Speiser, "Some Factors in the Collapse of Akkad," *Journal of the American Oriental Society* 72 (1952):97, n. 6; reprinted in E. A. Speiser, *Oriental and Biblical Studies: Collected Writings of E. A. Speiser*, ed. J. J. Finkelstein and Moshe Greenberg (Philadelphia: University of Pennsylvania Press, 1967), pp. 233–34, n. 6.
[72] Compare: ibid., pp. 97–101, reprint pp. 232–43; and William W. Hallo, "Gutium," *Reallexikon der Assyriologie und vorderasiatischen Archäologie*, vol. 3, ed. W. von Soden et al. (Berlin: Walter de Gruyter, 1971), 708–20.
[73] Ignace J. Gelb, "New Light on Hurrians and Subarians," *Studi Orientalistici in onore di Giorgio Della Vida* (Rome: Istituto per l'Oriente, 1956), pp. 378–92.

Year	Akkad	Lagash	Ur	Uruk	Umma	Gutians	Amorites	Hurrians
	ANARCHY	VARIOUS GOVERNORS	HIGH PRIESTESSES OF THE MOON GOD					
2160	Dudu		*Enmenanna*			Iarlagan V	Tudia	Dish-atal of Karahar
						Ibate	Adamu	
2150		Ur-Ba'u		Ur-nigin	Lugal-annatum	Iarlagan VI	Iangi	
				Ur-gigir		Kurum		
						Apil-kin		
				Kudda		...-rabum	Sahlamu	
2140	Shu-Durul	Gudea	*Enannepadda*			Irarum		Dish-atal of Urkish and Nawar
				Puzur-ili		Ibranum	Harharu	
						Hablum		
						Puzur-Sin		
2130				Ur-Utu		Iarlagan VII	Mandaru	
				Lugal-melam			Emsu	
2120	2121	Ur-Ningirsu		Utu-hegal		(?)	Didanu	Atal=shen of Urkish
		Pirigme					Hanu	
		Urgar						
		Nammahani						
				2114	Nammahani	Tirigan 2115		
2110			*Ennirgalanna*				Zuabu	

NOTE: Females are italicized. The Amorites listed here were not rulers but ancestors of the second-millennium royal houses of Babylon and Assur; their exact order is uncertain.

FIGURE 12 The successor states of Akkad (ca. 2160–2110).

perial collapse. Each city-state tended to go its own way, sometimes achieving significant cultural results but relatively lesser political ones. Given the
absence of major political events, synchronisms between the separate
dynasties may be more difficult to establish, but this is no warrant for
treating them as sucessive. Figure 12 represents one attempt to coordinate
what is known of the rulers and dynasties in the principal city-states of
this time. Of these, by far the most important was Lagash. Ur-Ba'u of
Lagash, though he did not gain a place in the King List, must have had
sufficient prestige to appoint his daughter, under the cult name of Enanne-
padda, high priestess of Nanna at Ur. He was succeeded by three sons-in-
law, of whom the greatest was Gudea, who seems to have extended his
domain as far as Uruk and Adab, if only briefly. In the best Lagash tradition (compare above, Section 2), he also made passing references in his
innumerable inscriptions to a triumph over Anshan and Elam, and to the
(re)construction of various fortifications. But with these exceptions, the
date formulas and inscriptions of all the late Lagashite governors (they
did not aspire to the royal title) are devoid of military exploits and devoted wholly to economic and religious pursuits: irrigation; trade; the
building, furnishing, and dedication of temples; and the installation of
their personnel. In this peaceful interlude, commerce, including foreign
trade, thrived, and both literature and sculpture flourished. Gudea was not
only remembered in the cult of the succeeding Ur III dynasty but is a
familiar figure to this day thanks to the magnificent statuary depicting him
and other members of his dynasty. And, to commemorate his dedication
of the Eninnu-temple at Lagash, Gudea's scribes composed a hymn that
remains the single most impressive piece of Sumerian creative writing.
Thus, a minor city-state laid the foundation for a new flowering of Sumerian culture in the ashes of the Akkadian empire.

FIGURE 13 "Basket-bearer"; bronze statuette of Ur-Nammu.

III

THE MIDDLE BRONZE AGE
ca. 2100–1600 B.C.

[1] AMORITES, PATRIARCHS, AND THE WESTLAND

We have seen that, at its height, the Sargonic empire embraced all of the Euphrates basin and much of the land lying beyond its great bend as far as the Mediterranean Sea. At the same time, the pharaohs of the sixth Egyptian dynasty maintained the Old Kingdom's control over the Sinai Peninsula and made its presence felt with repeated incursions into Palestine and southern Syria (see Figure 11, page 64). Both the Mesopotamian and the Egyptian spheres of influence included flourishing urban centers whose populations, though of unknown ethnic affiliations, were regarded as cultural equals of those of the two great empires and which supplied the latter, whether by way of trade or of tribute, with the lumber, metals, and other raw materials in which their hinterlands abounded. But between these two urbanized spheres of influence lay the semi-arid northern fringe of the Syrian desert, known today as the Hamad. This area, unable to support urban life, was the home of nomadic peoples known (perhaps on the basis of their most important tribe) as Amurru in the cuneiform sources and Amorites in the Bible. Their territory extended to the Euphrates at the mountain of Basar (modern Jebel Bishri), which the Sumerians therefore called the "highland of the Amorites," while in later Mesopotamian usage the geographical term Amurru came to designate an ever larger portion of Transeuphratia, until ultimately it embraced all of the "Westland."[1] From their mountain, the nomads posed a threat to Mesopotamia, for the Euphrates route led straight to the heart of Sumer and

---

[1] Compare above, p. 23, n. 45.

Akkad. Only the great citadel of Mari, some hundred miles downstream and across the river from Mount Basar, blocked their way; and already in pre-Sargonic times it had developed into an outpost of Sumero-Akkadian culture against this threat from the northwest, much as Lagash and Umma had against those from the southeast (compare Chapter II, Section 4). But the confrontation along the Euphrates proved fateful for the Amorites as well as for Mari, for it led to an irresistible dilution of nomadic patterns in the direction of seminomadic and, ultimately, urban institutions. The next half-millennium in this area is largely characterized by the tension between the desert and the sown, between country and town, between the wandering herdsman and the settled cultivator of the soil. Its history must be reconstructed from a variety of sources—archeological, epigraphic, and literary—and it remains full of gaps. But its outlines begin to suggest a definite pattern: gradual Amorite acculturation to the urban articulations that they encountered and eventually conquered, together with the survival of significant nomadic traits in the resulting amalgam.

As in the case of the Gutians (Chapter II, Section 6), the first reliable reference to the Amorites occurs in a date formula of Shar-kali-sharri, who claimed to have defeated them at Mount Basar. At his death, the great Sargonic empire disintegrated under the hammer blows of foes from beyond the Tigris; the Amorites on the opposite side of the Euphrates only provided the anvil. But, given the almost simultaneous collapse of the Old Kingdom in Egypt and, hence, of its influence in Asia, the Amorites were now in a position to assert themselves on their home ground, to infiltrate the entire "Westland," and ultimately to conquer much of Egypt and Mesopotamia themselves. They thus inaugurated a pattern that was to become almost paradigmatic in Near Eastern history: the seemingly natural centralization of imperial power in the valleys of the Nile and Tigris-Euphrates alternating, whenever that concentration proved too much to sustain, with an intermediate period when power shifted briefly to the intervening area of Syria-Palestine, an area that, by contrast, seemed destined by nature for political fragmentation.

In the anarchic half-century that followed the death of Shar-kali-sharri, (Chapter II, Section 6), unnamed Amorites already appear, side by side with Gutians, in economic texts from Umma. Gudea of Lagash, whose building materials came from as far away as Urshu, Ibla, and the Amanus, also imported building stone from the "mountain of the Amorites," referring thus both to Mount Basar and to Tidanum (elsewhere identified with Amurru). By the time of the Third Dynasty of Ur in the twenty-first century, the texts from Umma and Lagash show other Amorites, perhaps their descendants, already thoroughly sedentarized. They are still identified as Amorites by the scribes, but most of them already bear good Sumerian or Akkadian names and engage in agriculture and typical urban crafts. The contemporaneous Ur III texts from Drehem, however, and the slightly later ones from Isin, show an entirely different picture. Here the great majority of persons identified as Amorites actually bear Amorite names; indeed these and later names are to date the chief source for the reconstruction of the Amorite language, the earliest form of West Semitic (so called to distinguish it from Akkadian, or East Semitic), later and better known in such forms as Ugaritic, Phoenician, Hebrew, and Aramaic. These unassimilated Amorites were clearly regarded as foreigners, and they appear in the texts side by side with emissaries from the older cities of the northwest, such as Tuttul, Arman, Ibla, and perhaps even Byblos. It is important to note, however, that the scribes always distinguished carefully between the Amorites and other foreigners. Literary texts of neo-Sumerian date or origin are even more explicit: their stereotype Amorite is a tent-dweller of the mountain, unfamiliar with grain or cooked meat, with life in the city, or (worse yet) with death and burial in a proper grave—he is warlike, uncouth, and generally strange.[2] It seems clear that, at this stage of initial contacts, the Amorites had not yet adopted urban ways, and still represented a distinct cultural entity even in those cities where they may have taken up temporary residence.

In areas beyond the range of the cuneiform texts, the archeological record must be consulted for clues to the progress of Amorite sedentarization. The area of Mount Basar itself was hardly excavated until very recently,[3] but in Transjordan there is clear evidence of numerous walled villages with a significant sedentary population that seem to have sprung up in the twenty-second and twenty-first centuries. In Palestine at about the same time, the flourishing urban culture of the Early Bronze Age came to an abrupt end, to be succeeded by a seminomadic interlude and a wholesale change in styles of pottery, weaponry, burial customs, architecture, and other evidences of material culture. While there was no dramatic innovation in basic technology such as marked the beginning of the Bronze Age, most archeologists see in both the Transjordanian and the Palestinian developments the beginning of the Middle Bronze Age and attribute them directly or indirectly to the expansion of the Amorites.[4] Surface exploration of the southern desert of Palestine, the Negev, shows that it too sustained a significant sedentary population at this time. That situation was drastically changed, however, at the beginning of MB II

---

[2] Compare the summary by Giorgio Buccellati, *The Amorites of the Ur III Period*, Pubblicazioni del Seminario di Semitistica, Ricerche, vol. 1 (Naples: Istituto Orientale di Napoli, 1966), pp. 330–32.

[3] Ibid., p. 237, nn. 13–14a.

[4] Compare especially Kathleen M. Kenyon, *Amorites and Canaanites*, The Schweich Lectures of the British Academy (London: Oxford University Press, 1966), who prefers to regard MB I as an "intermediate" period between EB and MB.

times,[5] when both the Negev and Transjordan entered a period of protracted decline while the rest of Palestine and Syria shared a revival of urban life and developed a largely uniform material culture.

It is against this background that we must evaluate the Hebrew traditions of the so-called Patriarchal Age as these are preserved in the Book of Genesis and scattered through the rest of the Bible. It is generally conceded that these traditions were not put into writing before the time of King David, at the beginning of the first millennium, but scholarly opinion diverges widely as to the reliability and antiquity of the oral sources on which they are presumably based, not to mention the accuracy with which the written reflects the oral. The most radical view is that the written versions are so far from faithful to their oral antecedents as to represent new literary creations, reflecting at best the life and times of their authors and throwing no light on events or conditions of the times they presume to describe.[6] This view, however, forces one to posit alternative explanations of the origins of the written traditions and to ignore a certain amount of archeological data that tends to support them.[7]

A more moderate position regards these narratives as more or less authentic reflections of Late Bronze times. In particular they show numerous apparent parallels to law and society of the Hurrian culture attested in northern Mesopotamia at that time.[8] Some support for this position may be found in one genealogical-chronological pattern in the Bible, according to which the last patriarchs were separated from the conquest by only four generations. Other Biblical schemes, however, require a much longer interval, and many of the Hurrian parallels have lately been called in question. The most serious objection to the thesis comes from archeological

---

[5] Or, in Kenyon's terminology, the MB period proper (ca. 2000–1600). This period correlates roughly with the Old Babylonian and Old Assyrian periods in Mesopotamia, the Middle Kingdom and Second Intermediate Period in Egypt, and the Middle Minoan, Middle Helladic, and Middle Cycladic periods in Crete, Greece, and the Aegean respectively.

[6] According to Albrecht Alt and Martin Noth. See Martin Noth, *The History of Israel*, trans. Stanley Godman (New York: Harper & Bros., 1958), who begins the history of Israel with the conquest of the Promised Land at the start of the Iron Age.

[7] Compare John Bright, "The School of Alt and Noth: A Critical Evaluation," in idem, *Early Israel in Recent History Writing*, Studies in Biblical Theology, no. 19 (Naperville, Ill.: Alec R. Allenson, 1956), pp. 79–110; reprinted in *Old Testament Issues*, ed. Samuel Sandmel (New York: Harper & Row, 1968), pp. 159–95.

[8] Compare especially E. A. Speiser, "The Hurrian Participation in the Civilization of Mesopotamia, Syria, and Palestine," *Journal of World History* 1 (1953):311–27; reprinted in: *Oriental and Biblical Studies: Collected Writings of E. A. Speiser*, ed. J. J. Finkelstein and Moshe Greenberg (Philadelphia: University of Pennsylvania Press, 1967), pp. 244–69; and E. A. Speiser, *Genesis*, ed. William Foxwell Albright and David Noel Freedman, The Anchor Bible, vol. 1 (Garden City, N.Y.: Doubleday & Company, 1964).

surface exploration in the Negev, which proves it to have been totally devoid of occupation during the last three-fourths of the second millennium.[9] The patriarchal settlement and wanderings in southern Palestine
are, however, so much a part of the traditions that they cannot be assigned
to any locale other than the Negev. Thus the compromise solution cannot
be reconciled with the archeological evidence.

Both the literary and the archeological evidence are best served when
the patriarchal period is dated to the Middle Bronze Age.[10] This position
does not mean a literal acceptance of every word in Genesis. For example,
the camel nomadism described in Genesis 24 and elsewhere may well be
an anachronistic updating of a tale originally told about donkey-caravan-
eers.[11] Nor does it presume a blind faith in the reliability and non-
ambiguity of every artifactual relic. Instead, it stresses the overall com-
patibility of the Biblical and extra-Biblical sources with respect to the
general conditions of life, settlement, and movement in the area from Harran on the Balih River to the borders of Egypt (see Figure 17, page 90).
Within these limits, Biblical literature adds a welcome complement to the
fragmentary picture of the process of sedentarization and the survival of
nomadic, and especially tribal, vestiges.[12]

The political history of the Amorites is easier to trace. Kings of the
Third Dynasty of Ur conducted most of their aggressive campaigns on the
other side of the Tigris and did not attempt to reassert the Sargonic
hegemony on or beyond the Middle Euphrates. In his third year (ca.
2034), Shu-Sin of Ur was constrained to build a defensive wall, called "the
one which keeps Tidanum at a distance," or simply "the Amorite wall," an
event duly recorded in his date formulas, inscriptions, and correspondence.
But the wall did not hold them for long. Under Shu-Sin's son Ibbi-Sin, the
Amorites breached these defenses, helped to put an end to the dynasty,
and established themselves as rulers in most of the numerous city-states
into which Mesopotamia quickly disintegrated again. The same process was

---

[9] Compare especially: Nelson Glueck, "The Archeological History of the Negev,"
Hebrew Union College Annual 32 (1959):11–18; and idem, *Rivers in the Desert: A
History of the Negev* (New York: Farrar, Straus and Cudahy, 1959).

[10] Compare especially: William Foxwell Albright, *The Biblical Period from Abraham
to Ezra* (New York: Harper & Row, 1963), pp. 1–9; and John Bright, *A History of
Israel* (Philadelphia: The Westminster Press, 1959).

[11] Compare William Foxwell Albright, "Abram the Hebrew: A New Archaelogical Interpretation," *Bulletin of the American Schools of Oriental Research*, no. 163 (October,
1961):36–54.

[12] Compare: Roland de Vaux, O.P., *Ancient Israel: Its Life and Institutions*, trans.
John McHugh (New York: McGraw-Hill Book Company, 1961), pp. 3–15; and A.
Malamat, "Aspects of Tribal Societies in Mari and Israel," *La Civilisation de Mari*, ed.
J.-R. Kupper, XV⁰ Rencontre Assyriologique Internationale (Paris: Société d'édition
"Les Belles Lettres," 1967), pp. 129–38.

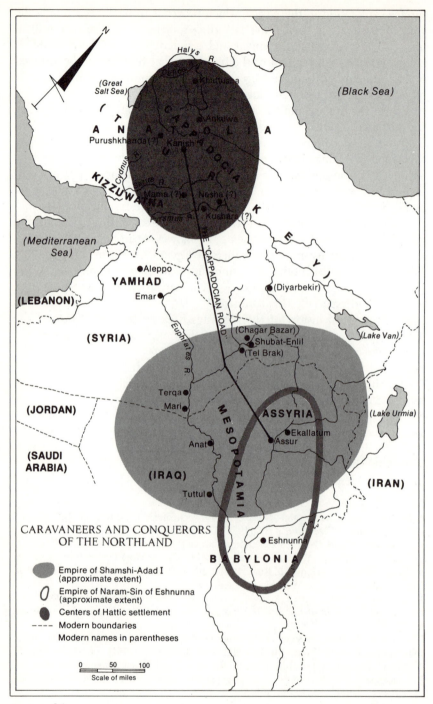

CARAVANEERS AND CONQUERORS
OF THE NORTHLAND

Empire of Shamshi-Adad I
(approximate extent)

Empire of Naram-Sin of Eshnunna
(approximate extent)

Centers of Hattic settlement

- - - Modern boundaries

Modern names in parentheses

Scale of miles

FIGURE 14

at work in the north, where in the twentieth century, the Assyrian traders in Anatolia included numerous Amorites,[13] and in the west, where great cities like Hasor arose. Even in the absence of texts, the massive fortifications and characteristic royal palaces of these western cities mark them clearly as real city-states. By about 1800, the cuneiform texts from Mari and Alalakh and the so-called Execration Texts from Egypt[14] show Amorite dynasties firmly entrenched throughout Syria and Palestine. After 1750, the Amorites penetrated as far as Lower Egypt, where they were known as the Hyksos.[15] In this process, the urbanization of the Amorites was consummated, and their language and culture were fused with those of the populations they ruled. The resulting blend produced new and distinctive cultures throughout the Asiatic Near East—Assyrian and Babylonian in the east, Canaanite and Ugaritic in the west—but their common Amorite component accounted for a considerable number of linguistic, literary, and institutional similarities.

[2] THE NEO-SUMERIAN RENAISSANCE: UR III
ca. 2100–2000 B.C.

Having surveyed the entire Middle Bronze Age from the point of view of the Amorites, we now return to lower Mesopotamia, which we left in the aftermath of the Sargonic collapse, divided between such petty-states as Lagash, Umma (under Gutian rule), Uruk (under its Fourth Dynasty), and a much reduced Akkad. Before the end of the twenty-second century, the centrifugal trend was reversed again when Uruk decisively defeated the Gutians. In later tradition, the event was celebrated as a dramatic example of divine retribution. In point of fact, the domination of the Gutians had rested only briefly and lightly on selected portions of the land, and the reconsolidation of the country did not follow immediately upon their expulsion. Utu-hegal, the conqueror of the Gutians, ruled at Uruk only briefly (seven years, six months, and fifteen days according to one version of the King List) and constituted the entire Fifth Dynasty of that city. He seems to have enjoyed some prestige in Sumer, settling a boundary dispute between Lagash and Ur in favor of Lagash, and to have restored Uruk's condominium with Ur, which he administered through a governor called Ur-Nammu, possibly his own son[16] (see Figure 13, page 70).

13 Julius Lewy, "Amurritica," *Hebrew Union College Annual* 32 (1961):31–74.
14 For their date, compare John van Seters, *The Hyksos: A New Investigation* (New Haven: Yale University Press, 1966), pp. 78–81.
15 Ibid, pp. 181ff. Compare pp. 250–51 for other proposed identifications of the Hyksos.
16 William W. Hallo, "Gutium," *Reallexikon der Assyriologie und vorderasiatischen Archäologie*, vol. 3, ed. W. von Soden et al. (Berlin: Walter de Gruyter, 1971), 708–20.

Ur-Nammu, however, was destined for bigger things. At Utu-hegal's death, if not before, he asserted the independence of Ur from Uruk by claiming or usurping certain traditional royal rights, such as refortifying the city, naming years after his own achievements, and assuming the title of King of Ur. At first he continued to stress his connections to Uruk, invoking the gods of that city as his personal deities and building temples to them. But he soon moved to secure the loyalty of Ur by a massive building program in honor of Nanna and Ningal, the chief deities of that city. At enormous expense, he built up the great terrace of Ur and erected on it a great ziggurat, or monumental stepped tower, destined to be imitated wherever Sumerian models influenced religious architecture (see Figure 15)[17] and reflected in the Biblical account of the Tower of Babel. To this day, the ruins of Ur preserve the essence of his architectural plans, although the actual structures were often repaired or rebuilt thereafter. In and around Ur, he devoted his energies to the reconstruction of the quays for overseas trade and to a substantial program of irrigation works, thus assuring the city of economic progress to match its new religious renown. Next he proceeded to rebuild the temples of the national Sumerian deities, Enlil and Ninlil, in Nippur, the traditional cult center of Sumer and Akkad. This won him the allegiance of the priesthood at Nippur, and in about his fourth year he was accordingly invested with the title of King of Sumer and Akkad. This coronation was commemorated not only in the (by now traditional) date formulas (compare Chapter II, Section 6), but also, like other outstanding events of his reign, in a royal hymn, a new medium introduced by Ur-Nammu (or perhaps by Gudea a few years earlier).[18]

Thus Ur-Nammu won religious legitimation for his political pretensions by rebuilding the ancient sanctuaries. He did so not only at Nippur, as duly noted in the *Tummal Inscription* (see Chapter II, Section 3), and at Ur, but also throughout the cities of Sumer and Akkad. His building and votive inscriptions, and to a lesser extent his hymns and date formulas, bear eloquent witness to this fact. They show that he built temples to the principal deities of Eridu (Enki), Uruk (Inanna), Larsa (Utu), Kesh (Ninhursag), and probably Umma (Shara), as well as to some additional deities (Nin-egal, Nin-gubla) at Ur itself. No doubt he also provided for the upkeep of these temples, and he took pains to install their high priests and priestesses. At Uruk and Ur his own son and daughter, respectively, were named to these high offices.[19]

---

[17] See Martin A. Beek, *Atlas of Mesopotamia: A Survey of the History and Civilisation of Mesopotamia from the Stone Age to the Fall of Babylon*, ed. H. H. Rowley, trans. D. R. Welsh (London: Nelson, 1962), Map 21 (facing p. 150).

[18] William W. Hallo, "The Coronation of Ur-Nammu," *Journal of Cuneiform Studies* 20 (1966):133–41.

[19] On the principle involved, see p. 44.

FIGURE 15   Ziggurat at Ur.

Another son was married to the daughter of the ruler of Mari, thus establishing friendly diplomatic relations with a city-state that, while independent of the Ur III empire, was a key factor in its defense against the Amorites (above, Section 1). Ur-Nammu's great stele at Ur also emphasizes his cultic and architectural interests: although it is carved in the style of the great victory stelae of Lagash and Akkad, only one of its ten registers, showing a prisoner led before the king, has any martial overtones.[20] The only instance in which we are certain that Ur-Nammu resorted to arms is when he fought, defeated, and killed Nammahani, the last independent ruler of Lagash and, like Gudea and Urgar before him, a son-in-law of Ur-Ba'u[21] (see Chapter II, Section 6), desecrating his monuments, and once more redrawing the common boundary with Ur, this time in favor of Ur. But Ur-Nammu showed foresight in victory. Lagash was left with a measure of sovereignty over its reduced territory, Nammahani's old viceroy was reappointed to govern it as a loyal servant of Ur-Nammu, and the king even built a new canal for the area. Thus Lagash was transformed into a province of the new empire. The same was true of the other ancient

[20] Leon Legrain, "The Stela of the Flying Angels," *The Museum Journal* 18 (1927): 74–98; and André Parrot, *Sumer: The Dawn of Art* (New York: Golden Press, 1961), Figs. 279–82.
[21] Nammahani was perhaps chief musician of the goddess Nin(ki)mar under Gudea: Edmond Sollberger, "Selected Texts from American Collections," *Journal of Cuneiform Studies* 10 (1956):11–13.

city-states. In return for pledging allegiance and contributing taxes and labor to the national coffers, they (or literally their deities) were confirmed in their old territorial claims, as duly registered in detailed cadastral stelae erected and copied at Nippur.[22]

Such literary, architectural, and administrative precedents marked the founder of the Ur III dynasty as an innovator comparable, if not equal, to the great Naram-Sin. But a still more enduring invention was his promulgation of the first "law code" known to history. Although at the end of the Dynastic Age Urukagina had attempted to restore the old ordinances, his attempt (apart from failing) was largely unsystematic and never emulated. But Ur-Nammu's code, which has only recently come to light and still is not completely recovered, represents a conscious effort to collect such actual legal precedents as might serve as a guide to future generations. These precedents were phrased in conditional form (for example, "suppose that/given that/if a man violated a virgin slavegirl without the owner's consent, that man pays five sheqels of silver)," and this form became normative for all ancient Near Eastern precedent law, (also called case law or casuistic law), not only in Sumerian but also in Akkadian, Hittite, and Hebrew. Some of Ur-Nammu's paragraphs were repeated in later compendia, others were replaced, and there was a general tendency to add to the corpus such cases as illustrated extreme and unusual conditions. It is thus difficult to regard it as a "code of laws," for it tended to be erratic in its coverage, often omitting typical or borderline cases. Indeed it is doubtful whether it was intended as binding on the courts, whose active role is well attested under Ur-Nammu's successors, and they never appealed to written law as the basis for their decisions. Nevertheless, the promulgation of the laws marked Ur-Nammu as the "shepherd" of his people, genuinely interested in justice for all, and in this respect a model for many subsequent kings.[23]

Ur-Nammu appears to have met his death in battle, a rare fate for later Mesopotamian kings. A hymn tells how his body was returned to Ur for an elaborate burial and gives in detail the Sumerian view of the netherworld.[24] The excavations at Ur have indeed uncovered the hypogeum, or underground vault, of his successors, though no trace of Ur-Nammu's tomb has been found. The bloody end of the pious and peaceful king was, in

[22] F. R. Kraus, "Provinzen des neu-sumerischen Reiches von Ur," *Zeitschrift für Assyriologie und vorderasiatische Archäologie* 51 (1955):45–75, esp. 64–68, and plates 1–5.

[23] For the latest edition, see J. J. Finkelstein, "The Laws of Ur-Nammu," *Journal of Cuneiform Studies* 22 (1968–69):66–82.

[24] Samuel Noah Kramer, "The Death of Ur-Nammu and his Descent to the Netherworld," *Journal of Cuneiform Studies* 21 (1967):104–22. Supplemented by C. Wilcke, "Eine Schicksalsentscheidung für den toten Urnammu," *Actes de la XVIIe Rencontre Assyriologique Internationale*, ed. André Finet, Publications, vol. 1 (Ham-sur-Heure, Belg.: Comité Belge de Recherches en Mésopotamie, 1970), pp. 81–92.

fact, a problem for the later tradition, which in some cases simply passed over his reign and concentrated on his even more illustrious son.

Shulgi succeeded to the throne of Ur about 2093 and reigned for forty-eight years. By the testimony of the date formulas, the first half of this long reign was devoted to the same peaceful pursuits that had occupied Ur-Nammu, notably the building, furnishing, and staffing of temples and, to a lesser extent, of royal palaces. But beginning with the twenty-fourth year, no less than fifteen year names record military triumphs, all on the other side of the Tigris, from Urbilum (modern Erbil) on the Upper Zab to Anshan in the south. The main target was apparently Simurrum, which was the object of no less than five campaigns, and the capture of whose ruler Tappan-darah was the principal event of Shulgi's reign recalled in the later omen literature. Other date formulas indicate that these campaigns were preceded by diplomatic efforts to achieve the same ends, notably dynastic marriages between Shulgi's daughters and the rulers of Anshan and Markhashi (Barakhshi), and that at the same time the king was securing his rear against the Amorite threat from the west by constructing a defensive wall at the narrow waist of the valley, where the Tigris and the Euphrates flow closest to each other (the so-called *bad-mada*, or "wall of the land"). A common purpose runs through all these measures: to blunt the eastern threat that had toppled the Akkadian empire and, if possible, to turn the tide decisively in Mesopotamia's favor. An economic motive might well have added urgency to this military strategy. The sources of numerous raw materials, especially lapis lazuli and tin (for the manufacture of bronze), lay in the northeast, and Shulgi was perhaps anxious to reopen the trade routes that provided access to them.

There is, at any rate, no doubt that the Mesopotamian economy began to flourish as never before, beginning in the second half of Shulgi's reign. The king saw to it, according to his twenty-first year name, that the field surveys were properly executed for the temples of Nippur,[25] and both this site and others, notably Umma,[26] presently provide massive documentary evidence to this effect, as previously only the archives of Lagash had done.[27] The thirty-seventh year was named for the founding of Puzrish-Dagan, identified with the modern mound of Drehem, a few miles southeast of Nippur, and now this site adds its documentation.[28] It housed the royal cattle pens that serviced the great temples of Nippur and, to a lesser extent, of Ur and Uruk. It accepted enforced and voluntary contributions in kind from both the central provinces and the foreign vassals of the

[25] Albrecht Goetze, "The Chronology of Šulgi Again," *Iraq* 22 (1960):151–53.
[26] T. Fish, "Chronological List of Ur III Economic Texts from Umma," *Manchester Cuneiform Studies* 5 (1955):61–91.
[27] Idem, "Chronological List of Ur III Economic Texts from Lagash," ibid., pp. 33–55.
[28] Idem, "Chronological List of Ur III Economic Texts from Drehem," ibid., pp. 92–114.

empire and routed them to their proper destinations. The meticulous bookkeeping of the royal scribes enables us to reconstruct the operation of this branch of the royal economy,[29] and other spheres of economy and administration are illuminated by the equally abundant archives of other sites. For example, the texts from Ur are particularly rich in evidence of trade and industry, including textiles and metals;[30] those from Lagash reveal the structure and operations of an elaborate judicial system,[31] and those from Umma include a relatively large number of letter-orders reflecting a kind of banking system involving disbursements in kind from royal storage centers.[32] A small but significant group of texts from various sites shows that foreign trade at this time was also a royal monopoly, with royal officials importing luxury items of all sorts by land and sea: copper and tin; exotic foods; resinous plants and aromatic woods; fruit trees and herbs; ingredients for tanning, dyeing, and cleaning; ship's lumber and even the prized tortoise shell. In return, the royal traders were able to offer the bulkier agricultural staples that Mesopotamia produced far in excess of its own needs: wool, barley, wheat, dates, dried fish, fish oil and skins, the last both unfinished and in the form of processed leather products. Deficit balances in this trade, if any, were made good in silver, which now began to serve the three classical functions of money: as a medium of exchange, as a unit of account, and as a standard of value. In the last aspect, long lists of commodities evaluated in silver provide us for the first time with an accurate price index of all the major components of the Mesopotamian economy.[33]

One of Shulgi's most interesting innovations, revealed by the archival texts from Drehem, is an elaborate schedule of monthly obligations levied

[29] Tom B. Jones and John W. Snyder, *Sumerian Economic Texts from the Third Ur Dynasty: A Catalogue and Discussion of Documents from Various Collections* (Minneapolis: University of Minnesota Press, 1961), esp. pp. 203–43; and Buccellati, *The Amorites of the Ur III Period*, pp. 274–302.

[30] For trade, see A. Leo Oppenheim, "The Seafaring Merchants of Ur," *Journal of The American Oriental Society* 74 (1954):6–17. For textiles, see Thorkild Jacobsen, "On the Textile Industry at Ur under Ibbi-Sîn," *Studia Orientalia Ioanni Pedersen . . . īdicata* (Copenhagen: E. Munksgaard, 1953), pp. 172–87; reprinted in Thorkild Jacobsen, *Toward the Image of Tammuz and Other Essays on Mesopotamian History and Culture*, ed. William L. Moran, Harvard Semitic Series, vol. 21 (Cambridge: Harvard University Press, 1970), pp. 216–29. For metals, see William W. Hallo, "Lexical Notes on the Neo-Sumerian Metal Industry," *Bibliotheca Orientalis* 20 (1963):136–42.

[31] Adam Falkenstein, *Die Neusumerischen Gerichtsurkunden*, 3 vols. (Munich: C. H. Beck, 1956–57).

[32] Edmond Sollberger, *The Business and Administrative Correspondence under the Kings of Ur*, Texts from Cuneiform Sources, vol. 1, ed. A. Leo Oppenheim (Locust Valley, N.Y.: J. J. Augustin, 1966); and William W. Hallo, "The Neo-Sumerian Letter-orders," *Bibliotheca Orientalis* 26 (1969):171–75.

[33] John B. Curtis and William W. Hallo, "Money and Merchants in Ur III," *Hebrew Union College Annual* 30 (1959):103–39.

on all the major Sumerian and Akkadian provinces through their governors. This rotating "liturgy" provided for the sacrificial requirements of the Nippur temples and, not incidentally, the maintenance of their sizable retinues. It conveniently institutionalized the relationship between the Ur III empire and those of its once independent city-states that were formerly united in the rather amorphous "Kengir League" (see Chapter II, Section 3). In its calendaric and religious aspects, it foreshadowed the amphictyonic taxation systems of the Solomonic kingdom in Israel and of Delphi and other cult centers in Greece.[34] The Nippur priesthood was not unmindful of these and other benefits conferred on it by the long-lived king. Fairly early in his reign, it permitted him to resume the divine status that had gone unclaimed since the collapse of the Sargonic empire, and apostrophized him in more royal hymns than any other Mesopotamian ruler before or after him.

The many-sided king was also remembered as a patron of learning. The great scribal schools of both Nippur and Ur traced their foundation to him,[35] and he himself claimed to have mastered the scribal curriculum. He was pictured as adjudicating between wood and reed in a "disputation" over their respective merits conducted in his palace at Ur, thus suggesting courtly patronage of this and other genres of the so-called wisdom literature.[36] He also figured prominently in the literary letters, another type of secular composition that became part of the scribal curriculum. These epistolary exchanges between the king and his high officials were inspired by actual events, if not actual documents, of the reign of Shulgi and his successors, and they serve as a welcome complement to the more laconic contemporaneous records. They were studied along with another type of letter, the letter-prayer, a ceremonial petition addressed in stereotyped phrases to a deity or deified king on behalf of a distressed individual.[37] Such fictitious exercises were designed to train future scribes for similar assignments in their later careers, as were the great lists of words, forms and phrases that now began to be compiled into canonical series[38] on the basis of attested occurrences in the accounts and contracts of the period. They provided a new systematization of the great lexical tradition that was always a hallmark of cuneiform learning. It was also probably at this time that the great epic cycles dealing with the Early Dynastic kings of

[34] William W. Hallo, "A Sumerian Amphictyony," *Journal of Cuneiform Studies* 14 (1960):88–114.

[35] Idem, "Review of Gadd and Kramer, *Literary and Religious Texts, First Part*," *Journal of Cuneiform Studies* 20 (1966):92, n. 33.

[36] Idem, "The Cultic Setting of Sumerian Poetry," *Actes de la XVIIᵉ Rencontre Assyriologique Internationale*, ed. Finet, pp. 116–34, esp. 117, n. 3. For these literary debates and other genres of wisdom literature, see Chapter VI, Section 4.

[37] William W. Hallo, "Individual Prayer in Sumerian: The Continuity of a Tradition," *Journal of the American Oriental Society* 88 (1968):71–89.

[38] Concerning the concept of canonicity, see Chapter VI, Section 2.

Uruk (Chapter II, Section 3) were put into their final form, for the kings of Ur traced their descent to those of Uruk, and Shulgi regarded Lugalbanda as his father and Gilgamesh as his brother. Even though most of the canonical Sumerian literature is to date known only in school copies of Old Babylonian date, much of it was no doubt created in Ur III times, which thus rates as a neo-Sumerian renaissance in cultural as well as political terms.

In addition to all these achievements, Shulgi surpassed even Naram-Sin of Akkad in the number of his progeny. Over fifty royal princes and princesses are known by name for the dynasty, and as many as half of these may have been children of Shulgi. Some were married off to foreign princes, others served as high religious or political functionaries, and two, Amar-Sin and Shu-Sin, succeeded Shulgi on the throne of Ur (see Figure 16).[39] According to the Old Babylonian omen tradition, Amar-Sin died from the "bite" of a shoe—that is an infected foot.[40] He and his brother reigned for nine years each, and both continued to pursue the policies of their father in all essentials. Each was deified upon his accession, and Shu-Sin even allowed temples to be built in his honor at Ur, Lagash, Adab and Eshnunna. The latter king's campaigns in the East, although noted only briefly in the date formulas, are described in detail on Old Babylonian copies of stelae erected at Nippur and Ur.[41] At the same time he defended himself against the increasing pressure of the Amorites with a major enlargement of the defensive wall intended to hold them at bay. But the empire of Ur survived his reign only briefly, and the combined threat of Amorites from the northwest and Elamites from the southeast proved the undoing of his son and successor, Ibbi-Sin.

[3] THE FALL OF UR AND THE RISE OF ISIN: EOB (EARLY OLD BABYLONIAN) ca. 2000–1900 B.C.

Like Naram-Sin of Akkad, but with considerably more justification, Ibbi-Sin of Ur survived in later memory as the epitome of the hapless ruler. Indeed, he was fated to end his days in exile, as the proud empire founded a century earlier by Ur-Nammu crumbled around him. His reign began auspiciously enough, with the tribute of the land flowing into the

---

[39] Edmond Sollberger, "Sur la chronologie des rois d'Ur et quelques problèmes connexes," *Archiv für Orientforschung* 17 (1954–56):20–23. Sollberger regards Ibbi-Sin too as possibly a son of Shulgi.

[40] Albrecht Goetze, "Historical Allusions in Old Babylonian Omen Texts," *Journal of Cuneiform Studies* 1 (1947):260–61.

[41] See most recently M. Civil, "Šū-Sîn's Historical Inscriptions: Collection B," *Journal of Cuneiform Studies* 21 (1967):24–38.

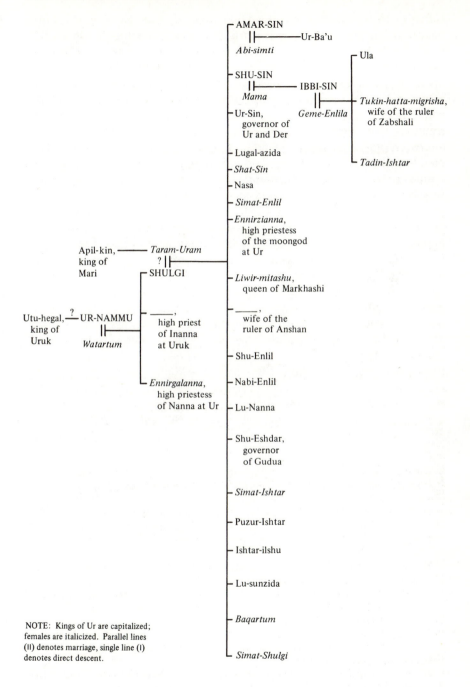

FIGURE 16 The royal house of Ur.

coffers of Ur to sustain its growing population. His coronation in the ninth month of Shu-Sin's last year was marked by special offerings,[42] and shortly thereafter he married a royal princess, perhaps his own sister. At this time he was still represented as a beardless youth on the seals he bestowed on his favored retainers,[43] and indeed, seal inscriptions remain the most characteristic relics of his reign in contrast to the more numerous building and votive inscriptions of his predecessors.[44] They suggest a burgeoning bureaucracy that augured ill for the kingdom's economic stability. Ibbi-Sin, moreover, proved unable to defend his kingdom against the Amorites. They breached the wall that Shu-Sin had only recently completed and began to assume control of the northern provinces early in the new king's reign. In short order, dated texts ceased at the major archives of Drehem (beginning of third year), Umma (fifth year), Lagash (sixth year) and Nippur (eighth year),[45] and the same is true of the smaller archives like Eshnunna and Susa.[46] Only those of Ur itself continued in abundance, faithfully dating by the king's formulas to the end of his long reign of twenty-four years. But Ur could not sustain its own population, let alone all those loyal to the king who now sought refuge behind its walls, without the continued tribute from the provinces. As this was more and more withheld, commodity prices soared, sometimes to sixty times their normal level, and the capital was confronted by the twin crises of inflation and famine. In desperation, Ibbi-Sin turned to the commander of his northern troops, a non-Sumerian from Mari named Ishbi-Irra, and with his help prolonged his own reign—but at a considerable price. Ishbi-Irra extorted, in return, full control of the province of Isin and of the nearby religious capital of Nippur and, consequently, claimed the fealty of the remaining Sumerian and Akkadian provinces.[47] These in many cases, however, de-

---

[42] Edmond Sollberger, "Remarks on Ibbi-Sin's Reign," *Journal of Cuneiform Studies* 7 (1953):48–50; and idem, "Texts Relating to Ibbi-Sin's Coronation," *Journal of Cuneiform Studies* 10 (1956): 18–20.

[43] Idem, "Three Ur-Dynasty Documents," *Journal of Cuneiform Studies* 10 (1956): 26–30; and J. Nougayrol, "Une forme rare de l'hommage au roi deifié," *Studia Biblica et Orientalia*, vol. 3 (Rome: Pontificio Istituto Biblico, 1959), pp. 276–81 and plates 19–20.

[44] William W. Hallo, "The Royal Inscriptions of Ur: A Typology," *Hebrew Union College Annual* 33 (1962):1–43, esp. 8.

[45] Compare: Fish, "Chronological List of Ur III Economic Texts from Umma"; idem, "Chronological List of Ur III Economic Texts from Lagash"; and idem, "Chronological List of Ur III Economic Texts from Drehem."

[46] Thorkild Jacobsen, "The Reign of Ibbī-Suen," *Journal of Cuneiform Studies* 7 (1953):36–47, esp. 38; reprinted in Jacobsen, *Toward the Image of Tammuz and Other Essays on Mesopotamian History and Culture*, ed. Moran, pp. 173–86.

[47] See the correspondence of Ibbi-Sin as translated by: Samuel Noah Kramer, *The Sumerians: Their History, Culture, and Character* (Chicago: University of Chicago Press, 1963), pp. 333–35; and P. van der Meer, *The Chronology of Ancient Western Asia and Egypt*, ed. William Foxwell Albright and A. de Buck, Documenta et Monumenta Orientis Antiqui, vol. 2 (Leiden: E. J. Brill, 1963), p. 45.

clared their own independence of Ur in a succession of actions that added up to a pattern of usurpation.[48] They began the process by withholding contributions of supplies for the daily and festival requirements of Ur, and of manpower for the economic and military needs of the empire, such as canal-dredging. Still avoiding an open break, they replaced the name of the deified Ibbi-Sin with that of their local patron deity in their monumental inscriptions and their personal names.[49] When these actions went unpunished, they proceeded to exalt their own governors, although they had been appointed by Ur, to royal (and, in some cases, divine) status and to name the years by their own date formulas. The final act of defiance was the rebuilding of the various cities' fortifications, for in permitting this the sovereign was obviously forfeiting his last chance to bring the provinces back into the empire by means short of war.

The pattern of usurpation, in whole or in part, can be followed in a number of important cities, including Assur, Eshnunna, Der, and Susa, all lying too far to the east to maintain their allegiance to the dying empire or to transfer it to Ishbi-Irra, as was the tendency among the more centrally located provinces. Ishbi-Irra seems to have followed a somewhat devious course in these difficult times, posing as Ibbi-Sin's defender against Amorites from the west and Subarians and Elamites from the east, yet allowing the king's powers to erode under their onslaughts and gradually arrogating them to himself. Although he was content with vaguely royal titles like "god of his nation" and "king of (his) territory,"[50] he was ready when, in the twenty-fourth year of Ibbi-Sin's reign and the fourteenth of his own, the king of Ur was conclusively defeated, his capital razed, and he himself carried into exile, apparently by the Elamites, ultimately to die and be buried in Anshan.[51] Ishbi-Irra sprang into action, chasing the Elamites out of the pillaged capital and claiming the legitimate succession to Ur and its reduced, but still substantial, empire. For the next four generations, his successors, though they may have used Isin as their administrative capital, proudly reigned under the more prestigious title of King of Ur. During all this time (ca. 2000–1900) they enjoyed the undivided loyalty of the national priesthood at Nippur and of the subordi-

[48] William W. Hallo, "Review of Die "Zweite Zwischenzeit" Babyloniens, by Dietz Otto Edzard," Bibliotheca Orientalis 16 (1959):237–38; and idem, "The Coronation of Ur-Nammu," Journal of Cuneiform Studies 20 (1966):136–38, nn. 49, 65, and 76.

[49] For the theophoric (that is, compounded with a divine name) character of many personal names, see Henri Linet, "L'Anthroponymie Sumérienne dans les documents de la 3e dynastie d'Ur," fasc. 180, Bibliothèque de la Faculté de Philosophie et Lettres de L'Université de Liège (Paris: Société d'Edition "Les Belles Lettres," 1968).

[50] Vaughn E. Crawford, Sumerian Economic Texts from the First Dynasty of Isin, Babylonian Inscriptions in the Collection of James B. Nies, Yale University, vol. 9 (New Haven: Yale University Press, 1954), Plate 93.

[51] Thorkild Jacobsen, "The Myth of Inanna and Bilulu," Journal of Near Eastern Studies 12 (1953):182–83, n. 50; reprinted in idem, Toward the Image of Tammuz and Other Essays on Mesopotamian History and Culture, ed. Moran, p. 346, n. 50.

nate governors of the central provinces. Contrary to a common misinterpretation of the so-called Larsa King List and of the Larsa Date List,[52] the later Amorite dynasty of that city did not demonstrably begin its rule until the end of this period. Its earliest members figure at the head of these lists not as ruling kings, but as ancestors,[53] tracing their descent back to a certain Naplanum, well known as an Amorite from beyond Mari in the account texts of the time of Shu-Sin and Ibbi-Sin.[54]

The century following the disappearance of Ibbi-Sin was thus one of uninterrupted peace in southern Mesopotamia, and the dynasty of Ishbi-Irra was at pains to stress its devotion to and perpetuation of the patterns set by the great kings of the Third Dynasty of Ur. The kings of both houses were listed in unbroken succession in king lists[55] and litanies,[56] and alike honored such cultic and ceremonial traditions as had grown up around the royal titles[57] and royal hymns.[58] The high priestess of the moon god at Ur, whom Ibbi-Sin had installed, survived his removal by several years before being succeeded by Ishbi-Irra's nominee. The Sumerian King List was composed, under Ishbi-Irra or his successors, precisely, it seems, to stress his dynasty's lawful inheritance of the claims of Ur and of nine other cities to have ruled Sumer by turns.[59] Their succession was expressed in the standard formula: "Ur was smitten with weapons; its kingship to Isin was carried"; though this can suggest a break in continuity, it had the opposite intent. Another significant document, the *Lamentation Over the Destruction of Ur*, describes the disaster that befell the city in such graphic terms that it was once thought to reflect the immediate reac-

[52] For a detailed study of both documents, compare Ettalene Mears Grice, *Chronology of the Larsa Dynasty*, Yale Oriental Series. Researches, vol. 4 (New Haven: Yale University Press, 1919). A date list is a document that lists in succession all the year names of a given ruler or dynasty; a local king list, such as that of Larsa, summarizes a dynastic date list by conveniently totaling the date formulas for each king.

[53] The third name on the list, Samium, is attested in this function in a newly published inscription. Compare Georges Roux, "Le Père de Gungunum," *Revue d'Assyriologie et d'Archéologie Orientale* 52 (1958):233–35.

[54] Buccellati, *The Amorites of the Ur III Period*, esp. pp. 356–59.

[55] Edmond Sollberger, "New Lists of the Kings of Ur and Isin," *Journal of Cuneiform Studies* 8 (1954):135–36.

[56] Carl Frank, *Kultlieder aus dem Ischtar-Tamūz-Kreis* (Leipzig: Otto Harrassowitz, 1939), pp. 57–109; with the revisions by J. J. Finkelstein, "The Genealogy of the Hammurapi Dynasty," *Journal of Cuneiform Studies* 20 (1966):102–03.

[57] William W. Hallo, *Early Mesopotamian Royal Titles: A Philologic and Historical Analysis*, American Oriental Series, vol. 43 (New Haven: American Oriental Society, 1957), esp. pp. 150–56.

[58] William W. Hallo, "New Hymns to the Kings of Isin," *Bibliotheca Orientalis* 23 (1966):239–47; and idem, "Royal Hymns and Mesopotamian Unity," *Journal of Cuneiform Studies* 17 (1963):112–18. See also Figure 18, page 98.

[59] See Chapter II, Section 2. For the different views on the date of and occasion for the composition of the King List, see M. B. Rowton, "The Date of the Sumerian King List," *Journal of Near Eastern Studies* 19 (1960):156–63.

tion of an eye-witness. In fact, it was composed two or more generations after the event, when the temples and sacred precinct were rebuilt, probably by Ishme-Dagan—a politically astute move designed to ingratiate the new dynasty with its Sumerian subjects, as was the simultaneous reconstruction of the sanctuaries of Nippur. But at the same time the lamentation was yet another gesture of piety toward the cultic traditions of the ancient capital, and its wailing tone must be understood as a formalized ritual, intentionally emphasizing the extent of the destruction at the hands of the foreign invaders in order to absolve the rebuilder of any sacrilege involved in the further demolition that was an inevitable prelude to reconstruction.

In the realm of daily life too, no less than in that of court and temple, the first century of the second millennium showed little change from the last of the third. The economy remained heavily étatist, with a large proportion of both the land and the means of production held by royalty or farmed out to favored retainers. International trade gradually passed out of the hands of merchant-officials who were in the direct service of the monarchy, and into those of private capitalists who invested their accumulated capital wherever profit beckoned—in overseas or overland trading ventures or in lending at high interest at home. (See Figure 17.) But the chief items of international trade remained largely the same as in the Ur III period, with luxury items of all sorts imported by land and sea in return for nonperishable staples in heavy demand.[60] As "exchangeable commodities," the latter continued to compete with money in the form of silver as a medium of exchange and a standard of value.[61] In the case of specific economic activities well documented in both the Ur III and the Early Old Babylonian periods, notably the leather industry, the techniques of production continued largely unchanged.[62]

Near the end of the twentieth century, however, this pattern of continuity with the neo-Sumerian traditions was abruptly broken. Lipit-Ishtar of Isin (1934–1924) proved to be the last member of the dynasty founded by Ishbi-Irra. The Amorite descendants of Naplanum, who perhaps until

[60] See above, Section 2.

[61] W. F. Leemans, *Foreign Trade in the Old Babylonian Period as Revealed by Texts from Southern Babylonia*, Studia et Documenta ad Iura Orientis Antiqui Pertinentia, vol. 6 (Leiden: E. J. Brill, 1960); and the review of this book by William W. Hallo, *Journal of Cuneiform Studies* 17 (1963):59–60.

[62] Compare, for example: Crawford, *Sumerian Economic Texts from the First Dynasty of Isin*; T. Fish, "Kuš Texts of the Isin Period," *Manchester Cuneiform Studies* 5 (1955):115–24; idem, "Umma/Lagash/Drehem Tablets Concerning Kuš," *Manchester Cuneiform Studies* 6 (1956):1–103; and Albrecht Goetze, "A Drehem Tablet Dealing with Leather Objects," *Journal of Cuneiform Studies* 9 (1955):19–21. In addition, see the detailed review (of Crawford, *Sumerian Economic Texts from the First Dynasty of Isin*), by L. Matouš, "Zu den ältesten ökonomischen Texten aus Isin," *Bibliotheca Orientalis* 13 (1956):135–40.

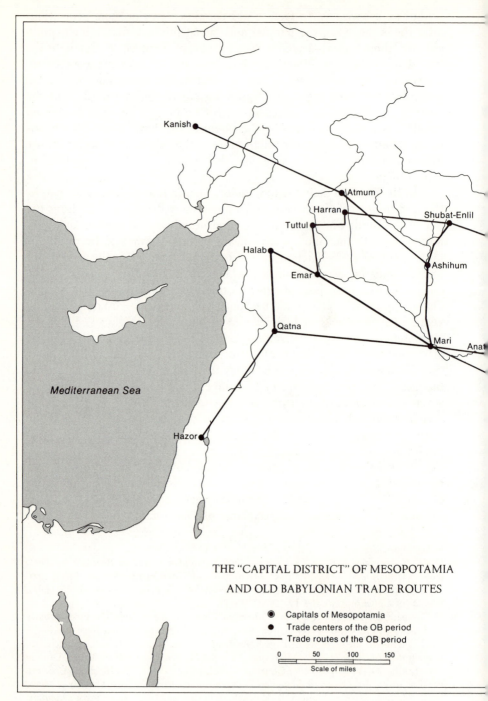

THE "CAPITAL DISTRICT" OF MESOPOTAMIA
AND OLD BABYLONIAN TRADE ROUTES

⊚ Capitals of Mesopotamia
● Trade centers of the OB period
—— Trade routes of the OB period

0   50   100   150
Scale of miles

FIGURE 17

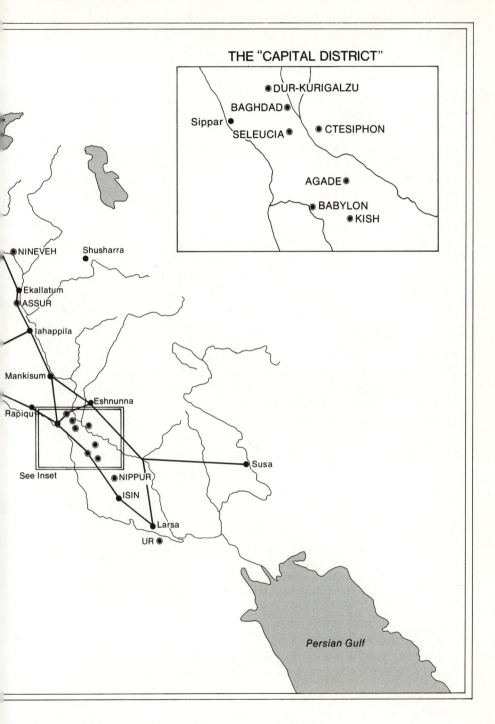

THE "CAPITAL DISTRICT"

● DUR-KURIGALZU

BAGHDAD●

Sippar ●
       SELEUCIA ●   ● CTESIPHON

                      AGADE●

                  ● BABYLON
                     ● KISH

●NINEVEH   Shusharra

●Ekallatum
●ASSUR

●Iahappila

Mankisum●

           ●Eshnunna
Rapiqu●

See Inset

●NIPPUR

●ISIN

●Larsa
●Susa

UR ●

Persian Gulf

then governed Lagash and other southern cities for the kings of Isin, established a dynasty of their own at the southern city of Larsa and soon took over Ur as well, although Isin continued to claim a nominal suzerainty over the ancient capital. Gungunum, the first Larsa dynast (1932–1906), may well have been impelled to these drastic steps by economic pressures. Two basic needs of his area were the overseas trade via the Persian Gulf on the southern frontier on the one hand, and a steady supply of sweet water from the northern frontier on the other. The Persian Gulf trade had languished since the sack of Ur, its principal port of entry, and was revived by Gungunum as soon as he had been entrusted with the administration of the city;[63] under his successors it assumed greater proportions than ever before.[64] As for the fresh water supply, an exchange of letters between Lipit-Ishtar and his general alludes to a military action by Gungunum to secure the waters of the great Adab Canal (also called the Iturungal), which directly or indirectly supplied most of the south with water.[65] Gungunum inaugurated a massive program of canal-building, which was emulated not only by his own successors at Larsa but also by the later kings of Kish, Babylon, Sippar, Eshnunna, and Isin, as indicated by date formulas from the period 1918–1760.[66] But while Gungunum and Lipit-Ishtar of Isin seem to have avoided an open breach, their successors were less careful. In 1897, Gungunum's son Abi-sare recorded a victory over Ur-Ninurta of Isin, which probably helped terminate the long reign of this first member of a new ruling house at Isin. This battle marked the end of the long peace that had characterized the twentieth century and ushered in more than a century of maximum political turmoil in which the authority of Isin was no longer recognized, even within the traditional borders of Sumer and Akkad, and a host of Amorite petty-states arose on every side. Disputes over water rights seem to have played a large part in the breakdown of the former unity, yet, ironically enough, the hydraulic needs of the country could have been met only by a unified effort to keep the watercourses free of silt and to allocate the limited water supply where it was most needed. The land paid dearly in loss of productivity as the salt water table rose and the tidal salt water was allowed to penetrate farther and farther inland.[67] Abi-sare and his successor, Sumu-el, both went far

[63] William W. Hallo, "A Mercantile Agreement from the Reign of Gungunum of Larsa," *Studies in Honor of Benno Landsberger on his Seventy-fifth Birthday April 21, 1965*, ed. Hans G. Güterbock and Thorkild Jacobsen, Assyriological Studies, no. 16 (Chicago: University of Chicago Press, 1965), pp. 199–203.

[64] Oppenheim, "The Seafaring Merchants of Ur."

[65] M. B. Rowton, "Watercourses and Water Rights in the Official Correspondence from Larsa and Isin," *Journal of Cuneiform Studies* 21 (1967):273.

[66] Dietz Otto Edzard, *Die "zweite Zwischenzeit" Babyloniens* (Wiesbaden: Otto Harrassowitz, 1957), pp. 112–16.

[67] Thorkild Jacobsen and Robert M. Adams, "Salt and Silt in Ancient Mesopotamian Agriculture," *Science* 128, no. 3334 (Nov. 21, 1958):1251–58.

north in an attempt to divert the waters of Isin to the benefit of Larsa.[68]
But they were repaid in kind for, before the end of Sumu-el's reign,
Larsa's water supply was in turn cut off, probably through foreign intervention, and the situation became so desperate that a *coup d'état* ensued.
The origin of the new ruler, Nur-Adad, like that of the family he displaced, seems to have been at Lagash, and he saved the interests of all the
southern cities by restoring their water supplies.[69] But the constant warfare
between Isin and Larsa at this time encouraged not only the emergence of
independent dynasties at cities such as Uruk, Kish, and especially Babylon,
but also the first interference in the affairs of southern Mesopotamia by
a king of Assyria, Ilushuma, who claimed to have restored the ancient free-
doms of several Babylonian cities about this time. Although the exact
nature of his intervention is hard to determine, it probably served to secure
the trans-Tigridian trade and military routes leading from Assur via Eshnunna and Der to Susa and, thus, to unite all those lands that had first
broken free from Ur and Isin. Der had already attempted to achieve some
such purpose by a campaign against Anshan, Elam, and Simash, as had
Eshnunna by the marriage of its princess to the ruler of Elam.[70] In any
case, Ilushuma symbolized the emergence of a new northern factor in the
history of Mesopotamia, and it is to the north that we now turn our
attention.

[4] CARAVANEERS AND CONQUERORS OF THE NORTHLAND
ca. 1900–1800 B.C.

We have seen that irrigation and trade played major roles in the
transition of southern Mesopotamia from the Sumero-Akkadian symbiosis
of the third millennium to the Akkado-Amorite patterns of the second.
The foothills and mountains encircling the great valley on the north and
east enjoyed adequate rainfall and immunity to the salinization of soil that
threatened the alluvial plains. But they shared with the south a growing
dependence on international trade and a rapid transfer of this trade from
royal to private hands. This is best illustrated by thousands of documents
from Cappadocia, written in the Assyrian dialect of Akkadian and representing the letters and records of Assyrian merchants who traveled with
their wares between Assyria and Cappadocia. Cappadocia is the classical

68 Stanley D. Walters, *Water for Larsa: An Old Babylonian Archive Dealing with
Irrigation*, ed. William W. Hallo, Yale Near Eastern Researches, vol. 4 (New Haven:
Yale University Press, 1970), pp. 143–66, esp. 159–65.
69 J. van Dijk, "Une insurrection générale au pays de Larša avant l'avènement de
Nūradad," *Journal of Cuneiform Studies* 19 (1965):1–25.
70 Thorkild Jacobsen, *Cuneiform Texts in the National Museum, Copenhagen* (Leiden:
E. J. Brill, 1939), pp. 6–9.

name of central Anatolia (Turkey). It is a landlocked upland crossed by important highways and fertile river valleys. It is bounded on the south by the Great Salt Sea (Tuz Göl), the Taurus Mountains, and the upper Euphrates River, and it embraced at various times greater or lesser portions of the basin of the Halys River (Kizil Irmak) toward the north.[71]

There are no written documents from Anatolia in the third millennium and no references to it in the contemporaneous sources from Mesopotamia. We may disregard also the later tales of Gilgamesh that allude to a campaign in this direction by the ruler of Uruk against the mythical monster Huwawa. But other legendary material of diverse type and provenance is unanimous and specific in crediting the Old Akkadian kings of the Sargonic period (see Chapter II, Sections 5 and 6) with influence in the Cappadocian area, and there must be an historical kernel to this material. Besides allusions in omens, chronicles, and geographical treatises, at least one historical romance, The King of Battle, relates how Sargon of Akkad honored the request of the defenseless merchants (perhaps Akkadian) of Anatolia and forced the king of Purushkhanda to come to terms with them. The tale recalls so many features of the situation in Old Assyrian times that one is almost inclined to see in it a transfer to Sargon of Akkad of traditions originally associated with Sargon I of Assyria. But the historical tradition insists on the Old Akkadian milieu and still claims Purushkhanda for the grandson of Sargon of Akkad, Naram-Sin. Perhaps this tradition should be respected, for under the latter, contemporaneous inscriptions and palaces attest to Akkadian influence at least as far north as Tell Brak, Chagar Bazar, and Diyarbekr. But in Anatolia, such influence definitely came to an end at this time, and there is no indication that the Ur III dynasty reestablished it.

With the turn of the millennium, Cappadocia emerged from legend into history. It was now the focus of an indigenous Anatolian culture known in the native sources as Hattic—that is, Hittite in the original sense of the word. It is not to be confused with the later Indo-European culture of the area that inherited the name. In this book, the term Hattic will be applied to the former,[72] and Hittite exclusively to the latter. Hattic culture is attested archeologically by a characteristic "Cappadocian" pottery found on both sides of the Halys River. More important, it is illuminated by over ten thousand "Cappadocian" texts, which reveal the nature and extent of Assyrian participation in this culture. Most of these tablets have so far been found at Kültepe (ancient Kanish) and, in smaller numbers, at

---

[71] The name of Cappadocia (and the Cappadox, or Deliçe, River) is derived from the Old Persian name of the satrapy, Katpatuka (probably a plural formation of Katpat), and this in turn has been compared to the old name of Cilicia, Kizzuwatna (which could be a Hurrian plural of Kizwat). In ancient translations of the Hebrew Bible, the Hebrew "Kaphtor" is translated as "Cappadocia."

[72] In some modern studies, this culture is termed proto-Hattic.

Boghaz Köy (ancient Khattusha) and Alishar (probably ancient Ankuwa); only a few doubtful examples have so far turned up in Assyria itself.[73]

The Assyrian traders began to penetrate Cappadocia soon after Assur won its independence from the Third Dynasty of Ur. They even brought with them reused seals dedicated to Ibbi-Sin, the last king of Ur. An inscription of the Old Assyrian king Erreshum I (ca. 1920–1900) seems to have served as a school text in the Assyrian quarter at Kanish. But the greatest flourishing of Assyrian influence was in the nineteenth century, when Assyrian traders regularly made the long trip from Assur to Kanish on donkeyback via a number of routes, bringing with them chiefly cloth from Assur and tin from across the Tigris (to be made into bronze in Anatolia) and selling it all over Cappadocia for gold, silver, and other metals.

The Assyrian trade was a highly organized one, dominated from Assur by a number of commercial families who subjected themselves to the discipline of the Assyrian *karum* (a kind of board of trade) at Kanish and the other major centers subordinated to it and of the *wabartum* (a kind of association of traders) at the smaller ones. These institutions in turn were governed and protected by treaties with the various native princes of the area, of whom the chief one was still, as in the third millennium, the "great prince" of Purushkhanda. The arrangement benefited both parties for at least three generations, with the indigenous princes providing a measure of military security in return for a share (in the form of gifts and customs duties) of the sizable profits realized by the Assyrians. The Assyrians did not exercise any political control over the local princes, who certainly did not belong to any great Assyrian empire, as has sometimes been argued. But they surely controlled the economic destinies of the area in their time. Although the Assyrians were quartered in the "suburbs" of each city, outside and below the walled citadel, they entered into numerous relationships with the natives, including marriage.

A number of the native princes of this and the following century are known by name. One of these is Warshama of Kanish, the addressee of a lengthy letter from another prince, Anum-khirbi of Ma'ama, who in turn is mentioned by one of the oldest Hittite texts yet recovered. Warshama seems to have lost his realm to a king of Kushara called Pitkhana and his son and successor, Anitta, who is known from the bronze point of a lance inscribed in cuneiform with his name and found on the citadel of Kanish.

[73] Louis Lawrence Orlin, *Assyrian Colonies in Cappadocia*, Studies in Ancient History, vol. 1 (The Hague: Mouton, 1970); M. T. Larsen, *Old Assyrian Caravan Procedures*, ed. A. A. Kampman and Machteld J. Mellink, Publications de l'Institut Historique et Archéologique Neerlandais de Istamboul, vol. 22 (Istanbul: Nederlands Historisch-Archaeologisch Instituut in het Nabije Oosten, 1967); and Paul Garelli, *Les Assyriens en Cappadoce*, Institut Français d'Archéologie d'Istanbul, Bibliothèque Archéologique et Historique, vol. 19 (Paris: Librairie Adrien Maisonneuve, 1963).

Both Pitkhana and Anitta are mentioned in several Old Assyrian documents from Kanish as well as in the later Old Hittite historical tradition, which recounts their struggles to win supremacy over their Hattic rivals. Perhaps it was in these struggles that the nineteenth-century level at Kanish was destroyed in a catastrophic fire.

At any rate, by about 1800 a new pattern had emerged. Assyria was deeply involved in constant warfare in Mesopotamia, while the Hattic natives confronted a new power, the Hittites. The last Assyrian caravan to Kanish is attested in letters to Zimri-Lim of Mari (ca. 1780), and while some Cappadocian tablets are preserved in the eighteenth-century levels there, they deal with different articles than were previously traded. The center of power was clearly shifting northward to Alishar and particularly to Khattusha. Here the new Hittites established a kingdom that rapidly displaced the older centers of Anatolian power at Purushkhanda, Kanish, Kushara, and Nesha. The end of the profitable trade with Cappadocia coincided with a major upheaval in Assur. The dynasty of Puzur-Assur I ended with Puzur-Assur II. Assyria was incorporated briefly in the empire of Eshnunna, which grew to its greatest extent under its last rulers, especially a certain Naram-Sin, who assumed the name and title of his great Sargonic namesake. But this interregnum was destined to be cut short from another quarter, Terqa on the Middle Euphrates.

According to the cuneiform geographical lists, there were at least three ancient Mesopotamian towns known as Terqa, and variant spellings such as Sirqa, Sirku, and Tirga suggest an etymology based on Semitic words for irrigation. The principal Terqa suits this etymology, since it is located on the Euphrates between a network of ancient canals paralleling that river, and about fifteen miles below the confluence of the Chabur River. It lies in modern Syria, about forty-five miles above the Iraqi border. Like the ancient cities of Mari, Anat (Hanat), and Tuttul farther downstream, it lay on the right bank of the Euphrates and, together with them, constituted a buffer zone between Syria and Babylonia.

The Middle Euphrates entered the orbit of Sumerian culture at an early date, as revealed both by the excavations at Mari, which have turned up architecture, sculpture, and artifacts in the best Early Dynastic style, and by the native Sumerian sources, which include an early ruler of Mari in their king lists and record the destruction of the city by Eannatum of Lagash (see Chapter II, Section 4). In return, the region bequeathed to Sumer (as it did later to Philistia and the west) its worship of the grain god Dagan. Thus Sargon of Akkad worshipped Dagan at Tuttul to assure himself of access to the "Upper Country" and, similarly, his grandson Naram-Sin credited his conquests in northern Syria to Dagan. By the neo-Sumerian (Ur III) period personal names composed with Dagan become common in Mesopotamia, and his worship became part of the official cult, at least at Puzrish-Dagan, the great livestock center of the religious capital at Nippur. A text from this site mentioning people from "Tirga" is the earliest documentary evidence of the city's existence.

The names of the earliest rulers of Terqa may be preserved for us in an unexpected source—the Assyrian King List. It incorporates a list of the ancestors of Shamshi-Adad I (ca. 1815–1782), which includes some typically Amorite names and others that are at home in the Middle Euphrates region. According to the same source, Shamshi-Adad bided his time in Babylonia while Assur was under the domination of the king of Eshnunna. But when the latter died, he swung into action, seizing first Ekallatum and then Assur itself. By a pious fiction, he traced his genealogy back to the presumed ancestor of Puzur-Assur I, thus strengthening his legitimacy at Assur. At the same time he remained mindful of his Amorite origins, sacrificing to his ancestral spirits in Terqa and rebuilding the great temple of Dagan there. Neither Assur nor Terqa, however, were destined to serve as his capital. Instead, the choice fell on nearby Ekallatum and Mari, respectively. In Ekallatum, Shamshi-Adad installed his crown-prince as governor; at Mari, newly captured from its own Amorite ruler, he appointed his younger and less able son. The extensive correspondence unearthed at the colossal palace of Mari includes numerous letters from the solicitous king exhorting the prince to greater efforts and holding up his older brother as a model.[74] As his own capital, the king chose Shubat-Enlil further north, from where he could govern the Chabur valley himself while keeping an eye on his sons. Thus the entire area between the Middle Euphrates and the Middle Tigris was united under one Amorite family from Terqa about 1800. Shamshi-Adad I not only conquered northern Mesopotamia but proved a capable administrator of a united realm at the very time when southern Mesopotamia underwent its greatest upheavals and fragmentation. Yet his achievements were destined to be surpassed, and his fame to be eclipsed, by a younger contemporary from the South.

[5] THE AGE OF HAMMURAPI
ca. 1800–1600 B.C.

Amorite and Elamite dynasties, firmly entrenched in the outlying reaches of ancient western Asia from Aleppo in the northwest to Susa in the southeast, were also dividing the thrones of Babylonia proper by the late nineteenth century. The chief contenders here were the Elamite dynasty of Larsa and the Amorite (or First) Dynasty of Babylonia. (See Figure 18.) At first fortune seemed to favor the former. Kudurmabuk, an

[74] See the large selection of letters translated by Jørgen Laessøe, *People of Ancient Assyria: Their Inscriptions and Correspondence*, trans. F. S. Leigh-Browne (London: Routledge and Kegan Paul, 1963), pp. 46–77.

Isin	Uruk	Larsa	Babylon (1st Dynasty)
ISHBI-IRRA (2017)		[Naplanum (2025)]	
		[Emisum (2004)]	[Ashmadu (2000)]
SHU-ILISHU (1984) IDDIN-DAGAN (1974)		[Samium (1976)]	[Abi-yamuta (1980)]
ISHME-DAGAN (1953)			[Abi-ditan (1960)]
LIPIT-ISHTAR (1934)		[Zabaia (1941)] Gungunum (1932)	[Mam-x-y-z (1940)]
UR-NINURTA (1923)			[Shu-x-y-z (1920)]
		Abi-sare (1905)	[Dadbanaya(?) (1900)]
BUR-SIN (1895)		Sumu-el (1894)	Sumu-Abum (1894)
LIPIT-ENLIL (1873)			Sumu-la-el (1880)
IRRA-IMITTI (1868) ENLIL-BANI (1860)	SIN-KASHID (1865)	NUR-ADAD (1865) SIN-IDINNAM (1849) SIN-ERIBAM (1842) SIN-IQISHAM (1840) SILLI-ADAD (1835) WARAD-SIN (1834)	Sabium (1844)
Zambia (1836) Iter-pisha (1833) Urdukuga (1830) Sin-magir (1827)	Sin-iribam (1832)		Apil-Sin (1830)
	Sin-gamil (1826) Ilum-gamil (1823) Eteia (1822) Anam (1821)	RIM-SIN I (1822)	Sin-muballit (1812) HAMMURAPI (1792)
Damiq-ilishu (1816)	Irdanene (1816) Rim-Anum (1809) Nabi-ilishu (1805)		
1794	**1802**		
		1763 Rim-Sin II (1741) 1736	SAMSU-ILUNA (1749)
			ABI-ESHUH (1711)
			Ammi-ditana (1683)
			Ammi-saduqa (1647)
			Samsu-ditana (1625)
			1595

NOTE: Ancestors or predecessors are bracketed; rulers recognized at Nippur are capitalized. Accession dates are given in parentheses.

FIGURE 18   Principal royal houses of the Old Babylonian Period.

Sealand (2nd Dynasty)	Eshnunna	Assur	Mari
	Ituria (2030)		
	Shu-ilia (2020)		
	Nur-ahum (2010)	Ushpia (2010)	
	Kirikiri (2000)	Kikkia (2000)	
	Bilalama (1990)	Akia (1990)	
	Ishar-ramassu (1980)	Puzur-Assur I (1980)	
	Usur-awassu (1970)		
	Azuzum (1960)	Shalim-ahhe (1960)	
	Ur-Ninkimara (1950)		
	Ur-Ningizzida (1940)	Ilushuma (1940)	
	Ipiq-Adad I (1930)		
	Abdi-Erah (1920)	Erreshum I (1920)	
	Shiqlanum (1910)		
	Sharria (1900)	Ikunum (1900)	
	Belakum (1890)		
	Warassa (1880)	Sargon I (1880)	
	Ibalpi-el I (1870)		
	Ipiq-Adad II (1860)	Puzur-Assur II (1860)	
	Naram-Sin (1840)	Naram-Sin (1840)	
Iliman (1793)			
	Dadusha (1819)	Erreshum II (1819)	Yaggid-Lim (1820)
		Shamshi-Adad I (1814)	Yahdum-Lim (1810)
			Sumu-Iaman (1794)
			Yasmah-Adad (1790)
Itti-ili-nibi (1733)	Ibalpi-el II (1785)	Ishme-Dagan I (1781)	Zimri-Lim (1780)
	1762		**1760**
		Mut-Ashkur (1740)	
		Rimuia (1730)	
		Asinum (1720)	
		Puzur-Sin (1710)	
		1700	
DAMIQ-ILISHU (1677)			
Ishkibal (1641)			
Shushi (1616)			
Gulkishar (1589)			
Peshgal-daramash (1534)			
Adara-kalamma (1484)			
Akurul-anna (1456)			
Melam-kurkurra (1430)			
Ea-gamil (1423)			
1415			

Elamite (or perhaps an Amorite who had assumed an Elamite name in the service of Elam) and chieftain of the buffer area between Babylonia and Elam known as Emutbal, succeeded in placing two of his sons in succession on the throne of Larsa in the troubled times that followed the reign of Sin-iddinam. Their sister, moreover, became high priestess of the moon god at Ur. She was another of that long line that reached back to Enheduanna (see Chapter II, Section 5), thus showing that the new dynasty enjoyed the traditional allegiance of the national Sumerian shrines.[75] While Warad-Sin reigned only a dozen years, his brother Rim-Sin ruled for sixty. He annexed Uruk and in 1794, halfway through his long reign, he finally put an end to the Isin dynasty, which although long since on the wane, had still played a considerable military role in its last years.[76] The event loomed so large in contemporaneous estimates that all of Rim-Sin's remaining years were named after it. Rim-Sin's devotion to the cult at Ur and elsewhere is attested briefly by date formulas and in greater detail by building and votive inscriptions,[77] by records of cultic expenditures,[78] and by literary compositions.[79] He also figures prominently in the diplomatic correspondence from Mari and contended on equal terms with Shamshi-Adad and with the powerful kingdom of Yamhad which ruled the area beyond the Euphrates from its capital at Halab (modern Aleppo).

Yet for all his achievements, Rim-Sin, like Shamshi-Adad, was destined to be overshadowed and eclipsed by his younger contemporary, Hammurapi of Babylon. Hammurapi was the sixth in a line of long-lived kings whose rule had passed smoothly from father to son since 1894 and was to continue to do so for five more reigns. His dynasty traced its forebears all the way back to the "Gutian period" (see Chapter II, Section 6), and claimed a common ancestry with the Amorite kings of Assyria.[80] The abundant documentation for Hammurapi's reign and the indelible impression he left on later generations of Babylonians have combined to make him one of the commanding figures of Mesopotamian history. He is most famous for his law code[81] as well as for achieving, if only briefly, the re-

[75] C. J. Gadd, "En-an-e-du," *Iraq* 13 (1951):27–39 and plates 13–14.

[76] William W. Hallo, "Oriental Institute Museum Notes No. 10: The Last Years of the Kings of Isin," *Journal of Near Eastern Studies* 18 (1959):54–72.

[77] Idem, "Royal Inscriptions of the Early Old Babylonian Period: A Bibliography," *Bibliotheca Orientalis* 18 (1961):4–14, esp. 10–11.

[78] See, for example: Edwin C. Kingsbury, "A Seven-Day Ritual in the Old Babylonian Cult at Larsa," *Hebrew Union College Annual* 34 (1963):1–34; and Baruch A. Levine and William W. Hallo, "Offerings to the Temple Gates at Ur," *Hebrew Union College Annual* 38 (1967):17–58.

[79] See, for example, C. J. Gadd, "Rim-Sin Approaches the Grand Entrance," *Iraq* 22 (1960):157–65.

[80] Finkelstein, "The Genealogy of the Hammurapi Dynasty."

[81] See the translation by Theophile J. Meek, *Ancient Near Eastern Texts Relating to the Old Testament*, 2nd ed., ed. James B. Pritchard (Princeton: Princeton University Press, 1955), pp. 163–80. Compare also Chapter VI, Section 6.

unification of Mesopotamia almost to its old Sargonic borders. His domestic policies can be studied in detail from his own voluminous correspondence, while his foreign policy is illuminated indirectly by letters from the
archives at Mari.[82] His schools maintained the old traditions of Sumerian
learning and at the same time promoted the flowering of a native literature in Akkadian. Any survey of Mesopotamian law and society, religion
and literature, learning and daily life (see Chapter VI) is inevitably and
in large measure a picture of Hammurapi's Babylonia as revealed by the
sources from or about his time.[83]

In later traditions the city of Babylon itself claimed an even greater
antiquity than its new dynasty, but in point of fact a date formula of Shar-
kali-sharri of Akkad (see Chapter II, Section 6) is the first mention of its
existence. It had constituted a rather minor province in the neo-Sumerian
empire and did not become the seat of an independent dynasty until over
a century after that empire fell. Its swift and spectacular rise to power
thereafter can be attributed to at least three factors: the smooth and
unbroken succession of long-lived rulers from a single family; the intensity
of the struggle between the other major powers of the time; and the personal genius of Hammurapi. The last factor was perhaps the most important, for a lesser personality would have fallen victim to these struggles
instead of emerging as the victor from them. A celebrated Mari letter
phrased the situation in classic terms: "There is no king who is (all-)
powerful by himself: ten or fifteen kings follow in the train of Hammurapi
of Babylon, as many follow Rim-Sin of Larsa, as many follow Ibal-pi-el of
Eshnunna, as many follow Amut-pi-el of Qatna, and twenty kings follow
in the train of Yarim-Lim of Yamhad."[84] But by an adroit alternation of
warfare and diplomacy, Hammurapi succeeded where others had failed.
He maintained the friendship of Rim-Sin of Larsa while that king was disposing of Isin, Uruk, and other rivals; then, in his thirtieth year, he broke
with Rim-Sin and, in defeating him, fell heir as well to all that Larsa had
conquered. He avoided challenging the mighty Shamshi-Adad I of Assyria
but defeated his successor two years after disposing of Rim-Sin. Three
years later, he conquered Mari, where the native dynasty had reestablished
itself after the Assyrian defeat, and had sought to maintain itself by ex-
changing not only diplomatic missions but also spies with Babylon. Eshnunna and other Trans-tigridian city-states fell to Hammurapi's armies
before the end of his reign, and only the powerful states beyond the
Euphrates—notably Yamhad and Qatna—escaped his clutches. The pro-

[82] See the selections and translations listed in A. Leo Oppenheim, *Letters from Mesopotamia* (Chicago: University of Chicago Press, 1967), pp. 78–110 and 202–06.
[83] Henceforth, the terms Babylonia and Babylonian will be applied to southern Mesopotamia and its culture.
[84] Compare most recently Jack M. Sasson, *The Military Establishments at Mari*, Studia
Pohl, vol. 3 (Rome: Pontifical Biblical Institute, 1969), p. 1.

logue to his laws proudly catalogues all these conquests, at the same time identifying the code in its preserved form as dating from the end of his reign.

It is important, in spite of all this, to see Hammurapi's political achievement in its proper perspective. His reunification of Mesopotamia, consummated at the end of his reign, survived it by only a few years. His son and successor, Samsu-iluna, had to surrender much of the new empire before he had ruled more than a decade. The south was lost to Iliman (or Ilima-ilu), who founded a new dynasty at the otherwise unknown city of Urimku (or Urukug). It maintained itself successfully against repeated attacks by Samsu-iluna and his successors and briefly succeeded them in the rule of Babylon itself, thus becoming the Second Dynasty of Babylon. More often it is known as the First Dynasty of the Sealand, after the title of one of its kings in later tradition. It seems to have rallied what was left of the adherents and traditions of the defunct kingdom of Isin and of Sumerian culture generally; its third king assumed the name of the last king of Isin, Damiq-ilishu, and by capturing Nippur seems to have earned the traditional claim to a Sumerian hymn in his honor. His successors took ever more ponderous and archaizing Sumerian names.[85] Meanwhile, across the Tigris, a new Rim-Sin, namesake and perhaps nephew of the long-lived king of Larsa, rallied the adherents of that royal house in its ancestral homeland of Emutbal. Most ominous of all was the emergence of a wholly new threat at an old center of power on the Middle Euphrates, Terqa. The special privileges Terqa apparently enjoyed under Shamshi-Adad had come to an end at his death (ca. 1782), for Zimri-Lim soon regained Mari for himself, and Terqa now became a province of the restored kingdom. Its governor, Kibri-Dagan, maintained a lively correspondence with Zimri-Lim, his sovereign, and with his colleagues at Mari, and more than a hundred of his letters are preserved in the archives of Mari. They provide a vivid picture of provincial administration in the Mari Age. Other letters, too, deal with Terqa at this time. One of the most interesting details the dream of an official in the temple of Dagan at Terqa in which this deity interrogated and instructed him concerning the chiefs of the "Benjaminite" nomads with whom Zimri-Lim was constantly concerned. The defeat of Mari by Hammurapi, about 1760, and its destruction two years later once more changed Terqa's fortunes, setting the stage for Terqa's independence after a brief time as part of the empire of Hammurapi and his successor.

As presumed capital of the independent kingdom of Hana, which inherited the Middle Euphrates when the empire of Hammurapi collapsed under Samsu-iluna, Terqa boasts one of the few documented dynasties in

---

[85] Raymond Philip Dougherty, *The Sealand of Ancient Arabia*, Yale Oriental Series. Researches, vol. 19 (New Haven: Yale University Press, 1932), pp. 11–27.

a period (ca. 1740–1570) when most of the surrounding area was gradually being plunged into a prolonged eclipse. Even so, we know little more than the names of the rulers, and not even their order is certain. Those attested by date formulas, seal impressions, or both are all of the Amorite type already familiar from the Mari texts, except for a certain Kashtili-ashu. His name belongs to a totally new ethnic element in Babylonian history, the Kassites. Indeed, the same name is borne by no less than four of the thirty-six Kassite kings who, calculating from the native king lists, ruled somewhere in Mesopotamia from about 1740 to 1160 B.C. If that rule was confined to Babylon, the native sources cannot be reconciled with the known fact that the dynasty of Hammurapi held Babylon at the very least until 1700[86] and their historical value in general is severely impugned. But if the first Kassite kings ruled at Terqa (for which there are also some other, if ambiguous, indications), then they could well have been contemporaries, not successors, of the last Amorite kings of Babylon. In that case Samsu-iluna's ninth year, which is named for the first Babylonian encounter with the Kassite host, and which falls in 1741 according to the chronology followed here, would coincide with the traditional beginning of Kassite rule. For a century and a half, the successors of Hammurapi continued to hold Babylon and its surrounding provinces, but the great empire which he had forged was much reduced in size. Not only was the north lost to the Kassites but the extreme south fell to the First Sealand Dynasty two or three years later. The final blow, however, came from a more distant quarter: Anatolia.

---

[86] This is an extreme solution, according to the so-called highest chronology; see Benno Landsberger, "Assyrische Königsliste und 'dunkles Zeitalter'," *Journal of Cuneiform Studies* 8 (1954):31–93, 106–33, esp. 120. Most solutions, including the one adopted here, prefer a date just after 1600 for the end of the Hammurapi Dynasty ("middle chronology"). In the "high chronology," the date is about 1650, in the "low chronology," about 1530. The significance of these dates (each of which rests on different lines of evidence) is that all prior dates in Mesopotamian history depend on them.

FIGURE 19   Kudurru (boundary stone) from the time of Marduk-apla-iddina I (?).

IV

FROM THE SACK OF BABYLON TO THE SACK OF TROY: THE LATE BRONZE AGE ca. 1600–1200 B.C.

[1] THE SACK OF BABYLON AND THE DARK AGES
ca. 1600–1500 B.C.

When the last Assyrian caravan left for Kanish about 1780 (Chapter III, Section 4), that city was embroiled in the struggle of the Hattic princes for supremacy in central Anatolia (Cappadocia). But by about 1740, the Hittites had become strong enough to found a royal house of their own. Within another century they moved their capital from Kushara to Hattusha in defiance of the heavy curse laid on that city by Anitta, the Hattic ruler who had razed it. Within a few generations the Old Hittite Kingdom had established itself throughout the former Hattic domains, and its kings began to look beyond the highlands of Anatolia and toward the fertile plains that lay to the south across the lofty Taurus and Antitaurus mountains. Both Hattushili I (ca. 1650–1620), who took his name from the new capital, and his adopted son Murshili I (ca. 1620–1595) fought with the kingdom of Yamhad, which still controlled the lands between the Taurus and the Euphrates. Urshu, Karkemish and other great cities along the way having been defeated or neutralized, Murshili then marched down the Euphrates. The way to Babylon lay open, with only the Kassites of Hana to bar the way. But apparently an accommodation was reached with them. Samsu-ditana (1625–1595) was no match for the Hittite conqueror. The dynasty of Hammurapi came to an end, and the entire Asiatic Near East was plunged into a Dark Age of a hundred years (ca. 1600–1500) when contemporaneous documentation virtually ceased and the sequence of events must be reconstructed from later sources. These inform us that Murshili returned home laden with plunder. But he was not the prime beneficiary of his own epochal campaign. On the contrary, his absence from Hattusha gave rebellion there its head, and soon after his return[1] he was assassinated by his brother-in-law, and the Old Hittite Kingdom entered several generations of bloody palace revolutions which temporarily put a complete stop to its international influence.

Instead of the Hittite invaders, the most immediate beneficiaries of the fall of Babylon apparently were the kings of the Sealand. We have seen that the first of these, Iliman or Ilima-ilum, had established himself in southernmost Babylonia as early as Samsu-iluma's reign and that the third, Damiq-ilishu, already claimed central Babylonia including Nippur (Chapter II, Section 5). Now their sixth king, Gulkishar, apparently completed the process, seizing northern Babylonia and the capital itself in the wake of the Hittite withdrawal. His hold on the city is not positively established, and it lasted at best only briefly, but long enough to qualify Gulkishar's entire dynasty for inclusion in the great Babylonian King List (King List A). Like the Sumerian King List, which outlined the history of Sumer and Akkad from the Flood to Hammurapi from the point of view of the scribes of Nippur, the Babylonian King List recorded the subsequent history of Babylonia from that of the priests and scholars of Babylon. It recognized at least ten dynasties from about 1900 to 600 as successive claimants to Babylon, which served each in turn as the actual, or at least ceremonial, capital during all this time. (See Figure 20.) The First Dynasty of the Sealand thus figured in it as the Second Dynasty of Babylon, the direct successor to the First, or Amorite, Dynasty (Hammurapi Dynasty). And even though Gulkishar had shortly to abandon Babylon again, as well as Nippur, tradition has it that the great schools at these two centers of learning found a refuge with him in the far south,[2] where the dynasty lasted through five more reigns before it was finally terminated in the fifteenth century by the Kassites, to whom we now return.

The Kassites, already ensconced on the Euphrates around Terqa, had not barred the Hittites on their way to Babylon. Within a few years,[3] they moved downstream themselves, seized Babylon from Gulkishar, and made

---

[1] But not necessarily at once as is sometimes argued; compare Albrecht Goetze, "On the Chronology of the Second Millennium B.C.," *Journal of Cuneiform Studies* 11 (1957):53–73, esp. 55.

[2] William W. Hallo, "Royal Hymns and Mesopotamian Unity," *Journal of Cuneiform Studies* 17 (1963):116–17.

[3] Two according to the scheme adopted here (compare Kurt Jaritz, "Quellen zur Geschichte der Kaššû-Dynastie," *Mitteilungen des Instituts für Orientforschung* 6 (1958):187–265, esp. 202–25). Twenty-four according to Goetze, "On the Chronology of the Second Millennium B.C.," p. 66.

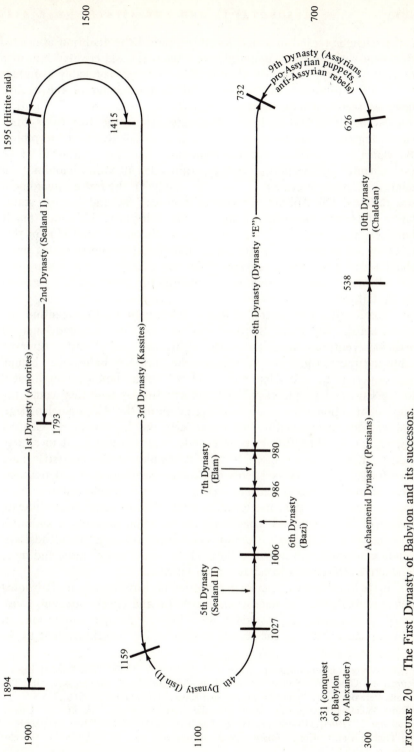

FIGURE 20   The First Dynasty of Babylon and its successors.

it the religious capital of a new Kassite empire. Later tradition associated this event with a certain Agum-kakrime (Agum II) and credited him with recovering the cult statue of Marduk from Hanaean (probably a mistake for Hittite) captivity. The political and military center of the empire, however, seems to have been moved north to a more strategic location, midway between the Tigris and Euphrates where the two rivers come closest together. This was the site of the wall repeatedly erected to protect Babylonia from invasion and incursion since the time of Shu-Sin of Ur (see Chapter III, Sections 1 and 2), who called it Muriq Tidnim. This name was later abbreviated to Mu-ti, or simply Ti; the fortress guarding it was renamed Dur-Apilsin, "fortress of Apil-Sin," by and for the grand-father of Hammurapi who rebuilt it in his fifth year (1826), and finally Dur-Kurigalzu, "fortress of Kurigalzu," when the first Kassite king of that name turned it into the unquestioned administrative center of his realm about 1400.[4] The massive remains of the new capital (modern Aqar-Quf) are still being excavated; they include one of the best-preserved ziggurats within Babylonia.

The Kassites had controlled the Middle Euphrates for a century and a half before they seized Babylon, and they were to rule Babylonia for over four centuries thereafter, longer than any other dynasty. After re-capturing the south from the Sealand, they restored Babylonia's bound-aries almost to those of Hammurapi. They became thoroughly acclimated to the land and people they ruled, perpetuating as best they could the study of traditional Sumerian learning, adopting the Akkadian language, and creating a new literature in it based partly on old themes (see Chapter VI, Section 4). The characteristic cylinder seal was elongated to accom-modate more elaborate inscriptions, and samples of the new style have been found as far away as Thebes in Greece. (See Figure 21.) A rich new array of divine symbols decorated the *kudurru*'s (boundary stones), per-haps to supplement the curse formulas directed at an increasingly illiterate audience. (See Figure 19, page 104.) At the same time, these kudurru's were indicative of a new pattern of social organization, a quasi-feudal sys-tem of land grants to favored retainers of the king whereby more and more productive acreage was withdrawn from taxation.

In political terms, the long centuries of Kassite rule in Babylonia were essentially years of stagnation, uneventful and largely peaceful. Occa-sional battles with the Assyrians were inflated to epic proportions in Assyrian literature,[5] but the Kassite monarchs were largely content to de-

---

[4] For the various identifications proposed, see: William W. Hallo, "The Road to Emar," *Journal of Cuneiform Studies* 18 (1964):67–68; and J. A. Brinkman, "Ur: The Kassite Period and the Period of the Assyrian Kings," *Orientalia* 38 (1969):325.

[5] Ernst Weidner, "Assyrische Epen über die Kassiten-Kämpfe," *Archiv für Orient-forschung* 20 (1963):113–16; and W. G. Lambert, "Three Unpublished Fragments of the Tukulti-Ninurta Epic," *Archiv für Orientforschung* 18 (1957–58):38–51. See also below, p. 116.

FIGURE 21   Kassite cylinder seal found at Thebes in Greece.

pend on what survived of Babylonian prestige in order to seek a place for themselves in the shifting kaleidoscope of Late Bronze Age international relations. Exchanges of gifts, dynastic marriages, alliances, embassies—all these as revealed by royal correspondence, especially from the archives of El-Amarna, show that Kassite Babylonia strove to maintain itself largely by non-military means. For the first two centuries of their rule we have virtually no contemporaneous documentation. When that becomes available again with Kurigalzu I or his immediate predecessors, it reveals little of interest for political history. The real center of political gravity had shifted north again, to the Chabur Valley, and to a different ethnic group, the Hurrians.

[2] HURRIANS AND HITTITES
ca. 1500–1350 B.C.

When Murshili the Hittite marched through northern Mesopotamia against Babylon, his real object was less to capture and loot that city than to harass the Hurrians who lay in his path, with their center of power in the valley of the upper Chabur River. The Chabur River is a tributary of the Euphrates, which it joins just above Terqa. Its lower half flows through a largely barren area, but its upper half forms the western leg of a triangle resembling a river delta in reverse; the many streams emptying into it from farther east (see Figure 17, page 90) embrace a fertile area that was occupied by the earliest agriculturists descending from the rain belt of Anatolia in the north. Without the aid of irrigation, it supported a large population in earlier times and is today dotted with numerous *tell*'s (ruin mounds) representing the remains of ancient settlements.[6] This "Chabur triangle" had been the seat of an independent Hurrian principality as early as the Late Sargonic period, as shown by the discovery of the foundation deposits of a certain Dish-atal of Urkish at the site of that ancient city (compare Chapter II, Section 6). Other Hurrian personal names in Sargonic and neo-Sumerian texts attest to the gradual growth of this new population throughout the Near East in the late third millennium. By Old Babylonian times, Hurrians are found from Shashrum (Shushara) in the east[7] to Alalakh in the west, while the existence at Mari of incantations translated or adapted into Hurrian already reveals this language in its characteristic role as a vehicle for the transmission of Babylonian culture.[8] Absorbing many of the earlier Babylonian traditions, the Hurrians played a crucial role in transmitting them beyond Babylonia to Assyria, to Palestine and Phoenicia and, indirectly, even to Greece. Their most conspicuous impact was on Hittite culture: religious, literary, and historical texts from the royal Hittite archives at Hattusha all betray strong Hurrian influence, and one can speak of a real Hurro-Hittite symbiosis in Anatolia.

But if the Hittites were receptive to Hurrian cultural influences, they were less hospitable to Hurrian political expansion. After Murshili's assassination, the Hurrians invaded Anatolia and the Hittites, for their part, campaigned in northern Syria.[9] Such see-saw warfare across the mountain barriers that separated the Anatolian plateau from the lowlands of northern Mesopotamia and Syria characterized the political relations of Hittites and Hurrians for three or four centuries, and it would be fruitless to detail them here. In any case the first century is obscured by the documentary silence of the Dark Age. When this lifted across northern Mesopotamia about 1500, the Chabur triangle emerged as the center of the new kingdom of Mitanni, ruled by a small Indo-Aryan aristocracy and a large Hurrian nobility. Throughout the fifteenth and much of the fourteenth centuries, Mitanni stretched from the Mediterranean on the west

[6] William W. Hallo, "Habor River," *The Biblical World: A Dictionary of Biblical Archaeology*, ed. Charles F. Pfeiffer (Grand Rapids, Mich.: Baker Book House, 1966), pp. 273–75.

[7] Jørgen Laessøe, *The Shemshāra Tablets: A Preliminary Report*, Arkaeologisk-Kunsthistoriske Meddelelser, vol. 4, no. 3 (Copenhagen: Ejnar Munksgaard, 1959).

[8] E. A. Speiser, "The Hurrian Participation in the Civilization of Mesopotamia, Syria, and Palestine," *Journal of World History* 1 (1953):311–27; reprinted in *Oriental and Biblical Studies: Collected Writings of E. A. Speiser*, ed. J. J. Finkelstein and Moshe Greenberg (Philadelphia: University of Pennsylvania Press, 1967), pp. 244–69.

[9] Goetze, "On the Chronology of the Second Millennium B.C.," pp. 55–56.

to Assyria, east of the Tigris. Its capital was at Washukanni, a site that has not yet been recovered, and our documentation comes, therefore, from the more distant outposts of the kingdom, notably Alalakh[10] and Ugarit in the west and Nuzi and Arrapkha in the east. Its military strength may well have rested on the horse. If the horse was not actually introduced to the Near East by the Indo-Aryans and Hurrians of Mitanni, it certainly figured prominently in their military strategy both as a mount and for pulling a light chariot. Handbooks of horse-raising and horse-racing have also been preserved from this milieu. The many other innovations introduced into the Near East by the Hurrians were especially conspicuous in the realm of social and legal institutions.[11]

Apart from Mitanni, the Hurrians established a number of other viable states at this time, notably in what later came to be known as Cilicia. Cilicia is the classical name of the Mediterranean littoral south of the Taurus Mountains in Turkey, from Paphlagonia in the west to the Amanus Mountains in the east (see Figure 14, page 76). At its eastern end, this littoral broadens into a fertile valley watered by the Pyramus, Sarus, and Cydnus Rivers (Ceyhan, Seyhan, and Tarsus Cay). This portion was known in classical times as Cilicia Pedias, Campestris, or simply Cilicia proper, to the Hittites as Kizzuwatna (Kizwatna), to the Assyrians as Quwe, to the neo-Babylonians as Hume, and to the Egyptians as Kode or Qedi. According to some Egyptologists, the western portion of Cilicia (Cilicia Aspera or Tracheia) was called Keftiu (Biblical Kaphtor), though this name is more generally held to designate Crete and perhaps the Aegean coasts as well. The name Cilicia is probably derived from that of the Chilakku people who were the dominant ethnic group in the neo-Assyrian period. Like much of the surrounding littoral, Cilicia was an important link in the trade routes of the ancient Near East and was subject to influences, by land and sea, from all neighboring cultures.

By about 1650, eastern Cilicia was clearly under Hittite control, for Hattushili I (1650–20) and Murshili I (1620–1595), the outstanding Old Hittite kings, seem to have moved freely down the Pyramus River during their campaigns in Syria. But with the death of Murshili about 1595, the Hurrians asserted themselves in Cilicia, as elsewhere, and presently Cilicia enjoyed two centuries of precarious independence. The first attested Cilician king, Ishput-achshu, son of Paria-watri, is known both from his own inscription and from a Hittite record. His bilingual bulla from Tarsus on the Cydnus River proclaims him "great king" in cuneiform and in a prototype of hieroglyphic Hittite writing, while the Hittite archives

[10] Compare Sir Leonard Woolley, *A Forgotten Kingdom: Being a Record of the Results Obtained from the Excavation of Two Mounds, Atchana and Al Mina, in the Turkish Hatay* (Baltimore: Penguin Books, 1953).
[11] Speiser, "The Hurrian Participation in the Civilization of Mesopotamia, Syria, and Palestine."

contain references to and fragments of a bilingual (Hittite and Akkadian) treaty between Ishput-achshu, king of Kizzuwatna, and Telepinu, the Hittite king (ca. 1525–1500). Cilicia maintained its independence throughout the fifteenth century. One of its kings, Pallia, or Pillia, concluded treaties with the Hittite king Zidanta II (ca. 1480–1470) and with Idrimi of Alalakh, although the latter claims to have ravaged the strongholds of eastern Cilicia. Idrimi's successor, Niqmepa, appealed to Saushtatar of Mitanni against a Shuna-shura (I), who may have been Pillia's successor in Kizzuwatna. In the time of Arnuwanda I (ca. 1440–1420), Kizzuwatna even expanded beyond the Cilician borders as far east as Urshu and Washukanni. But the increasing power of the new Hittite empire, and the rise of rival Hurrian states, particularly Mitanni, soon put an end to these pretensions. Perhaps as early as the reign of Hattushili II (ca. 1420–1400), Patta-tishu of Kizzuwatna concluded a treaty with the Hittite empire, though still on terms of equality. Under Tudhalia III (ca. 1400–1380), the city of Kizzuwatna itself already belonged to the Hittites, who in turn lost it to Mitanni, and the last independent king of Kizzuwatna, Shuna-shura II, was compelled to conclude a treaty reducing him to a vassal, albeit a privileged one, of the great Hittite king Shuppiluliuma (ca. 1375–1335). Under his successors, Kizzuwatna, its boundaries reduced, seems to have been a province or protectorate of the Hittite empire. As such, its merchants enjoyed extra-territorial rights under Hittite protection as far away as Ugarit.[12]

The city of Ugarit boasted one of the best harbors on the eastern Mediterranean, and the one closest to the island of Cyprus. It was thus the natural emporium for the copper and other products of that important island throughout the Bronze Age. After emerging from Hurrian domination, Ugarit enjoyed a golden age (ca. 1440–1360) when it maintained its independence by judicious alliances with the great powers. It ruled over a not inconsiderable territory in the valley of the Lower Orontes River, and its administration of these lands is well attested by numerous documents, chiefly written in Akkadian cuneiform. But Ugarit is most famous for the library of literary texts which it has been yielding to almost continuous excavations since 1929. These literary texts in large part employ an entirely different system of cuneiform writing from the administrative texts. It is a system intrinsically identical with the later Phoenician "alphabet," with which it shares a common ancestry; among other curiosities it enables us to trace the order of our own alphabet back to the middle of the second millennium.[13] More important, it was the

---

[12] Cyrus H. Gordon, "Abraham and the Merchants of Ura," *Journal of Near Eastern Studies* 17 (1958):28–31; and idem, "Abraham of Ur," *Hebrew and Semitic Studies presented to Godfrey Rolles Driver*, ed. D. Winton Thomas and W. D. McHardy (Oxford: Clarendon Press, 1962), pp. 77–84.

[13] William W. Hallo, "Isaiah 28:9–13 and the Ugaritic Abecedaries," *Journal of Biblical Literature* 77 (1958):324–38.

vehicle for an epic literature which not only rates great interest in its own right, but also illuminates the Hebrew Bible both by its themes and by its poetic diction. These and other textual discoveries have given Ugarit a special significance in Near Eastern archeology.

There were, however, numerous other city-states along the entire length of the Syro-Phoenician coast at this time. Their fortunes are briefly but brilliantly illuminated during the second quarter of the four-teenth century, thanks to the international correspondence discovered at El-Amarna in Egypt.[14] This correspondence reveals the entire area in con-tention as a prize in a three-cornered struggle between the Egyptians, the Mitannians, and the Hittites. The various local princes wavered between a vassalage of dubious loyalty to one or another of these great powers and a precarious independence from all of them. Their struggles were further complicated by the presence throughout the area of a disaffected social stratum known as the Habiru or Hapiru from whom the Biblical term "Hebrew" is derived.[15] At first, the advantage seemed to lie with Egypt, whose empire had once reached to the Euphrates and which still claimed the nominal allegiance of most of the area. Mitanni for its part drew strength from the fact that many of the cities were ruled by princes of the same stock, either Hurrian or Indo-Aryan, as the kingdom of Mitanni itself. But the Hittites boasted the greatest military genius of the time in the person of Shuppiluliuma (ca. 1375–1335), and by a combi-nation of warfare and diplomacy he emerged supreme in the struggle, reducing the Hurrians to relative impotence, and redrawing the border be-tween the Hittite and Egyptian spheres of influence to his own ad-vantage. And yet the ultimate beneficiary of all these developments was destined to be none of these principals, but a party who (as was so often true in the ancient Near East) was, so to speak, waiting in the wings: Assyria.

[3] THE EMERGENCE OF ASSYRIA
ca. 1350–1200 B.C.

The land of Assyria took its name from that of Assur, a city whose history and topography are better known than most others in ancient Mesopotamia, thanks to both extensive excavations and a group of cultic texts listing and describing the temples of the city in such detail that it has come to be known as the divine directory of Assur.[16] Its description

---

[14] See pp. 268–75; and Edward F. Campbell, Jr., "The Amarna Letters and the Amarna Period," *The Biblical Archaeologist* 23 (1960):2–22.

[15] Moshe Greenberg, *The Ḫab/piru*, American Oriental Series, vol. 39 (New Haven: American Oriental Society, 1955).

[16] For the latest discussion of these and related texts, compare G. van Driel, *The Cult of Aššur*, Studia Semitica Neerlandica, vol. 13, ed. M. A. Beek et al. (Assen: van Gorcum, 1969).

may therefore serve as a paradigm for other great capital cities of Mesopotamia.[17]

Topographically, Assur resembles a child's top in ground plan, its concave sides following the Tigris on the east and its ancient branch (now dry) on the north, while the convex side followed the southwestern crest of the elevation on which the city was built. The latter side was fortified by a massive wall and this in due time by a second, outer wall and a moat enclosing, on the extreme southeast, a new suburb that stretched along the Tigris. A quay-wall ran the length of the northern and eastern river fronts.

Most of the monumental buildings fronted on the heavily fortified northern Tigris quay. From west to east, they included: the "gate of the smiths," the "new palace," the Anu-Adad temple with its twin ziggurats, the "old palace," the great Enlil ziggurat (later rededicated to Assur), and the temple of Assur, called Esharra. Behind and south of this imposing façade, there stood two somewhat smaller, older temple complexes, sacred respectively to Ishtar and Nabu and to Sin and Shamash. Other landmarks of the heavily fortified city included thirteen gates and an open area between the two southern walls that was given over to two parallel rows of inscribed stelae of great historical interest; the northern one commemorated the Assyrian kings from Adad-nirari I (who acceded about 1300) on, as well as prominent queens such as Sammu-ramat (the Semiramis of Greek legend); the southern one was reserved for the high officials who, after the king, gave their names to the Assyrian years.[18] Just outside the city walls to the northwest, a special house was built for the akitu, or New Year's festival.

Assur lay behind the northernmost end of the Hamrin (ancient Ebikh) mountains, which, straddling the Tigris from northwest to southeast, form a natural barrier against Babylonia. From the Babylonian point of view, the city was thus the gateway to the north country, which they called either Subartu or simply the land of Assur, Assyria. The latter usage was adopted by the Assyrians themselves, but the geographical concept covered by the term varied with the country's changing fortunes.

The prehistoric periods of Assyria are well attested at numerous sites, first antedating and then paralleling developmental stages in Babylonia. The city of Assur was exposed to Old Sumerian influence at its height (early third millennium), as shown by the layout of the archaic Ishtar temple and by its statuary. By about 2300, the Sargonic kings of Akkad ruled the valleys of the Upper Chabur, Tigris, and Adhem rivers, as attested by Akkadian art, architecture, and texts from sites such as Tell Brak and Gasur (Nuzi) and by native historical traditions. At Assur itself,

[17] For details, see Walter Andrae, *Das Wiedererstandene Assur* (Leipzig: J. C. Hinrichs, 1938).
[18] For the system of dating by so-called eponyms, see p. 61.

a certain Abazu inscribed a statue as a sign of his allegiance to Man-ishtushu of Akkad, and later Assyrian tradition recalled him or a name-sake as one of those early kings who still "dwelled in tents." Babylonian control of Assyria was reasserted by the neo-Sumerian kings of Ur, who fought a long series of wars in the area; one of them, Amar-Sin, ruled Assur itself through a viceroy named Zariqum.

Assyria first emerged briefly as an independent state with the col-lapse of the Ur III dynasty, about 2000. At this time, a certain Ushpia and his son Kikkia built the original main temple and walls of Assur, and though the new state may not at first have expanded significantly beyond the city limits, its influence was felt as far away as Cappadocia, where Assyrian merchant colonies flourished in the time of Puzur-Assur I and his descendants (Chapter III, Section 4). His dynasty ended with Puzur-Assur II about 1850, and Assyria once more fell under a succession of foreign rulers, this time for almost five hundred years. First it became part of the kingdom of Naram-Sin of Eshnunna and then of that of Shamshi-Adad of Terqa and his successors. Finally, after the last of these had been killed in an abortive attempt at reasserting native leadership under a certain Puzur-Sin (ca. 1700), it became a vassal of the Hurrian state of Mitanni. Later Assyrian historians obscured this fact in the Assyrian King List and in the royal inscriptions which recalled earlier rulers and events. They did so for the period of Amorite domination (ca. 1840–1650) by creating the pious fiction that Naram-Sin was the son of Puzur-Assur II and by tracing Shamshi-Adad's ancestry all the way back to Ushpia, the very founder of Assur's independence. For the period of Hurrian domination (ca. 1650–1360) they achieved the same purpose by elevating the vassal-governors of Assur to royal status, claiming for all of them descent from an obscure ancestor called Adasi. They were not, however, distorting history willfully, but rather giving formal expression to a very real sense of continuity which centered on the worship of Assur, the deity from whom their city took its name. They thus provide an interesting parallel to the Israelite experience as canonized in the Hebrew Bible. In both instances, it was the reality of an unbroken religious tradi-tion which permitted an ethnic group to lay claim to the memories or monuments surviving from the Middle Bronze Age and to link them to later political institutions

In Assyria, these political institutions got their chance when Mitannian power began to collapse in the middle of the fourteenth century. The first known claimant to the title "king of the land of Assyria" was Assur-uballit I (ca. 1362–1327), and the foundation of the Assyrian king-dom may be credited to him, for all his predecessors back to the old Assyrian rulers had contented themselves with the title "governor of the city of Assur" or "governor of the god Assur." The new title was favored, henceforth, together with new royal names which emphasized the consciousness of a new era in the history of a state otherwise much given to the preservation of tradition; the recurrent Shamshi-Adad's, Ishme-Dagan's, and Erreshum's of the previous three centuries had recalled the Amorite overlords of the Hammurapi period;[19] in their stead, the Middle Assyrian kings introduced such new royal names as Shulmanu-asharid and Tukulti-apil-esharra which even in their more familiar Biblical guise (based on their neo-Assyrian namesakes) of Shalmaneser and Tiglath-pileser still convey some of their sonorous majesty. The Middle Assyrian kings traced their descent back to Puzur-Assur III, an obscure fifteenth century governor of Assur who provided an onomastic link to the period of Old Assyrian independence and a genealogical one to the house of Adasi; but they broke with the tradition of fraternal succession which had characterized that dynasty hitherto. Beginning with Assur-uballit I, the royal succession passed in the normal manner from father to son.

All these formal changes were but the preliminaries to more far-reaching developments in the military and diplomatic spheres. Throwing off the Hurrian overlordship of Mitanni and disdaining that of Kassite Babylonia which claimed to have inherited it, the Assyrians began to negotiate on a footing of equality with all the great powers of their time, as well as to show their mettle in battle, chiefly with the Kassites. Indeed, the fortunes of Assyria and Babylonia were henceforth closely linked; dynastic intermarriages and treaties alternated with breaches of peace and adjustments of the common border in favor of the victor. A synchronistic king list recorded these contacts in the first systematic attempt to correlate the histories of two discrete states before the Biblical Book of Kings (which made the same attempt for the divided monarchy of Israel and Judah). This synchronistic style was cultivated by the Assyrian historians along with other historical genres, while the court poets created a whole cycle of epics celebrating the triumphs over the Kassites. The king, portrayed in heroic proportions, figured as the peerless protagonist of the latter, and from this combination of sources we deduce, for example, that Enlil-nirari (ca. 1329–1320) fought with Kurigalzu II, or "Kurigalzu the Younger" (ca. 1345–1324), and that Enlil-nirari or Adad-nirari I (ca. 1307–1275) encountered Nazi-maruttash (ca. 1323–1298) at the battle of Suqaqu on the border between Assyria and Babylonia. The Assyrians generally claimed the upper hand in these encounters with the Kassites, who were on the wane; but a deep-seated respect for the older culture and religion of Babylonia, which they regarded as ancestral to their own, constrained them from following up on their advantage at first.

This restraint was dropped by Tukulti-Ninurta I (ca. 1244–1208), one of the few intriguing personalities in the long line of Assyrian kings who were more often so true to form that they are barely distinguishable one

---

[19] That Hammurapi himself ever seized the city of Assur is so far not proved.

from another.[20] So far from respecting the sanctity of Babylon, he took its defeated king (Kashtiliashu IV) into Assyrian captivity together with the statue of Marduk, its god; he razed the walls of the city and assumed the rule of all of Babylonia in his own person. At home, he claimed almost divine honors and, not content with an extensive building program at Assur, he moved across the Tigris to found a whole new capital on its eastern bank, naming it Kar-Tukultininurta ("Quay of Tukulti-Ninurta") after himself. But in all this he aroused increasing enmity, both for the sacrilege against Babylon and its god and for the heavy exactions of his military and building programs. A reaction set in and, led by the king's own son and successor, the more conservative party imprisoned the king in his new capital and set fire to it. The fame of Tukulti-Ninurta was such that garbled features of his reign are thought to be preserved both in Biblical and Greek literature: in Genesis 10, his prowess as conqueror and hunter in the name of Nimrod;[21] in the Greek legends, "King Ninos" and the building of his new capital, "the city of Ninos";[22] and, in the Greek recollections surrounding Sardanapalos, his fiery death there.[23] Separating fact from legend, it is clear that his death marked a new eclipse of Assyrian power destined to last for almost a century.

[4] THE FALL OF TROY AND THE END OF THE BRONZE AGE
    ca. 1200 B.C.

The Late Bronze Age was characterized by a constantly shifting balance of power among a half-dozen major states, each ruled by a different ethnic element. The end of the Bronze Age was precipitated by still other ethnic groups, as distant events unleashed a wave of migrations that altered the political complexion of the entire Near East (see Figure 22). If there was any single first cause of these upheavals, it may conceivably have been the fall of Troy.[24] This event, dated traditionally about 1200 B.C. (or, on the basis of the archeological evidence, about 1250),[25] is properly a part of Greek history, but the whole civilized world was profoundly

[20] Horst Klengel, "Tukulti-Ninurta I, König von Assyrien," *Das Altertum* 7 (1961): 67–77.

[21] E. A. Speiser, "In Search of Nimrod," *Eretz-Israel* 5 (1958):32*–36*; reprinted in *Oriental and Biblical Studies*, ed. Finkelstein and Greenberg, pp. 41–52.

[22] Hildegarde Lewy, "Nitokris-Naqî'a," *Journal of Near Eastern Studies* 11 (1952): 264–86, esp. 266–71.

[23] Ibid.

[24] Carl Nylander, "Zur Moortgat-Festschrift: Troja, Philister, Achämeniden," *Berliner Jahrbuch für Vor- und Frühgeschichte* 6 (1966):203–17.

[25] Denys L. Page, *History and the Homeric Iliad* (Berkeley and Los Angeles: University of California Press, 1966), pp. 73–74.

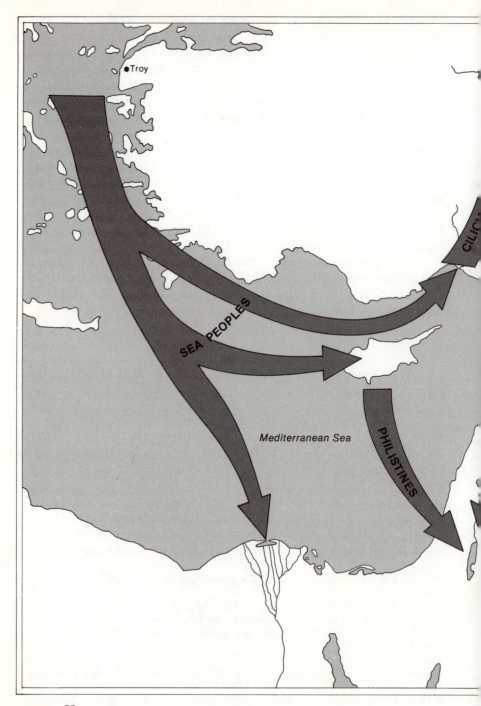

FIGURE 22

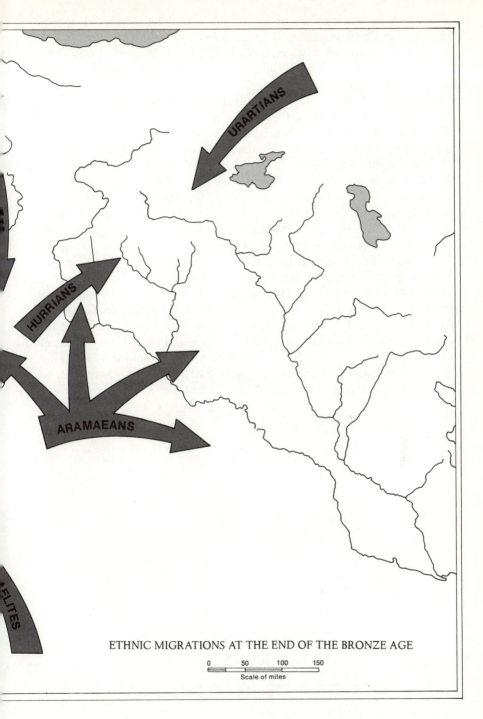

ETHNIC MIGRATIONS AT THE END OF THE BRONZE AGE

0   50   100   150
Scale of miles

affected by its repercussions or by the subsequent fall of the Mycenaean cities of the Greek mainland. The survivors of these catastrophes fled by sea, not across the open water, but along the coasts, seeking new lands to conquer and settle. Known collectively as Sea Peoples, individual groups are identified, particularly in Egyptian sources, by such designations as Philistines, Sicilians, Tyrrhenians, Etruscans, and Sardinians. Wherever, as in Egypt, the established powers were strong enough to withstand them, they pushed on elsewhere and have thus left their names scattered across the Mediterranean to this day. One of the first lands to fall to their onslaughts was Cilicia. Its Hurrian population fled northeast across the Taurus to topple the Hittite empire and establish the province of Cappadocia, while the Hittites in turn fled southeast into northern Mesopotamia to found the state of Hattina on the debris of the fallen kingdom of Mitanni. The Hurrians of Mitanni, blocked by the resurgence of the Assyrians on the east and the simultaneous invasions of the Aramaeans from the south, appear to have escaped northeastward into the mountainous regions around Lake Van, there to establish the kingdom of Hurri, the forerunner of the later Urartu and Armenia.[26] In the southwest, meanwhile, the Israelites were moving from the desert into Canaan to divide it with the Philistines invading it by sea. Finally in the Babylonian southeast, the waning dynasty of the Kassites gave way to a new ruling house, the so-called Second Dynasty of Isin (founded 1158). Thus, in the short span of a century, the Near East took on a wholly new aspect, and new protagonists were to rule its destinies in the Iron Age.

[26] For the dispute concerning the connections between Urartu and Armenia, compare Warren C. Benedict, "Urartians and Hurrians," *Journal of the American Oriental Society* 80 (1960):100–104.

FIGURE 23 Vassal treaty of Asarhaddon with Ramataia.

[V]

THE END OF THE ANCIENT NEAR EAST: THE IRON AGE
ca. 1200–539 B.C.

[1] THE NEAR EAST AT THE BEGINNING OF THE IRON AGE
ca. 1200–860 B.C.

Meteoric iron was known and sporadically used at least as early as the Bronze Age, but terrestrial iron was virtually unknown outside of Asia Minor, where it had already been mentioned in Old Assyrian commercial documents. The Hittites were the first to develop a substantial iron metallurgy, which involved the fusing of molten iron with the help of bellows.[1] With the collapse of their empire, about 1200 B.C., the Hittites' iron monopoly was broken, and the superiority of the new medium for tools and weapons was quickly and widely recognized. The Bible recalls, for example, the advantage it gave the Philistines over the Israelites in the eleventh century.[2] Archeologists thus are generally agreed on about 1200 as the start of the Iron Age, although they differ on its end, which while most often equated with the beginning of the Persian period, in a sense can be said to await the start of the Atomic Age. At best, the term is a mere convention for a period that can be understood, particularly in the Near East, more adequately from the explicit testimony of its written records than from its artifacts.

As we have seen, the new age dawned on a radically transformed Near East. In Palestine, Philistines and Israelites contended with each other

[1] O. R. Gurney, *The Hittites* (London: Penguin Books, 1952), pp. 82–84.
[2] William Foxwell Albright, *The Archaeology of Palestine* (Harmondsworth, Middlesex: Penguin Books, 1949), p. 110.

and with the surviving Canaanites for the possession of the "promised land," and the outcome was in doubt until Saul, David, and Solomon forged the united monarchy out of the disparate tribes with their jealously guarded tribal heritages. In Syria and northern Mesopotamia, a similar struggle ensued between the neo-Hittite and Aramaean newcomers to the area. A number of city-states, however, successfully fused these two elements into an Aramaeo-Hittite or Syro-Hittite culture. Its peoples were probably increasingly Aramaic in daily speech but favored a Hittite dialect, Luwian(?), and the so-called Hittite hieroglyphic script for their monuments, which themselves were often provincial hybrids of many different artistic styles. In this way such city-states as Carchemish, Guzana, Tell Ta'-yinat (probably the ancient Kunulua, capital of Hattina),[3] and Til Barsib were able to maintain an independent course for a time before they finally were incorporated into the expanding Assyrian empire in the east or the Aramaic nation-state that eventually emerged around Damascus in the west.[4] Palestine and Syria were thus evolving comparable constitutions out of divergent backgrounds to meet the challenges of a new age.[5]

In Babylonia, the various dynasties that succeeded the Kassites (see Figure 20, page 107) had only indifferent success in coping with the Aramaean influx. The Second Dynasty of Isin left a certain impact on later literature,[6] and in Nebukadnezar I it included a worthy predecessor to his later neo-Babylonian namesake.[7] But between these two great figures there are few Babylonian kings whose achievements deserve our attention.[8] We must focus, instead, on Assyria and Israel.

Assyria was the one major power in western Asia that survived the upheavals at the end of the Bronze Age. It is true that the assassination of Tukulti-Ninurta I (ca. 1204) plunged Assyria into a period of weakness when it contended on uneven terms with a briefly renascent Babylonia and with the ubiquitous Arameans. But under Tiglath-pileser I (ca. 1115–1077), it once more reasserted itself. Actual territorial growth was at first slow. Ex-

---

[3] David Ussishkin, "Building IV in Hamath and the Temples of Solomon and Tell Tayanat," *Israel Exploration Journal* 16 (1966):104–10.

[4] William W. Hallo, articles on Carchemish, Gozan, Tell Ta'yinat and Til Barsib, *The Biblical World: A Dictionary of Biblical Archaeology*, ed. Charles F. Pfeiffer (Grand Rapids, Mich.: Baker Book House, 1966), pp. 165–69, 270–72, 575, and 584–86.

[5] For a detailed analysis, see Giorgio Buccellati, *Cities and Nations of Ancient Syria: An essay on Political Institutions with Special Reference to the Israelite Kingdoms,* Studi Semitici, vol. 26 (Rome: Istituto di Studi del Vicino Oriente, 1967).

[6] Compare, for example, William W. Hallo, "Akkadian Apocalypses," *Israel Exploration Journal* 16 (1966):231–42, with the comments of J. A. Brinkman, A *Political History of Post-Kassite Babylonia 1158–722 B.C.*, Analecta Orientalia, vol. 43 (Rome: Pontificium Institutum Biblicum, 1968), p. 129.

[7] W. G. Lambert, "The Reign of Nebuchadnezzar I: A Turning Point in the History of Ancient Mesopotamian Religion," *The Seed of Wisdom: Essays in Honor of T. J. Meek*, ed. W. S. McCullough (Toronto: University of Toronto Press, 1964), pp. 3–13.

[8] Brinkman, A *Political History of Post-Kassite Babylonia 1158–722 B.C.*

pansion into the Babylonian south was hindered by religious scruples which Tukulti-Ninurta I had defied at his peril. Eastward and northward, Assyrian ambitions were stymied by even more warlike tribes of the mountains who cast envious eyes at the growing wealth of the Assyrian cities along the Tigris. But in defending these frontiers, the Assyrians evolved a military machine of unequaled efficiency and prepared to unleash it in the one direction that remained open to them, the west. At first, they contented themselves with expeditions in quest of plunder, although dignified in the royal inscriptions as collection of tribute. Typically, the Assyrian army marched downstream along the Tigris, or the parallel Wadi Tartara, as far as the Babylonian frontier, then crossed to the Euphrates which it followed upstream as far as possible before turning north and east in a great arc to return home. By the time of Assurnasirpal II (ca. 883–859), these expeditions assumed almost annual regularity, and the towns and cities in their path knew only too well that they must pay the tribute demanded of them or face the fury of a military assault. The "calculated frightfulness" of Assurnasirpal[9] is documented not only in his inscriptions but even more graphically in the monumental reliefs with which he decorated his palaces, especially at Kalah (modern Nimrud). They are vivid illustrations both of Assyrian art and of the Assyrian character as these asserted themselves in the newfound confidence of an age of expansion.

In Israel, meantime, the united monarchy (ca. 1020–930) did not survive Solomon and his imperial ambitions. But the twin kingdoms of Israel in the north and Judah in the south remained potentially the principal fulcrum for the political see-saw of the time, with Egypt on one end and Assyria on the other. Thus the stage was set for a protracted period of confrontation between Assyria and Israel.

[2] THE ASSYRIAN RESURGENCE
859–783 B.C.*

When Shalmaneser III (see Figure 24) succeeded his father, Assurnasirpal II, in 859 B.C., he inherited a kingdom on the ascendant. His ruthless if artistic predecessor had been a master of military tactics. If he was

[9] A. T. Olmstead, *History of Assyria* (New York: Charles Scribner's, 1923), pp. 81–97.

* This and the next two sections are adapted from William W. Hallo, "From Qarqar to Carchemish: Assyria and Israel in the Light of New Discoveries," *The Biblical Archaeolgist* 23 (1960):34–61, to which the reader is referred for extensive documentation and detailed bibliography. See also the updated version in *The Biblical Archaeologist Reader*, vol. 2, ed. David Noel Freedman and Edward F. Campbell, Jr. (Garden City, N.Y.: Doubleday & Company, Anchor Books, 1964), pp. 152–88. The original version was reprinted in The Bobbs-Merrill Reprint Series in European History, E-95.

FIGURE 24 Statue of Shal-maneser III.

not equally accomplished in military strategy or in diplomacy, the new king supplied these wants. Where Assurnasirpal's object had been little more than plunder, Shalmaneser's expeditions bore the earmarks of a grand design. He measured his capacities, annexed those areas he could, imposed regular annual tribute on those still strong enough to maintain, as loyal vassals, a measure of autonomy, and sought trade relations with others who were too powerful or too distant to be reduced to vassalage. The repeated hammer blows of Shalmaneser's armies were directed with an almost single-minded dedication and persistence against Assyria's western neighbors and brought about the first direct contact between Assyria and Israel.

In Israel, the year 859 marked the sixteenth of King Ahab, son of Omri. He too inherited an expanding kingdom, newly entrenched at Samaria, which sought by trade, conquest, and alliance to secure its place in the developing constellation of ninth-century powers. Moab acknowl-edged Ahab's sovereignty over Gilead-Gad and sent him tribute (2 Kings

3:4); Sidon's alliance and trade were no doubt won together with the hand of Jezebel, the daughter of its king (1 Kings 16:31); Jehoshaphat of Judah, Ahab's contemporary, made peace with him (1 Kings 22:45), an alliance further cemented by marriage (2 Chronicles 18:1). These successes were achieved no doubt in the time of Assurnasirpal, who, though he reached the Mediterranean and claimed receipt of tribute from as far south as Tyre, apparently left Israel undisturbed in the enjoyment of successful diplomacy and domestic prosperity.

The accession of Shalmaneser changed this situation. From now on, an annual campaign by the king or his commander-in-chief became a commonplace, so much so that it began to serve as an auxiliary system of dating in Assyria, producing the so-called *Eponym Chronicle*, which provides us with a record of the major military (or, occasionally, religious or civil) events of each year from the middle of the reign of Shalmaneser to the first years of Sennaherib. The king's inscriptions supply the details.

The Assyrian inscriptions inform us of the Battle of Lutibu near Zinjirli (Sam'al), where in 858 Shalmaneser met the combined forces of Sam'al, Hattina, Carchemish, and Adini, a north Syrian confederacy that succeeded in checking Shalmaneser's march toward Cilicia and his control of the strategic routes to Asia Minor. Undaunted, Shalmaneser concentrated his next effort against the nearest of the allies, Bit Adini. This area, lying between the river Balih and the westernmost part of the Euphrates, was ruled by the Aramaeo-Hittite Ahuni from his fortress at Til Barsib (modern Tell-Ahmar) on the east bank of the Euphrates. In three successive campaigns (857–855), Shalmaneser chased Ahuni from his capital and renamed it after himself, annexed Bit Adini to Assyria, and captured Ahuni. A hundred years later, Amos was to recall the downfall of perhaps this very "scepter-wielder from Bet-Eden" (Amos 1:5), and its fate still served Assyria as an intimidating example another fifty years later (2 Kings 19:12; Isaiah 37:12). In 854, the Assyrian success was consolidated with an expedition to Mt. Kashiari (Tur Abdin) at the headwaters of the Chabur River.

The lesson of Shalmaneser's tenacity was not lost on the kingdoms of Syria and Palestine. Ben-Hadad II of Aram-Damascus had for two years been attacking the Israelite Ahab deep in his own kingdom, but in the face of the common threat, the two made peace (I Kings 20). Together with Cilicians, Egyptians, Arabians, Ammonites, and various Phoenician contingents, both joined a grand alliance under Jarhuleni of Hamath, which met Shalmaneser at Qarqar on the Orontes River in 853. Thus a new south Syrian confederacy was created, comparable to the north Syrian confederacy that had engaged Shalmaneser in the first five years of his reign.

Shalmaneser claimed an overwhelming victory at Qarqar, but there are several indications that the confederacy actually carried the day. First of these is the total silence in which the Bible passes over the event. Had Ahab and his allies really suffered the massive defeat the Assyrian annalists attributed to them, an account of the battle would certainly have served the didactic purposes of the Book of Kings. Equally telling is the fact that Shalmaneser's next three campaigns (852–850) were conducted considerably closer to home, while Damascus and Israel, two of the principal partners in the coalition, renewed their old conflict. It was, apparently, immediately after the engagement of Qarqar that Ahab broke with his late ally by assaulting Ramoth-Gilead (1 Kings 22). Jehoshaphat of Judah accompanied Ahab and appointed Jehoram his coregent just before his departure. Ahab should have taken a similar precaution, if such it was, for, though Jehoshaphat survived the expedition, Ahab did not, and his successor Ahaziah was displaced, before a year had elapsed, by another of his sons, a namesake of the Judahite coregent. Much of Elisha's ministry must have fallen during the reign of this Israelite Joram, and it is then that we can thus place the siege of Samaria by Ben-Hadad II of Damascus (2 Kings 6:24ff.). Whether this was in reprisal for Ahab's breach of the alliance or not, it produced conditions of cannibalism in the besieged city— which were later to be paralleled in Mesopotamia in the closing years of the Assyrian empire.

Perhaps the most important clue to the effectiveness of the south Syrian coalition at Qarqar in 853 is the fact that it opposed Shalmaneser again in 849, 848, 845, and 841. And only after the last of these encounters could Shalmaneser truthfully claim the submission of the western states, for whom 841 was in many ways a critical year.[10] More than a century later, the prophet Hosea recalled the triumphal march across the now prostrate westland by "Shalman," that is, Shalmaneser (Hosea 10:14).[11] Otherwise, the Biblical record is again silent regarding the Assyrian's role, but it reflects the unsettled conditions of the time in its account of the accession of Hazael in Damascus, Jehu in Israel, and Athaliah in Judah (2 Kings 8:7–15, 25–29; 9:1–28). The result of the Assyrian success and the upheavals in Palestine was the extinction of the house of Omri in Israel and its survival in Judah in the person of Athaliah. Athaliah was a daughter of Ahab and Jezebel, the widow of Jehoram, and the mother of the short-lived Ahaziah. Her triple claim to royal authority enabled her to sit first behind, then beside, and finally on the king's throne, and her career seems the more credible in the light of three Mesopotamian queens —Sammuramat, Nakia (Zakutu), and Adad-guppi—whose roles are emerging ever more clearly.

[10] Compare Y. Aharoni and Ruth Amiran, "A New Scheme for the Sub-division of the Iron Age in Palestine," *Israel Exploration Journal* 8 (1958):171–84.
[11] Michael C. Astour, "841 B.C.: The First Assyrian Invasion of Israel," *Journal of the American Oriental Society* 91 (1971):383–89.

Among the members of the much reduced south Syrian coalition, only Hazael of Damascus posed a threat to Shalmaneser, and a single punitive expedition by Shalmaneser (838) was not enough to deter the Syrian usurper. Nevertheless, Jehu in Israel, a loyal Assyrian vassal, and Joash in Judah, who came to the throne in Jehu's seventh year (835), bore the brunt of Hazael's military designs. And Shalmaneser was therefore able to turn his attention once more to north Syria and the lands beyond it. The campaigns of 839–828 were directed primarily against the northwest, although the Medean and Armenian frontiers received some attention in 834–831.

Shalmaneser III's reign nevertheless ended in disaster. In the midst of a two-year campaign against the northeastern frontier, he had to face the Great Revolt in Nineveh and other Assyrian centers that occupied the next six years of the *Eponym Chronicle* (827–822). As a result of this upheaval, all of Shalmaneser's western conquests were nullified. Although Shamshi-Adad V, his son and successor, was able to quell the revolt in his second year (822), he had to acknowledge the temporary overlordship of Babylon for this purpose. His recorded campaigns were directed first against the north and then, when he felt powerful enough to throw off the Babylonian vassalage, against his recent sovereign there. But the areas west of the Euphrates were lost, and Til Barsib on the Euphrates became the westernmost outpost of Assyrian influence. Excavations at Til Barsib show that this citadel remained under Assyrian control throughout the period of weakness that followed. But a degree of independence was manifested even in such relatively nearby areas as the middle Chabur Valley, where the priestdom of Mushezib-Ninurta is attested by a votive seal of this period.

Hazael of Damascus, meanwhile, continued his depredations against Israel and Judah unchecked by Assyrian restraints. The death of Jehu in 814 even enabled him to march through the length and breadth of Palestine in order to capture Gath (2 Kings 12:18), for both events seem dated to the twenty-third year of the long reign of Joash of Judah. Nor did the accession of a new Assyrian king in 811 immediately relieve Jehoahaz, the son and successor of Jehu, of the Aramaean pressure. For Adad-nirari III was a mere child when his father died, and for four years his mother Sammuramat (the Semiramis of Greek legend) ruled in his name. When, in 805, he was at last able to turn his attention against the Aramaeans, he was regarded as a veritable deliverer by Israel (2 Kings 13:5).

The reign of Sammuramat and Adad-nirari III indeed marked a partial recovery in the general decline that followed the Great Revolt. The new excavations at Kalah show that this residence city was now thoroughly rebuilt. In the northwest corner of the outer city, Adad-nirari erected his own palace. Within the citadel area proper, two smaller palaces, the so-called Burnt Palace and the high-lying AB palace, were built, as was a great temple of Nabu called Ezida, like its Babylonian prototypes. The cult of Nabu, thus introduced into Assyria, meant a cultural reconciliation with Babylonia, perhaps at the instigation of the Babylonian queen mother. The completion of the new temple was marked by the dedication of two statues at its entrance inscribed on behalf of Adad-nirari and Sammuramat, the inscriptions ending in the well-known lines: "In Nabu trust: trust in no other God!" They were dedicated by Bel-tarsi-ilumma, the new governor of Kalah, who is known not only as eponym for the year 798 but from administrative tablets found in the governor's palace that was newly erected for him in the citadel of Kalah at this time.[12]

Thus Kalah was transformed into a major—perhaps the major—capital of Assyria. Undoubtedly, too, it became a staging area for military operations, which began to regain some of their old effectiveness, even during Adad-nirari's minority. The Medes and the Mannaeans were attacked in the east, while the way to the west was opened with the recapture of Guzana (Tell Halaf) in 808. The archive of Guzana's governor, Mannu-ki-Assur, which was discovered on this site, shows clearly the close supervision that Adad-nirari presently exercised over this important outpost. The king's coming of age was marked by the previously mentioned campaign against Damascus and Palashtu. Israel too, under its Assyrian designation of House of Omri, appears among the willing tributaries of this campaign, which was followed by strikes against more northerly Syria (Arpad, Hazazu, Ba'li, 805–803) until, in 802, the Mediterranean itself was reached. (One more campaign to the west is recorded in the *Eponym Chronicle* for 796.) It was directed against Mansuate in north central Syria, and is commemorated on a newly found stela on which, among others, Jehoash of Israel is recorded as offering tribute, presumably coming to Damascus for this purpose.[13]

But Adad-nirari could not hold the west. For the rest of his reign, his armies were engaged closer to home, north, east, and south of Assyria. At the same time, the Urartian kings of what later became Armenia began to make their influence felt, and until their pretensions were decisively challenged by Tiglath-pileser III at Kummuh in 743, they were apparently recognized as overlords of the Anatolian country reaching to the Mediterranean, as far south even as Aleppo. Thus Adad-nirari's claim that "the country of the Hittites, Amurru-country in its full extent, Tyre, Sidon, Israel ("the land of Omri"), Edom, Philistia (Palestine), as far as the shore of the great sea of the setting sun" all acknowledged his sovereignty and paid him tribute was true at best temporarily.

[12] See William W. Hallo, "The Rise and Fall of Kalah," *Journal of the American Oriental Society* 88 (1968):772–75.
[13] Stephanie Page, "A Stela of Adad-nirari III and Nergal-ereš from Tell al Rimah," *Iraq* 30 (1968):139–53 and plates 38–41; and idem, "Joash and Samaria in a New Stela Excavated at Tell al Rimah, Iraq," *Vetus Testamentum* 19 (1969):483–84.

[3] *DIVIDE ET IMPERA:* THE CONSOLIDATION OF THE NEO-ASSYRIAN EMPIRE 782–722 B.C.

When Shalmaneser IV succeeded his father, Adad-nirari III, in 783, both Judah and Israel were firmly ruled by two long-lived princes who had taken over the throne in the lifetime of their fathers. Azariah of Judah had begun his coregency in 791, the sixth year of his father, Amaziah; Jeroboam II had begun his in 793, the fifth year of his father, Jehoash, becoming sole ruler of Israel in Shalmaneser IV's first regnal year (782). Elsewhere, too, the new Assyrian king found powerfully entrenched rulers. During his reign and that of his successor, Assur-dan III, Urartu was ruled by Argishti I, who continued the Urartian domination of Syria. He attacked Assyria from both east and west, and the six campaigns of Shalmaneser IV against Urartu between 781 and 774 were really defensive actions. Even the central provinces maintained only a tenuous loyalty to Assyria, for the various governors ruled in virtual independence of the king at Kalah. One of them, Shamshi-ilu, inscribed his own monuments at Kar-Shalmaneser (Bit Adini) in quasi-royal style, and even after this fortress had to be abandoned he virtually ruled the empire as *turtanu* (commander-in-chief).

Shalmaneser IV was succeeded by his brother Assur-dan III in 773, but the situation did not change materially. Although the new king attacked Damascus once (773) and Hatarika (Biblical Hadrach; see Zechariah 9:1) on the Orontes three times (772, 765, 755), the main direction of Assyrian military efforts, such as they were, continued to be south and east. There are few historical records for this reign, as for the preceding one, but the *Eponym Chronicle* reveals the Assyrian weakness clearly enough. For the first time—except 810—it specifies that the king and his armies stayed at home (768), and it repeats this information three more times (764, 757, and 756). The Assyrian weakness was aggravated by plagues (765, 759) and internal revolts (763–759).

The third son of Adad-nirari III succeeded to the throne of Assyria in 755 under the name of Assur-nirari V. Assyrian fortunes had now reached a nadir, and half of Assur-nirari's decade of rule was spent at home. The campaign of his first regnal year (754) was directed against Arpad, and its temporary success can be seen in the famous treaty he concluded with Mati'-ilu of Arpad. But its clay was hardly dry before Mati'-ilu broke the agreement to enter into a similar vassal relation with Bar-Gayah. The stelae inscribed with the latter treaty constitute one of the most important documents for the study of Old Aramaic.[14]

In the first half of the eighth century, then, Assyrians, Aramaeans,

---

[14] Joseph A. Fitzmyer, S.J., *The Aramaic Inscriptions of Sefire,* Biblica et Orientalia, vol. 19 (Rome: Pontifical Biblical Institute, 1967).

and Urartians fought each other to a standstill in Mesopotamia and Syria. Given the internal stability prevailing in Judah and Israel at the same time, it is no wonder that the divided kingdom briefly regained the economic strength and territorial extent of the Solomonic empire. Judah exploited the southern desert (2 Chronicles 26:1–15) and its land and sea routes, while Israel won back all the Transjordanian lands lost to Hazael and much Aramaean territory besides (2 Kings 14:25, 28).

Yet the very prosperity enjoyed by the petty kingdoms of Syria and Palestine nourished the seeds of their destruction, and those astute enough to see this (Amos 1–2) knew that it could not outlast the fortuitous coincidence of stability in the west and weakness in Assyria. It required only a turn of the wheel of fortune to bring the Assyrians down on Israel once more (Amos 6:14). And so it was. Jeroboam II died in 753 after a reign of forty-one years (twenty-nine of them as sole ruler), and his son Zechariah was unable to perpetuate the dynasty of Jehu. Within the year, his throne was usurped, first by Shallum and again (752) by Menahem. Even Menahem's rule did not go unchallenged for a later view assigned all of Menahem's ten years to his successor-by-usurpation, Pekah.[15] In Judah, meanwhile, the long reign of Azariah (Uzziah) ended in illness, and, in 750, he turned over effective power to his son and successor, Jotham. Thus ended forty years of internal stability and external prowess for Israel and Judah.

In Assyria, however, the change of rulers had the opposite effect. Here, too, rebellion was the order of the day. This time it broke out in Kalah, and although the excavations have not turned up any physical evidence of its virulence, it served to sweep away the old ruling family and pave the way for a new resurgence. In the excavator's words, Assur-nirari "perished in Kalhu . . . as the result of a revolution which reflected the culmination of discontent at the end of nearly forty years of disastrous Assyrian weakness."[16] Perhaps Israelite tradition reflected the memory of these forty years by attaching the legend of the near-collapse of Nineveh to Jonah, a prophetic contemporary of Jeroboam II or, conversely, by assigning the Jonah of legend to the reign of Jeroboam (2 Kings 14:25).[17]

Tiglath-pileser III (744–727) was a usurper, and the Assyrian King List excavated at Dur-Sharrukin, though dated 738, stops with his predecessor, Assur-nirari V. But the new king was perhaps of royal blood, and a later copy of the Assyrian King List even calls him the son of his predecessor.[18] He was certainly the beneficiary of the revolt that unseated Assur-

---

[15] Compare Edwin R. Thiele, "Pekah to Hezekiah," *Vetus Testamentum* 16 (1966): 88–107, esp. 86–89.

[16] M. E. L. Mallowan, "Excavations at Nimrud, 1949–1950," *Iraq* 12 (1950):172.

[17] For the exegetic problem involved, compare William W. Hallo, "On the Antiquity of Sumerian Literature," *Journal of the American Oriental Society* 83 (1963):175, n. 68.

[18] Ignace J. Gelb, "Two Assyrian King Lists," *Journal of Near Eastern Studies* 13 (1954):209–30, esp. 229, n. 108.

nirari and even arrogated that ruler's last year to himself instead of following Assyrian practice and counting his regnal years from the New Year succeeding his predecessor's death. He and his first two successors changed the whole balance of power in the Near East, destroying Israel among many other states and reducing the rest, including Judah, to vassalage. They found Assyria in a difficult, even desperate, military and economic situation, but during the next forty years they recovered and consolidated its control of all its old territories and reestablished it firmly as the preeminent military and economic power in the Near East. (See Figure 25.)

The Assyrian campaigns of the next four decades not only assumed a new intensity but also covered greater distances in more numerous directions than ever before. Israel felt the effects of the new policy almost at once. In 743, the year of his own eponymate, Tiglath-pileser was in Arpad, apparently to receive homage from the loyal kings of the west and to direct the launching of a massive campaign against those Anatolian, Syrian, and Palestinian rulers who did not at once submit. Among the tributaries was Menahem of "the Samarians" (that is, Israel), while Azariah of "the Judeans" (that is, Judah) was prominent among the rebels. Menahem's position at this late stage of his reign was insecure. Not only did he feel it necessary to submit to Assyria "in order to secure the kingship in his hand" (2 Kings 15:19), but also his son Pekahiah, who succeeded him in the following year, was presently killed in the revolt of Pekah.

The exact course of Tiglath-pileser's first great campaign against the west (743–738) is difficult to follow. But various details are emerging from obscurity. Evidently the Assyrians were simultaneously organizing the nearer Syrian provinces under Assyrian administration, regulating the successions to their liking in the middle tier of states, and waging war against the more distant ones. The semiautonomous Assyrian proconsulships were broken up into smaller administrative units and their governors thereby deprived of the virtually sovereign power that the interval of royal weakness had allowed them to assume. The Urartian empire in northern Syria was destroyed, Pisiris of Carchemish became a loyal vassal, and the main cities of northern Phoenicia were annexed and formed into the new province of Unqi after Tutannu of Unqi had been sent as booty to Assyria. Presently, Phoenician cities as far south as Tyre and Sidon occupied the attention of the royal administration at Kalah. In more northerly Sam'al, Panamu II was installed by Tiglath-pileser in an attempt to end a troubled period that witnessed the assassination of his father, Bar-Sur.

Faced with these and similar examples, Menahem of Israel had probably sought Assyrian support for his eventual successor by payment of tribute. If so, that support was ineffectual, for Pekahiah had reigned only two years, when, in 740–39, the revolt of Pekah unseated him in what certainly represented an anti-Assyrian reaction. In Judah, Azariah died in the

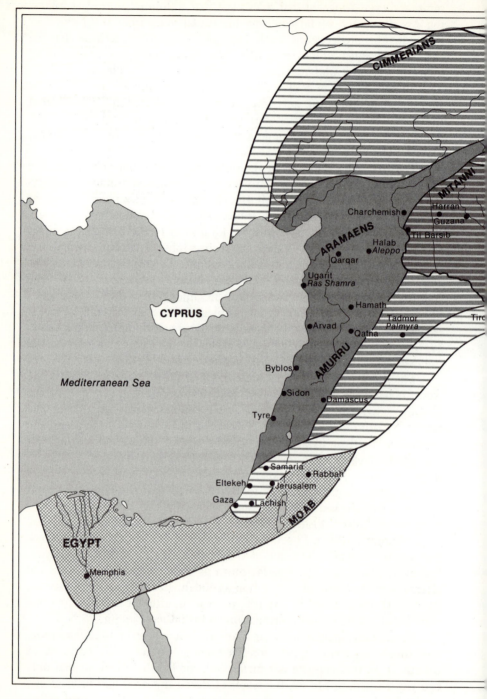

FIGURE 25

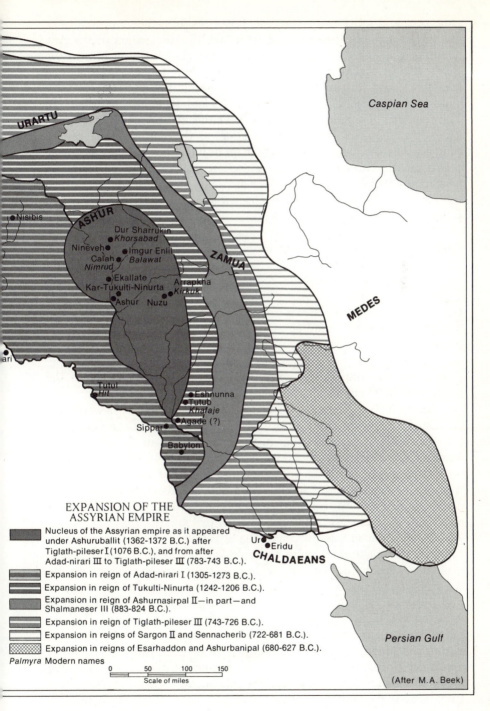

EXPANSION OF THE
ASSYRIAN EMPIRE

Nucleus of the Assyrian empire as it appeared
under Ashuruballit (1362-1372 B.C.) after
Tiglath-pileser I (1076 B.C.), and from after
Adad-nirari III to Tiglath-pileser III (783-743 B.C.).

Expansion in reign of Adad-nirari I (1305-1273 B.C.).

Expansion in reign of Tukulti-Ninurta (1242-1206 B.C.).

Expansion in reign of Ashurnasirpal II—in part—and
Shalmaneser III (883-824 B.C.).

Expansion in reign of Tiglath-pileser III (743-726 B.C.).

Expansion in reigns of Sargon II and Sennacherib (722-681 B.C.).

Expansion in reigns of Esarhaddon and Ashurbanipal (680-627 B.C.).

Palmyra Modern names

0   50   100   150
Scale of miles

(After M.A. Beek)

same year, and Jotham, the coregent, began his sole reign. Apparently he was still enough of a free agent to undertake the subjugation of the Ammonites on the other side of the Jordan, for they do not appear in the early tribute lists of Tiglath-pileser; they had paid tribute to Azariah (2 Chronicles 26:8), and Jotham forced them to continue this practice for three years (2 Chronicles 27:5), after which we find them paying tribute to Tiglath-pileser alongside Ahaz of Judah. During the three-year interval in which Tiglath-pileser turned his attention to the northern and eastern frontiers, Ahaz became coregent of Jotham in Judah in what may well have been a pro-Assyrian coup designed to appease Tiglath-pileser on his imminent return to the west. His payment of tribute is, at any rate, in marked contrast with the anti-Assyrian and expansionist policies of Azariah and Jotham.

The second phase of Tiglath-pileser's western activities falls in the three years 734–732. According to the *Eponym Chronicle*, these were marked by one Assyrian campaign against Philistia and two against Damascus. The focus of anti-Assyrian resistance was now Rezin of Damascus. Tiglath-pileser's strategy was to attack the various lesser allies beyond Damascus first and then, having isolated Rezin, to turn on Damascus itself. This strategy was the more appropriate as he was already master of the Phoenician cities. Those that had not been included in the province of Unqi were now united in a new province around Hamath, bordering, presumably, on Unqi in the north, the House of Omri (Israel) in the south, and the House of Haza'ili (Damascus) in the east.

According to 2 Kings 16:7 (see also 2 Chronicles 28:16), however, the Assyrian strategy was inspired by Ahaz's call for help. Rezin had paid tribute as early as 743 and again in the same year(?) in the company of Menahem of Israel. Now, however, emboldened by Tiglath-pileser's preoccupation in the north, he conspired with Pekah of Israel and perhaps with the Philistines and Edomites in a new anti-Assyrian coalition. No doubt the coalition was intended to include Judah too, but there effective power was in the hands of the pro-Assyrian party and the coregent Ahaz, even though Jotham was still alive. The Syro-Ephraimite coalition sought, therefore, to substitute a more tractable king in Judah. Ahaz, however, maintained his throne without yielding to the coalition, backed up, no doubt, by Isaiah's reassurances. Under attack from all sides, he called on Tiglath-pileser for help, and Assyria's campaign against Philistia ensued. Ashkelon and Gaza were defeated, and Gezer too was captured. Tiglath-pileser accepted tribute from Judah and her eastern neighbors, Ammon, Edom, and Moab, but dealt more severely with Israel. Judging by 2 Kings 15:29, the Northern Kingdom was shorn of most of its territory, including all of Gilead and much of Galilee. The inhabitants were exiled (see also I Chronicles 5:26), perhaps because Pekah had drawn much of his strength from across the Jordan; the huge stronghold of Hazor was destroyed; and the proud Kingdom of Israel was reduced to little more than a vassal state, which Isaiah and Hosea now properly enough called simply Ephraim, where Amos had still called it Joseph. The utimate step of incorporation into the Assyrian provincial system remained, under these circumstances, little more than a formality. It was postponed for a decade because, while Tiglath-pileser was successfully concluding his siege of Damascus in 732, a pro-Assyrian revolt in Samaria finally cost Pekah his life and elevated the last northern king, Hoshea, who was a loyal Assyrian vassal. If Tiglath-pileser did not actually put Hoshea on the throne, as he claims, he was certainly not dissatisfied with the regulations of the succession.

Throughout the west, the royal successions were similarly regulated to Assyria's satisfaction. About 733, the Assyrian vassal Panamu II had died fighting loyally at his master's side before Damascus, and his son Bar-Rekub received the throne of Sam'al from Tiglath-pileser, as he admitted freely in his own inscription. At the same time Ambaris of Tabal was recognized as vassal king of Chilakku (Cilicia). Damascus fell in 732 and, with Rezin dead, was at last incorporated into the Assyrian empire (2 Kings 16:9). In Judah, at the same time, Tiglath-pileser had the satisfaction of seeing the loyal Ahaz become sole ruler upon the death of Jotham.

Tiglath-pileser's second western campaign was thus even more decisive than the first, and from the Taurus Mountains in the north to the border of Egypt in the south, the entire Mediterranean littoral now paid him homage, whether as province or as vassal kingdom. If the vassals, such as Israel and Judah, Tabal and Cilicia, and even Carchemish, were not at once reduced to provinces, it was because Tiglath-pileser's attention was once more diverted elsewhere. In 731, a rebellion broke out in Babylonia, and a certain Mukin-zeri replaced the loyal Nabu-nadin-zeri. Tiglath-pileser moved energetically against this threat at his rear. At the New Year's festival in Babylon in 729 and again in 728, he himself "seized the hands of Bel," that is, he led the statue of Bel (Marduk) in procession in the gesture of legitimation and ostensible submission to the Marduk priesthood that was traditionally demanded of Babylonian kings. He thus successfully challenged Mukin-zeri's claim to the kingship, and was duly enrolled in the Babylonian King List, where he appears under his nickname of Pulu, a name that passed, more or less intact, also into the later Jewish and Greek accounts of his reign. The Mukin-zeri rebellion occupied Tiglath-pileser until the end of his reign. When he did finally turn his attention to Damascus again in 727, it was his last recorded act; judging by the *Eponym Chronicle*, Shalmaneser V took the throne before the campaign had really started.

The new king's brief reign of five years (726–722) is so far illuminated by hardly any inscriptions. Were it not for records from Babylonia (where he reigned as Ululai) and Israel, he would scarcely even be credited with the capture of Samaria, his greatest achievement. During his first regnal

year he stayed in the land, apparently content not to interfere with the
Phoenico-Palestinian rebellion that had, almost inevitably, greeted his
accession (see 2 Kings 17:4). But in 725 he began his countermeasures.
Shechem was captured, Samaria invested, and a siege of Tyre begun at the
same time. The five-year siege of Tyre was destined to be completed by
Sargon, but Samaria fell in August or September 722, Hoshea having been
deported sometime before. Shalmaneser V died in December of the same
year, after the fall of Samaria, and those scholars who argued that 2 Kings
17:6 and 18:10 implied as much seem now definitely to be proven right.
Although Sargon may have shared as second-in-command in the siege of
Samaria, he misappropriated his predecessor's triumph late in his own reign
in order to fill the gap in military activities that loomed in his first year.

The exile Shalmaneser V imposed on Samaria was no more severe
than Tiglath-pileser's exile of the Trans-Jordanian Israelites ten years
earlier. Nor was he the king who repopulated Samaria with the motley
victims of other campaigns. If the events of 722 nevertheless had an
enormous impact on Jewish religious thought, it was because the literary
prophets saw in them the first decisive fulfillment of their collective interpretation of history, as the Babylonian exile of Judah was to be the second.
The exiles themselves were probably quickly acclimated in such strongholds of Assyro-Aramaean symbiosis as Guzana (Gozan) and the Chabur
region (2 Kings 17:6; 1 Chronicles 5:26). They may soon have penetrated
even the capital cities of Assyria, for presently we find such Israelite royal
names as Menahem at Kalah and Hoshea at Nineveh.

[4] PAX ASSYRIACA: THE SARGONID KINGS
ca. 721–627 B.C.

The accession of Sargon inaugurated the beginning of a new "Sargonid" branch of the royal family and the closing chapter in the period of
Assyrian conquest and expansion. The seventeen years of Sargon's reign
were marked by almost continuous warfare, and his later scribes would
have it appear that every single year witnessed a major campaign. It is this
conceit that was responsible for a number of chronological contradictions
within the records of Sargon's reign. In light of new historical sources,
however, it is now possible to resolve these contradictions and to adduce
some important new synchronisms with Biblical history and literature.

The change of Assyrian rulers was, as usual, greeted by a rebellion.
In the west it was led by a certain Yaubidi, a commoner who, having succeeded in seizing power in Hamath and winning followers
among the newly conquered cities of Damascus, Simirra, Arpad, Hatarika
and Samaria, found allies in the still independent Hanuni of Gaza

and in Re'e, the commander-in-chief of Lower Egypt. However, Sargon did not move at once to quell the rebellion. Like Shalmaneser V before him, he seems to have spent his first regnal year in the land. When he did open hostilities in 720, it was first against the south. At the battle of Der, before the Iranian foothills, the Assyrians met the combined forces of Humbanigash of Elam and Marduk-apla-iddina II (the Biblical Merodach-baladan), the new king of Babylonia who was destined to be a focus of anti-Assyrian resistance for a generation. Since this king was left in control of Babylon for a decade following the battle, it is apparent that Sargon won at best a partial victory at the Battle of Der, which is unusually well documented. With the recovery of Merodach-baladan's version on a barrel-cylinder from Uruk which Sargon brought to Kalah and replaced with his own, we now have three different accounts of the battle. Victory is claimed in almost the same terms for Humbanigash by the *Babylonian Chronicle*, for Sargon, and now for Merodach-baladan, whom the *Babylonian Chronicle* had contemptuously dismissed as arriving too late for the action. We are thus warned against an uncritical reading of our primary sources even where they rely on eye witnesses.

Against the western rebellion Sargon was considerably more successful. Yaubidi was defeated near Qarqar and executed; Hamath, his base of operations, was destroyed together with Hatarika (the Biblical Hadrach), and the other rebellious cities, including Samaria, were recaptured. The subjugation of Judah—that is, its payment of tribute—was a natural consequence. The campaign climaxed in Sargon's victorious sweep of the Philistine coast. Eqron and Gabbatunu (Biblical Gibbeton) were razed along with Gaza, the center of Philistine opposition, and the Assyrians advanced to the very gates of Egypt, which for the first time was defeated and forced to pay tribute. Finally, the siege of Tyre begun by Shalmaneser V was brought to a successful conclusion during this campaign.

Thus Sargon showed in no uncertain manner that he was prepared to carry on in the aggressive footsteps of his two predecessors. And he saw to it that the lessons of his energetic campaigning would not be lost on his subjects and vassals. At Dur-Sharrukin ("Sargonsburg," today Khorsabad), he spent most of his reign erecting for himself an entirely new capital city and a magnificent palace, whose walls were decorated with reliefs illustrating this and subsequent campaigns. The execution of Yaubidi and other rebels was depicted in realistic detail in Hall VIII as a warning to visiting princes, while Hall V was given over to the rest of the campaign of 720. It would be no wonder if Sargon's first western campaign left a deep impression on Judah, and, indeed, it has been argued that it was referred to with awe in a prophecy as late as Zechariah 9:1-5, whose topographical allusions can now all be linked to this campaign.

A respite followed for the west, but it lasted only two years (719–718), during which Sargon was engaged in the far north. In 717, Carchemish conspired against Assyria, and Sargon unleashed a two-year show of strength (717–716) throughout the entire west, effectively quelling whatever opposition was left from 720. Carchemish was defeated and incorporated into the empire, another Assyrian province was organized in Palestine, and captive Arabian tribes were settled in Samaria. Finally, Sargon marched to the Egyptian border once more and, according to a newly published fragment from Assur, defeated Shilkanni (Osorkon), king of Egypt, at the city of the River of Egypt, probably identical with Raphia-Rapikhu.

In the midst of these events occurred the death of Ahaz of Judah, the "broken rod" of Isaiah 14:28–32. The historical Isaiah had perhaps never been such a partisan of Ahaz as his later editors made him out to be; he either sensed or himself contributed to the decisive change in Judaean policy implied by Hezekiah's accession. Sargon did not recognize the change (or more likely was already on his way back to Assyria). Otherwise he surely would have invaded Judah at this time, instead of waiting until 712. Certainly Hezekiah showed his hand at once, for the proclamation of his Passover, together with an invitation that embraced not only Judah but the new Assyrian province in Israel as well, fell in his first or second year (715 or 714). By these, he inaugurated not only a great religious reform but also an anti-Assyrian policy, both of which, resumed by Josiah, ultimately enabled Judah to survive Assyria.

In the meantime, Sargon was again occupied on the northern frontier, carving out new provinces and waging mountain warfare of the type made famous by the account of his eighth campaign.[19] But the diversion was short-lived, for in 712 Palestine once more felt the full impact of Assyrian arms. Sargon stayed in the land according to the *Eponym Chronicle*, confirming Isaiah's statement that his commander-in-chief, the turtanu, led the operations and contradicting the claims of Sargon's annalists that the king led the operation in person. The provocation for Sargon's third and last western campaign came from Ashdod, where a certain Iamani or Iadna had been elevated to kingship by the anti-Assyrian party in a rebellion that implicated all the southern states including Judah and Lower Egypt. Ashdod was captured in the same year (712) and organized into a new Assyrian province; Lower Egypt was given to the Nubian ruler of Upper Egypt as a reward for extraditing Iamani; Judah was defeated; and foreign captives were settled in the Philistine cities. A Kalah letter mentioning the tribute of Egypt, Gaza, Judah, Moab, Amon, Edom, and Eqron may date from this campaign, following which a period of relative stability settled over the area.

[19] A lengthy document in the form of an "open letter" to the god Assur. Compare: A. Leo Oppenheim, "The City of Assur in 714 B.C.," *Journal of Near Eastern Studies* 19 (1960):133–47; and Edwin M. Wright, "The Eighth Campaign of Sargon II of Assyria (714 B.C.)," *Journal of Near Eastern Studies* 2 (1943):173–86.

For the rest of his reign (710–705), Sargon was occupied largely with the restless Aramaeans penetrating Babylonia from the Sealand at its extreme south. Indeed, it is possible to see in the sequel to Isaiah's Ashdod prophecy a reference to the Sealand campaign of 710. The ever-dangerous Merodach-baladan was removed from the throne of Babylon, and Sargon himself "took the hands of Bel" and assumed the kingship of Babylon (709). Merodach-baladan was allowed to remain as prince of Bit-Jakin (see below, Section 5), but soon his capital of Dur-Jakin was destroyed, and the mission he sent to Hezekiah (2 Kings 20:12ff.; Isaiah 39) must be dated during his subsequent exile. An important new Kalah letter, probably written by Sargon to the crown prince Sennaherib about this time, refers to Merodach-baladan as Apla-iddina, thus throwing light on his curious patronymic in the Biblical account. The letter is concerned primarily with war and diplomacy on the northern frontier, and it was there that Sargon met his death in battle in 705.

The accession of Sennaherib symbolized in many ways the start of a new phase of the Assyrian impact on western Asia. No longer did the Assyrian army march annually toward new conquests. The *Eponym Chronicle*, which had dated the years by campaigns since Shalmaneser III, typically enough ends with the first years of Sennaherib. Only eight campaigns, plus two conducted by his generals, marked the twenty-four years of his reign, and the royal annalists made no attempt to edit the record (as they had with Sargon) in order to make it appear otherwise. Assyrian power was, in fact, approaching the natural limits of which it was capable, and the thrusts that were now made into more distant regions such as Persia, Central Anatolia, or Egypt were either repulsed or only temporarily successful. Although the warlike ideals of their forebears continued to color the records of the later Sargonids, the impression of sustained militarism that they convey is an exaggerated one. The real spirit of the time is revealed, on the one hand, by such marvels of civil engineering as Sennaherib's aqueduct at Jerwan[20] and, on the other, by the greatly increased attention to administrative matters reflected in the growing amount of royal correspondence. Literature and learning too came into their own, and the vast library assembled by Assurbanipal at Nineveh is only the most dramatic expression of the new leisure. In spite of their protestations to the contrary, the later Sargonid kings were inclined to sit back and enjoy the fruits of empire.

The new *Pax Assyriaca* stabilized the relations of Assyria and her western vassals to some extent. Where we have outlined no less than six major Assyrian campaigns to the west in the preceding forty years, there were only three of comparable magnitude in the nearly sixty years that

[20] Thorkild Jacobsen and Seton Lloyd, *Sennacherib's Aqueduct at Jerwan*, Oriental Institute Publications, vol. 24 (Chicago: University of Chicago Press, 1935).

followed—namely, Sennaherib's invasion of Judah in 701, Esarhaddon's capture of Sidon in 677, and the more or less continuous decade of warfare in and against Egypt by Esarhaddon and Assurbanipal (673–663).

Sennaherib's campaign against Hezekiah in 701 is well known. We have an unusually complete account of this event told from both sides—if indeed it was a single event. In part because of the very different interpretations put on it by the Biblical and the Assyrian sources, some have argued that there were actually two contests between Sennaherib and Hezekiah and that the Assyrians won the first but lost the second. This theory is plausible, for it would not be out of character for the Deuteronomist to dismiss the defeat of a good king in three verses, nor for Sennaherib to pass over his defeat in total silence. By the same reasoning, however, we would have to suppose that there had been two or even three battles of Der. And it is difficult to see where in Sennaherib's reign a second campaign against Judah could be placed. His exploits are well known through 691 and do not include any further attacks on Palestine; even the campaigns against Cilicia and Tilgarimmu (696–695) were conducted by his generals. And by this time, Hezekiah was "sick unto death," and Manasseh was coregent of Judah; the account of 2 Kings 18:17–19:35 would make little sense in this context.

Manasseh reigned for fifty-five years (696–642), forty-five of them as sole ruler. It was probably his loyalty to Assyria, both politically and culturally (2 Kings 21), that enabled him to hold the throne for this unprecedented length of time. Even the assassination of Sennaherib in 681 did not entice him to revolt as it did Babylonia.[21] Moreover, the new Assyrian king made sure that the next succession would proceed more smoothly. Fragments of eight *tupkallu*'s, "grand tablets," found at Kalah in 1955, show how Esarhaddon in 672 forced his Iranian vassals to swear to support the accession of his sons in Assyria and Babylonia after his death. (See Figure 23, page 122.) Similar treaties may well have been imposed on the western vassals. Esarhaddon's planning bore fruit, and for seventeen years his designated successors ruled the empire side by side, Assurbanipal from Nineveh and Shamash-shum-ukin from Babylon. But in 652, civil war broke out between the two brothers. It was won by Assurbanipal after four years of bloody warfare, and the price was heavy: the *Pax Assyriaca* had been irreparably broken, and the period of Assyrian greatness was over.

The last forty years of Assyrian history were marked by constant warfare in which Assyria, in spite of occasional successes, was on the defensive for the first time in a century. The principal historical source for these years is the *Babylonian Chronicle*, recently augmented by important new

---

[21] For the evidence, see: Weidner, "Hochverrat gegen Asarhaddon," *Archiv für Orientforschung* 17 (1954–56):5–9; and René Labat, "La Mort du roi d'Elam," *Archiv Orientální* 17 (1949):1–6.

finds. Assyrian royal records are sparse, and even the order of the eponyms is uncertain after 648.

The new state of affairs was not without its repercussions in Judah. Although Amon succeeded his long-lived father, Manasseh, in orderly enough fashion in 642 and continued his father's pro-Assyrian policies (2 Kings 21:20ff.; 2 Chronicles 22:22), the unrest that gripped the empire (Elam revolted in 641) spread to Judah. Amon was murdered after just two years of rule in what was certainly an anti-Assyrian move. It was probably a part of the uprising of all the western territories that Assurbanipal moved quickly to quell in 640. Even Samaria may have joined the revolt, for the foreign populations that "Asnappar"[22] settled there could well have been prisoners of the Elamite revolt. At the approach of the Assyrian king, the "people of the land" grew faint-hearted, slew the rebels, and made Josiah king (2 Kings 21:24; 2 Chronicles 33:25), thus apparently avoiding further Assyrian retribution.

But Josiah was no mere Amon. By 632, "though he was still a young man," he began to revive the anti-Assyrian political and religious policies of Hezekiah, and the death of Assurbanipal in 629 or 627[23] assured the success of these policies. In the latter year, his twelfth, Josiah annexed the Assyrian provinces of Samaria, Gilead, and Galilee, enabling him to extend his reforms, including presently the Deuteronomic reform (622), to all of Israel. The last kings of Assyria were powerless to oppose him, nor were they a match for the great coalition of Media, Babylon, and Palestine that now began to close in on them. The complete annihilation of the Assyrian capitals—Nineveh, Kalah, Assur, Dur-Sharrukin—between 615 and 612 is attested in part by the *Babylonian Chronicle* and even more graphically in the archeological evidence from these sites. Its impact on the contemporaneous world can still be measured in the prophecies of Nahum, and possibly of Zephaniah. Only Egypt remained loyal to Assyria, and Pharaoh Neko's efforts to aid the last remnants of Assyrian power at Harran under Assur-uballit II were seriously impaired by Josiah at Megiddo (609).[24] Four years later, the Battle of Carchemish finished what Josiah had begun: Egypt bowed to Nebukadnezar II of Babylon and a new era opened for the entire Near East. Lacking an army to fill its coffers with the tribute of its neighbors, or a monarch to divert the waters of a dozen rivers to its fields and cities, Assyria became deurbanized, returning to a primitive stage of civilization such as it had not known for two thousand years. When, finally, it reemerged as the vassal kingdom of Adiabene under the Parthians of the first century of our era, a supreme irony of history decreed that its royal house convert to Judaism.

---

[22] Apparently a reference to Assurbanipal in Ezra 4:9 ff.

[23] For the latest discussion of this moot question, compare Julian Reade, "The Accession of Sinsharishkun," *Journal of Cuneiform Studies* 23 (1970):1–9.

[24] See p. 293.

[5] DECLINE AND FALL: THE CHALDAEANS
626–539 B.C.

Babylonia contributed to the final downfall of the Assyrian imperial colossus and seemed to be its most immediate beneficiary. Thus the focus of attention shifts back to the south, which we had left in the aftermath of the first Nebukadnezar (ca. 1126–1105) and his brother Marduk-nadin-ahhe (ca. 1100–1083). The latter fought a number of engagements with his Assyrian contemporary Tiglath-pileser I (1115–1077), but both monarchs presently had to turn their efforts against a common danger: the Aramaeans. Over the next two centuries, both Assyria and Babylonia were increasingly preoccupied with this threat to their borders, and in Babylonia there are inconclusive indications of a growing Aramaean component within the country itself. These southeastern Aramaeans, however, were not given as readily to sedentarization as their linguistic kinsmen in contemporary Syria and northern Mesopotamia (above, Section 1). They appear chiefly as loosely organized seminomads, roaming the frontiers of the settled areas and raiding them for the sake of plunder whenever the opportunity arose.

In this regard they must be distinguished from the Chaldaeans, who first appear in the cuneiform records in the ninth century. The Chaldaeans ultimately adopted the Aramaic script and language, which the Bible even refers to as the "script and language of the Chaldaeans" (Daniel 2:4), but the confusion is not found in the cuneiform sources. Though perhaps related to the Aramaeans, the Chaldaeans of Babylonia were organized into strict tribal groupings called houses, each recognizing the leadership of its own hereditary chieftain. They occupied major cities within the Babylonian frontiers and were contending for the kingship of all of Babylonia by the beginning of the eighth century. Apparently they found many adherents among other Babylonian groups, whom they may have inspired with visions of the restoration of past glories. By 747, they had stabilized the country enough so that the accession of Nabunasir (Nabonassar) was regarded as inaugurating a new era. The calendar was stabilized; monthly diaries were kept listing astronomical observations together with fluctuations in such matters as commodity prices, river levels, and the weather; and the outstanding events of each year were entered into a valuable new historiographic record, the *Babylonian Chronicle*. In Hellenistic astronomy, the "Nabonassar Era" was recognized as a turning point in the history of science, and the very term Chaldaean came to mean astronomer.

Nabonassar himself was not demonstrably a Chaldaean; indeed he seems to have enlisted the help of his greater Assyrian contemporary, Tiglath-pileser III (744–727), in his struggles against both Chaldaeans and Aramaeans. If so, the step proved as fateful as Ahaz's invoking of the same ruler's help in the west (above, Section 3). In both cases, there ensued over a century of conflict between native nationalists and pro-Assyrian elements. Tiglath-pileser went so far as to assume the throne of Babylon himself in violation of Assyria's traditional respect for Babylonia's greater antiquity and its role as birthplace of much of Assyria's religious and cultural heritage. Before him, only Tukulti-Ninurta I (above, Section 1) had dared to take this step, which he had paid for with his life in a revolt inspired at least partially by Assyrian revulsion against it. But Tiglath-pileser III's successors followed his example, ruling Babylonia either in their own persons or through their appointees and throwing down the gauntlet to Babylonian nationalism. The challenge was accepted by the Chaldaean Merodach-baladan II, who defied both Sargon and Sennaherib and twice succeeded in regaining Babylonia's independence from Assyria (721–710 and for nine months in 703) before he was driven conclusively from the scene.[25] Even the precautions of Esarhaddon were not proof against the spirit of insurrection: as we have seen (above, Section 3), Shamash-shum-ukkin raised the standard of revolt against his own brother, thus seriously weakening Assyria. When Kandalanu, whom Assurbanipal installed in his stead in 647, died in 627, the basis for a Babylonian reassertion had thus already been laid.

For a year, Babylonia was without a recognized ruler. Then the throne was seized by Nabopolassar, who established a new dynasty, generally known as the neo-Babylonian or Chaldaean Dynasty.[26] With equal justice it might be called the Third Dynasty of the Sealand, or the Dynasty of Bit-Iakin, for, although it is impossible to prove Nabopolassar's actual descent from this southernmost and strongest of the Chaldaean tribes, his career certainly followed the pattern of earlier members of the house of Iakini (Figure 26). Like many of them, he began his public career as governor or ruler of the Sealand, a virtually hereditary position to which he was appointed, or in which he was confirmed, by the Assyrians; and, like some of them, he used this base as a springboard to the rule of all of Babylonia when Assyrian power faltered. Although the Assyrian military machine continued to be a highly effective instrument for almost twenty years, Nabopolassar successfully defended Babylonia's newly won independence and, with the help of the Medes, finally eliminated Assyria itself. Under his son and successor, Nebukadnezar II (604–562), the Chaldaean empire fell heir to most of Assyria's conquests and briefly regained for Babylonia the position of the leading power in the ancient world.

[25] J. A. Brinkman, "Merodach-Baladan II," *Studies Presented to A. Leo Oppenheim June 7, 1964* (Chicago: The Oriental Institute of the University of Chicago, 1964), pp. 6–53.
[26] A. T. Olmstead, "The Chaldaean Dynasty," *Hebrew Union College Annual* 2 (1925):29–55.

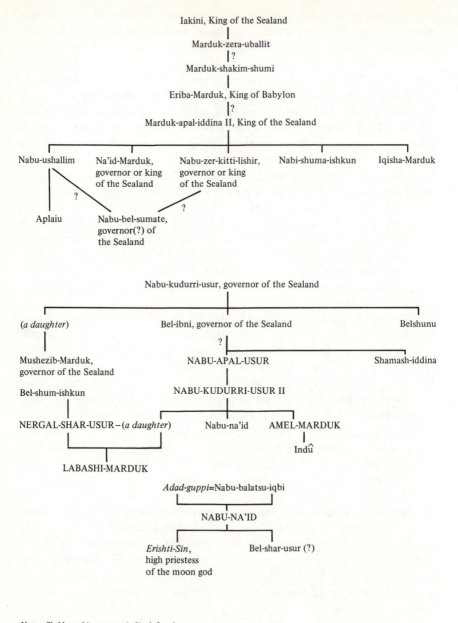

FIGURE 26   The House of Iakini (Bit Iakin) and the Chaldaeans.

Nebukadnezar's conquest of Jerusalem and Judah, with the exile of the Judean aristocracy to Babylonia, is the most famous of his many triumphs, but his own inscriptions prefer to stress his more peaceful achievements. These certainly matched his foreign conquests. He reconstructed Babylon in its entirety, filling it with magnificent temples and palaces and turning the city into one of the wonders of the ancient world (Figure 27). Its fame traveled far and wide with those who had seen it, and even after its destruction by Xerxes in 478 its ruins fired the imagination of later ages, from Herodotus, who described them in detail in the same century,[27] to the German excavators who uncovered them in the twentieth century A.D.[28] Even Nebukadnezar's contemporaries were moved by his achievements to catalogue the topography of the restored capital in all its details, thus providing an unrivaled description of an ancient city.[29] Among its more noteworthy sights were the ziggurat, the famous hanging gardens (which, however, might go back to Merodach-baladan II), and the museum attached to Nebukadnezar's new palace. Here the king and his successors brought together statues, stelae, and other inscribed relics of the then already long antiquity of Mesopotamia. This neo-Babylonian interest in the monuments of the past[30] thus complemented the neo-Assyrian efforts to collect the literary heritage of Babylonia that climaxed in the creation of the library of Assurbanipal.

The same antiquarian interest characterized the rule of Nabonidus, who succeeded to the throne of Babylon in 556 after the three brief reigns of Nebukadnezar's son, son-in-law, and grandson. He was not related to the royal Chaldaean house, although he was the namesake of a son of Nebukadnezar, whom he had served as a high diplomatic official as early as 585.[31] The biography of his mother, Adad-guppi, is preserved on inscriptions from Harran, an important commercial and religious center in northern Mesopotamia, from which we learn that she lived for 104 years (650–547).[32] Her long devotion to Harran and its deity may help to ex-

[27] O. E. Ravn, *Herodotus' Description of Babylon*, trans. Margaret Tovborg-Jensen (Copenhagen: Nyt Nordisk Forlag-Arnold Busck, 1942).

[28] Robert Koldewey, *The Excavations at Babylon*, trans. Agnes S. Johns (London: Macmillan and Co., 1914).

[29] Compare most recently William L. Moran, "A New Fragment of DIN-TIR-KI = Bābilu and enūma eliš VI 61-66," *Studia Biblica et Orientalia*, vol. 3, Oriens Antiquus (Rome: Pontificio Istituto Biblico, 1959), pp. 257–65 and plate 18. Also compare above, p. 118, for Assur.

[30] Compare Godefroy Goossens, "Les recherches historiques à l'époque néo-Babylonienne," *Revue d'Assyriologie et d'Archéologie Orientale* 42 (1948):149–59.

[31] On one interpretation, he may even have claimed descent from the last neo-Assyrian kings. See Hildegarde Lewy, "The Babylonian Background of the Kay Kâûs Legend," *Symbolae ad Studia Orientis Pertinentes Frederico Hrozný Dedicatae*, vol. 2, ed. V. Čihař et al. (Prague: Orientální Ustav, 1949), pp. 35–36.

[32] C. J. Gadd, "The Harran Inscriptions of Nabonidus," *Anatolian Studies* 8 (1958): 35–92 and plates 1–16.

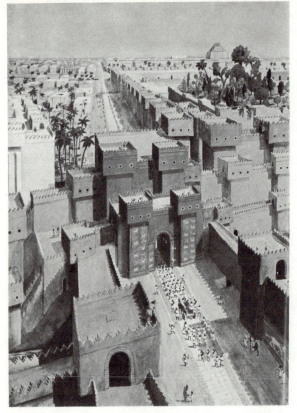

FIGURE 27   Recon-
struction of Babylon
under Nebukadnezer II
(after Unger).

plain her son's similar, but more fateful, preoccupation.[33] While it is
uncertain precisely when Harran had passed from Aramaean hands to
direct Assyrian rule, it is clear that it was one of the first of the more
distant provinces to do so. It always enjoyed a special status within the
empire, was loyal to the king when other provinces revolted, was never
the object of a recorded Assyrian campaign in the first millennium, and
even harbored the last Assyrian defenders when the capital cities of the
empire had already collapsed. It was at Harran that the last Assyrian king,
Assur-uballit II, made a final desperate attempt to save and restore the
empire, and it was not until he fled Harran in 609 that the fate of Assyria
was conclusively sealed.

Virtually alone among the former Assyrian strongholds, Harran recovered some of its old glory under the neo-Babylonians and survived for

[33] R. P. Dougherty, *Nabonidus and Belshazzar: A Study of the Closing Events of the
Neo-Babylonian Empire*, Yale Oriental Series Researches, vol. 15 (New Haven: Yale
University Press, 1929).

many centuries thereafter as the center of successive forms of the worship of the moon god Sin.[34] According to Adad-guppi's biography, Harran lay desolate (that is, in the possession of the Medes) for fifty-four years (610–556) until, at the very beginning of the reign of Nabonidus (555–539), a vision informed him, in words strangely reminiscent of Isaiah 44:28–45:1, that Marduk would raise up "his young servant" Cyrus to scatter the Medes. In obedience to the divine injunction, Nabonidus presently rebuilt the great temple of Harran, and reconsecrated it to Sin. At the same time he singled out the other centers of moon worship, at Ur in Babylonia and at the oasis of Teima in Arabia, for special attention. The latter move, which carried Babylonian arms for the first time all the way to Yatrib (modern Medina), was particularly fateful. Though it may have been inspired by reasonable strategic or even commercial considerations,[35] it was regarded as an act of outright madness by the Babylonians and as a self-imposed exile of the king by later legend. The Book of Daniel associates this sojourn of seven years[36] in the desert with Nabonidus' more famous predecessor, Nebukadnezar, but new finds from Qumran show that other Jewish traditions linked it with the correct king.[37] In any case, his sojourn in Arabia was resented by the population of Babylon, and the veneration of Sin there and at Harran and Ur was regarded as a veritable betrayal of Marduk, the national deity. Led by the Marduk priesthood, Babylon turned against Belshazzar, the son whom Nabonidus had left behind at the capital, and delivered the city into the waiting hands of Cyrus the Persian. In a bloodless conquest (539), he assumed control of all of Babylonia and rang down the curtain on the last native Akkadian state.

[34] Julius Lewy, "The Late Assyro-Babylonian Cult of the Moon and its Culmination at the Time of Nabonidius," Hebrew Union College Annual 19 (1946):405–89; and Hildegarde Lewy, "Points of Comparison Between Zoroastrianism and the Moon-cult of Ḥarrân, A Locust's Leg: Studies in Honour of S. H. Taqizadeh, ed W. B. Henning and E. Yarshater (London: P. Lund, Humphries, 1962), pp. 138–61.

[35] W. Röllig, "Erwägungen zu neuen Stelen König Nabonids," Zeitschrift für Assyriologie und Vorderasiatische Archäologie 56 (1964):218–60, esp. 243–52.

[36] Or, in the cuneiform sources, ten years.

[37] Rudolf Meyer, "Das Gebet des Nabonid: Eine in den Qumran-Handschriften wiederentdeckte Weisheitserzählung," fasc. 3, Sächsiche Akademie der Wissenschaften, Sitzungsberichte, philologisch-historische Klasse, vol. 107 (Berlin: Akademie-Verlag, 1962); and W. Röllig, "Nabonid und Tēmā," Compte Rendu de l'onzième Rencontre Assyriologique Internationale (Leiden: Nederlands Instituut voor het Nabije Oosten, 1964), pp. 21–32.

FIGURE 28 Varieties of cuneiform texts.

[VI]

MESOPOTAMIAN CULTURE: A SURVEY

[1] SCRIPTS AND LANGUAGES

Writing, according to the latest theories, was invented in southern Mesopotamia for the first and perhaps the only time. The oldest written texts come from Uruk toward the end of the fourth millennium B.C. They were impressed on clay tablets with a reed stylus and then baked. The signs, though linear in form, are no longer purely pictographic, as in some of the preliterate drawings on clay, but considerably conventionalized representations of concrete objects. The new invention must have quickly proved its worth, for it apparently provided the stimulus to the beginning of pictographic writing in Egypt and Persia (proto-Elamite) by about 3000.

During the third millennium, important developments affected both the inner structure and the outer form of cuneiform writing, as well as the uses to which it was put. It was soon found that the reed stylus left various forms of wedgelike impressions on clay, and the characteristic cuneiform signs gradually became normative, at first on clay and later, by imitation, also on stone and other hard surfaces. In the process, the original pictorial associations of the signs were largely lost, a process completed when the direction of writing was later changed by ninety degrees. At the same time, the principle of phonetization was introduced, freeing writing from its dependence on representational depiction, and enabling it to render not only the separate words but also the individual sounds (including the grammatical elements) of the inventors' language and, within limits, of other languages as well. Armed with this potent technique, the new script was mastered by a growing class of scribes, trained with the help of writing exercises that began to take the form of a fixed curriculum very early in the third millennium and that laid the basis for later literary and monumental writings.

It is not certain what language the inventors of writing spoke. It may have been one that later Mesopotamian scholarship alluded to as "the vernacular" (Sumerian *kakasega*, Akkadian *ša têlti*) and which originally supplied some of the simplest syllabic values, such as HA, HU, and HI. Other traces of a linguistic substratum in Mesopotamia survive, for example, in geographical names and in a significant group of professional names ending in *-ar*, which can be correlated with the skills of the late prehistoric period as attested by archeological discovery—for instance, potter and carpenter. But without doubt, the language that first fully exploited writing and phonetization was Sumerian.

Sumerian was the language of southern Mesopotamia and its environs at the emergence of the historical period. It was probably not native to Mesopotamia but introduced, perhaps via the Persian Gulf, from somewhere to the east, perhaps the Indus Delta or Valley. On linguistic grounds it has hitherto been impossible to link it, even remotely, with any other known language or language family; of the innumerable candidates put forward so far, perhaps Dravidian has the best chance to prove an ultimate cognate.

Throughout the third millennium, Sumerian was the principal spoken and written language of Mesopotamia, and it continued to serve as a written language in the second millennium, during which it gradually gave way as a spoken language to Akkadian, and as a learned written language in the first millennium, during which Akkadian, in its turn, was giving way to Aramaic.

The recovery of Sumerian passed through a number of stages. After the initial decipherment of cuneiform in the 1840's (see below, Section 6), there was doubt for a time as to the very existence of a pre-Semitic linguistic stratum in Mesopotamia. This was followed, after the discovery of native Sumerian sites such as Lagash at the end of the nineteenth century, by the attempt to translate the early Sumerian economic and historical texts as well as the late, and somewhat artificial, bilingual religious texts with the help of their Akkadian translations. Since about 1940, the unilingual Sumerian literary texts, as preserved chiefly in copies of the Old Babylonian (Hammurapi) period, have received the major share of attention. Their interpretation has been greatly aided by the recovery of native Mesopotamian lexical and grammatical lists.

Sumerian emerges from all these sources as a so-called agglutinative language, in which grammatical elements are added seriatim to both ends of a nominal or verbal stem, with or without the resulting modifications in the stem or affixes that regularly characterize inflectional languages. The resulting nominal and verbal chains are combined in varying numbers to produce the typical Sumerian sentence. The distinction between verb and noun is basic, but any verb may be nominalized by the addition of the relative suffix, and the language as a whole prefers stative or even passive constructions to the active verbal sentences that characterize the Semitic and Indo-European languages.

Semites must have settled in Mesopotamia as early as the Sumerians, infiltrating particularly northern Mesopotamia and originating most likely from Arabia and the Syrian desert. Only a scattering of personal names and loan-words in Sumerian contexts linguistically attest their presence in the first half of the third millennium, but after 2500, Sumerian cuneiform was quickly adapted for the writing of complete Semitic texts. These begin to occur in great numbers with the dynasty of Sargon of Akkad and his successors (see Chapter II, Sections 5 and 6), although earlier texts exist. They are written in a dialect known as Old Akkadian, which together with a few contemporary Semiticisms in Egyptian texts, represents the oldest written evidence of Semitic speech anywhere. This dialect was fairly uniform over a wide area, from Elam (Susa) in the southeast to Assyria (Assur, Nuzi, Tell Brak, Diyarbekir, etc.) in the north and Mari in the west, as well as in the central Sumero-Akkadian areas. Linguistically, Old Akkadian was distinguished from later forms of East Semitic by the retention of a larger number of proto-Semitic phonemes and morphemes; its lexicon, and to some extent its morphology, shared with later Akkadian dialects a growing infusion of Sumerian elements. This resulted from the long symbiosis of the two ethnic groups which ended in a virtual bilingualism and a progressive differentiation of Akkadian from all other Semitic languages. Orthographically, Old Akkadian was distinguished by a monumental calligraphy, generously and esthetically executed like the contemporaneous representational art.

Old Akkadian survived, to some extent, the neo-Sumerian renaissance at the end of the third millennium, but not the irruption of the new wave of Semitic-speaking peoples known in the native sources as Amorites. These settled (and by about 2000 conquered) both Assyria and Babylonia and broke the linguistic unity of the Old Akkadian period. Henceforth, two dialects of Akkadian may be distinguished—Assyrian in the north and Babylonian in the south. Old Assyrian was written as far away as Anatolia, where it is found on the Cappadocian tablets. Because of its greater intimacy with the Sumerian sources of learning in the south, Babylonian tended to become the language of culture in both areas. But the distinction between the two dialects remained largely phonologic and orthographic. In addition to these two major dialects, traces of other Semitic languages and dialects written in cuneiform may be found in marginal areas, such as Elam, Nuzi, Mari, Ugarit and Canaan. The widest spread of Akkadian was registered by the Middle Babylonian dialect, which became the lingua franca of the Near East in the middle of the second millennium. At El-Amarna, it was employed for international diplomatic correspondence, and the presence of literary texts in the Egyptian archive shows that it was studied by the native scribes. In the first millennium, Akkadian and cuneiform gradually gave way to Aramaic and its easier mode of writing. The former was still used sporadically in the Macedonian and Seleucid chancelleries of Babylonia, but it was at last abandoned for all time in the era of the Arsacids (Parthians).

The great span of time and area to which speakers of Akkadian carried cuneiform stimulated the development of similar scripts all around Mesopotamia. In most cases, the Sumero-Akkadian system of cuneiform was taken over intact; in some, it inspired the creation of an entirely new cuneiform syllabary. Naturally, Sumero-Akkadian literature and learning were absorbed more readily by the former group, which included Elamite, Kassite, Hurrian, Hittite, and Haldian (Urartian). In fact these peoples adapted and transmitted Mesopotamian literary and religious traditions in the second half of the second millennium; much of Babylonian literature probably took its final form under the Kassites, while the Hurrians are generally considered the intermediaries between Babylonian myths and their counterparts in the Bible and, via the Hittites or Phoenicians, in Greek literature. Using the Sumero-Akkadian syllabary in more or less its received form and function, the Hurrians and Hittites also produced a new literature in their own languages, including not only the indigenous Hattic or proto-Hattic (Hittite, properly speaking) of Anatolia, but also the Indo-European dialects that supplanted it: Neshite (that is, what is commonly called Hittite), Palaic, and Luwian.

In Elam, the old pictographic script and its linear successor were abandoned as early as the Sargonic period in favor of a modification of Sumero-Akkadian cuneiform for writing the native language (neo-Elamite). In Armenia, (Urartu, Biblical Ararat), another modification of the same system was used for royal monuments of a native dynasty, written both in Assyrian and Urartian during the first half of the first millennium.

The influence of Sumero-Akkadian culture was less direct where wholly new systems of cuneiform writing sprang up under Mesopotamian stimulus. This happened first at Ugarit. Although standard cuneiform was employed there in the fifteenth century for writing Sumerian, Akkadian, and Hurrian, a kind of cuneiform rendering of the newly invented West Semitic script of Palestine-Syria was employed for writing native religious texts and occasional temple records, letters, and the like on clay. Finally, the Achaemenid Dynasty of Persia created a new and simplified cuneiform syllabary for writing Old Persian.

[2] ARCHIVES, MONUMENTS, AND THE SCHOOLS

It is possible to classify cuneiform literature in broad linguistic groups, roughly contemporaneous with the dialects of Sumerian, Akkadian, Hittite, and so forth, already mentioned above. However, a typological classification is more useful. It cuts across linguistic boundaries because the underlying conditions of literary productivity were the same wherever clay and reed were the basic writing materials. If a man wished, for example, to record a transaction in the realm of daily affairs, he would write it once on a clay tablet, which would then be baked in the sun, or fired in an oven for greater durability, and deposited in an archive for future reference. Such was the inspiration, no doubt, of the very first written records from Uruk, which consist of simple tallies of cattle entrusted to herdsmen by their owners. Such documents were not expected to last for more than a few generations at most, although in fact they have often proved extremely durable. Since their normal destination was an archive, they may be described as *archival texts*.

Archival texts are by far the most numerous of all cuneiform records, comprising, among other types, accounts, letters, contracts, and court decisions and representing every period and area of cuneiform attestation, such as Fara (Shuruppak) in the pre-Sargonic period; Tello (Lagash-Girsu) in the whole second half of the third millennium; Djoha (Umma) and Drehem (Puzrish-Dagan) in the neo-Sumerian period; Kultepe (Kanish) in Old Assyrian Anatolia; Tell Hariri (Mari) and Atchana (Alalakh) in Old Babylonian Syria; Nippur, Sippar, Larsa, Kish, Ur, and so on in contemporary Babylonia; Amarna in Egypt, Ta'anah in Canaan, and Nuzi across the Tigris in the Middle Babylonian period; Nimrud (Kalah) and Kuyunjik (Nineveh) in Assyria and Uruk in Babylonia at the end of the independent existence of each.

If, on the other hand, the intention of the writer was to create a document to last for all time, he resorted instead to one of two devices: either he produced it in numerous duplicates, or he inscribed it on what was apparently considered a more durable material, such as stone. In the former category are royal building inscriptions on clay nails and clay bricks, the latter often mass produced, from Sargonic times on, with the help of a brick stamp. In the latter category are seals, building inscriptions on pivot stones and foundation deposits, and votive inscriptions on precious objects of all kinds from simple plaques to life-size statues. Such inscriptions became part and parcel of the monuments on which they were inscribed, and may therefore be designated *monumental texts*. They include most of the so-called historical inscriptions of the kings of all periods—although in the native view these royal inscriptions were essentially building records, and their historical information was, strictly speaking, incidental. They were clearly intended for the information of later rebuilders and were usually concealed from contemporaneous eyes by the masonry of the building. Similarly, royal and private votive texts were conceived of primarily as perpetual surrogates for the donor, conveying the prayer inscribed on them before the god. Even promulgations of legal reforms or restorations, such as the so-called codes of Ur-Nammu, Lipit-Ishtar, and the kingdom of Eshnunna, probably originated on stelae like that of Hammurapi and may have had little practical effect. Only seal inscriptions had a more mundane motive, their impressions on legal texts serving as signatures for those who could afford them, while others had to substitute fingernail marks or the imprint of the fringes of their garment. However, one may add to the category of monumental texts those *kudurru's* (boundary stones) in which royal grants of land or exemptions from feudal obligations were memorialized.

The third major category of cuneiform texts consists of those, written on clay in a limited number of duplicates, whose perpetuation was secured by frequent copying. Since this was a process that typically took place in the schools, one might refer to such texts as school texts were it not for the fact that this term has come to designate only those among them that represent writing exercises of beginning scribal pupils. Moreover, in the process of copying such texts each new generation of scribes gradually modernized, adapted, selected, and finally fixed them in a prescribed textual form governing such matters as their division into *iškaru* (books—literally, "series"), *pirsu* (sections, or subseries), *tuppu* (chapters—literally, "tablet"), and *šumu* (verses—literally, "name") and the sequence of these. Thus, for all practical purposes, they developed into a literary canon, and may best be designated as literary or, better, as *canonical texts*.

The major cuneiform canons covered all branches of ancient thought, but it is appropriate to begin a survey of them with the texts that, at one time or another, formed the basic curriculum of the scribe, for the scribal education was basic to all careers, whether in the clergy, army or civil service, and even monarchs and princes proudly recalled their early schooling. The earliest school texts go back to the very beginning of writing at Uruk; they are long sequences of signs and sign groups that gradually assumed a fixed order. They are attested throughout the third millennium all over Sumer and even Elam. One particularly interesting example is by the Sargonic governor of Lagash himself.

But our best information comes from the Old Babylonian school at Nippur, for which we can reconstruct not only a good part of the curriculum but also, thanks to contemporaneous essays on the subject, many other details of school life. Instruction began at that time with a list of some 450 cuneiform signs, learned in a fixed order and written out repeatedly one beneath the other, typically on lentil-shaped school tablets (of which many have survived), until the pupil's hand approached the master's sample in excellence. The Old Babylonian students, unlike those of the third millennium, were no longer native speakers of Sumerian, however, and their sign list was therefore soon furnished with an explanatory column that gave some nine hundred of the commonest Sumerian values of these basic signs. Thus, for example, the first sign, A, was explained as having the pronunciations á, ya, duru, e, and a; and these five lines constituted a typical day's lesson. The first equation, á=A, moreover, gave its name to the entire series (book). With the disappearance of Sumerian, even as a second language, after the Old Babylonian period, á=A was replaced as primer by a series that, beginning with the equation ea=A= *nâqu* ("cry out"), added the basic Akkadian translation to each of the Sumerian signs in a third column. The old á=A series, for its part, was gradually expanded, first to eight and later to forty-two tablets (chapters), beginning with the same equation but serving as an advanced compendium of historical cuneiform orthography. (It is interesting to note that, like most of the later West Semitic alphabets, all these sign lists began with the "basic sound" A.)

Having mastered the writing and pronunciation of the simpler cuneiform signs, the student next embarked on learning, by rote and by hand, a long succession of syllabaries and lexical lists, covering in their totality every conceivable sphere of terminology. These constitute a classified and, in part, annotated roster of Sumerian forms, words, and phrases. The later versions added Akkadian translations, and thus constitute for the modern lexicographer an invaluable key to both Sumerian and Akkadian.

In the Nippur school, the first of these texts was the syllabary tu-ta-ti, which organized the newly learned signs phonetically. It was followed by the first exercise in meaningful combinations of signs, using for this purpose personal names, beginning with the baby names me-me, pa-pa or a-a, a-a-a, and continuing with more complicated ones. More advanced and, in part, later texts dealt with complex signs, with grammatical elements and constructions, with dialectal Sumerian, particularly the "Emesal" dialect, with foreign languages such as Kassite, and with special topics such as legal terminology, god names, personal names, and temple names. The most ambitious lexical list of all is *Urra* which in twenty-five chapters provides a truly encyclopedic survey of the observed world, including such categories as woods, reeds, leathers, metals, stones, vessels, foods, plants, animals, and geographical and professional names. In later times, this and other texts in their turn led to the creation of explanatory texts, which added a simpler or more modern Akkadian equivalent in a fourth column. Similar commentaries were also occasionally produced for the more complicated Akkadian literary texts, and perhaps from these sources originated the last stage in the Mesopotamian lexical tradition: "synonym lists," which no longer explained Sumerian words at all, but instead defined difficult or dialectal Akkadian ones by simpler Akkadian equivalents.

Of course, the scribal curriculum was never confined entirely to purely lexical and grammatical texts. Sumerian syntax could hardly be learned except from connected prose and poetry, and the schools have preserved for us Sumerian literary works that appeal even to modern literary tastes. Later, Akkadian literary works took their place in the curriculum too. Thus we know, for example, that an early version of the Flood story (Atrahasis legend) followed directly upon the me-me pa-pa series. In the elementary curriculum of the Old Babylonian period, the Sumerian proverbs, among several other categories, were particularly popular, as shown by the numerous school tablets inscribed with extracts from the canonical collections. However, all such texts can be better described in the context not of scribal education but of religious literature and of higher learning.

[3] THE PREDICTION AND CONTROL OF EVENTS

Of all the manifestations of learned speculation in Mesopotamia, the most characteristic was divination. It reflected the official world view, as espoused by court and temple, as well as the popular belief of the masses. Beginning with scattered allusions in Sumerian sources, it developed into the largest single category of Akkadian literature in terms of sheer numbers of texts. A staggering number and variety of techniques, each with its own exhaustive handbooks, became a distinguishing mark of later Akkadian culture both in Mesopotamia and wherever that culture was exported, imitated, or even ridiculed abroad. Thus the Biblical prophets derided the arts of the Mesopotamian diviners for, alone among cuneiform literary genres, the literature of divination had no precise parallels in Biblical or other early Near Eastern writings, just as Biblical prophecy, alone among Biblical genres, is unparalleled in cuneiform.

The basic assumption of the mantic, or divinatory, Weltanschauung is diametrically opposed to that of modern science. Whereas the scientific view assumes a causal relationship between phenomena, the mantic view assumes what may be called a symptomatic association between events. Thus the occurrence of a given symptom is believed to herald the same disaster (or good fortune, as the case may be) in all future days. If events prove otherwise, the correlation is not itself invalidated; rather, it is assumed that minor variations in the symptom or other, concomitant, symptoms were operative. Hence the ever more refined and detailed prognostic lists, many of which are purely theoretical and remote from any observed event; hence also the spread of divinatory techniques to ever new fields of observation. The multitude of resulting omens displays the same descriptive and classificatory approach that inspired the lexical lists; it has no room for speculative or abstract thought.

The oldest techniques—and technicians—of divination as attested in sporadic Sumerian allusions are based on the interpretation of dreams and on the observation of the entrails of slaughtered sheep (or goats) and their configurations.[1] Livers were the favorite organ studied for the pur-

[1] Adam Falkenstein, " 'Wahrsagung' in der Sumerischen Überlieferung," *La Divination en Mésopotamie Ancienne et dans les régions voisines*, XIVᵉ Rencontre Assyriologique Internationale (Paris: Presses Universitaires de France, 1966), pp. 47–68.

pose, and this branch of divination is therefore called hepatoscopy. But other organs were also utilized, hence the more general term extispicy, or divination by means of the exta. Beginning in Old Babylonian times, the findings of this and all other methods of divination were collected in systematic handbooks, in which each entry took the form "if the organ has the shape X, then the outcome of the campaign (business venture, sickness, or the like) will be Y." This "casuistic" formulation is identical with that of the law codes, which are attested earlier; whether it derived from them cannot yet be determined.

Because extispicy was tied to the sacrificial cult, it was favored as a mantic technique by the kings, who were at all times the major patrons of the cult. Before embarking on military campaigns or other affairs of state, they commissioned appropriate animal sacrifices to the gods and, while the priests consumed the meat that the deity (in the form of his statue) had ostensibly left uneaten, the entrails were put to good use in the search for a favorable omen. It goes without saying that the diviners were not above contriving to elicit favorable omens for undertakings that their royal patrons had already determined on. But they could also be objective, and they duly recorded the real events (as against the mere prognostications) that ensued after a particular omen had been taken. In some cases they even molded a model to show the particular configuration of a liver that had proved especially ominous, like the one inscribed "This is the omen (literally, liver) which befell King Sin-iddinam (of Larsa) when he sacrificed in the temple of Shamash at the Elunum (festival and died)."[2] Such omens were preserved for future reference, for if they were ever observed again, they demanded elaborate prophylactic rituals if the identical fate was not to ensue once more.

A group of "historical" omens thus came to be collected from the results of hepatoscopy and certain other mantic techniques, and associated with successive kings of the historical tradition beginning (if we disregard the purely fictitious omens about Gilgamesh) with Sargon of Akkad. Although their *protases* ("if-clauses") are purely mantic, their *apodoses* ("then-clauses") preserve real historical information. Indeed they form a unique and characteristically Mesopotamian variety of historiography.[3] This was recognized by the ancient Babylonians and Assyrians themselves, who abstracted the historical omens from the much larger mass of omens in general, and combined them into special collections.[4] In the present work, the evidence of the historical omens has been repeatedly invoked.

---

[2] William W. Hallo, "New Texts from the Reign of Sin-iddinam," *Journal of Cuneiform Studies* 21 (1967):96–97. See Figure 28, page 150, second row, center, for this liver model.

[3] J. J. Finkelstein, "Mesopotamian Historiography," *Proceedings of the American Philosophical Society* 107 (1963):461–72.

[4] L. W. King, *Chronicles Concerning Early Babylonian Kings*, 2 vols. (London: Luzac, 1907).

But if extispicy was well suited to the needs and resources of the state, it was beyond the means of the average private citizen. He too wanted foreknowledge of divine intention and pleasure for his more modest undertakings, but could not afford a sacrificial animal each time. A variety of cheaper methods developed quickly to serve his needs. Some of these were also connected with the cult, as for instance the technique of libanomancy, that is, observing the configurations of smoke rising from a censer when incense was burned. Others were simply popular practices widely attested in the Near East as shown by Biblical references, derogatory or otherwise. Lecanomancy, for example, involved pouring oil into water, or vice versa, and studying the resulting configuration (compare Genesis 44:5).[5] Belomancy required the shooting of arrows (see I Samuel 20:20ff.; Ezekiel 21:26),[6] while cledonomancy found ominous significance in a chance response or remark elicited or overheard from a designated stranger (see I Samuel 14:8ff.; I Kings 20:30ff.).[7] Finally, a practical means of assuring a propitious choice of alternatives was psephomancy, the casting of dice or *pūrū* (lots) comparable to the Urim and Thumim of the Israelites or to the *pûr* of Haman (Esther 3:7).[8] One such lot, in the form of a cube inscribed with a prayer and the name of a candidate for the Assyrian eponymate, has even been found. (See Figure 28, page 150.)

Like extispicy, these miscellaneous popular techniques all involved induction (or impetration, in the terminology of classical [Roman] divination), that is, the eliciting of a divine response by the intervention of human initiative, and for some of them, the results obtained were collected in Old Babylonian handbooks. But unlike extispicy, these techniques did not continue to flourish, and the "inductive" method gave way more and more to that of intuition (or oblation in classical terms). This approach assumed that the divine purpose was inherent everywhere (pantheism) and that it was not necessary to go to elaborate lengths to elicit it, but rather to acquire specialized knowledge in order to interpret it. This newer approach went hand in hand with an increasing specialization and professionalization of the diviner's art, much of which was ultimately consigned

---

[5] Giovanni Pettinato, "Zur Überlieferungs geschichte der aB-Ölomen texte," *La Divination en Mésopotamie Ancienne et dans les régions voisines*, pp. 95–107; and idem, *Die Ölwahrsagung bei den Babyloniern*, Studi Semitici, nos. 21 and 22 (Rome: Istituto di Studi del Vicino Oriente, 1966).

[6] Samuel Iwry, "New Evidence for Belomancy in Ancient Palestine and Phoenicia," *Journal of the American Oriental Society* 81 (1961):27–34; and W. W. Struve, "Die Frage der Existenz eines Pfeilorakels in Sumer," *Proceedings of the 25th International Congress of Orientalists, 1960*, vol. 1 (Moscow: International Congress of Orientalists, 1962), pp. 178–86.

[7] A. Leo Oppenheim, "Sumerian i n im . . . g a r, Akkadian egirrû = Greek Kledon," *Archiv für Orientforschung* 17 (1954–56):49–55.

[8] Erica Reiner, "Fortune-telling in Mesopotamia," *Journal of Near Eastern Studies* 19 (1960):23–35.

to the status of a secret lore. Here, too, as in the case of inductive divination, a rough distinction between private and public omens is possible.

The oldest intuitive technique is oneiromancy, the interpretation of dreams.[9] Many of the dream omens collected in *Ziqīqu*, the late Assyrian "Dreambook," strike us as exceptional because, in them, the associative principle makes some sense in modern terms; for example, a dream of the loss of one's cylinder seal is taken to portend the death of a son. This is also the case, at times, in the medical omens, a work consisting of six parts and forty chapters, and known by its first line as "When the conjuration priest comes to the house of a sick man," or by its contents simply as *sakkikû*, "symptoms."[10] Here we find more or less reasonable diagnostic and prognostic correlations side by side with typically symptomatic ones. The so-called physiognomic omina, collected in the treatise *alandimmû*, are based on the appearance of facial and bodily characteristics in the client or in persons he encounters; they incidentally provide a candid description of human types unmatched before Petronius.[11]

All three of these well-documented, intuitive techniques were suitable for private individuals. The fate of the king, however, and thus of the state, was more often observed in three other spheres of divine manifestation: in the heavens, on earth, and in the accidents of birth. Although it reached great scientific heights in neo-Babylonian times, astronomy originated in the service of divination. The principal textbook of astrological divination, called *inūma Anu Enlil*, "when (the great gods) Anu and Enlil," was variously attributed to Oannes-Adapa, the first antediluvian sage, or even to Enki (Ea), the god of wisdom. Astrologers were known as "Inuma-Anu-Enlil scribes," and continued to add to the corpus by observation as late as neo-Assyrian times.[12] The terrestrial omens formed an even longer series, dealing in nearly two hundred tablets (chapters) with all manner of things encountered in daily life. It began with the city, and is therefore known by its first entry as *šumma ālu*, "if a city."[13] The series

[9] A. Leo Oppenheim, "The Interpretation of Dreams in the Ancient Near East," *Transactions of the American Philosophical Society*, new series, vol. 46, part 3 (Philadelphia: American Philosophical Society, 1956), pp. 179–373; idem, "Mantic Dreams in the Ancient Near East," *The Dream and Human Societies*, ed. G. E. von Grunebaum and Roger Caillois (Berkeley and Los Angeles: University of California Press, 1966), pp. 341–50; and idem, "New Fragments of the Assyrian Dream-book," *Iraq* 31 (1969): 153–65 and plates 35–36.

[10] J. V. Kinnier Wilson, "Two Medical Texts from Nimrud," *Iraq* 18 (1956):130–46 and plates 26–27; and idem, "The Nimrud Catalogue of Medical and Physiognomical Omina," *Iraq* 24 (1962):52–62.

[11] Ibid.

[12] D. J. Wiseman and Margaret Howard, "Assyrian Writing Boards," *Iraq* 17 (1955): 3–20 and plates 1–3.

[13] Compare David B. Weisberg, "An Old Babylonian Forerunner to *šumma ālu*," *Hebrew Union College Annual*, 40–41 (1969–70):87–104, for a newly published example of the genre.

šumma izbu, "if a foetus," deals with monstrous births, human and animal (teratoscopy), whose ominous significance is underlined by numerous reports on the subject preserved from the royal archives.[14] One such report even specifies that the twin-tailed and eight-legged pig born to a slaughterer in Babylonia was pickled in brine, perhaps to satisfy a sceptical inspector, and goes on to quote the appropriate meaning of the occurrence from the canonical series.

As though all this were not enough, the will of the gods also involved a time dimension: not only had an undertaking to be inherently propitious, but its timing had to be favorable. Thus there developed menologies, quasi-divinatory texts that stated whether a month was favorable or unfavorable for any given undertaking, and hemerologies that indicated what undertakings were or were not propitious for every day of each month.[15] The series *iqqur ippuš,* "he tore down [a house] and wants to rebuild it," and *inbu bēl arhim,* "fruit [that is, moon], lord of the month," illustrate these two genres.

The assumption behind all Mesopotamian divination was that events were predictable if one could but learn the symptoms that accompanied or presaged them. This assumption rested on an even more fundamental one: that both symptom and event were equally expressions of some sort of divine or demonic will. It was thus not enough to foretell the future; one had also to assure that it came to be or, if necessary, to reshape it by appeal to the powers behind events. Thus a second great field of Mesopotamian cultural expression consisted of cultic acts and their accompanying formulas, which brought the ancient Mesopotamian into direct contact with the numinous and can therefore be regarded as truly religious expressions. These formulas range all the way from the primitive magic of the conjurations to the sublime psalmody of the literary prayers and take us into the realm of poetry.

Poetry is often attested earlier than prose, and Mesopotamian poetry is no exception to this rule. Some of the earliest extant examples of Sumerian literature consist of conjurations and incantations. The rich religious poetry in Sumerian, although most of it has survived only in Old Babylonian copies, undoubtedly dates, for the most part, to the third millennium. It had an elaborate system of classification and notation, apparently for musical accompaniment, but this, like the comparable terminology of the Biblical psalms, is largely obscure to us. Instead, we may divide it by modern categories into hymns to gods, to kings, and to

---

[14] Erle Leichty, "Teratological Omens," *La Divination en Mésopotamie Ancienne et dans les régions voisines,* pp. 131–39.

[15] For treatments of the subject in English, compare: S. Langdon, *Babylonian Menologies and the Semitic Calendars,* Schweich Lectures on Biblical Archaeology, 1933 (London: The British Academy, 1935); and Peter Hulin, "A Hemerological Text from Nimrud," *Iraq* 21 (1959):42–53.

temples and into lamentations over the destruction of cities and over the death of Dumuzi and equivalent deities.

The Old Babylonian period also witnessed the first flourishing of Akkadian poetry, which developed a special dialect for its hymns and epics. The former display an originality and freshness which thereafter gradually disappear in both Sumerian and Akkadian hymns. The religious poetry of post-Old Babylonian times (ca. 1500–150) is characterized by essentially stock poetic phrases put together in endlessly varied combinations to produce hymns and prayers, liturgies, litanies and laments, conjurations, and incantations of increasingly stereotyped form. At their best, some of the later creations achieved considerable excellence of expression, as, for instance, the prayers to the gods of the night or the literary prayers to Marduk, Shamash, and Ishtar; but this was rarely the case in the most characteristic of later Akkadian prayers, the *šu-ila* "lifting of the hand."

Not all cultic texts, however, were poetic in form. Especially as they approached the magic end of the scale, they tended to become more prosaic. In such texts, the recitation of formulas increasingly gave way to prescriptions for cultic operations until, in ritual tablets like that of the series *bīt rimki* "house of the [ritual] bath," the entire tablet consisted of instructions to the sorcerer or his client, and the texts to be recited were only referred to by their titles. Among these were the major collections of conjurations such as *šurpu* and *maqlû* (both "burning"), the *namburbi*, "incantations against every kind of evil," and specific collections of spells against *utukki limnūti* (evil spirits), *mītūti namrūti* (appearing ghosts), and *asakkû maršūti* (infectious diseases). Finally, one can mention such evidence of the more popular religious spirit as the amulets against demons like Lamashtu and Pazuzu, inscribed less often with real texts than with magical gibberish and designs and drawings.

[4] BELLES-LETTRES AND SCIENCE

If the future were to be predicted and controlled on a symptomatic basis, the present could best be explained on an historical basis. Here, too, Mesopotamian thought rejected causality in the Western sense. Human mortality, for example, was the result, not of an experimentally verifiable decline in cell growth, but of an "historically" attested loss of a divinely intended immortality with which mankind had originally been endowed (myth of Adapa). The fall of a great kingdom like Akkad was caused, not by a decline in military and economic power under its last, weak kings, but by the sacrilegious excesses of the earlier, powerful ones ("Curse of Agade").[16] Convinced that his destiny could be, indeed had to be,

---

[16] See above, p. 63.

fathomed, the Mesopotamian savant thus had an equally keen, if less practical, curiosity about his past and about the origin of all things. To this curiosity we owe the most famous portion of cuneiform literature and that which, next to the wisdom literature, has the most claim to be regarded as truly belletristic by critical standards.

In modern terms, it is common to divide this literature into myths, epics, and historical tradition, according to whether its protagonists are gods, early kings of heroic or even legendary stature, or more recent, fully historical kings. But these distinctions hardly reflect the native Mesopotamian view of the past, in which gods, heroes, and men either figured side by side or readily assumed each other's qualities. Thus the divine protagonists of a myth like *The Wooing of Inanna*[17] really represent eternal human types: Inanna the impetuous young girl; Utu (the sun god) her overly cautious elder brother; Dumuzi, like Abel, the typical shepherd; Enkimdu, like Cain, the typical farmer. Such a myth is no more a religious document for its divine stereotypes than a modern play is for its Biblical ones. On the other hand the later traditions concerning early kings frequently treat them as gods, a status rarely accorded to Mesopotamian kings in their lifetimes. Between these two extremes, the *Epic of Gilgamesh* characteristically describes its hero as two parts divine and one part human. Nevertheless the distinctions may be retained for convenience.

The early Sumerian myths are nearly all etiological, viewing the present existence of various phenomena of the material and human world as the result of primordial events involving a limited number of the principal deities. Thus, for example, the moon is the product of the rape of the goddess Ninlil by the god Enlil according to the *Myth of Enlil and Ninlil*.[18] The functions and properties of all manner of rocks and stones were assigned to them by the warrior god Ninurta based on whether they sided with or against him in *lugal-e* (his mythical exploits).[19] The cycle of myths about Inanna and Dumuzi seems to begin with the descent of Inanna to the netherworld;[20] in order to make good her release from the Land of No Return she must deliver the lamented Dumuzi as a pawn, and his incarceration becomes symbolic of the desiccation of the irrigated arable land in the month of Dumuzi (Tammuz in Hebrew, approximately our June or July).

[17] Thorkild Jacobsen, "Mesopotamia," *The Intellectual Adventure of Ancient Man*, ed. Henri Frankfort and H. A. Frankfort (Chicago: University of Chicago Press, 1946), pp. 166–68.

[18] Ibid, pp. 152–56.

[19] On this myth, see most recently J. V. Kinnier Wilson, "Lugal ud melambi nirgal: New Texts and Fragments," *Zeitschrift für Assyriologie und vorderasiatische Archäologie* 54 (1961):71–89.

[20] See most recently Samuel Noah Kramer, *The Sacred Marriage Rite: Aspects of Faith, Myth, and Ritual in Ancient Sumer* (Bloomington, Ind.: Indiana University Press, 1969), pp. 107–21.

The largest number of Sumerian myths relate to Enki, god of wisdom, friend of mankind, and ultimate source of all invention. In separate myths he creates gods and men, establishes cults and crafts, transfers the arts of civilization from pristine Eridu to Uruk, organizes the world order as a whole, even allotting a place in life for freaks and misfits, and saves mankind from the Flood.[21] The Flood occupies a prominent place in Mesopotamian tradition. It marks the end of the mythical age peopled only by gods, by shadowy antediluvian monarchs of incredible longevity, and by their *apkallu* (semi-divine counselors), Promethean mediators who bring Enki's wisdom to mankind.

After the Flood, however, kingship, in the Sumerian concept, was brought down from heaven, and an heroic age was ushered in, which is the theme of the Sumerian epic literature. Its heroes are in the first place the semi-legendary kings and high priests of Uruk: Enmerkar, Lugalbanda, Dumuzi the fisherman, and Gilgamesh. But their contemporaries from north (Kish) and east (Aratta) also figure in the epics, and brief allusions elsewhere show that the entire period had captured the imagination of the later Sumerians.[22]

Myth and epic both served to describe the remote past. But to capture the immediate past, let alone the great doings of his own sovereign, in appropriate form, the Sumerian scribe had recourse instead to literary forms modeled much more closely on contemporaneous monumental and archival genres. The favorite subjects of this historical tradition were the first great Semitic kings of Akkad, notably Sargon and Naram-Sin, and the last Sumerian kings of Ur, notably Shulgi and Ibbi-Sin. They and other dynasts, such as Utu-hegal of Uruk and Anu-banini of Lullubu, were the subjects of creative compositions phrased in the style of royal compositions, law codes, and letters, as well as of copies that claimed more or less faithful descent from original models. Along with the hymns to, for, or by the princely figures from Sargon's time to beyond Hammurapi's, they have left a rich picture of the political and historical philosophies of early Mesopotamia.

The foregoing picture of Sumerian "historical" literature is based entirely on Old Babylonian copies. Clearly the Akkadian-speaking Babylonians were firmly under its spell. It is no wonder that Akkadian literature continued in the paths marked out by Sumerian. Some of the Sumerian texts were translated verbatim;[23] some were considerably rewritten; a few were abandoned outright, particularly certain genres like the royal hymns,

---

[21] Compare most recently Samuel Noah Kramer, "Enki and His Inferiority Complex," *Orientalia*, new series, 39 (1970):103–10.

[22] Compare above, Chapter II, Section 3.

[23] For some reason, the Sumerian text was always retained with the Akkadian translation, resulting in bilingual texts usually arranged in alternating lines of Sumerian and Akkadian.

which were more suited to the divine concept of kingship that went out of vogue in Old Babylonian times. Of Akkadian adaptations, the best-known example is the Babylonian *Epic of Gilgamesh,* which in its final form wove the separate episodes of the Sumerian Gilgamesh cycle into one superb composition with a central theme and continuous plot.

In addition, there were at all times new compositions in Akkadian, though rarely employing forms not already utilized for Sumerian. Among such texts that have, at least so far, no apparent Sumerian antecedents are myths like that of Adapa or Irra, epics like that of Etana and the Eagle, and historical romances concerning not only traditional figures like Sargon (for example, *šar tamhari,* "the king of battle") and Naram-Sin (for example, "the king of Cutha") but also more nearly contemporaneous kings like Tukulti-Ninurta I of Assyria.

Regarding the likely audience of these texts, one is quickly drawn to the conclusion that they must have been intended in the first place for royal edification. Only thus can we account for their preoccupation with kings and courts and their relative unconcern with either the popular or the sacred sphere. Of course, the best epics, such as the *Epic of Gilgamesh,* have great popular appeal and even begin with the address to a universal audience. And the best myths found a place in the cult; we know that *enūma eliš,* the "epic of creation," was recited in the neo-Babylonian *akitu* (New Year's festival), like hundreds of purely cultic texts whose recitation is enjoined in this or that ritual. More often it was the other way around: texts that we regard as myths were originally only pretexts for incantations to ward off the evils they described, like toothache (*The Worm and the Toothache*), broken shoulder-blades (*Adapa*) or pestilence (*Irra*). But, for an example of literature directed to and in part originating with the common man, we turn to the wisdom literature.

Literacy and memorization tend to be mutually exclusive, and Mesopotamia, with its early, and at times widespread, literacy, gives little indication of ever having harbored a sizable oral tradition.[24] However, with the various genres commonly described as wisdom literature, we come closest to the realm of popular (as opposed to learned) productions, and in a number of cases they were apparently transmitted orally both within ancient Mesopotamia and beyond. Of these genres, the first attested in writing consists of proverbs, a few of which are found as early as the Old Sumerian (Fara) period.[25] Probably by neo-Sumerian and certainly by Old Babylonian times, these Sumerian proverbs had been thoroughly adapted for and adopted into the school curriculum, in perhaps a score or more different collections grouped in part by subject. Only a fraction of

[24] Jørgen Laessøe, "Literacy and Oral Tradition in Ancient Mesopotamia," *Studia Orientalia Ioanni Pedersen . . . Dicata* (Copenhagen: E. Munksgaard, 1953), pp. 205–18.
[25] See, for example, W. G. Lambert, "Celibacy in the World's Oldest Proverbs," *Bulletin of the American Schools of Oriental Research* 169 (February, 1963):63–64.

these survived into neo-Assyrian times, either in Sumerian or Akkadian, side by side with new Akkadian proverb collections or occasional maxims quoted in other contexts. Many of these sayings, fables, and miniature essays recur in the popular wisdom of other cultures, such as the Aramaic version of Ahiqar (now known to have been derived from an Akkadian original), the Aesopic fables, and *The Arabian Nights* (for example, "The Poor Man of Nippur").

Proverbs and fables were thus the most durable wisdom genres, but there were others. All are represented both by unilingual Sumerian versions and by later bilingual or wholly Akkadian examples. The poetic essays on the themes of theodicy and the suffering of the righteous, such as "Let me praise the lord of wisdom," have sometimes been compared to the Book of Job. The *adaman-duga* (literary debates) to determine the relative merits of various professions, materials, animals, or plants seem like enlargements on the theme of II Kings 14:9. The *nariga*, "instructions," attributed to gods and antediluvian kings like that concerned with agriculture have been dubbed *Georgica* with an eye to Vergil. But all these analogies pale before the undeniable uniqueness of these compositions in their own right.

Nowhere is this uniqueness more in evidence than in a special group of essays dealing with life in the Old Babylonian schools. These extremely candid vignettes provide a clue to the probable audience for most of the wisdom literature: the school itself and, in later periods, the scribal guilds.

Seen as a group, the various wisdom texts attest to a practical morality that ranges from downright cynicism to the highest ethical standards. They are equally free from the active superstition of the mantic texts and the passive resignation of the hymns and prayers.

Scribal education was the foundation of the civil, priestly, and mantic professions, but it could also lead to the equivalent of post-graduate specialization in one of the purer sciences. Indeed there was a *bit mummi* (academy) that gathered the leading scholars of each age. Presumably this was the source of the learned treatises that ancient Mesopotamia has left us in such fields as mathematics, astronomy, and medicine. Once more, the fundamental achievements in these fields may be attributed to the Sumerians, who devised the sexagesimal system of counting and the place notation of expressing numbers, as well as some of the basic terminology of arithmetic, and who made the initial identifications and classifications of stellar and biological quanta. But beyond this, the major breakthroughs seem to have been achieved in mathematics in the second millennium and in medicine and astronomy in the first millennium by the Semitic and other heirs of Sumerian culture. Again, it will be found convenient to exemplify these achievements in the light of the canonical series (books), although it should not be forgotten that numerous (in many cases far more numerous) noncanonical tablets existed by their side. The latter took the form of individual problem texts in mathematics; in astronomy they were diaries for one or more months, almanacs and other texts for single years, and observations of specific planets, including the moon, for one or more years; in medicine, they might consist of individual case histories cured by surgery, medication, or incantation.

The oldest existing copies of the mathematical series appear to date to the Middle Babylonian period. Although their exact composition is not yet restored, it is already clear that there were several separate series, or at least sub-series, of as yet unknown name or names. Even those presumably fragmentary samples of mathematical series that have so far come to light contain well over a thousand problems. These series are characterized by the extreme brevity and large number of examples illustrating a common solution to variants of the same basic algebraic problem. They may include the answer to the problem but never the steps leading to the correct answer; it was reserved for the individual problem texts to make these explicit. The seriatim character of the mathematical series is again in keeping with the Mesopotamian organization of knowledge generally: By tireless repetition and by piling example on example, the Mesopotamian illustrated a general principle or its application, but he never stated it as a general principle. Thus the Pythagorean theorem was well known in practice, and numerous problem texts illustrate the ability to handle 3:4:5 or 5:12:13 right triangles, even with such high numbers as rule out the possibility of a purely pragmatic solution. Yet the theorem as such was never stated, and the whole notion of a Euclidean theorem and its proof was entirely foreign to the Mesopotamian approach. Indeed, geometry in general was a relatively neglected aspect of mathematics in Mesopotamia when compared with either Egypt or Greece. It was treated rather as a subdivision of algebra; so, for example, typical, basic geometrical relationships were recorded in long lists of "coefficients" side by side with purely metrological and algebraic relations. For the rest, most of the emphasis was on arithmetic and algebra. It has even been stated that numerological and pictorial conceptualizations are mutually exclusive, and that Mesopotamian scholarship from the first stressed the former.

The same characteristic applies to Mesopotamian astronomy. Apart from the purely astrological omen series, *inūma Anu Enlil*, the principal series here is called *mul-apin* ("plow-star"=Cassiopeia) after its first entry. This lists the principal fixed stars of the Mesopotamian heavens and groups them by their locations. The oldest extant copies of this series date from seventh-century Assyria. But we know that celestial observations in Babylonia go back at least to the end of the Old Babylonian period, thanks to the famous "Venus Tablets" of Ammisaduqa (ca. 1646–1628). These still may have served primarily the needs of divination, but Babylonian astronomy is one field where later generations made decisive improvements. The newer techniques emancipated astronomy from astrology and served particularly the requirements of the calendar, specifically of the reconciliation of solar and lunar years. By a combination of accurate observation and astute calculation, both based on their unmatched arithmetic notation, the neo-Babylonians were able to construct a completely predictable nineteen-year cycle of intercalary months, which reconciled lunar and solar years with a degree of accuracy that still evokes admiration; it freed the Babylonian calendar from observation long before the Jewish calendar, which it directly inspired. This Babylonian achievement may be associated with the accession of Nabunasir (747), at which time the native *Babylonian Chronicle* and the *Ptolemaic Canon* also began. Other refinements of astronomical calculations and observations continued to be made in the various centers to the very end of attested cuneiform documentation in Arsacid times.

Medical and surgical practice is well attested from early times on by legislation, individual case histories, and professional designations (the Sumerian *a-zu*, "knower of waters or liquids," eventually passed into Aramaic as *asya*, "physician"). But the first connected treatises in this field now seem to consist of a neo-Sumerian pharmacopeia—lists of prescriptions with full details as to the ingredients and the method of preparing and applying them, although, oddly enough, without any indication of the diseases for which they were to be used. The Old Babylonian period has, for once, left us no immediate descendants of this genre, although their existence is clear from the testimony of their lineal descendants in Akkadian texts from the Hittite capital of Hattusha. It remained for the scribes of Assurbanipal to organize the received traditions into explicit textbooks covering every manner of disease and its cure. Such compendia as *šumma amēlu sulam maris*, "if a man is sick with coughing," or *šumma amēlu pûšu kabtu*, "if a man's mouth is heavy," show the extent to which the official corpus of medical knowledge had grown since neo-Sumerian times. But they also show the extent to which magical or ritual considerations had diluted the purely medical therapy of the earlier period. This is not surprising, for diagnostics too had become, so to speak, a branch of divination generally, and the great textbook of *sakikkû* (medical symptoms) was so thoroughly interspersed with nonmedical portents that it has been considered above with the mantic texts.

[5] RELIGION

The religion of Mesopotamia was closely bound up with its culture as a whole. Most of our knowledge of economic activity comes from the archives of temples, which, under royal or priestly patronage, frequently monopolized industrial and commercial life. Historical data were recorded by kings in monuments constituting or memorializing dedications to the gods, and at various periods the scribal schools were closely attached to temples and numbered priests among their graduates as well as their instructors. The arts of divination presuppose a theology of deism and demonism and can be considered a practical expression of that theology. The literary texts used divinities for heroes or made deities out of their protagonists, while the wisdom literature taught a morality not devoid of religious ethics. Even the scientific literature found application in the ritual needs of court, priesthood, and laity.

Yet to obtain a real understanding of Mesopotamian religion, we must concentrate on those activities and beliefs that brought men into direct contact with the divine qua divine. In terms of literature, this means primarily the ritual or cultic texts, which (as we have seen above) reflect chiefly the official cult and beliefs. There was at all times a popular religion as well, which concentrated on appeasement of hosts of petty demons (as we know from simple, grotesque charms and amulets) and rejected the official pantheon in favor of its own preferred deities, including the nameless generic *ilum*, "god." But the great mass of textual and artistic evidence reflects the official religion, and it is from this evidence that we gain most of our knowledge of the three basic components of such religion: dogma, practice, and personnel.

During the entire span of ancient Mesopotamia's recorded history, its official credo was polytheism, the belief that diverse deities guide the destinies of men and nature. Henotheistic tendencies occasionally developed as this or that deity assumed a commanding position for a limited time or in a specific place. More often, the polytheism tended toward pantheism, as the number of divinities multiplied and all phenomena were gradually invested with numinous qualities. Mesopotamian polytheism retained to the end its characteristic tolerance of all claims to divine status and worship and thereby its unsurmountable antipathy to an exclusive monotheism.

The bewildering multiplicity of divine and demonic forces challenged the orderly mentality of the Mesopotamian. He learned early to systematize and classify his deities, delimiting the realm of and assigning the appropriate rank to each in a hierarchic pantheon. One principle of organization was chronological or genealogical: the greater gods were conceived as descendants of one another, with successive generations displacing their defeated predecessors at the head of the pantheon. But these theogonic speculations had little importance outside the mythology, whence they passed also into the theogonies of Asia Minor, Phoenicia, and Greece. A more practical organization of the pantheon was the cosmological and geographical one. In this system, earth, sea, and sky were respectively the realms of the great gods Enlil, Enki, and An, who also divided the starry heavens among them. And, on the inhabited earth, each city was sacred to one god and/or goddess in particular, as Ur to the moon god Nanna (equated with Akkadian Sîn); Larsa to the sun god Utu (Akkadian Shamash); Uruk to An(u), the god of heaven, and Inanna (Ishtar), the "lady of heaven"; Nippur, the ancient center of Sumerian religion, to Enlil, the "chief executive" of the Sumerian gods; Babylon to Marduk, who took Enlil's place in Babylonian mythology; and Assur to the god of the same name, who replaced Enlil for the Assyrians. Finally, the Mesopotamian worshiper resorted to a typological systematization of his gods. In this scheme, all of the numerous deities were gradually subsumed under the heading of twelve or thirteen major ones in one of two ways: a local or foreign deity either was equated with one of the national gods on the basis of function or character or was considered a descendant or servant of one of the greater gods. In some cases deification could actually serve the taxonomic interest and inclination of the Mesopotamians: It could signalize the isolation of a distinctive phenomenon with predictable characteristics, as when Justice and Righteousness were acknowledged as minor deities in the court of the sun god Utu (Shamash), patron deity of the law. This deification served as an intellectual alternative to abstract conceptualization, which was largely alien to Mesopotamian thought. And it did not necessarily imply worship. Worship was reserved for those deities whose divine immutability threatened to give way to caprice in demonic or human guise. We know relatively little of the popular demonology, but the great gods in all their anthropomorphic individuality were the constant objects of cultic appeals to revert to their true divine nature.

The major outlines of the cult follow from and illustrate these basic dogmas. If there was no one supreme, all-powerful god, if every deity's powers were circumscribed chronologically, locally, or typologically, then safety demanded that the greatest possible number of gods be appeased. Thus kings vied with one another in constructing new temples to additional deities, and worship typically involved successive offerings at all the separate chapels of a single temple complex or all the different shrines of a given city. The major festivals as well as the regular services at all periods were therefore characterized by a kind of rotation of devotions and sacrifices to a prescribed succession of deities. The procedures followed in such cases are known from numerous and detailed archival records of sacrificial materials, chiefly animals, usually specifying, among other things, their origin and disposition. Such records were kept conscientiously at all temples from pre-Sargonic times on, and reveal patterns of cultic obligations that must have followed a number of carefully worked out procedures. Even though there are few or no prescriptive cultic texts of the early periods comparable to, say, the sacrificial instructions of Leviticus, such texts begin to appear in later times and confirm the impression of an elaborate set of rituals for all occasions.

A religious literature and ritual as pervasive as that outlined obviously required a large and extensive clergy. Indeed, standard Akkadian dictionaries list more than thirty different professional designations and epithets that can be translated as priest or priestess. Strictly speaking, however, only the terms *šangû* and *ēnu* (masculine) and *šangîtu* and *ēntu* (feminine) designate priests as such in the native texts. They are derived from Sumerian *sanga* and *en*, applied equally to priestesses (in the service of gods) and priests (in the service of goddesses). Most of the other terms describe professions or skills that might (or might not) be exercised in the temple but did not necessarily imply the priestly or sacred status of their bearer.

Nevertheless, there are some major professions so intimately identified with the cult that they can be best described in clerical terms. In the center of the actual temple ritual stood the *ašipu* (Sumerian *išib*), the specialist in the incantations and conjurations that formed the core of cultic texts. On him also devolved the rites of expiation and purification. The king himself might play the role or assume the title of *ašipu*, thus combining sacred and secular roles as had the old Sumerian *en* of the goddess Inanna at Uruk, who was originally both priest and lord of his city. But the cultic core of Mesopotamian religion merged on its more primitive side into divination and on its more advanced side into literature, and where these areas impinged on the cult other functionaries held sway. The widest competence seems to have been demanded of the *mašmašu*, who not only handled purifications and incantations like the *ašipu* but also, to judge from a detailed curriculum of his craft, had to master many of the canonical divination series and their appropriate rituals. More specialized professionals, however, were available for specific forms of divination. Thus the *barû* (seer) was particularly at home with extispicy and lecanomancy, the *šā'ilu* (inquirer) with oneiromancy, and the *mahhû* (ecstatic) with cledonomancy (see above for these techniques). At the other end of the scale, the proper delivery and accompaniment of hymns and even epics were not left to amateurs either, and at least two specialties were distinguished among musicians: the *kalû* (lamenter), noted for a falsetto voice and for using *eme-sal*, the "thin" dialect of Sumerian, and the *nāru* and *nārtu* (male and female singers of hymns), who likewise accompanied themselves on musical instruments. It goes without saying that this brief sampling does not exhaust either the roster of religious personnel in Mesopotamia or their functions.

[6] GOVERNMENT

The early Mesopotamian empires represented the apex of a governmental structure that descended through provinces, cities, and boroughs to reach into the daily life of the clan, the family, and the individual. These plateaus of political organization can best be studied in the approximate order of their historical emergence—which also, to some extent, reflects their relative importance.

The city was one of the basic constituents of that nexus of human inventions which we call civilization and which is generally held to have emerged in southern Mesopotamia, for the first time anywhere on the globe, in the fourth millennium B.C. Almost from their very beginning, these cities were distinguished by defensive walls and a central area of monumental buildings, including one or more temples. (In later times, this area tended to cluster at the highest elevation, either within the city or straddling its wall, and to be surrounded by a particularly strong wall of its own to form a citadel.) Thus fortified, the city became the nucleus of the first political organism attested by the native traditions, the city-state. This organism held sway also over as much of the surrounding territory as it could physically reach and as much of that territory's population as could fit within its walls in time of war or brigandage. Such territory consisted of open, unincorporated grazing and agricultural land and of unfortified villages. (In feudal periods, much of this land was organized into estates along tribal and clan lines.) At all times, military outposts secured the countryside and its principal roads.

Within the city itself, administration of justice and probably certain other governmental functions were delegated to the borough, or what properly can be called the quarter since there were typically four of them in each city, defined by the four principal city gates where the two intersecting main streets of the town met the city wall. In the otherwise heavily developed residential portions of each city, the open space around the inside of the great gates afforded room for the transaction of public business and assured the presence of citizen-witnesses, drawn from interested parties to lawsuits as well as from idle bystanders. (In later times, it is also possible to see the rudiments of an even more localized system of political organization by wards, based on streets or open spaces elsewhere in the quarter.)

It was natural for certain early city-states to expand their hegemony, by military conquest or political prestige, to neighboring city-states and thus to lay the foundations of that other political organism typical of Mesopotamia, the empire. Native traditions, indeed, insisted that all of Mesopotamia had been united from the beginning under the hegemony of a succession of different, but always single, cities. This is a patent fiction, projected into the past by later imperialists, but it underlines the sentiment in favor of attempts at unification. Such sentiment was unquestionably a political reality, well attested by other evidence, particularly from the religious sphere. In the imperial system, existing cities were not deprived of all fortifications or of all control of their surrounding territory. Rather, their traditional political and religious loyalties were often respected and their administration sometimes placed under their native leaders, although these, of course, had to demonstrate their loyalty to the central power and to supply their quota of taxes, in money or in kind, and of men for *corvée* or military duty. These payments took various forms, from a monthly obligation to supply the needs of the religious capital to an annual liturgy due from the eponym. But all obligations alike devolved on the provincial governor and, through him, on the provincial populace. The independent city-states of one period were repeatedly transformed into the provinces of the next, and a more or less precarious balance was struck between central and local power.

The outstanding examples of successful imperial organization in Mesopotamia include the empire of Sargon of Akkad and his immediate successors (twenty-third century), the Third Dynasty of Ur (twenty-first century), Babylon under Hammurapi and his son (eighteenth century), the neo-Assyrian empire of Tiglath-pileser III and the Sargonid kings who succeeded him (eighth to seventh centuries), and the neo-Babylonian kingdom (sixth century). In almost all of the intervals between these relatively short periods, Mesopotamian unity was more an ideal than a reality, and centralization of power was frustrated by opposing tendencies. One of these was Mesopotamia's exposure to the disruptive consequences of foreign invasion and infiltration, particularly upon the collapse of the empires of Sargon and Hammurapi under their successors. Another was the polarization of political strength around two or more separate centers, notably Sumer and Akkad in the pre-Sargonic periods and Babylonia and Assyria in the late second millennium. In the latter case, the centrifugal pull was strengthened by feudalism, the dominant socio-economic basis of political organization in much of Mesopotamia's middle ages. Unity was further hampered by the peculiar Mesopotamian phenomenon of petty-statism, which flourished particularly in the interval between Ur III and Hammurapi and witnessed the coexistence, sometimes peaceful sometimes warlike, of numerous medium-sized kingdoms in a constantly shifting pattern of alliances. Nevertheless, it is the periods of unity that are by far the most brilliantly illuminated by both texts and artifacts, and it is their character that tended to impress itself, both on the later "Oriental despotisms" that inherited the rule of Mesopotamia and on the assessments of the Mesopotamian experience in the Bible (see especially the Book of Daniel) and in modern scholarship.

The early Mesopotamian king represented the apex of a system of governmental institutions that endured through all the successive phases of Mesopotamian political development. These institutions were rearranged in different configurations with each new constitutional pattern, whether imperialism, feudalism, or petty-statism, and with each new distribution of power, whether this involved its concentration, polarization or diffusion.

But they had an enduring character independent of these temporary configurations and can be validly considered in some isolation from them.

Mesopotamian kingship derived from a number of sources of which the most important were religious and economic. By a peculiarity of Sumerian religious organization, priestesses served as chief ministrants to gods, while priests similarly served goddesses. In cities sacred to a goddess, therefore, the chief religious power was in the hands of male officiants who succeeded very early in capturing secular leadership as well. Thus the earliest attested *en* combines both the meaning of high priest and that of lord. Most of the early city-states, however, were sacred to male deities, and the office of high priestess was inevitably detached from, and eventually usually subjected to, the secular leadership. These cities produced the typical Mesopotamian king under a title (*lugal*, Akkadian *šarru*), whose semantic origin lies somewhere in the economic sphere as master, owner, patron—that is head of a large household. The original domain of the king was the city-state, but with the necessary modifications, the institution of kingship was adapted to the larger imperial organisms of Mesopotamia. It is sometimes also argued that Mesopotamian kingship originated in a temporary military leadership which, like that of the Roman dictator, was at first conferred only for the duration of a military crisis.

The figure of the king was pivotal in the structure of all of Mesopotamian government and society, as that of the god was in Mesopotamian religion, and nearly everything known of Mesopotamian literature and art revolved around these two poles. Sometimes the two were even fused, notably from the later Sargonic to the Early Old Babylonian periods (twenty-third to nineteenth centuries), when the kings of Akkad, Ur, Isin, and some other cities demanded and received divine honors during their lifetimes. At all times the king was conceived of as enjoying a special relationship to the gods, bearing epithets as their offspring, elect, protégé, earthly instrument, and supreme devotee. In Mesopotamia, the concept of royal responsibility for the discharge of religious and ritual obligations took the place of the Israelite concept of national and individual requirements of piety and morality, and the nation was thought to suffer or prosper in accordance with royal, not national, behavior. At the same time, Mesopotamian kingship never experienced the total identification with divinity prevalent in Egypt.

The duties and prerogatives of Mesopotamian kingship were equally pivotal in the nonreligious spheres, both civil and military. The king could, if he chose, initiate legislative reforms, public works, or war. He was the court of last resort in law and commander-in-chief of the army. In practice, however, both his privileges and his burdens were shared and defined by other elements of government.

If the neo-Sumerian myths and epics echo an earlier state of affairs, then the institution of the assembly may be as old as kingship itself. In the cosmic state of the myths, the chief god ruled his pantheon at the pleasure of one large assembly of the other gods, including a sort of senate of the fifty senior deities, while the epics show the city-state with a kind of bicameral legislature. Thus Gilgamesh, opposed by the senate of Uruk, appealed to the assembly of the younger, arms-bearing patricians to secure his city's consent for war in a manner suggestive of Rehoboam in Israel (I Kings 12). The Old Assyrian colonies of Asia Minor (ca. nineteenth century) knew of similar assemblies by the name of "young and old," and were required to convoke them in specified contigencies. A unicameral assembly presided over by the king is also attested as the highest judicial tribunal in contemporary Babylonia, while on the local level, the elders of each town formed a kind of council to assist the mayor. And they survived as such even into neo-Assyrian times.

The *vox populi* was not, however, a major factor after the earliest periods of Mesopotamian history. True, the king and his officials could be petitioned by the individual either by letter or in person, and as a final resort, a frustrated populace could always find a champion to raise the standard of revolt and to redress its grievances—and his own—as a usurper. But by and large, constitutional organs for collective expression of the popular will were conspicuously absent in Mesopotamia.

The king was the supreme judge and court of last resort, and there were also certain judicial areas that, at least in the Old Babylonian period, fell under royal jurisdiction in the first instance. But during most periods there was a far-flung judiciary system to which was delegated most of the litigation so prevalent in Mesopotamia. An elaborate judicial system is attested from neo-Sumerian times on, involving rotating panels of judges and court bailiffs, deputies, and scribes, as well as elaborate procedures for taking sworn testimony or administering promissory oaths. It is difficult to assess the role of written law in this connection. Certainly the collections of precedents promulgated by the kings of Ur, Isin, Eshnunna, and Babylon were not codes of laws. That is, they made no attempt to provide universal criteria of culpability, nor were they cited, or even necessarily followed, in the determination of lawsuits. But they were studied in the schools (the code of Hammurapi was studied for a thousand years after its promulgation) and must have formed part of the education of scribes and judges. And they inspired later collections of casuistic legislation: Middle Assyrian, Hittite, and Israelite. As late as neo-Babylonian times, a draft of a new lawbook was still in the making.

It is impossible to draw a sharp line between the private and public economies of Mesopotamia, but in many periods the public sector of the economy far outweighed the private in importance. Like cities, the accumulation of capital was a *sine qua non* of civilization, and the greatest concentrations of wealth naturally clustered around palace and temple, in shifting proportions. In addition to the inevitable taxes and tithes due to these institutions, reinvestment in major enterprises of various kinds—agricultural, industrial, and commercial—helped to multiply their wealth.

Beginning in Middle Babylonian times, a new balance was struck between the public and private sectors with the emergence of a guild system of economic organization under which the principal crafts were grouped into real or, more often, fictitious clans united by a common ancestral or family name. The guilds were apparently successful in maintaining a measure of discipline and self-government, and in the case of the scribal craft, it is actually possible to trace the existence of several such clans for over a millennium. The guilds thus filled a serious governmental vacuum during the feudal period in which they originated, and they survived beyond this period to the very end of cuneiform times.

The executive power of Mesopotamian government was vested securely in three well-entrenched institutions that owed their ultimate allegiance to the king: the army, the bureaucracy, and the priesthood. Entrance into all three was often on a hereditary basis and, in the more literate periods, normally required a scribal type of elementary education. (The scribal schools were therefore probably under royal patronage, although at times they were conducted under temple auspices.) All the three "services" were hierarchically organized, with some of the most detailed evidence dating from the first millennium. At that time the chiefs of the three services formed a kind of inner cabinet for the Assyrian king, and followed him as eponyms, that is, in giving their names to the year, a mark of their high status. Their functions were somewhat interchangeable, but generally the army was represented by the marshal (the *tartān* of Isaiah 20:1; II Kings 18:17) and the chief cup-bearer (the *rab-shāqēh* of II Kings 18f.; Isaiah 36f.); the priesthood by the chief temple(?) steward (*abarakku*, sometimes compared to the *abrēk* of Genesis 41:43); and the bureaucracy by the governor of the (capital) district (*shakin māti*) and then by all the provincial governors (see the *paḥôt ūs'gānim* of Jeremiah 51:23 et passim) in an order that in earlier centuries, was determined by lot (*pûru*) and later assumed a fairly fixed form (see Esther 3:7, 9:24, 26). A *pûru* is shown in Figure 28, page 150, second row, right.

The priesthood was not always equally subservient to the state. At times it enjoyed considerable autonomy or even dominated the secular arm. In both Assyria and Babylonia, it was generally conceded that kings held office by the grace of the god of their city or land, which they administered on his behalf. If a king was defeated or deposed, it was a sign of divine displeasure. Special precautions were taken to protect the king from dangers portended by evil omens. These developed over the centuries into an elaborate ritual that consumed much of the ingenuity of priests and diviners. The voluminous literature of divination, together with the recitations and prescriptions appropriate to each omen, absorbed an increasing share of priestly activity. In this sense, the later priesthood can be truly regarded as an arm of Mesopotamian monarchy.

[7] THE LOSS AND RECOVERY OF CUNEIFORM

When Cyrus entered Babylon and restored its neglected cults, the priests of Marduk hailed him as a deliverer from what they considered the treachery of the last neo-Babylonian king. A similarly benign policy allowed the Judean exiles, among others, to return to Jerusalem and reconstruct their political and religious autonomy there. But these policies had an ulterior motive: Cyrus was prepared to respect national sensibilities only to the extent that they served to weld together a new empire greater even than its Babylonian and Assyrian predecessors. At its greatest extent, the "Fifth Great Oriental Monarchy," as the Persian empire has been called,[26] embraced "one hundred and twenty-seven provinces from India to Ethiopia."[27] Babylonia became one of the most prominent of these provinces, thanks to its great agricultural wealth, its commercial importance, its historical renown, and its central location. Nonetheless, it became only a province. Since the end of the fourth millennium, Babylonia had been the home of a succession of independent dynasties that, no matter how diverse their origins, felt some sense of continuity with one another. In large measure, the unifying link in these twenty-five centuries had been the cuneiform script. Now even that link to the past was threatened. The Persian overlords adapted cuneiform to their own languages, Old Persian and Elamite, as well as learning Akkadian, and usually inscribed their monuments[28] with identical texts in all three languages, thus providing modern decipherers with the important trilinguals. But for administrative purposes they favored the vastly simpler Aramaic script, and this script and the Aramaic language quickly became the medium of communication all over the empire. Cuneiform survived in Babylonia for another five hundred years, but in gradually narrower circles. The great temples of Babylon and Uruk were centers of a lively and prosperous economic resurgence in these centuries as they passed successively under the rule of the Persian Achaemenids, Alexander the Great, the Greek Seleucids, and the Parthian Arsacids. Private business houses, like that of

[26] George Rawlinson, *The Five Great Monarchies of the Ancient Eastern World*, vol. 4 (London: John Murray, 1867).
[27] Esther 1:1.
[28] F. H. Weissbach, *Die Keilinschriften der Achämeniden*, Vorderasiatische Bibliothek, vol. 3 (Leipzig: J. C. Hinrichs, 1911).

"Murashu and Sons," flourished at Nippur.[29] Indeed, the economic texts (contracts, letters, and accounts) of Late Babylonian date are exceeded in number only by those of the neo-Sumerian period. They illustrate the common historical experience that cultural and commercial life can flourish in the absence of political independence.[30] Thanks to the unity of much of the Near East under the Persians and of major portions of it under their Hellenistic successors, many of the achievements of Mesopotamian culture continued to spread widely through the ancient world. But the fountainhead of this culture was fast running dry. A last renaissance of cuneiform learning can be detected at Uruk in the Seleucid period, where old Sumerian texts were once more being copied and even new ones were created in the old styles. But presently this effort too died out. The last cuneiform texts, chiefly from Babylon, were concerned exclusively with astronomy; apparently the astronomers were the final guardians of the knowledge of cuneiform. The last dated tablet now known is an astronomical diary text from the year A.D. 75.

The collapse of Assyrian and Babylonian civilization was so complete that its peoples, monuments, beliefs, languages, and scripts were buried as if by a second Flood. The names of its cities, rulers, and gods were lost to memory except in sundry local traditions, in the neglected works of Arab geographers, and in scattered and garbled allusions in Greek and Jewish literature. Assyro-Babylonian civilization bequeathed a legacy—to the arts, science, religion, and statecraft—of fundamental importance to all later ages, but that civilization itself was wholly obliterated, and only its disinterment by modern archeologists has been able to reveal the extent of the debt.

The western rediscovery of ancient Assyria[31] dates back to the Middle Ages. Both Rabbi Benjamin of Tudela and Rabbi Petahiah of Ratisbon (Regensburg) visited Mosul in the late twelfth century, and the former correctly identified the nearby ruins of Nineveh. But their accounts were not generally available before the late sixteenth century, when a steady succession of travelers from Europe brought back reports of the buried cities of Mesopotamia. One of the earliest and most prominent among these was the Italian nobleman Pietro della Valle, who not only revisited Nineveh but was the first to identify the ruins of Babylon (1616). In addi-

[29] Guillaume Cardascia, Les Archives des Murašû: une famille d'hommes d'affaires Babyloniens à l'époque Perse (455–403 av. J.-C.) (Paris Imprimerie Nationale, 1951).
[30] Compare, for example, David B. Weisberg, Guild Structure and Political Allegiance in Early Achaemenid Mesopotamia, Yale Near Eastern Researches, vol. 1 (New Haven: Yale University Press, 1967).
[31] See in detail, Svend Aage Pallis, Early Exploration in Mesopotamia with a List of the Assyro-Babylonian Cuneiform Texts Published Before 1851, The Royal Danish Academy of Sciences and Letters, Historisk-filolgiske Meddelelser, vol. 33, no. 6 (Copenhagen: Ejnar Munksgaard, 1954).

tion, he was the first to bring back inscribed bricks from Babylon and Ur, to publish (1658) facsimile copies of other inscriptions from Persepolis, the ancient capital of the Achaemenid Persians in southwestern Iran, and to recognize that they all employed the wedge-shaped characters which, by 1700, figured in a Latin treatise by Thomas Hyde as *dactuli cuneiformes*. Among numerous other travelers to Persia, which in the late seventeenth and the eighteenth centuries was far more attractive than Mesopotamia to Europeans, Carsten Niebuhr of Denmark deserves special mention. His copies of various inscriptions from Persepolis (1778) were the first to be both comprehensive and accurate enough to serve as the foundation for serious efforts at decipherment.

By 1800 it was clear that the cuneiform script contained the secrets of Mesopotamian antiquity, just as hieroglyphics held Egypt's. Unlike the Rosetta Stone, admittedly, the trilinguals from Persian sites (Persepolis, Pasargadae, Naksh-i-Rustam, Mount Elvend, Behistun) were composed in three different cuneiform scripts, all equally illegible. It was quickly realized, however, that the trilinguals represented royal Achaemenid inscriptions, and this proved the key to deciphering the simplest of the three scripts, Old Persian. Georg Friedrich Grotefend, working with Niebuhr's copies in his study at Göttingen, correctly identified twelve of the Old Persian cuneiform signs as early as 1802. Edward Hincks, an Irish priest, independently reached substantially similar results. In each case, the sign groups representing the royal names, their patronymics, and the royal titles were successfully isolated and then compared with the Achaemenid names and titles imperfectly known from Hebrew, Greek, and later Persian sources. But it remained for Henry Creswicke Rawlinson, the "father of Assyriology," to scale the rock at Behistun, to copy there the long trilingual inscription of Darius I,[32] and to present the world with the first substantial, connected Old Persian text properly deciphered and reasonably translated.

With this beginning the other two cuneiform scripts soon yielded their secrets, the most complicated one turning out to be Babylonian cuneiform, the key to the inscriptions from Mesopotamia itself. In 1857, the Royal Asiatic Society formally examined separate translations of the eight-sided prism inscribed with the annals of Tiglath-pileser I that had been submitted by Rawlinson, Hincks, Jules Oppert, and H. F. Talbot; although these four pioneers independently tackled the newly found text, their translations were sufficiently in agreement to persuade a previously sceptical world that Babylonian cuneiform had indeed been deciphered.

Lured by the imminent decipherment of cuneiform, the first English and French expeditions began, in 1842, a determined search for the lost cities and treasures of Mesopotamia that occupied the next four decades.

---

[32] This he did at great personal danger, from 1835 to 1837 and from 1844 to 1847, between his military and diplomatic duties.

Its most conspicuous successes were scored in the northeastern part of the country, the ancient Assyria, and the whole field of study thus newly opened soon acquired the name of Assyriology.

The first spectacular discoveries were made in 1843–44 at Khorsabad, where Paul Emile Botta, newly appointed French consul at Mosul, excavated Dur-Sharrukin, the great capital city built by Sargon II of Assyria at the end of the eighth century B.C. The paintings and drawings made *in situ* by E. N. Flandin for Botta's five magnificent volumes (1849–50) and the original sculptures with which the Louvre opened its Assyrian Gallery in 1847 opened Western eyes to the grandeurs of Assyrian archeology. From 1852 to 1855, Victor Place resumed the French efforts at Dur-Sharrukin.

Meanwhile an Englishman, Austen Henry Layard, had already begun to excavate the other Assyrian capitals, beginning with Kalah (Nimrud) in 1845, Nineveh (the twin mounds of Kuyunjik and Nebi Yunus) in 1846, and Assur (Qal'at Sherqat) in 1847. After seven seasons of sensational discoveries, especially at the first two sites, he was succeeded in 1851 by Hormuzd Rassam. By 1854, the latter had recovered the bulk of the great library of Assurbanipal at Nineveh, which to this day remains the most important single source of Akkadian literature. Thereafter the Crimean War brought all excavation in the area to a temporary halt.

In 1872, George Smith discovered the eleventh tablet of the *Gilgamesh Epic* and its version of the Flood narrative among the riches thus brought to the British Museum, and interest in further excavations was renewed. For four years Smith continued to mine the vast treasures of the library at Nineveh before an early death overtook him on the way back to Aleppo (1876). From 1878 to 1882, Rassam reentered the picture, and then interest in Assyria was for the time being exhausted as attention was directed instead to Babylonia.

The southern half of Mesopotamia had by no means been overlooked during the four spectacular decades of excavations in Assyria, but the results there were not considered impressive until Ernest de Sarzec began to unearth Lagash (Telloh). In a series of expeditions between 1877 and 1900, he laid bare a whole new civilization—the Sumerian—whose very existence, sketchily outlined by the Assyrian tablets, was till then still a matter of dispute.[33] Subsequent French excavations at the site, and clandestine operations in the intervals, helped bring to light a whole new millennium in human history.

Meanwhile American excavations at Nippur (1889–1900) uncovered the religious capital of the Sumerians, with a library rivaling that of Assurbanipal in importance and antedating it by more than a thousand years.

---

[33] Compare Tom B. Jones, ed., *The Sumerian Problem*, Major Issues in History, part 1, ed. C. Warren Hollister (New York: John Wiley & Sons, 1969), pp. 3–47.

Other expeditions before the First World War identified numerous other ancient Babylonian sites such as Babylon, Sippar, Borsippa, Kisurra, Shuruppak, Adab, and Kish. Improvements in stratigraphic[34] techniques in the field and the cumulative evidence of the inscriptional finds permitted the gradual construction of a chronological sequence and the recognition of certain significant cultural epochs. The extensive French excavations at Susa in Elam, begun in 1897, also proved significant, for this ancient capital of Iran was for millennia a faithful mirror of Mesopotamian influences and a repository of some of the precious booty from that area, notably the Stela of Hammurapi inscribed with his laws.

Assyriology between the wars (1919–39) was characterized by expanding horizons, both in field archeology and in philologic results. Not content with such brilliant discoveries as those of Sir Leonard Woolley at Ur (1922–34) and of the German expedition to Uruk (1928–39), excavators ventured beyond the boundaries of mandated Iraq to discover unsuspected, additional cultures built around derivative and, in part thoroughly different, cuneiform scripts. Boghaz-Köy in Anatolia harbored the remains of Hattusha, capital of the Hittites through much of the second millennium B.C., as well as an extensive literature in a number of languages, some of them Indo-European in character. At Ras Shamra on the north Syrian coast, the clay tablets of Ugarit included some of the earliest northwest Semitic literature. The Urartian inscriptions of first millennium Armenia were collected and treated systematically at this time, and renewed efforts at Susa and Persepolis in southwestern Iran yielded significant new finds in Old Persian, Elamite, and the proto-Elamite scripts.

At the same time, philologic tools and methods were being considerably refined. Individuals like François Thureau-Dangin, who put on a sound basis such diverse essentials as the origin of the cuneiform script, the Sumerian and Akkadian syllabaries, chronology, royal inscriptions, and even mathematical texts, combined a sweeping mastery of the entire field with a rigorous scientific approach to details. Their works are still standard. The British Museum and such other centers of sizable and still growing collections of cuneiform texts as Oxford, Berlin, Paris, Philadelphia, Cambridge (Mass.), and New Haven (Conn.) inaugurated or continued systematic editions of texts in autograph copies. Journals devoted primarily to Assyriology flourished in France and Germany, to be joined by new ones in England and America after the Second World War. An almost feverish resumption of both excavation and publication followed the war, with the most significant new results in many respects coming from the French excavations at Mari on the Middle Euphrates in Syria.

While significant new discoveries continue to be made in the field as well as in the museums, the discipline of Assyriology faces its second cen-

---

[34] On archeological strata and their chronological significance, see above, p. 10, n. 17.

tury since the decipherment of cuneiform with a degree of maturity. Excavations of additional sites and publications of new texts will continue to require the inevitable revisions of current views, but these revisions are being accommodated to an increasingly more complete understanding of the total picture of ancient Mesopotamia.

New centers and new names have contributed their share to postwar Assyriology. American influence has been strongest in the lexical field, with Benno Landsberger and the Oriental Institute at Chicago leading the way, and in the recovery of Sumerian literature, under S. N. Kramer and Thorkild Jacobsen. In Russia, two flourishing schools of Assyriology focus respectively on economic texts and on Urartian materials, the former at Leningrad around I. M. Diakonoff, the latter at Tiflis with M. de Tseretheli and others. Vigorous studies are also being pursued in the homelands of the cuneiform sources, notably in Turkey and Iraq.

Substantial syntheses of the materials already recovered are likely to occupy the attention of most Assyriologists for some time to come. In textual terms, such syntheses include: critical editions of literary, or canonical, compositions; tabular compendia of the data contained in economic, or archival, tablets, using computers where necessary to cope with the large number of texts and entries; and new editions of historical and votive texts, together with the monuments on which they are found, as a sound basis for the chronological outline on which all other historical judgments must rest. When these three fundamental syntheses have been achieved, the way will be open for the definitive interpretation of the cuneiform evidence and its full integration into the record of human achievement.

[2] EGYPT

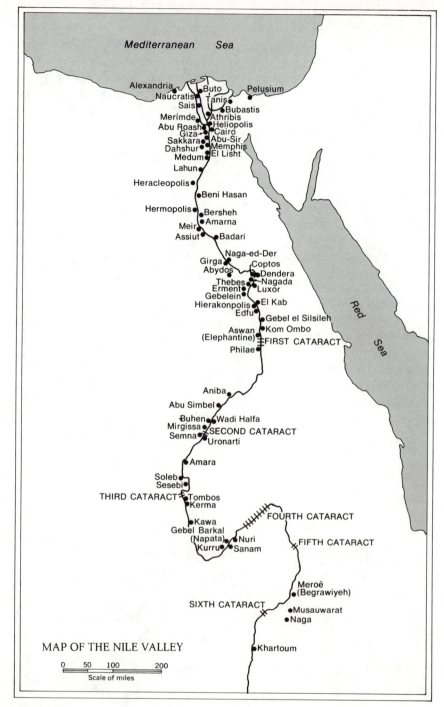

Mediterranean Sea

Alexandria
Naucratis
Sais
Merimde
Abu Roash
Giza
Sakkara
Dahshur
Medum
Lahun
Heracleopolis
Beni Hasan
Hermopolis
Bersheh
Amarna
Meir
Assiut
Badari
Naga-ed-Der
Girga
Abydos
Thebes
Erment
Gebelein
Hierakonpolis
Edfu
Aswan
(Elephantine)
Philae

Buto
Pelusium
Tanis
Bubastis
Athribis
Heliopolis
Cairo
Abu-Sir
Memphis
El Lisht

Coptos
Dendera
Nagada
Luxor
El Kab
Gebel el Silsileh
Kom Ombo
FIRST CATARACT

Red Sea

Aniba
Abu Simbel
Buhen
Wadi Halfa
Mirgissa
Semna
SECOND CATARACT
Uronarti
Amara
Soleb
Sesebi
THIRD CATARACT
Tombos
Kerma
Kawa
Gebel Barkal
(Napata)
Kurru
Nuri
Sanam
FOURTH CATARACT
FIFTH CATARACT
Meroë
(Begrawiyeh)
SIXTH CATARACT
Musauwarat
Naga
Khartoum

MAP OF THE NILE VALLEY

0   50   100   200
Scale of miles

FIGURE 29

VII

INTRODUCTION: THE LAND AND ITS PREHISTORY; CHRONOLOGY AND HISTORIOGRAPHY

The rains in the highlands of Abyssinia and central Africa feed the White and Blue Niles and their tributaries, causing the Nile in Egypt to rise in the summer and crest in September and October. Before the construction of modern dams, the result was the inundation of the greater part of the cultivated land by water and water-borne earth, a gift stored by man's irrigation basins and dikes. The rich cultivation thus made possible along the river and in the Delta in the north was the focus for one of the earliest and most significant experiences in the history of man.

The continuity of Egyptian history and prehistory is remarkable, and the land itself played a dominant role in its settlement. Egypt is formed by a belt of cultivable soil deposited annually by the inundation of the Nile, a trajectory of some 750 miles from the red granite outcroppings at Aswan northward to the Mediterranean at Damietta in the east and at Rosetta in the west.[1] (see Figure 29.) At times this belt of crops extends several miles from each side of the river, while elsewhere, particularly in

[1] For a general description of Egypt in terms of its subsequent development, see: William C. Hayes, *Most Ancient Egypt* (Chicago: University of Chicago Press, 1964); and I. E. S. Edwards, T. G. H. James, and A. F. Shore, *A General Introductory Guide to the Egyptian Collections in the British Museum* (London: British Museum, 1964), pp. 1–21.

the south in Nubia, the desert cliffs come directly to the banks and allow no cultivation. The Egyptians called their fertile belt *Kemit*, "the black land," and the viselike desert regions on either side *Deshret*, "the red land."

[1] THE EARLIEST "EGYPTIANS"

Northeast Africa in the wetter climate of the Oligocene was the home of now extinct species of primates and other mammals, and we have learned a considerable amount about them from the recent study of their remains in the deposits in the Fayyum, a lake depression connected to the Nile in the western desert.[2] In Paleolithic times, hunters and gatherers inhabited the desert regions, and traces of man (in the form of flint tools) are frequent in the deserts and on the successive terraces cut by the Nile as it fell to its present level. Toward the end of the Paleolithic and Mesolithic ages there may have been contacts between the Fayyum area, Tibesti in the west, and the Sudan. The transition from a hunting, fishing, and gathering economy to one based on agriculture and the domestication of animals, elsewhere regarded as stages in the "Neolithic Revolution," is curiously absent from the record so far compiled for Egypt. This transition is better attested in the foothills of the Zagros in Iraq and Iran as well as in Syria and Palestine.

Following this gap in Egypt is a sequence of stages attested by numerous cemetery sites in Upper (that is, southern) Egypt. From the earliest (Tasian-Badarian) stage onward, there is evidence not only of animal domestication, agriculture, and pottery-making, but also of weaving and the use of copper.

The successive predynastic stages, designated as Badarian, Amratian, Gerzean, and Semainean, were each named after a site where cemeteries have been excavated by Petrie and others.[3] They are also known as Badar-

[2] Elwyn L. Simons, "Early Relatives of Man," *Scientific American* 211, no. 1 (1964): 5–62, and idem, "Earliest Apes," *Scientific American* 217, no. 6 (1967):28–35.

[3] For a comprehensive view of the Predynastic Period, see Elise J. Baumgartel, "Predynastic Egypt," fasc. 38, *Cambridge Ancient History*, rev. ed. (Cambridge: Cambridge University Press, 1965). Consult also Hayes, *Most Ancient Egypt*. For the main formulation of his seriation of the predynastic stages, see Werner Kaiser, "Zur inneren Chronologie der Naqadakultur," *Archaeologia Geographica* 6 (1957):69–77. For a dramatic, overall view, see V. Gordon Childe, *New Light on the Most Ancient East*, 4th ed. (London: Routledge & Kegan Paul, 1953) and later reprints. For a critical review and survey of our present knowledge and gaps, see A. J. Arkell and Peter J. Ucko, "Review of Predynastic Development in the Nile Valley," *Current Anthropology* 6, no. 2 (April, 1965):145–66; and Bruce G. Trigger, *Beyond History: The Methods of Prehistory* (New York: Holt, Rinehart and Winston, 1968). On the earliest stages, consult Fred Wendorf, Rushdi Said, and Romuald Schild, "Egyptian Prehistory: Some New Concepts," *Science* 169, no. 3951 (1970):1161–71.

ian, Negada I (Amratian), Negada II (Gerzean), and Negada III (Semainean). Few settlements of these periods have been excavated, for most of them lie in the fertile land now well under the present-day water table. However, the cemeteries exhibit a pattern of continuity from the earliest times to the advent of the historical period (ca. 3000 B.C.). Bodies were generally placed in shallow pits in a flexed or contracted position, the head frequently to the south facing west. Food offerings in pottery vessels were accompanied by a supply of equipment for life in the next world: tools, harpoons, combs, palettes for the grinding of eye paint, jewelry, and magical figures and amulets. A buff ware of the Negada II and III stages with reddish-purple painted designs provides insight into a hunting, fishing, and gathering economy to which grain cultivation and animal domestication had been introduced. Flint knives and blades exhibit a high degree of mastery, particularly the flaked knives hafted in ivory, which often have processions of animals arranged in horizontal registers. From the terminal predynastic period (ca. 3200–3000 B.C.) there is a series of ceremonial slate palettes with extremely fine scenes of the hunt, animals, and battles. These were evidently deposited in temples to commemorate the gratitude of a chief to his patron god.

Contacts with other areas were not insignificant. Cylinder seals of a type well attested in the Mesopotamian protoliterate period have been found in Egypt, one in a grave of late Negada II date.[4] A class of buff pottery, with a kind of wavy rib on opposite sides serving as a hand hold, was adapted from Syrian and Palestinian wares. Motifs in art, such as the leonine creatures with serpentlike, intertwined necks (see Figure 30, page 200), have clear Mesopotamian sources and parallels.[5] Representations in art of boats of a Mesopotamian type, as well as of a bearded hero figure between two animals, form part of the shared repertory and indicate influence from the east at this time. In addition, the Tigris-Euphrates region may well have provided the inspiration for the niched architecture of the first two dynasties.

More problematic is the origin of writing. In both Mesopotamia and Egypt different but similar systems appeared at approximately the same time. The available evidence gives the Mesopotamian system a slight priority in time, so the idea of writing may have been transmitted to Egypt from there.

The language first evidenced in Egypt continued, though with constant change, for some 4,500 years, from archaic Egyptian around 3000 B.C. through Coptic, which lasted until the end of the medieval period. The

---

[4] Helene J. Kantor, "Further Evidence for Early Mesopotamian Relations with Egypt," *Journal of Near Eastern Studies* 11 (1952):239–50; and idem, *Chronologies in Old World Archaeology*, ed. Robert W. Ehrich (Chicago: University of Chicago Press, 1965).

[5] Henri Frankfort, *The Birth of Civilisation in the Near East* (London: Benn, 1951).

latter was written with Greek consonants and vowels, while the former was written with hieroglyphs or cursive variations of them. It is through writing that Egyptian history becomes a subject for study.[6]

[2] RECONSTRUCTING THE PAST

The study of ancient Egyptian history in its varied aspects is a highly specialized, yet wide and far-reaching discipline. In years, it may be considered to cover a period from the beginning of Egyptian history, about 3000 B.C., to the conquest of Egypt by Alexander the Great in 332 B.C.[7] In area it comprises the Nile Valley, the Delta and the outlying areas in the northeasternmost part of Africa. The discipline is not confined to Egyptologists. Predynastic Egypt, in many of its phases, is increasingly the domain of the prehistorian and the anthropologist concerned with settlement patterns and typologies. Hellenistic Egypt, a vast source of materials in the Greek papyri, is the scholarly world of the classical papyrologist. Egypt in the Coptic period is studied mainly by the historian of religion for its Christian and Gnostic texts, or by the legal and social historian for its rich and varied business documents.

Within the field of Egyptology itself, scholars have specialized in a number of areas: texts, grammatical analysis of the stages of the language, architecture, sculpture, and painting. By the same token, however, Egyptology is wide-ranging. History, religion, archeology, art and architecture, literature, social structure, land use and ownership, economics, the ancient fauna and flora, and ancient science, astronomy, and medicine are all part of the scheme. Egypt's contacts with the rest of the world involve Africa, Syria and Palestine, Anatolia, Mesopotamia, Persia, and Greece and the Aegean world. The subject is limited in time and area but almost unlimited in the multiple aspects and wider implications of one particular time span and small part of the world.

[6] For a brief and interesting account of the stages of the language, the writing system, and the literature preserved, see Sir Alan H. Gardiner, *Egyptian Grammar*, 3rd ed. (Oxford: Oxford University Press, 1957), pp. 1–24.
[7] Recommended histories in English are: Sir Alan H. Gardiner, *Egypt of the Pharaohs* (Oxford: Oxford University Press, 1961); John A. Wilson, *The Culture of Ancient Egypt* (Chicago: University of Chicago Press, 1951); and James Henry Breasted, *A History of Egypt* (New York: Charles Scribners, 1905), to cite only a few. A more detailed work, useful for reference and citation of the literature on the various periods and problems is Étienne Drioton and Jacques Vandier, *L'Égypte*, 4th ed., "Clio:" Introduction aux études historiques. Les peuples de l'Orient Méditerranéen, vol. 2 (Paris: Presses Universitaires de France, 1962). Particularly recommended is Eberhard Otto, *Ägypten: Der Weg des Pharaonenreiches* (Stuttgart: W. Kohlhammer, 1953). Fascicles of *Cambridge Ancient History*, rev. ed., now in preparation, are cited throughout this volume. An invaluable adjunct is William Stevenson Smith, *The Art and Architecture of Ancient Egypt* (Baltimore: Penguin Books, 1965).

The Egyptians had no real sense of history in the classical or modern sense.[8] There are no extant Egyptian histories; even chronicles and annals do not extend beyond a single reign or lifetime. Our history is based largely on annals and isolated biographical inscriptions found by chance, such as those of Weny and Harkhuf in the Old Kingdom and Ahmose, the son of Ebana, in the New Kingdom. (Royal and nonroyal annals are always centered on the individual, the king, or the noble of that particular inscription.) The present-day historian must, therefore, fit together isolated data in order to reconstruct a plausible sequence of events as a basis for reconstructing the larger picture of the forces of historical development at work.

We have a comprehensive system of expressing dates, such as A.D. 1971 or 1557 B.C. But the Egyptians, with their ahistorical world view, had no concept of a continuous era. In the first dynasties the years were given names such as "year of erecting the Min Temple." Later, in the Old Kingdom, a cattle census, taken every other year, formed the basis for a system of dating. Thus the year of the first census and the year after would be either the first and second or the second and third years of a reign, depending upon whether the census was taken in the king's first year. When annual census-taking was initiated in Dyn. 6, the consecutive censuses became equivalent to our concept of consecutive years. But since the numbering started all over again when a new king took office, it is impossible to determine the length of time between Year 5 of one king and Year 47 of another without an accurate record of the length of the first king's reign and a list of the intervening kings that includes the length of their reigns.

The basic framework for the study of Egyptian history is the system of dividing its long span into thirty dynasties, or periods, to which a thirty-first was added. The original division is the work of an Egyptian priest named Manetho, who wrote in the early third century B.C., after the conquest by Alexander the Great.[9] Manetho, wishing to stress to his royal patron the antiquity of Egypt, came at an opportune time. Of his history only garbled excerpts and a garbled summary remain. The latter begins with a list of gods, demigods, and spirits of the dead and continues with the thirty dynasties of mortal kings. The divine beings have unrealistically long reigns (for example, 727¾ years). Usually the lengths of the reigns

[8] On the Egyptian concept of history, see: Ludlow Bull, *The Idea of History in the Ancient Near East*, ed. Robert Dentan (New Haven: Yale University Press, 1955), pp. 3–33; Eberhard Otto, "Geschichtsbild und Geschichtsschreibung in Agypten," *Die Welt des Orients* 3 (1966):161–76; idem, "Zeitvorstellungen und Zeitrechnung im Alten Orient," *Studium Generale* 19 (1966):743–51; H. Ranke, "Vom Geschichtsbilde der alten Aegypter," *Chronique d'Égypte* 6 (1931):277–86; and Erik Hornung, *Geschichte als Fest* (Darmstadt: Wissenschaftliche Buchgesellschaft, 1966).
[9] W. G. Waddell, ed., *Manetho*, Loeb Classical Library (Cambridge: Harvard University Press, 1940); and Wolfgang Helck, *Untersuchungen zu Manetho und den ägyptischen Königslisten* (Berlin: Akademie Verlag, 1956).

and the total of years for each dynasty are given, as well as the capital town and occasional bits of cryptic information about the reign. Although it is frequently difficult to determine the criteria used in dividing the span of history into thirty dynasties, the system has been retained for convenience.

A more general and meaningful pattern is that of major eras and intermediate periods: the Early Dynastic Period (Dyns. 1 and 2); the Old Kingdom or Pyramid Age (Dyns. 3 through 8); the First Intermediate Period (Dyns. 9 and 10, and preconquest Dyn. 11); the Middle Kingdom (postconquest Dyn. 11 and Dyns. 12 and 13); the Second Intermediate Period (Dyns. 14 through 17); the New Kingdom or Empire Period (Dyns. 18 through 20, of which Dyns. 19 and 20 are designated as the Ramesside Period); the Third Intermediate Period (Dyns. 21 through 25); the Saite Period (Dyn. 26); and the Late Dynastic Period (Dyns. 27 through 31).

The view of history expressed in this scheme is one of periods of stability and achievement alternating with periods not as well documented. In contrast to the Old, Middle, and New Kingdoms, the intervening periods were eras of relatively weak political stance, interference from "foreigners," a decrease in monumental public building, a divided or multiple kingship in the land with rival, contemporary dynasties, and a restructuring of society. Our documentation does not show them as periods of mere anarchy or hopeless confusion. They were productive in terms of literature, and within them was formed the basis for changes in religion and the organization of the state. We often learn more about the state in a period of weakness than when it functioned at its most efficient level. The major periods, on the other hand, saw a strong, centralized monarchy ruling the entire land, a stable bureaucracy with effective means for taxation, firm control of the borders, the exploitation of quarries and mines, as attested by the records inscribed at the Wadi Hammamat and Sinai, considerable activity in the building of temples and royal and private funerary structures, and a high level of achievement in the major arts of architecture, sculpture, and painting.

A study of the records reveals a pattern in which a ruler arises from the south and reunifies the country after a period of weakness. At the beginning of Egyptian history, Menes inaugurated the double kingship of Upper Egypt and Lower Egypt in the Thinite region of Abydos and dominated the north from Memphis. The First Intermediate Period ended, and the Middle Kingdom began, with the conquest of the northern Herakleopolitan state by Nebhepetre Mentuhotpe of Thebes and the subsequent establishment of a new residence city just south of Memphis by Amunemhet I. The Second Intermediate Period ended, and the New Kingdom began, with the expulsion of the Hyksos by the Theban brothers Kamose and Ahmose and the founding of Dyn. 18. A reflection of the Egyptians' awareness of the pattern of their history is seen in a procession of statues of kings of the New Kingdom represented in carved relief in the Ramesseum. The procession ends with statues of Ahmose, Nebhepetre Mentuhotpe, and Menes. This extraordinary choice of earlier kings can be explained only as a recognition of their status as the founders of the New Kingdom, the Middle Kingdom, and Dyn. 1. The pattern of restructuring from the south is repeated with the conquest of Egypt by the Sudanese Piankhy of Dyn. 25, a force that eventually led to the end of the Third Intermediate Period and the establishment of the Delta dynasty of the Saites in Dyn. 26.

In laying out a framework for the chronology of ancient Egypt, on which any history must be based, there are several important categories of evidence. The first is the king lists. Next to Manetho in importance is the very fragmentary papyrus document of the Ramesside period known as the Turin Royal Canon, now in the Egyptian Museum at Turin.[10] It begins with the reigns of the gods and continues with a period of *akhu* (spirits) and the followers of the falcon god, Horus. The long list of mortal kings begins with Menes and extends through the Second Intermediate Period, with major gaps due to the sorry state of preservation of the manuscript. The length of each reign is given in years, and sometimes in months and days as well, and there are several summations and subtotals. Of particular interest is a summation of 955 years from Menes to the end of the Old Kingdom, as well as a missing subtotal from Menes to the end of Dyn. 5. With the Turin Royal Canon, we have an early precedent, with lengths of reigns and summations but with fewer "dynasties," for the Manethonian division.

Still another list from which much is to be learned is the royal annals represented by the Palermo Stone and related fragments.[11] These inscription fragments, taken together, were copied in stone from a papyrus list of consecutive regnal years grouped under the name of the ruling king. The various worn-down fragments, of which the largest is in the Palermo Museum in Sicily, may derive from more than one list. Although the last reigns noted are those of Dyn. 5, to which the fragments are assigned, it has been suggested that the inscription is a copy made in Dyn. 25.[12] The name of the king, apparently followed by that of his mother, is given in one line. The second and third lines are divided into compartments by vertical lines, the second designating the year (a year name incorporating

---

[10] Sir Alan H. Gardiner, *The Royal Canon of Turin* (Oxford: Griffith Institute, 1959).
[11] For a recent reconstruction of the Palermo Stone annals, see Werner Kaiser, "Einige Bemerkungen zur ägyptischen Frühzeit," *Zeitschrift für Ägyptische Sprache und Altertumskunde* 91 (1964):86–125. Concerning a newly found fragment, see J.-L. de Cénival, "Un nouveau fragment de la pierre de Palerme," *Bulletin de la Société Française d'Égyptologie* 44 (1965):13–17.
[12] Wolfgang Helck, *Geschichte des alten Ägypten* (Leiden-Köln: E. J. Brill, 1968), p. 28, n. 2.

events of the year), and the third the height of the Nile. Then follow the regnal years of the next king with similar data. When the document was complete, the reader could add the years for each reign to determine the total from the beginning to the point where the list ended. He also had for reference the names of the years to determine their proper sequence. The brief events making up the year name are extended for the later reigns and provide some bits of "historical" information. Although dedications of specific temples or festivals are mentioned along with campaigns against neighboring tribes and the importation of wood, presumably from the Lebanon, for boatbuilding, they are hardly annals in our sense. Of partic- ular interest, however, is the partially preserved section at the top of a frag- ment, with the names of predynastic kings designated by their crowns as kings of Lower Egypt. A fragment in the Egyptian Museum shows the hieroglyphs for king with the double crown of Upper and Lower Egypt in the same position. (See lower figure, page 202.) Presumably there was a list, without year names or Nile heights, of kings of Upper Egypt, followed by kings of Lower Egypt (Palermo Stone top), and concluding with kings of Upper and Lower Egypt (Cairo fragment).

The best known and preserved of the dynastic king lists, however, is the dedication scene in the Temple of Seti I of Dyn. 19 at Abydos.[13] Here Seti I, accompanied by his son, the future Ramses II, invokes offerings for the past kings of Egypt, whose cartouches are lined up to form a list. There are fifty-six kings from Menes through the end of Dyn. 8, two rulers of Dyn. 11, seven of Dyn. 12, eight of Dyn. 18, and two (including Seti I) of Dyn. 19. Notable omissions are the Herakleopolitans of Dyns. 9 and 10 in the First Intermediate Period, the rulers of Dyn. 13 and the Second Intermediate Period, and, in Dyn. 18, Hatshepsut and the "heretic" rulers of Amarna (Akhenaten as well as Smenkhkare, Tutankhamun and Ay). The "ancestor chamber" in the earlier (Dyn. 18) festival temple of Thut- mose III at Karnak also lists the kings. Here they are not placed in a coherent chronological order, since the main purpose of the list was to provide offerings for their cults. The list is of some importance, however, since it reflects the local, as opposed to the Memphite, tradition. Rulers of the Old Kingdom figure to a minor extent, for Thebes was not a major area at that time. On the other hand, the Egyptian rulers of the Second Intermediate Period figure prominently. Still another list is to be found at Sakkara on the wall of a Ramesside official, Tjuenroy, "festival manager of all the gods, overseer of work on all monuments of the king, royal scribe, and chief lector priest." He invokes daily offerings by Ramses II for kings beginning with Anedjib of Dyn. 1. Dyns. 11 and 12 are in order but copied inversely from the rest of the text. Although the Dyn. 18 section is dam-

---

[13] Gardiner, *Egypt of the Pharaohs*, p. 49.

aged, the same omission of the Amarna heretics observed in the Abydos List is necessitated by the reconstruction.

Thus the early Ramesside kings evidently paid attention to the records of their past, and a tradition of the double kingship of Upper and Lower Egypt, going back to Menes, was recognized. Since some rulers were omitted intentionally, the lists cannot claim unprejudiced veracity. To fill in the gaps and correct these sources for our reconstruction of the framework, we can make use of the contemporaneous inscriptions, royal and private, and what remains of the business documents and accounts. The private sources for history and chronology take precedence over the royal ones. If Manetho and the Turin Royal Canon indicate that a certain king ruled seven years while an account of meat deliveries indicates that he ruled ten years, the latter generally has more validity. Similarly, if a noble indicated that he was born under one king, promoted under a second, appointed to high office under a third, and buried under a fourth, the relevant portions of the combined reigns must fit within one lifetime.

The curious avoidance of the use of a continuous era is based in part upon a cyclical rather than a linear concept of history. The inundation, the agricultural seasons, and the schedule of religious festivals are cyclical; so too are the regnal years of a king. Occasionally a literary tale is set in the times of an early king, or it is said that a certain building or medical prescription dates to the time of a particular king; and statues are dedicated to past kings, or their cults are renewed. But the linear progression of time is not exploited. For the Egyptians, the king was supreme, the vanquisher of their traditional enemies: the Nubians to the south, the Libyans to the west, and the Semites to the northeast. A scene of a Libyan victory in the pyramid temple of Sahure of Dyn. 5 was copied in the mortuary complex of Pepy II at Sakkara in Dyn. 6 and still later at Kawa in the Sudan in Dyn. 25. And perhaps the Sahure scene was copied from a still earlier source. We would tend to regard the copies as plagiarisms, as indeed they are. To the Egyptian mind, however, the scene signified merely that the king successfully vanquished Libyan enemies, a constant recurrence. So, too, lists of captured towns were copied in the New Kingdom from one king by the next, and the mention of a certain Palestinian town in one inscription does not of itself guarantee that the pharaoh actually captured it. The real matter is a statement of victory fleshed out with details often cribbed from earlier sources.

Egyptian chronology is thus a piecing together of data within a framework based on the king lists and associated documents and supplemented by various contemporaneous inscriptions.[14] It must be checked against

---

[14] Erik Hornung, *Untersuchungen zur Chronologie und Geschichte des neuen Reiches* (Wiesbaden: Otto Harrassowitz, 1964).

synchronisms with western Asia. If the Egyptian king received a letter from an Assyrian king or met him in battle, they obviously were contemporaries. There are also rare astronomical dates, such as certain star risings indicated in Egyptian texts, that can be plotted in time at specific intervals. On this basis, Year 7 of Sesostris III of Dyn. 12 is estimated to fall in 1872 B.C. The carbon 14 dates based on analysis of the half life of carbon in organic materials are, without a proposed corrective factor, generally later than the dates arrived at by Egyptologists.[15] Dating is a complex matter still under study.

[3] SOME CULTURAL BACKGROUND

This is basically a political history, an account from the time of the earliest settlers who left written documents to the conquest by Alexander. Yet a brief word is in order on some more general cultural matters, for they relate to the history we are telling.

Religion, as mentioned in connection with the kingship in the next chapters, is part and parcel of Egyptian civilization rather than merely an aspect of it. If an Egyptian had been asked to outline the history of his country, he would certainly have started with its creation out of a watery abyss and the coming into being of the various gods and their cycles. Several of these accounts are to us mutually contradictory. His description would name the gods and perhaps their main cult centers in the land, indicate their attributes, and demonstrate their power.

An Egyptian's account of history would seem a conflation of myths and a series of rituals whereby these myths were acted out, frequently by a sort of player-king. This king built temples for the gods to ensure their well-being and obtain their favor. He engaged in the role-playing activity of slaying the foe, whether mortal enemy or animal. It is doubtful that our Egyptian's account would have included such specifics as the names of the pyramid-builders, Snefru, Cheops, Chephren, and Mycerinus, or even Thutmose III, Hatshepsut, Akhenaten, and Ramses II. Battles, such as Megiddo and Kadesh, and the Hyksos and Persian dominations might also have been accorded scant treatment or none at all.

The language of the ancient Egyptians is written with a system of picture signs. A sign, representing a consonant, a group of consonants, or the word for the object depicted, can also serve merely as a picture at the end of a group of consonants indicating the meaning or category of the word (for example, legs for a verb of motion). The language so written

---

[15] H. S. Smith, "Egypt and Carbon-14 Dating," *Antiquity* 38 (1964):32–37; Minze Stuiver and Hans E. Suess, "On the Relationship Between Radiocarbon Dates and True Sample Ages," *Radiocarbon* 8 (1964):534–40.

was an offshoot of the stock represented in the so-called Semitic languages, which include Akkadian (Assyrian and Babylonian), Hebrew, and Arabic. While Egyptian in its oldest stage is quite dissimilar to the oldest stages of the Semitic languages, there are a number of cognate words and a similarity, often masked, to the verbal structure of Semitic. The stages of the language are Old, Middle, and Late Egyptian, Demotic, and Coptic, and the development is in many ways parallel to that from Latin to French or Spanish. The formal script, in which the pictures are usually recognizable, is called hieroglyphic. It was used for inscriptions on stone and carved or painted on wall surfaces. A cursive version of the same script, bearing roughly the same relation to the former as our handwriting does to letterpress or typescript, is called hieratic. The hieroglyphs were simplified so that the original picture is not immediately recognizable. This cursive variety, used for business documents and literary texts, was usually written with a reed or rush pen in black or red ink on papyrus, a sort of vegetable paper made from the stalks of the papyrus plant. Texts were generally written horizontally from right to left, the opposite of our system, but they were also written, for reasons of symmetry, from left to right or vertically from top to bottom.

The literature of the Egyptians includes narratives, books of wisdom, poems, and a large body of religious texts. Several of the compositions of the Middle Kingdom became school texts in the New Kingdom. The *Story of Sinuhe*, for example, is represented by several papyri (texts written on papyrus) in the Middle Kingdom and numerous *ostraka* (limestone flakes) and potsherds of the New Kingdom, each with several lines or more of the composition.

The Egyptian scribe was responsible for the considerable amount of written material of which only a minute fraction has survived. In a profession corresponding more to that of our accountant, the scribe was called upon to render the elaborate accounting required by the diverse branches of the pharaonic government. Not unnaturally there grew up a literature about the scribe's superior life and its advantages, such as the oldest of these compositions, the *Satire on the Trades*, which outlines the sorry lot of all other men. This attitude is also seen in the following extracts:

Look for yourself with your own eye. The professions are set before you. The washerman spends the whole day going up and down, all his body is weak through whitening the clothes of his neighbors every day and washing their linen. The potter is smeared with earth like a person one of whose folk has died. His hands and his feet are full of clay, he is like one who is in the mire. . . . A carpenter, the one who is in the workshop, carries the timber and stacks it. If he renders today produce of yesterday, woe to his limbs! The shipwright stands behind him to say to him evil things. His outworker who is in the fields, that is tougher than any profession. He spends the whole day laden with his tools, tied down to his tool-box. . . .

But the scribe, it is he that reckons the produce of all those. Take note of this.[16]

In the *Satirical Letter* of the Ramesside period, one scribe taunts his colleague for ineptly calculating the workmen necessary for a ramp construction. These pieces about the scribe's lot, copied and recopied in a series of papyri, are interspersed with administrative letters abounding in technical terms to tax the scribe's knowledge—the parts of the chariot, deliveries of exotic plants and materials, and foreign place names—as well as hymns to the gods.

Through these exercises and set pieces of the apprentice scribes we learn much of the cultural setting of the ancient Egyptians in the same way as the wall reliefs and paintings provide illustrations of their lives and times.

[16] Ricardo Caminos, *Late-Egyptian Miscellanies* (London: Oxford University Press, 1954), pp. 384–85.

FIGURE 30 Narmer Palette: front and back. (Dyn. 1.)

VIII

THE EARLY DYNASTIC PERIOD

[1] DYNASTIES 1 AND 2

Historical Egypt begins at the end of the Predynastic Period, with the establishment of the double kingship in the first dynasty.[1] According to the records, the founder of the double kingship was named Menes. But the precise circumstances are not as clear as one would wish, for it is still not possible to identify Menes beyond doubt as a specific king in Manetho's list.

Sources clearly imply that there existed a predynastic line of kings of *Shemau* (Upper Egypt), the area in historical times that extended northward from the first cataract in the Nile, at Aswan, to the apex of the Delta just south of Memphis, near modern Cairo. (See Figure 29, page 186.) These kings were designated by the title *ny-swt*, "one who belongs to the sedge plant." This sedge title is conveniently translated as "King of Upper Egypt."

---

[1] For selected readings on the period of the first two dynasties, see: I. E. S. Edwards, "The Early Dynastic Period in Egypt," fasc. 25, *Cambridge Ancient History*, rev. ed. (Cambridge: Cambridge University Press, 1964); Walter Bryan Emery, *Archaic Egypt* (Baltimore: Penguin Books, 1961); Werner Kaiser, "Einige Bemerkungen zur ägyptischen Frühzeit," *Zeitschrift für Ägyptische Sprache und Altertumskunde* 86 (1961):39–61, and idem, "Einige Bemerkungen zur ägyptischen Frühzeit," *Zeitschrift für Ägyptische Sprache und Altertumskunde* 91 (1964):86–125.

Their characteristic headdress was a tall white crown with a bulbous terminal at the top (see below), and their protective goddess was the vulture goddess of Nekhen. A parallel line of kings ruled *To-mehu* (the northland or Delta area). Their title is *bity*, "the one of the bee," the symbol of the north. This title is translated as "King of Lower Egypt."

Their characteristic crown was a red wickerwork headdress with a tall element at the back and a curious, thin piece with a fiddle-head curve in front (see below). The protective goddess was the cobra or uraeus goddess Wadjet. There is no term for king, although *ny-swt*, or *nsw*, and later *per-aa*, "pharaoh," came to serve that function.

As noted earlier, the Palermo Stone shows some of the predynastic kings' names along with the hieroglyph for a king wearing both the red and white crowns, implying a predynastic union of north and south.

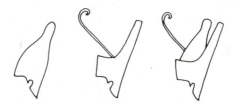

Although only one individual and name is involved, there is the constant, if eventually almost meaningless, alternated and combined use of the sedge-chief and bee-chief titles. It has been argued that this double kingship is really an artificial construct to maintain the integrity of each kingdom—that even in the beginning there was only one king who conciliated both parts of the land by holding the title of ruler of each. More likely there were predynastic rulers of each kingdom, and the founder of the double kingship, Menes, annexed the title of his unsuccessful opponent.

[2] DYNASTY 1

The kings of the united kingdom during the first dynasty are best known through their Horus names, whereby they are identified as the incarnation of the falcon god, Horus. The name, written in a rectangle representing the façade of a building, palace, or temple, is surmounted by a falcon.

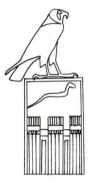

The Horus names of rulers in the first dynasty are Rosette-Scorpion, Narmer, Aha, Djer, Djet, Den, Anedjib, Semerkhet, and Qa.

Rosette-Scorpion is known only from ceremonial, *ex-voto* mace heads found in the temple at Hierakonpolis. Wearing the crown of Upper Egypt, he is shown with a hoe in the ritual of digging a canal. His name is written with a seven-petaled rosette above a scorpion. On a damaged mace head from the same deposit, a king wearing the Lower Egyptian crown is shown seated before a vanquished enemy, and the same signs have been plausibly restored in front of him.[2] Although neither name occurs in the Horus façade, they appear in the same position as the name in front of the figure of Narmer as Lower Egyptian king on the Narmer Palette, making it clear that Rosette-Scorpion stands for a king's name, arguments to the contrary notwithstanding.[3] The top row of the better-preserved mace head, which shows the standards of Upper Egypt with dead birds hanging from them, reflects a conquest of the northerners by a southern federation. Perhaps the scene of the vanquished enemy on the other mace head commemorates the same event. Thus Rosette-Scorpion, or Scorpion, may well have claimed the double kingship.[4] The rosette with seven petals may be an early title for the kingship and may represent a connection with Mesopotamia, where the rosette appears on many objects.

Perhaps the real founder of Dyn. 1 was Narmer. The major monument of his reign is a ceremonial, *ex-voto* slate palette from the temple at

[2] A. J. Arkell, "Was King Scorpion Menes?" *Antiquity* 37 (1963):31–34.

[3] Elise J. Baumgartel, "Scorpion and Rosette and the Fragment of the Large Hierakonpolis Mace Head," *Zeitschrift für Ägyptische Sprache und Altertumskunde* 93 (1966):9–13.

[4] Winifred Needler, "A Rock-drawing on Gebel Shaikh Suliman (near Wadi Halfa) Showing a Scorpion and Human Figures," *Journal of the American Research Center* 6 (1967):87–91.

Hierakonpolis. (See Figure 30, page 200.) The top of the shield-shaped palette shows on both sides a pair of cows' heads with human faces, representing the goddess Hathor and, between them, the Horus name of the king in the palace façade rectangle. The name, written in hieroglyphs of a fish and a chisel or pin, is conventionally read as Narmer. On one side the upper register shows Narmer, with the Upper Egyptian crown, brandishing a mace and clutching the hairknot of an enemy identified by the hieroglyphs for harpoon and pool of water. A curious group in the upper right seems to indicate that Horus is delivering into captivity an enemy from the papyrus land, the Delta.

The king is followed by a courtier who is bearing the king's sandals and a spouted jar. The courtier, designated by two hieroglyphs—the seven-petaled rosette and a wooden club—is perhaps the servant of the man whose title is written with the rosette. In the lower register, each of two enemies, running or swimming, is identified by a single hieroglyph, most likely a place name. On the other side of the palette (which measures about twenty-four inches high), the top register represents a visit to a battlefield. The king, here wearing the crown of Lower Egypt, is preceded by four standard-bearers and an official who may be the crown prince. A courtier follows with sandals and jar; above him is a rectangle with the hieroglyph designating a building. On the battlefield are ten corpses, their heads between their legs. The three hieroglyphs are a door, a bird, and a boat, evidently a geographical designation or the phrase, "a boat journey to the Great Door." The central register represents two leonine beasts with interlaced, serpent-like necks, held by two trainers. (The circle formed by the interlacing animal necks was used for grinding eye paint.) In the lower register a bull tramples an enemy while knocking down the walls of a fortified enclosure.

The document before us is susceptible to divergent interpretations both as a whole and in detail. The main question asked of these representations, rightly or wrongly, is whether the palette commemorates the conquest of Lower Egypt by the king of Upper Egypt, the resulting unification of the country, and the identification of Narmer as Menes. The answer is not clear. It is possible that the group with the falcon delivering the northern captive to the king actually represents the presentation of the Delta northland to the ruler of Upper Egypt. Some argue that the hieroglyphs for harpoon and pool identify the main captive as the representative of the harpooner's domain, while others maintain that it is "Wash," the enemy. The procession to the battlefield with the king wearing the Lower Egyptian crown may represent the subjugation of either an outlying portion of the Delta, called the Great Door, or the capital at Buto. The intertwined, serpentlike, leonine beasts can be read as the union of north and south, and the victorious bull as the king destroying an enemy encampment.

Thus the monument can be read as the conquest of the north by the south, as events forming part of this campaign, as the subduing of rebellions subsequent to the conquest, or as a general statement of victory of the ruler over his enemies. Such is the ambiguity inherent in our imperfect understanding of these representations, a kind of ambiguity that we will have to face on numerous occasions as we attempt to read the historical content of Egyptian records. For example, the king wears the northern crown on his visit to the battlefield. Is this a case of adding insult to injury, of the king visiting the slain soldiers while wearing the crown of their king? I rather think that the king is visiting Buto or an outlying area in the Delta and is shown, quite naturally, wearing the headdress appropriate for the king of the north. The latter view is supported if we accept the restoration of the name of Scorpion, apparently a predecessor of Narmer, on the fragment of the broken mace head with the king wearing the northern crown. In this case Narmer would not be the earliest king to alternate the crowns.

This rather lengthy treatment of the Narmer Palette is justified, for it illustrates a number of points. The size of the king relative to the others represented indicates his importance. Superimposed registers are features characteristic of Egyptian art for millennia to come, as is the pose of the human figure: head, legs, and feet in profile and the upper torso in frontal view. Most significant are the sculptor's accomplished artistry and high standard of workmanship; the proportions are well worked out, and the detail is clear. This sober level of achievement inspired the best Egyptian art throughout its history.

Since Scorpion, Narmer, Aha, and others are represented as leading battles with the enemy, the idea of a formal union of the two areas at a specific time may be an illusion. During these early reigns, the power of the king over that of his confederates and opponents may have developed gradually through a series of alliances and a succession of battles. Once accomplished, the union would have been regarded as part of the concept of kingship, credited to the founder of the dynasty and renewed by each successive king.

The generally accepted sequence is Scorpion, Narmer, Aha, Djer, Djet, Den, Anedjib, Semerkhet, and Qa, with an early king Ka, or Sekhen, omitted. (See Appendix.) The dynasty, encompassing a total of some 210 years, seems to have originated at Hierakonpolis, a major town of the south (where the Scorpion and Narmer documents were found), and later shifted northward to Abydos. The third major site is Sakkara, the necropolis of Memphis in Lower Egypt.

Archeologically the dynasty is well attested. At Abydos the rulers from Narmer on built relatively small tombs below the desert cliffs at some distance from the cultivated land.[5] Although the superstructures are beyond reconstruction, they probably were of fill with brick retaining walls. A stele, or vertical stone slab, with the ruler's Horus name was set up on either side of an offering slab. Around the tomb there was usually a rectangle of dependents' graves—small, roofed burial pits for the courtiers and artisans. Most graves had a crude stele with the individual's name and occasionally his title or profession. The regularity of these graves, often long ditches with walls forming individual graves, and their close proximity to the main tombs imply that burials were made at one time. The suggestion has been made that the courtiers and artisans were killed or stunned and buried alive so they might accompany and serve the ruler or prince in the hereafter. Also included were his concubines, court dwarfs, and hunting dogs.

Between these tombs in the distant desert and the cultivated land several large rectangular structures have been identified as funerary palaces and storehouses for the rulers. These too have been plundered, so thoroughly in some cases that only the barest outline of the ground plan is traceable. If later practice is any guide, these buildings could have served as vast storage depots for grain and other needs of the ruler in his life after death. They may have included models of his administrative buildings and even real structures for his cult, for he continued to be venerated after his death with offerings and ceremonies. There were no specific roadways between the tombs and their respective funerary palaces. Like the tombs, the palaces were usually surrounded by rows of courtiers' graves. Through statues of himself the king magically lived on in this palace after his death.

Abydos was the ceremonial cult center of the god Khenty-amentiu, whose name means "foremost of the westerners." He soon became identified with Osiris, the god of regeneration and the halls of judgment, who assumed his name as an epithet: Osiris, Foremost-of-the-Westerners. The Temple of Osiris, now razed, was the main feature of Abydos, a cult and visitation place of the first magnitude. (See Figure 29, page 186.) Perhaps the cult of Khenty-amentiu in the first dynasties explains the early shift of emphasis from Hierakonpolis to a site farther north. At Hierakonpolis, however, a major temple enclosure was developed with Horus and Hathor as the main deities.

[5] Barry J. Kemp, "The Egyptian First Dynasty Royal Cemetery," *Antiquity* 41 (1967): 22–32.

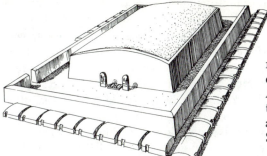

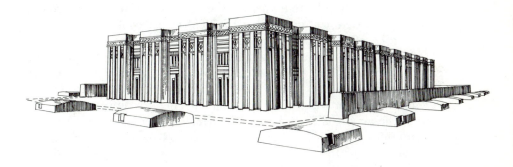

FIGURE 31   Reconstruction of the Merneith Tomb at Abydos and a tomb of her time, with surrounding wall and subsidiary tombs, at Sakkara (after Lauer).

The first dynasty is also well represented in the north by a series of tombs at Sakkara, Abu Rawwash, Giza, Helwan, and Tarkhan. Most significant of these is Sakkara.[6] On the edge of the desert fifteen imposing, rectangular tombs overlook the verdant valley, Memphis, and the cliffs on the other side of the Nile. To a limited extent the elaborately niched brick tombs resemble gigantic sarcophagi. The burial apartment is generally below ground, while the compartments containing vast stores of equipment are above ground. One tomb of the reign of the Horus Aha is about 158 feet long by 72 feet wide overall. North of it were several miniature replicas of buildings, including granaries and a grave for a wooden boat. In a later tomb of the same dynasty, a low bench lining all four sides was decorated with about three hundred clay bulls' heads. Provided with real horns, they either warded off evil spirits or represented the royal cattle. In the reign of Anedjib, the tomb of the official Nebitka was stepped on three sides and later masked by the traditional niched paneling. During the reign of the last ruler of the dynasty, a noble, Merika, built a tomb with an extensive statue chapel of several rooms on the north. On the west side niches were painted to resemble elaborate, woven textiles lashed on a frame with thongs. The patterns, geometric designs in gaudy colors, remind one of the colorful tents set up in present-day Egypt during Muslim memorial services.

[6] For an account, see Emery, *Archaic Egypt*.

If the separate functions of tombs and funerary palaces at Abydos have been properly interpreted, then the Sakkara tombs represent a combination of both functions in the same structure. They are magnificent buildings with valuable tomb equipment. Mainly unknown, the persons who erected them were powerful governors of the north or officials with northern family connections. The tombs are dated by seal impressions on wine-jar stoppers and wooden and ivory labels attached to boxes, leather bags, and other containers. In addition to the king's name, the name of the official responsible for provisioning the tomb is often found in these brief texts. (In fact, the great officials of the time are known only from these inscribed jar sealings and labels.) Since he was usually one of the chief administrative officers of the land, the tomb may well have been his own. Here too subsidiary graves were laid out so that the tomb-owner could continue to be served in his afterlife by his contemporaries.

Of the kings' immediate families little is known. The queen of Aha was Neith-hotpe, "the goddess Neith is pleased." (Neith was the goddess of Sais, a town in the Delta.) Neith-hotpe may have been of northern origin, and her marriage may represent an alliance between south and north. The same goddess figures in the name of Mer-Neith, an important queen associated with Djer, Djet, and Den—perhaps the daughter of the first, the wife of the second, and the mother of the last. She may also have been the mother of Anedjib.

The origin of this first of many dynasties is as intriguing as it is obscure. Manetho cites This (Tjeni) as the main town in the area of Abydos, and the time of the first two dynasties is frequently known as the Thinite Period. As noted above, Egyptian tradition implies the existence of predynastic rulers of Upper Egypt and of Lower Egypt, each section presumably having numerous tribal chieftains. In time a single ruler unified most of Upper Egypt and another most of the Delta. Dyn. 1 represents a further unification of both lands under one king. On the early mace heads and the Narmer Palette are standards later associated with the traditional *nomes* (districts) of Upper Egypt; the political base of the king thus reflects a confederacy of districts allied through mutual interests. There is also the possibility, however, that some foreign elements combined with indigenous ones in the setting up of the dynasty.

Upper Egypt comprised some twenty-two nomes by the beginning of the Old Kingdom; through subdivision and newly won areas, the Delta eventually comprised twenty nomes, with the main towns on water courses leading to the Mediterranean. (In light of the Delta flood pattern, these towns were frequently developed on high land, turtlebacks in geological terms, that remained dry at flood time.) Each nome became known for its principal town and outlying areas. Local deities were worshipped in the main temple, and political and religious authority was combined in the same individual.

A major factor in establishing political power was evidently the organizational ability to distribute irrigation waters. A central authority was necessary to ensure the proper control of the Nile flood waters for irrigation, because the building of embankments and a canal network involved more than one community. Yet the management of simple basin irrigation could not have in itself laid the groundwork for oriental despotism and the rise of civilization.

Although ancient Egypt was isolated from her neighbors by the desert to the east and west of the Nile, by the barren lands to the south (with river traffic interrupted by granite barriers), and by the sea to the north, there is evidence of constant interchange. In the last stage of the Predynastic Period, Mesopotamian cylinder seals of the Protoliterate Period have been found in Egyptian cemeteries, and the idea of the cylinder seal was almost certainly derived from Mesopotamia. The niched architecture of Egyptian tombs and funerary palaces may represent a brickwork translation of timber paneling, but it more likely reflects a kind of architecture developed in early temples in Mesopotamia. Several artistic motifs are borrowed directly or indirectly from Mesopotamian sources. The animals with intertwined necks are represented on seal impressions from Uruk in southern Mesopotamia. Furthermore, the idea of writing with pictographs, as noted above, was attested earlier in the Tigris and Euphrates areas. These elements indicate that dynastic Egypt developed at a time of various stimuli from Mesopotamia.[7] It is unlikely, however, that the founders of the first dynasty were invaders from outside. Various routes were available, and most of the Mesopotamian elements can be explained by trade. The coastal route through Palestine and the Sinai Peninsula is the traditional bridge between Egypt and Asia. There were also caravan routes from the Red Sea to the Nile Valley through the eastern desert. The best known of these, the Wadi Hammamat, runs from modern Qus on the Nile to Qosseir on the coast, where the Nile is nearest the Red Sea. Shipping along the Red Sea coast also may have linked Egypt and Asia.

The rapid advances made in the first dynasty, as indicated by the funerary architecture and grave goods, astonish us, as does the extent of Egyptian activity outside the Nile Valley. Pottery incised with the name of Narmer has been excavated at Tell Gat in Palestine. An official of Aha named Het is known from a clay jar stopper from Toshka found in Nubia. South of the second cataract at Gebel Sheikh Soleiman, near Buhen in the Republic of the Sudan, a rock drawing indicates a successful battle under Djer, and the name of Scorpion may be present there. Perhaps the copper tools deposited as grave equipment in the tombs at Sakkara came from there. Both Djer and Den may have sent missions to the inhospitable inhabitants of Sinai. The name of Djet was inscribed on a rock outcropping

[7] Henri Frankfort, *The Birth of Civilisation in the Near East* (London: Benn, 1951).

in the desert some fifteen miles east of Edfu in the Nile Valley, along one of the later routes to the Red Sea. Some of the tombs at Abydos and Sakkara contain oil jars of a Syrian type and coniferous wood brought most likely from the Lebanese hillsides. Although these indications are few, they show a wide geographical distribution of Egyptian contacts with other parts of the ancient world.

The events cited in the year names on the Palermo Stone and related fragments and on the wooden and ivory labels rarely contain material helpful to the historian. The data consist largely of the celebration of rituals (particularly those of a recurrent nature) and the holding of festivals and census projects (events normally occurring every two or three years)—for example, the ritual appearance of the king of Upper Egypt and Lower Egypt or the less frequent Sed festival, a sort of jubilee and renewal rite for the king. The founding of chapels and casting of cult statues also play a part in these records. Much rarer are the citations of events we would consider historically pertinent: the smiting of Nubia and the building of a border fortress under Aha, the smiting of Asia (Sinai?) under Djer, and the smiting of the Iuntiu (eastern Libyans) under Den. The census, which tends to be cited with its count, is, however, very useful for chronology. For example, consecutive years of Nyneter of Dyn. 2 are recorded on the Palermo Stone thus:

Year X + 5 Horus worship, 5th occasion of counting.[8]

X + 6 Appearance of the King of Lower Egypt, 2nd occasion of the Sokar festival.

X + 7 Horus worship, 6th occasion of counting.

X + 8 1st occurrence of the worship of Horus-of-the-sky, settlement of the towns Shem-Re and North-house.

In any case, only a fraction of the year names is preserved, and even in these years major historical events may have been omitted in favor of rituals more meaningful to the compilers.

[3] DYNASTY 2

Manetho's division into dynasties sometimes appears arbitrary, reflecting a break when none seems to have occurred. This is not the case for the beginning of Dyn. 2, for there are indications of a serious change at the end of Dyn. 1. The great tombs of the nobles at North Sakkara end abruptly after the reign of Qa, although there are later tombs of Dyn. 2 to the west. It appears that some of the Dyn. 1 tombs were thoroughly plundered, then set on fire. No royal tombs or funerary palaces at Abydos can be assigned to the first half of Dyn. 2. On stone bowls of Dyn. 1 the

[8] The ordinal notations refer only to the particular reign.

new ruler's name was customarily added to that of his predecessor—some vessels were inscribed with as many as four names. However, there is no carry-over on these vessels from Dyn. 1 to Dyn. 2. The year dates of Qa are missing in the preserved portion of the Palermo Stone documents, and the few container tags in the tombs are unfortunately not instructive. Even though the Turin Royal Canon records no break, it seems a new royal family came to the throne after a period of unrest.

This change in dynasty raises an interesting question. There is evidence of a political reorganization as well as a new emphasis in the structure of the state religion. Was the new political configuration a cause or an effect of the religious changes? (A similar question arises with the advent of Akhenaten in Dyn. 18.) Unfortunately, we presently have no means of answering this.

The new rulers seem to have deserted the royal cemetery at Abydos for a royal necropolis south of the Dyn. 1 cemetery at Sakkara. The superstructures of these Dyn. 2 tombs were completely razed, at least by the time of the building of the pyramid of Unis in Dyn. 5, but two series of well laid out and extensive substructures have been uncovered and assigned to two of the first three rulers of the dynasty. There seems to be a new emphasis on the sun god Re without a diminishment of the dynastic god Horus. Later in the dynasty there will be an emphasis on the brother-uncle of Horus, the god Seth. The Horus names of the first two rulers are Hotepsekhemwy, "the two powerful ones are pleased," these being the brother-gods, and Re-neb, "[my] lord is Re." The third ruler, Nyneter, celebrated the usual Horus festivals and the Memphite Circuit of the Apis Bull. He also founded a settlement called Shem-Re, "what Re goes around." The real change seems to have come to a head with the ruler named Peribsen. Unlike his predecessors, he used the Seth animal over his name rectangle in place of the falcon Horus. (See below.)

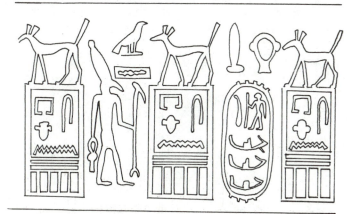

So basic a departure must reflect a political or religious step of considerable significance; it was accompanied by a shift of the royal necropolis back to Abydos, where Peribsen built his funerary palace and tomb. He appears to have been followed by the Horus Khasekhem, "the powerful one appears," known from documents from Hierakonpolis, and the Horus-and-Seth Khasekhemwy, "the two powerful ones appear," the latter a conciliatory(?) name incorporating both gods. The similarity between the two names suggests that there may have been but one ruler, Khasekhem, who, for political or religious reasons, chose to alter his name.

From historical events in Dyn. 2 not much can be gleaned. The major internal problem is certainly reflected in the change from the Horus to the Seth name and the resulting compromise expressed in the combined Horus-and-Seth name. It is difficult to speculate on the political origin or result of a situation that found its expression in an essentially religious context. The present interpretation of the Horus-Seth dyad is that Horus was the Lower Egyptian representative and Seth his counterpart in Upper Egypt. The Seth Peribsen may have asserted the superiority of the south by partially denigrating the deity of the conquered north. Alternatively, Peribsen may have controlled only the south, a rival king having taken over the north. Various complex theories have been advanced, including one that the same individual bore two names simultaneously—that of the Seth Peribsen in Upper Egypt and that of the Horus Sekhemib in Lower Egypt.

The times were disturbed. Khasekhem records the defeat of a northerner (or Libyan prince, tribe, or region) named Besh, perhaps the political heir of the much earlier Wash, whose defeat is represented on the Narmer Palette. On two statue bases from Hierakonpolis a mass of fallen enemies is depicted with legends indicating on one statue 48,205 defeated and on the other 47,209; and a relief fragment from Hierakonpolis shows the king kneeling on a prostrate enemy representing Nubia.

The second dynasty ends with Khasekhemwy, the only king in Egyptian history to bear the Horus-and-Seth name. His personal name, also included in the Horus-and-Seth rectangle, reads "the two lords are satisfied with him." (See below.)

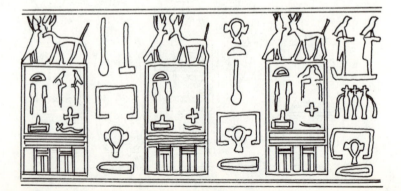

Thus the names show a clear reconciliation between the gods. Because a tomb has been located at Abydos for Khasekhemwy but not one for Khasekhem, it is not unlikely that, as suggested above, Khasekhemwy is a change in name effected by Khasekhem and only one individual is involved. Khasekhemwy is the first Egyptian ruler represented by name in the Egyptian temple deposits at Byblos, near modern Beirut, although a fragmentary vessel with the name of Peribsen is said to have come from there. By the end of Dyn. 2, prosperity and control of the entire land seem to have been achieved again.

The length of time covered by the first two dynasties is considerable—some four and one-half centuries. We calculate it by beginning with the usually accepted astronomical date of 1872 B.C. for Year 7 of Sesostris III of Dyn. 12, which in turn provides 1991 for the beginning of Dyn. 12. The 143 years in the Turin Royal Canon for Dyn. 11 then places the beginning of that dynasty in 2134 B.C. If Dyn. 9 and 10 began at the same time as Dyn. 11, the addition of 2134 to the Canon figure of 955 years from Menes to the end of the Old Kingdom gives a date of 3089 for the foundation of Dyn. 1. Since the duration of Dyns. 3 through 8 can be estimated on various grounds as approximately five hundred years, this leaves a long span of 455 years for Dyns. 1 and 2. It seems prudent to assign about 210 years to the eight kings of Dyn. 1, even though a summation of 253 years and individual reigns totaling 263 years were recorded by Manetho. The king lists and contemporary records do not provide a satisfactory order of kings and lengths of years for Dyn. 2. The Manethonian total of 302 seems excessive, and one might settle for around two hundred years. In all discussions of Egyptian chronology it must be remembered that the data are drawn from different types of sources of varying historical value: actual year dates of rulers, the Turin Royal Canon of Dyn. 19, and the late and often demonstrably inaccurate remains of Manetho's history. These facts, reasonable hypotheses, and guesses provide the basis for a tentative reconstruction, and new facts or interpretations may well alter the picture. For example, if Manetho recorded a reign as seventy-one years and this seems to be an error for seventeen years, there is an appreciable change.

IX

THE PYRAMID AGE:
THE OLD KINGDOM

The Pyramid Age follows the Early Dynastic Period and is so named because the surviving monuments are pyramidal royal tombs and associated funerary buildings.[1] Dyn. 3, at the beginning of the period, lasted about seventy-three years and represents a transition from the Early Dynastic Period. Dyns. 7 and 8, at the end (reckoned by some scholars as part of the First Intermediate Period), amounted to little more than twenty-one years. The core of the Old Kingdom, Dyns. 4 through 6 (2613–2181), was an age in which Egypt became the major civilization of the world, rivaled only by Sargon's kingdom of Akkad on the Tigris and Euphrates. For some 432 years, a long span for a period of prosperity, Egypt was essentially isolated on the international scene, although trade connections were maintained.

The almost antihistorical nature of the record is more evident here than in any other era of Egypt's development. The succession of kings, the probable length of their reigns, their genealogies, the names and offices of an increasingly observable officialdom, a few royal decrees, the great pyramid buildings, scenes and texts from the cult chambers of the royal and private chapels built at the tombs, an occasionally attested trade mission abroad or skirmish on the borders, the isolated find of an Egyptian object in Asia Minor or Crete, and the votive objects in Egyptian temples at Byblos and in the Sinai—these are the strands with which the historian must work. From them we can learn something of the nature of the kingship and the administration of the land, particularly at the end of Dyn. 5

[1] For an outline of the period with comprehensive references, see William Stevenson Smith, "The Old Kingdom in Egypt and the Beginning of the First Intermediate Period," fasc. 5, *Cambridge Ancient History*, rev. ed. (Cambridge: Cambridge University Press, 1962). For a general view with illustrations, see Cyril Aldred, *Egypt to the End of the Old Kingdom* (London: Thames and Hudson, 1965).

and in Dyn. 6, from which pyramid temple scenes and private mastaba reliefs are extensive.

In coming to terms with ancient Egypt, we are aware of images mirrored repeatedly, each dimmer and less complete than the last. We are at a vast remove in time, space, and mentality. The picture of an ancient civilization reflected in its plundered cemeteries and in the surviving temples is of necessity extremely distorted. We have some evidence, for example, of the farmer in the fields and the grains he cultivated, but it derives from an artist's representation on the walls of his master's tomb chapel. In one scene a sarcastic peasant says to his lazy companion, "We do not know of anyone who has died from his work." The details are preselected and likely to have been copied from a model by then already several centuries old. Yet our task is to question more deeply and attempt an assessment of the relative economic prosperity of all classes. We must make constant adjustments for the fact that so much of our material comes from tombs and not from the houses of the people. Business contracts, letters, and other correspondence from the cemeteries naturally refer to cult matters. A document dealing with the sale of a house may on closer inspection concern the sale of a tomb. Letters to a dead relative may request his interference with a dead enemy who troubles the dreams of the living and is thought to be responsible for the writer's calamities.[2]

In the Pyramid Age the Egyptian world was administered by a king who was also a god. It is perhaps difficult for us to understand the concept of a god-king, but there can be no question as to the evidence. The term *nuter*, or *natar*, used to designate a god, is also applied to the king. He is called "the good god" ("good" also meaning perfect or complete), while a real god is designated as "the great god." The queen is considered the god's wife. In Coptic translations of the Old and New Testaments the same term for god is used. The king as a god administers the world on his own behalf, not intrinsically on behalf of his people or the gods, but according to set principles. The overall principle is *maat*, the idea of order, justice, and truth. At times the nature of the king's relationship to the world of the gods seems to be contractual—on a purely business basis. In exchange for his building of temples and provision of offerings, the gods maintain the equilibrium of the state, the continuation of the king's power, and, almost incidentally, the welfare of the people. Since the king by definition acts according to *maat*, he cannot err or be evil.

Religion, so woven into the fabric of the Egyptian state, is difficult to isolate.[3] Significantly, the Egyptian language lacks a word for religion, for

[2] For a general account with references, see William K. Simpson, "The Letter of the Dead from the Tomb of Meru (N3737) at Nag'ed-Deir," *Journal of Egyptian Archaeology* 52 (1966):39, n. 2.
[3] For discussions of Egyptian religion and thought, see: Jaroslav Černý, *Ancient Egyptian Religion* (London: Hutchinson's University Library, 1952); Henri Frankfort et al., *Before Philosophy* (Baltimore: Penguin Books, 1946); and idem, *Kingship and the Gods* (Chicago: University of Chicago Press, 1948).

the concept is unthinkable in Egyptian terms. Yet such specific ideas as prayer, offerings to the gods, humility, and a wide variety of other concepts relating to ethics and religion are represented in the language. In the wisdom or instruction literature, particularly of a later stage, the idea of the truly silent man (as opposed to the hothead) becomes dominant. The king is said to be loved by the gods, and the gods love mankind, but the idea of man loving the gods is not represented. For the Egyptian mentality, religion was operative in much the same way as our physical laws of gravity. It included explanations of how the world came into being, many of which are to us mutually exclusive. But characteristically, Egyptian thought saw all these statements as valid. It had a sort of attic complex; ideas were stored in the attic of the mind, never to be discarded. Horus and Seth are brothers, and yet in the same text Seth is the uncle of Horus. The king is the son of Re, the sun god, and yet he is the incarnation of Horus, the son of Osiris. The "and yet" is our modern way of indicating an inconsistency not incongruent to the ancients.

The concept of the pyramid and mastaba is like that of the state. The pyramid towers above the desert plain, itself high above the valley.[4] Visible for miles—upstream, downstream, and on the other side of the Nile—it is an ever present reminder of the glory and might of the absolute monarch. It symbolizes a ramp or staircase to heaven for the king's spirit. At its base a cult and offering temple was the scene of busy activity involving a host of officials and laborers. As a land-owner and major employer, the pyramid corporation was a significant economic force. Surrounding the pyramid, low, rectangular tomb superstructures with slightly sloping sides and flat tops were laid out like many gravestones in a modern cemetery. These were the mastaba tombs and tomb chapels of the favored who surrounded their lord in death as in life. The huge difference in size between the pyramid and even the largest mastaba reflects the relative importance of king and official. This contrast, maintained to the end of the Old Kingdom, was mitigated by the small-scale pyramids of the queens near their lord's pyramid. Nevertheless, with time the pyramids tended to decrease in size and the mastabas to increase.

[1] DYNASTY 3

The transition indicated by Manetho and the Turin Royal Canon from Dyn. 2 to Dyn. 3 appears in the archeological record to have been smooth. Perhaps the lack of a male heir resulted in a northerner marrying the daughter of Khasekhemwy, or possibly the first kings of Dyn. 3 were the sons of his queen, Nymaathap.

The contemporaneous documents and the king lists are difficult to

[4] I. E. S. Edwards, *The Pyramids of Egypt*, rev. ed. (London: Penguin Books, 1961); Leslie Grinsell, *Egyptian Pyramids* (Gloucester: John Bellows, 1947).

reconcile. The order and number of the kings, as well as the length of
their reigns, are not well established by the king lists or their actual monuments. Judging from the royal tombs, the kingship was centralized at
Memphis from the beginning of Dyn. 3 to the end of the Old Kingdom.
The first kings of the dynasty opened up the turquoise quarries and perhaps the coppermines on the Sinai Peninsula.

The dynasty is overshadowed by the monuments of the Horus Neterirykhet (later called Djoser), probably its second ruler,[5] following his
brother, the Horus Sanakhte. The Horus Sekhemkhet followed Djoser and
was in turn followed by the Horus Khaba and then Huni. Djoser and
Sekhemkhet built step pyramids at Sakkara, and a layer pyramid slightly
to the north is assigned to Khaba. To Huni is assigned the step pyramid,
later converted to a true pyramid, at Medum.[6] It was completed by Snefru,
the founder of Dyn. 4, and it is logical to consider it the pyramid of his
predecessor if not one of his own. Two unexcavated pyramid complexes of
this general period are visible in the aerial photographs of Sakkara. They
may belong to additional kings, one of whom may be Sanakhte. A shrine
built by Djoser at Heliopolis illustrates the fine relief carving achieved at
this time and the northern connections of the dynasty. In the south, a
Ptolemaic stele from the island of Sehel at the first cataract reflects the
tradition of Djoser's association with the region. A cartouche of Huni has
also been found in this region.

Djoser's place in history is based on his tomb and associated buildings.
(See Figure 33). It has a rectangular enclosure over a mile in perimeter.
Its master builder, Imhotep, regarded in later times as a great sage and
physician, was eventually considered a god. The monumental complex of
the step pyramid, now excavated and partly restored, seems as extraordinary and exciting as it is puzzling and ambiguous. (The latter features, of
course, are entirely the result of our failure to comprehend the architect's
building task and to penetrate the meaning of the parts of the complex.)
Three or perhaps four major program factors are at work in the design
concept. The first is the creation of a royal burial place, represented by the
rectangular granite chamber beneath the pyramid and perhaps by the similar, smaller square chamber beneath the southern enclosure wall. The sec-

[5] For accounts of the buildings of the Djoser complex and the other step pyramids of
the dynasty, see: Edwards, *The Pyramids of Egypt*, rev. ed.; J.-Ph. Lauer, *Histoire
Monumentale des pyramides d'Égypte*, vol. 1 (Cairo: Institut Français d'Archéologie
Orientale, 1962); and H. Ricke, *Bemerkungen zur ägyptischen Baukunst des alten
Reichs*, vol. 1 (Cairo and Zurich: Borchardt-Institut für Ägyptische Bauforschung und
Altertumskunde in Kairo, 1944).
[6] The step pyramid rises in several giant steps to its summit. The layer pyramid is
constructed with a similar end result by adding successive revetments to a core. The
true pyramid was achieved at first by filling in the sides of a layer or step pyramid to
create four smooth planes. Once this form was achieved, the earlier ones were abandoned.

FIGURE 33 Model of the Step Pyramid complex of King Djoser at Sakkara (by Lauer). (Dyn. 3.)

ond factor is the provision in both structures of underground apartments for the king's spirit, the vast stores of grain northwest of the complex, and the caches of stone vessels beneath the pyramid. The third element is the creation of a theatrical set of varied structures (none real in the sense of being truly functional) elaborately grouped within the enclosure wall. Was this three-dimensional theater set ever conceived for the use of human players? Or was it a ghostly stage for the entrances and exits of actors from the spirit world? Related to the last question is a fourth theme, the problematic use of the real buildings, the entrance colonnade, and the double temple or palace on the north of the pyramid for the perpetuation of the king's cult. Indeed, it is as if this vast, architectonic fantasy was created expressly to be abandoned, left as an earthly town for the private use of the dead king's spirit and his associates, the gods.

In the standard pyramid complex of the Old Kingdom only the first and fourth of these elements found architectural expression: the provision for the burial and the provision for the cult. The underground apartments and storerooms are not present. The theatrical set of dummy buildings is translated into the allusive, secondary order of relief representations in the cult temple. The themes entering the building program of the Djoser complex, insofar as we can attempt imperfectly to reconstruct them, seem more diverse than those of later complexes. In Dyn. 5 there is a parallel set of pyramids and sun temples for each king. It seems altogether probable that these separate structures are polarizations of themes existing side by side in the unity of the Step Pyramid enclosure. The emphasis on the Sed festival jubilee rites seen in the court of the Step Pyramid is apparent in the Neuserre sun temple reliefs of Dyn. 5. The great north altar of the Step

Pyramid may be expressed later in the central obelisk of the Neuserre sun temple.

From the technical point of view, the complex realizes a startling and even sensational translation of brick, reed, and wattle construction into stone. This is exhibitionism, a tour de force attaining dignity through its seriousness of purpose, extraordinary dimensions, and the excitement implicit in working in the medium of stone. The ideas, however, were not new. For example, the dummy buildings are part of a scheme already seen in the Dyn. 1 mastabas at North Sakkara. And it is possible to infer the existence of a northern temple and dummy building among the now destroyed superstructures of the Dyn. 2 royal tombs at Sakkara.

But the innovative aspect of the Step Pyramid complex is stamped on all its details, none more so than in the change of plan that resulted in the alteration of a square, mastabalike structure into a six-stepped pyramid. The tradition, so inaugurated, was difficult to emulate. The complex of Sekhemkhet to the southwest was left unfinished. The layer pyramid assigned to Khaba toward the end of the dynasty betrays no new ideas, although its ruined condition and apparent lack of an enclosure with subsidiary buildings make it a poor example. The exuberance of technical mastery and exploration is seen in Djoser's monument alone, in the experiments with fluted and fasciculated columns, column bases, capitals (the papyriform shaft and capital at the north building), shadows of imaginary beam ends in the enclosure wall, opened portals frozen in their sockets, picket fences sculptured in stone, and all the tricks of an illusionistic yet serious trompe l'oeil.

The salient features of the Step Pyramid are many. It expresses the concept of a god-king requiring of his people the extensive service embodied in this structure. It is the working out of a complicated series of functions, still ambiguous to us, involving spirit actors and the infinite repetition of the jubilee. The original square superstructure, extended and built up in the course of several changes to form a ramp or staircase to heaven, is the dominant feature. Throughout there is the expression of Imhotep's genius in using stone rather than brick and light materials used for the prototypes.

A single mastaba of the time deserves mention, the Sakkara tomb of a scribe and courtier named Hesy-re, among whose titles and offices is that of chief dental physician.[7] On one side of an enclosed corridor east of his mastaba are painted representations of his funerary equipment: oils, chairs, tables, beds, game boards, chests, and the like. The chests are frequently shown with their contents visible, as if by X-ray vision. On the other side are eleven niches paneled with wood. These show Hesy-re standing and seated with his scribe's equipment. (See Figure 34.) The artistry of these carved panels was never surpassed in any of the following dynasties.

[7] J. E. Quibell, The Tomb of Hesy (Cairo: Department of Antiquities, 1913).

FIGURE 34 Wood relief showing the official Hesy-Re as a scribe. (Dyn. 3.)

[2] DYNASTY 4

The apex of the Pyramid Age is reached with Dyn. 4. In this and the following two dynasties each ruler built a pyramid complex. While it may seem unwarranted to lay so much stress on the building of royal and private tombs, it is from these structures and the surrounding mastaba tombs that the major portion of our information about the times is derived.[8] Of other Old Kingdom building, not even the great temples of the gods at Abydos, Heliopolis, and Memphis can now be traced.

It will be most convenient to describe the basic elements of a standard pyramid complex before discussing the features of any specific monument. The chief element was the pyramid itself. It developed initially by filling each side of a stepped pyramid, making a smooth, even surface. Within the body or below it was a simple chamber or series of chambers reached by a low-ceilinged, sloping corridor. In the main chamber the king was buried in a stone chest, or sarcophagus. From the end of Dyn. 5 the

[8] Edwards, *The Pyramids of Egypt*, rev. ed.; and Ricke, *Bermerkungen zur ägyptischen Baukunst des alten Reichs*, vol. 2 (1950).

walls of these chambers were inscribed with religious texts and spells relating to the king's journeys in the afterlife. Presumably such inscriptions
had been stored in earlier pyramids on papyrus. The function of the pyramid was twofold. First, it was the symbol of the king's power and connection with the sun god. Second, it served as his final resting place. After
burial the corridor was blocked and its entrance concealed with the intent
that the burial should remain intact for eternity.

Next in importance after the pyramid was the temple at its base to
the east, facing the valley. It consisted of a private section near the pyramid, which contained a stele and an offering slab for making offerings to
the dead king. Here the king was frequently represented in relief receiving
the offerings of his court and meeting the assembled gods as he emerged in
spirit from his pyramid. A larger section of the temple incorporated an
open court surrounded by an arcade, and in the northwest section was an
altar or offering slab. The court and surrounding chambers served as the
scene for the perpetuation of the deceased king's cult, the main features of
which were the rituals performed in front of his statues to make them live
and partake of food offerings. An extensive wall enclosed the pyramid and
part of the temple, with the latter interrupting it on the east side of the
complex. Within its precinct was a small satellite pyramid, which may
have been for the burial of the king's *ka* (spirit) or of his crowns. Outside
the wall were small pyramids for the principal queens. The later examples
had their own relatively small temples on the east side, complete with
offering slab and false-door stele. Outside the wall, mastaba tombs for the
main officials of the reign and their descendants were laid out. From the
mortuary temple on the east side down to the valley was a processional
avenue generally designated as the causeway. Walled with stone and frequently roofed, it was in many cases decorated with bas reliefs at both
ends and along its entire length. A small temple at the end of the causeway served as the entrance to the complex and had a landing stage along
the canal where the processional boats were moored. In it, rites relating to
the preparation of the king's body for burial were performed, and a temporary embalming tent may have been erected on its roof. In the vicinity of
the valley temple were houses for the staff of the pyramid foundation,
virtually a company town of officials, priests, scribes, accountants, field
workers, and laborers.

Snefru, the founder of Dyn. 4, appears to have built three huge pyramids. The first of these, at Medum, was converted from a stepped to a
true pyramid, and it is thought to have been the pyramid of Huni, the last
ruler of Dyn. 3, although no trace of his name has yet been found at the
site. The mortuary temple on the east side is extremely simple, lacking the
cult-temple element with open court and altar. The site is otherwise best
known for two double mastabas, the first of the vizier Nefermaat and his
wife, Atet, famous for its painted scene of geese, and the second of the

army commander Rehotpe and his wife, Nofret, known for an extraordinary pair of seated statues with their colors remarkably preserved.

The second of the three pyramids is the Bent Pyramid at Dahshur, a site between Medum and Sakkara. The angle of the facing changes abruptly about halfway up, probably because structural difficulties, creating cracks inside the mass, indicated that a lesser angle and a correspondingly lighter weight of stone might salvage the project. The mortuary temple on the east side is austere in comparison with later pyramid temples. A causeway leads from a point near a corner of the enclosure wall to a lower temple generally thought to be the valley temple. However, the plan of this temple and its location some distance short of the valley suggest that it may have been the functional counterpart of the cult temple and that the true valley temple, still to be located, may lie farther to the east. The temple is noted for its reliefs, among which is a procession of the personifications of the farms of the Egyptian nomes, each with produce for the king's cult. These farms or estates are arranged by nome and follow one another in the traditional sequence. The pyramid, curiously, has two distinct burial apartments, one reached from the north face in the standard scheme and the second reached from the west face. The latter was provided with a strange timber and stone filling. A passage in the Palermo Stone records the king's purchase of timber, presumably from Lebanon, and it is perhaps this very shipment that is represented in the pyramid. The significance of this double arrangement remains a mystery. It has been ingeniously proposed that the two slope angles could be extended visually to suggest two superimposed pyramids, each with one burial chamber.

The third of Snefru's pyramids is the North Stone Pyramid at Dahshur, about a mile north of the Bent Pyramid. Its angle follows the gentler slope of the upper part of the Bent Pyramid, as if the architects determined not to try again the steeper angle that brought the earlier project to its strange conclusion. Like all the pyramids, it was entered and plundered in antiquity, and much of the finer stone casing was removed. Its temple on the east, causeway, and valley temple have not yet been excavated.

Snefru is reputed to have been a benign and beneficent king. His cult continued to be celebrated for centuries at the site of the Bent Pyramid temple, and the literary narratives of the Middle Kingdom held him in reverence. Neither the continuation of his cult into the Middle Kingdom nor its revival in Ptolemaic times can be explained solely as the result of the prudent management of the funds of his temples.

The Horus Medjedu, King of Upper and Lower Egypt, Khnum-Khufwy (better known as Khufu or Cheops) succeeded his father, Snefru, and selected the desert promontory of Giza as the site for the largest of the pyramids. Although its most noticeable quality is its single, massive geometric form, its internal ascending corridor and Grand Gallery represent a majestic architectural tour de force. The pyramid, 481.4 feet high and 756 feet to a side at the base, covers 13.1 acres. The building of the final burial chamber was preceded by that of two others during the construction of the pyramid. Although the plan of the mortuary temple can be made out, the causeway and valley temple are lost beneath the modern village at the site.

The tomb of Hetepheres, queen of Snefru and mother of Cheops, was plundered during her son's lifetime. The burial equipment, including the empty sarcophagus, was then secretly reburied near the Great Pyramid with no superstructure to mark its location. Discovered and excavated by an expedition of the Boston Museum of Fine Arts, it contained the queen's carrying chair, a bed, and a portable tent frame, all of wood covered with gold leaf and the queen's titles and name in hieroglyphs. It seems doubtful that, when the reburial was effected, the officials told the king her body had been stolen for its jewelry.

No historical information about the reign of Cheops has survived, although Herodotus recounted his reputation as a cruel monarch. In the Middle Kingdom much was stripped from his pyramid temple structure to be used for a pyramid at el Lisht.

After a twenty-five-year reign, Cheops was succeeded by Redjedef (Djedefre), a king who, following tradition, built a pyramid complex isolated from those of his predecessors. The unfinished pyramid at Abu Rawwash, north of Giza, is assigned to his brief reign. Khafre (Chephren), his successor, built his complex at Giza just south of that of Cheops. It measures 471 feet high and 708 feet to a side, not much less than the Great Pyramid that it seemingly rivals because of the lay of the land. The outline of the mortuary temple as well as a fair portion of the valley temple and causeway are preserved. The valley temple, with monolithic red granite pillars and architraves, is still an impressive building. Several austere diorite statues that formed part of the cult have been discovered. A natural rock outcropping near the valley temple was transformed by the king's sculptors into a guarding sphinx, the well-known monument still extant. Of the reign of Chephren little else is known. After his death the throne may have been occupied by one or two of his sons, Hordedef and Baefre, but their reigns, if they took place at all, were short.

The next king of importance was Menkaure (Mycerinus), the builder of the third pyramid at Giza. Although considerably smaller in size, its lower part was encased with red granite instead of limestone, and it must have been intended to rival the others in material if not in enormity. Again, historical data are sparse for the reign. In the valley temple, a statue of the king and his queen was found (see Figure 32, page 214), as well as several triad statues of the king, a deity, and a personification of one of the Egyptian nomes.

At the death of Menkaure the program of pyramid-building and the concepts related to it changed, at least temporarily. Shepseskaf, who ruled five years, built instead an impressive, sarcophaguslike, rectangular super-structure for his tomb considerably south of Giza and Sakkara. Perhaps the sun religion of Re, of which the pyramids were an expression, suffered a sharp diminution in emphasis at this time, or perhaps the economy could not tolerate such massive programs. Except for the shape of the monu-ment, however, Shepseskaf's complex was essentially like the traditional pyramid complex, with temple, causeway, and presumably valley temple. After an ephemeral successor or two, the dynasty of Giza pyramid builders came to an end about 120 years after its foundation by Snefru.

[3] DYNASTY 5

In Dyn. 5, a new line of rulers came to the throne, and traditions reflect this change in several ways. The main lines of the development of Egyptian civilization were not interrupted, nor was there a drastic up-heaval in the bureaucracy. But there appeared an even more marked em-phasis on the royal cult of Re.

A papyrus of the Second Intermediate Period consists of stories of magicians of the past recited to Cheops by his sons.[9] The last of them concerns a living magician who foretells the end of Cheops' line through the birth of triplets to the wife of a priest of Re. Attending are the god Khnum and the birth goddesses who give the infants names that are ob-viously puns on those of the first three rulers of Dyn. 5—Userkaf, Sahure, and Neferirkare Kakai. The tale breaks off when a crocodile seizes a maid-servant about to inform the king of these events. From an historical point of view, the significance of the story lies in its premise that the new line of kings is unrelated to Cheops' dynasty and in the parentage of the new line through a priest of Re.

The first ruler of the dynasty, Userkaf, built his modest pyramid not at Giza, where the pyramids and mastabas of Dyn. 4 dominated the desert edge, but in the vicinity of the Step Pyramid of Djoser at Sakkara. The small chapel on the east side of his pyramid is separated from the larger cult temple, which is placed, exceptionally, on the south side, perhaps to receive the sun's rays during a greater part of the day or else merely to take advantage of the terrain. Several miles to the north Userkaf constructed a large shrine to his sun god, the Re particularly associated with the king. It apparently had an obelisklike element as its focal point and, with offer-ing court, causeway, and valley building, resembled a pyramid complex.

[9] Adolf Erman, *The Ancient Egyptians: A Sourcebook of their Writings*, trans., A. M. Blackman, introduction by William K. Simpson (New York: Harper & Row, 1966), pp. 36–47.

During the dynasty each king built a pyramid complex and a sun temple complex.[10] Just as the king was a god, so Re was the king of the world, requiring the trappings of an Egyptian pharaoh. The curious architectural concept embodied in the sun temples was perhaps derived from the altar in the northern section of the Step Pyramid enclosure. This may be the sun temple cited in a short text of a contemporary of Djoser and Sekhemkhet.[11] In any case, we do not know the precise meaning of the royal sun temples and their relationship to the great temples of the gods, no longer surviving at Heliopolis, Abydos, and other centers.

Userkaf's sun temple sparked a somewhat similar development just to the south at Abu Sir, where his successor, Sahure, and two later kings of the dynasty, Neferirkare Kakai and Neuserre, built pyramids. Thus, Abu Sir was to the first part of Dyn. 5 what Giza was to Dyn. 4. A curious feature of the Abu Sir pyramids is the diversion of the long causeway from the pyramid complex of Neferirkare Kakai. King Neuserre demolished the upper part of the causeway and changed its route so that it led to his own pyramid. Neuserre also built an extensive sun temple nearby at Abu Gurob. Here are bas reliefs concerning the Sed Festival and the foundation rites of a temple, as well as an extensive, though fragmentary, scene of seasonal activities and the migratory habits of birds and fish. Officials whose families had used the Giza and Sakkara cemeteries continued to build their mastabas there. Sakkara in particular was favored by the great officials when the last ruler of Dyn. 5 and the first ruler of Dyn. 6 built their pyramids there.

The pyramid of Sahure is the classic example for Dyn. 5. The mortuary temple reliefs show the king hunting, fishing, and catching birds. The significance of these scenes goes beyond appearances, for they were meant to represent the king continuing these pursuits after death and to illustrate the maintenance of order and the productive domination of nature. A major section shows a mission to Syria and its successful return with bears and jars of oil. Previously mentioned is the scene, later copied elsewhere, of a conquest of the Libyans and a recording of the booty by the goddess Seshat. The Abu Sir pyramids show extensive traces of copper used for drainage channel plugs. The copper was obtained from Buhen at the Second Cataract or from the Sinai Peninsula.

A very fragmentary papyrus archive, providing a glimpse into the management of the Abu Sir pyramids at the end of Dyn. 5 and into Dyn.

[10] Erich Winter, "Zur Deutung der Sonnenheiligtümern der 5. Dynastie," *Wiener Zeitschrift für die Kunde des Morgenlandes* 54 (1957):222–33; Werner Kaiser, "Zu den Sonnenheiligtümern der 5. Dynastie," *Mitteilungen des Deutschen Archäologischen Instituts, Abteilung Kairo* 14 (1956):104–16.
[11] Hans Goedicke, "Bemerkung zum Alter der Sonnenheiligtümer," *Bulletin de l'Institut français d'archéologie orientale* 56 (1957):151–53.

6,[12] deals mainly with the affairs of the funerary temple of Neferirkare Kakai. There are lists of persons employed in the many jobs relating to the temple as well as tables of duties performed regularly by the priests and the names of those assigned. Many individuals mentioned are known through relief representations of them among the king's courtiers or through their own nearby tombs. Some of their titles, such as royal hairdresser, indicate their role at the king's court more than their official function. One document is a pass allowing a certain official to enter an offering area to which admittance was usually forbidden. There is mention by name of various chambers, passageways, gates, and doors; temple objects, including those in need of repair, are listed in inventories. Accounts of income and distribution of food and cloth appear in ledgers, with headings, totals, and notes in red ink. Significantly, the oldest dated fragment appears to have been written over fifty years after the burial of the king, attesting to the continuance of his cult in the reigns of his successors.

The dynasty ended with Menkauhor, whose pyramid may lie to the east of that of King Teti of Dyn. 6 at Sakkara; Djedkare Isesi, whose pyramid lies between Sakkara and South Sakkara; and Unis, who built his pyramid just south of the Step Pyramid. Unis's pyramid is best known for the reliefs on the long causeway to its valley temple and for the first occurrence of pyramid texts in its subterranean chambers.[13] The pyramid texts are a collection of magical and religious utterances, often obscure, that aided the dead ruler in taking his rightful place in the company of the gods. These texts were inscribed on the walls of the burial chamber and other chambers in the pyramids of Dyn. 6. Parts of the hieroglyphs for certain animate beings were superstitiously eliminated so that fish, birds, or men could not magically come alive and injure the dead king. Similar elements appear later, in modified form, in the Middle Kingdom Coffin Texts, a group of spells inscribed on the wooden coffins of officials of early Dyn. 12. In the New Kingdom and later, the Coffin Texts were replaced in turn by papyrus scrolls of the *Book of the Coming Forth by Day*, better known as the *Book of the Dead*. The Unis causeway reliefs include scenes of columns and their bases delivered by barges from Aswan, a conflict with the Shashu nomads east of the Delta, an expedition by sea to Syria, and a group of famine-stricken Bedouin. The content and meaning of the last scene are not clear to us.[14] Are these enemies or Egyptians to whom the king is bringing food?

12 P. Posener-Kriéger and J.-L. de Cénival, *The Abu Sir Papyri*, Hieratic Papyri in the British Museum, Fifth Series (London: British Museum, 1968).
13 Alexandre Piankoff, ed. and trans., *The Pyramid of Unis*, vol. 5, Egyptian Religious Texts and Representations (Princeton: Princeton University Press, 1968).
14 Siegfried Schott, "Aufnahmen vom Hungersnotrelief aus dem Aufweg der Unaspyramide," *Revue d'égyptologie* 17 (1965):7–13.

The length of the dynasty is estimated at 150 years, from Userkaf through Unis. Quarrying, mining, contact with Byblos and the Levant, and trade missions to Punt on the Red Sea (under Sahure) and to Nubia are all attested. The chief internal development was the appearance of the royal sun temple, a feature that did not occur before or after except for the indication of a sun temple in the reign of Djoser.

[4] DYNASTY 6

A break at the end of Dyn. 5 is noted by the Turin Royal Canon. Evidently it represents more a change in the ruling family than an upheaval in the state. The already crowded area of Sakkara was the site of the first royal tomb of Dyn. 6, the pyramid of Teti, founder of the dynasty. His reign, estimated by some to have been as short as twelve years and by others to have been as long as 32½ years, has left little historical information, but the large tombs of the officials attest to a smooth transition from Dyn. 5 as well as the stability and prosperity of the land. Teti's successor, Userkare, ruled briefly, followed by Pepy I, whose reign was perhaps as long as forty-nine years. We are uncertain of the lengths of their reigns because we cannot precisely date the beginning of annual, rather than biennial, cattle counts. W. S. Smith reckoned Pepy I's reign as forty-nine years on the basis of the citation of the twenty-fifth count.[15] At the other extreme, H. W. Helck as recently as 1968 maintained that, on the basis of the Turin Royal Canon, the reign was only twenty years and regarded the twenty-fifth count as reflecting part of a previous reign when Pepy I and Userkare were joint rulers.[16] The rulers of this time seem to have been heavily dependent on the loyalty of the provincial governors, as evidenced by Pepy I's marriage to two daughters of an Abydos official named Khuy. Their brother, Djau, was the vizier. From the biography of Weny (discussed below), we learn that a harem conspiracy occurred involving a judgment against the principal queen. The next two rulers, Merenre Antiemsaf and Neferkare Pepy II, appear to have been half-brothers born at the end of the king's reign. The first is assigned a reign of six or fourteen years. Pepy II, on the other hand, appears to have had the longest reign in Egyptian history and perhaps in all history. The Turin Royal Canon credits him with upwards of ninety years. One version of the epitome of Manetho indicates that he "began to rule at the age of six and continued to a hundred." Although modern scholars have questioned this, it remains

[15] Smith, "The Old Kingdom in Egypt and the Beginning of the First Intermediate Period," fasc. 5, *Cambridge Ancient History*, rev. ed., p. 49.
[16] Wolfgang Helck, *Geschichte des alten Ägypten* (Leiden-Köln: E. J. Brill, 1968), pp. 71–72.

to be disproved. The king's pyramid at South Sakkara is of moderate size, but its reliefs were preserved well enough to be reconstructed on paper. They provide an extensive repertory of scenes, including the Libyan conquest copied from the Sahure complex. Each of Pepy II's main queens had a smaller pyramid, including a chapel with reliefs and a burial chamber with pyramid texts. The imposing valley temple, reached by a double flight of stairs, was a fitting entrance to Pepy II's complex.

Pepy II was succeeded by the short reigns of Netjerykare and a ruling queen, Nitocris, with whom the dynasty ended. The great Memphite kingdom, with expeditions into the Sudan, missions to Byblos, contacts as far as Anatolia in Turkey, and the organization to build the mighty pyramids, had come to an end. Yet the land of Egypt continued to be ruled from Memphis during the eight years assigned to the nine kings of Dyn. 7 and the approximately thirteen years during which six kings of Dyn. 8 attempted to carry on the tradition of the great pyramid-builders.

[5] THE OFFICIALS AND ADMINISTRATION

The god-kings of the Old Kingdom ruled with the loyal and able aid of a host of officials, many of whom were clearly men of outstanding ability. Imhotep, who served Djoser, was remembered for over two thousand years by his countrymen for his wisdom and his ability as a builder and as a physician. Although he does not seem to have been a member of the royal family, we know that in Dyn. 4 great officials were usually close relatives of the king. As time progressed, however, they were less often directly related to the rulers. Still, throughout Egyptian history offices tended to be hereditary. In the Old Kingdom there are examples of sons assuming their fathers' positions with the king's consent. There were cases in which an official petitioned the king to appoint the official's son as a "staff of old age," whereby the son assisted his father and presumably acquired the office and all its emoluments on his father's death.

The great office in the land is generally known by the Arabic term *vizierate*. Nefermaat, the vizier of Snefru, was succeeded by a son of Snefru, Kanefer, but he in turn was succeeded by Nefermaat's son Hemiunu in the reign of Cheops. The kings ruled in a patriarchal fashion through their family, but there were cases of able nonroyal men who rose to the highest offices. The main example at the beginning of Dyn. 6 is Weny. However, his contemporary, Mereruka, known to thousands through his mastaba tomb at Sakkara, owed his office of vizier partly to his marriage to a daughter of King Teti.

The land was administered through central offices charged with granaries, assessments, taxes, and disbursements of salaries. In addition, each nome was governed by a *nomarch*, the Egyptian title corresponding to governor, and by local officials. The system is not entirely clear to us. In Upper Egypt, from Elephantine (Aswan) in the south to just upstream of Memphis, there are twenty-two nomes in the traditional lists. Several lists of the twenty-two nomes are represented in the Old Kingdom. The designation of northern and southern nomes of the same name in several cases suggests that the lists of twenty-two go back to a time when there were fewer. They are always listed from south to north, U.E. 1 (Upper Egypt 1) being Elephantine, U.E. 4 Thebes, U.E. 8 This (Abydos), and so on. The standards borne on the Narmer and other early palettes and on mace heads may represent these nomes.

The administration of the north is less fully understood because documents are sparse. It is certain that the list of twenty nomes was not established until later. Land development and a sort of colonization added to the number of nomes, as did the large border areas split into nomes.

Certain gods and their corresponding goddesses and sons are associated with particular nomes. Thus Osiris, Isis, and Horus represent a triad associated with Abydos. Amun, the goddess Mut, and the moon god Khonsu form the Theban triad. Thoth, regarded as the god of writing, is associated with Hermopolis in U.E. 15.

In the Old Kingdom, although each nome was theoretically governed by a nomarch, royal officials were in charge of royal missions in two or more nomes. Dyn. 5 officials bore such titles as "overseer of Upper Egypt," "overseer of the Head of the South," "overseer of the Middle Upper Egyptian Nomes," and "overseer of the Northern Upper Egyptian Nomes." It has been suggested, therefore, that the kings attempted to rule through a governor of the south under whom were deputy governors of the tripartite south[17]—which in effect eliminated the twenty-two nomarchs as independent political forces. In both Upper and Lower Egypt the royal farmlands, known as "estates," must have further curbed the partial autonomy of the nomarchs. At the end of the Old Kingdom the nomarchs of Coptos (U.E. 5) held the governorship of the south.

Our information comes in large part from titles of officials and from the reliefs in their mastaba tombs. In the early Old Kingdom these tombs tended to be near a royal pyramid. In Dyn. 5 and, particularly, Dyn. 6, the nomarchs usually cut their tombs out of the cliffs overlooking their respective nomes, dramatically indicating a sense of independence.

Most of the mastabas of the early Old Kingdom, in Dyn. 4, have relatively small chapels. The texts found there are formulas relating to the funerary offerings of food, cloth, and the like from farms bestowed by the king, as well as offering stones, lintels, and other works by the royal

---

[17] Hans Goedicke, "Zu *imy-r' šm'* und *tp šm'* im Alten Reich," *Mitteilungen des Instituts für Orientforschung* 4 (1956):1–10.

masons and sculptors. Biographical details are rarer than general statements such as, "I gave food to the hungry, clothes to the naked, and I ferried across the river the man without a boat." In the reign of Neferirkare of Dyn. 5, the tomb inscriptions of the vizier Washptah record details of his death. The king was in the process of inspecting building work carried out under the vizier's supervision when he noticed that Washptah had suddenly collapsed. The vizier was carried to the court but the physicians, with their medical scrolls, proved unable to revive him. His tomb was erected by royal favor near the pyramid of Sahure at Abu Sir. Occasionally royal letters are incorporated into the tomb inscriptions. At a tomb chapel at Giza, the vizier Senedjemib recorded the letters of King Isesi of Dyn. 5 praising him for his prowess in planning certain buildings.

The two best-known texts that provide biographies of unusual interest are those of Weny at Abydos and Harkhuf at Aswan. Weny began his career under King Teti, the first king of Dyn. 6.[18] In the reign of Pepy I he obtained a judicial office and a priesthood of the king's pyramid town, and, in addition, acted as a royal confidant, for which he was rewarded with tomb equipment: a limestone sarcophagus and lid, a stone offering door, two window frames, and the traditional offering slab. He boasted that he replaced four men in one of the offices to which he was appointed. A conspiracy in the harem necessitated legal proceedings against the queen, and Weny was delegated to this commission, although it was not the kind of matter dealt with by a man of his station. During state visits to outlying towns, Weny organized the journey and the king's accommodations at each stop. This administrative ability was tested by a special appointment to lead a large force including men from the twenty-two nomes of Upper Egypt, both sides of the Delta, and several areas of Nubia and Libya against the Asiatics. After five expeditions, the army returned safely, having overturned the enemy's walls and felled their fig trees and vines. At one juncture a force was sent by boat to attack near a ridge "in the north"— an area that has been conjectured to be in the Wadi Tumilat on the way to the Red Sea,[19] Mons Cassius on the Suez Peninsula,[20] or Mount Carmel in Palestine. In the reign of Pepy I's successor, Merenre, Weny was made Governor of Upper Egypt, from Elephantine (u.e. 1) in the south to Aphroditopolis (u.é. 22) in the north, and managed the tax collection throughout. He was in charge of quarrying expeditions for granite and

[18] James Henry Breasted, *Ancient Records of Egypt*, vol. 1 (Chicago: University of Chicago Press, 1906–07), pp. 291–324; Sir Alan H. Gardiner, *Egypt of the Pharaohs* (Oxford: Oxford University Press, 1961), pp. 94–98; and John A. Wilson, *Ancient Near Eastern Texts Relating to the Old Testament*, James Pritchard, ed. (Princeton: Princeton University Press, 1950), pp. 227–28.

[19] Hans Goedicke, "The Alleged Military Campaign in S. Palestine in the Reign of Pepi I (VITH Dynasty)," *Revista degli Studi Orientali* 38 (1963):187–97.

[20] Helck, *Geschichte des alten Ägypten*, p. 73, n. 12.

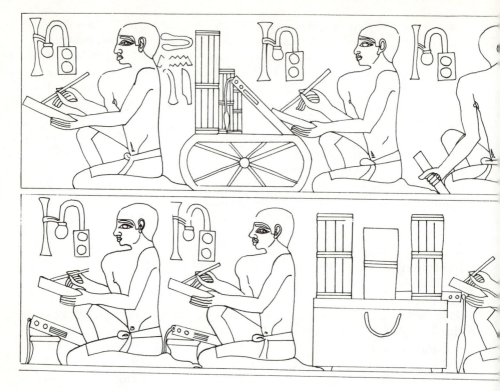

FIGURE 35   Detail of scribes at work drawn from a carved relief in the mastaba

diorite for the king's pyramid. A recently discovered rock text in the Wadi Allaki, the gold mining region of Nubia, attests to his visit there. At the first cataract at Aswan he excavated five channels in the rock for the passage of ships, and Merenre made an official appearance there to receive the homage of the Nubian kinglets.

Harkhuf too was Governor of Upper Egypt (or perhaps actually a subgovernor for the southern third of Upper Egypt) in the reigns of Merenre and Pepy II. His tomb was cut in the cliffs on the west side of the river at Aswan. The text on the façade records his journeys into Nubia and farther south on the king's business, and black Africa can be said to enter history with this important inscription.[21] Considerable scholarly study has been devoted to identifying the places he visited with areas in the Sudan. Among the produce of Nubia are listed ivory and ebony, the latter term in fact de-

[21] Breasted, *Ancient Records of Egypt,* vol. 1, texts 325–36 and 350–54; see also Elmar Edel, *Ägyptologische Studien,* ed. O. Firchow (Berlin: Akademie Verlag, 1955), pp. 51–75; D. M. Dixon, "The Land of Yam," *Journal of Egyptian Archaeology* 44 1958):40–55; and Elmar Edel, "Inschriften des alten Reiches. XI," *Zeitschrift für Ägyptische Sprache und Alterumskunde* 85 (1959): 18–23.

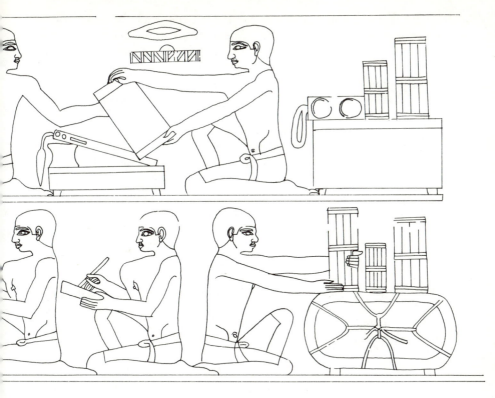

tomb of the official Ti at Sakkara (after Wild). (Dyn. 5.)

rived from the hieroglyphic *hebny*, an Egyptian word borrowed from an African language. On one of these expeditions Harkhuf obtained a dancing dwarf, and Pepy II, then a child, commanded Harkhuf to bring the dwarf home immediately. In the child-king's letter he told Harkhuf to check ten times every night and see that the dwarf was well, and he admonished him to see that the dwarf did not fall into the water. Harkhuf wrote, "My Majesty desires to see this dwarf more than the produce of Sinai or Punt."

The mastaba tomb chapels at Sakkara dating from Dyns. 5 and 6 are filled with relief scenes of numerous subjects.[22] (See Figure 35.) In addition to the main scene of the official before his table of offerings, there are scenes of life on a great farm, butchering cattle, raising fowl, fishing, hunting birds in the marshes and wild game in the desert, fashioning statues in the workshops, boys and girls engaging in tug-of-war and games, athletics, dancing, and men being brought before the assessors and beaten for under-

[22] See Prentice Duell, ed., *The Mastaba of Mereruka*, 2 vols. (Chicago: University of Chicago, Oriental Institute, Sakkara Expedition, 1938).

payment of taxes. Rarer scenes of the funeral rites and the procession of wailing mourners are also depicted. The man for whom the tomb chapel was built is shown in pursuits such as hunting and fishing and being carried in his sedan chair. Sometimes details of his profession appear in the tomb reliefs. For example, a scene of the circumcision of boys is shown in the tomb of Ankhmahor, a physician. In general, the owner is shown as a large figure viewing the life on the estate. Is he represented as a living figure, watching the activities that took place in his lifetime? Is he a ghost, so to speak, watching the continuation of his affairs from the world of the dead? Or is the entire scene in the hereafter, indicating that his activities continue after his death? These are questions still difficult to answer.[23] Absent from the repertory of scenes is any real emphasis on public or private religion as such. The owner is not shown entering a temple or praying. Neither are the gods, so frequent in royal pyramid reliefs, shown in the reliefs of mastabas or rock-cut tombs. The absence of these scenes, which do appear in the New Kingdom, is significant. It indicates a certain respect and distance between the world of the Old Kingdom nonroyal funerary cult and that of the gods. It also emphasizes the correspondingly close relationship between the king and the gods—the king alone has direct access to the divine world, and other men are largely dependent on him for their position in that world.

[6] THE END OF THE OLD KINGDOM

The powerful state of the pyramid-builders did not long survive the death of Pepy II, and the causes for its collapse are complex. The overlong reign of Pepy II was certainly detrimental to the Egyptian state. A later fragmentary literary text indicates curious nocturnal visits by the king to one of his generals. A sort of lethargy in the national conscience, economic woes, and loss of credibility in a state based on the concept of a god-king combined to bring the era to an end. Although incursions of Asiatics are attested by contemporaneous inscriptions, it is doubtful that the Memphite state succumbed to an outside force; it appears to have collapsed through internal weakness. A factor contributing to its demoralization and impoverishment must have been the cumulative expenditure of manpower and land on the building and maintenance of the royal pyramids. The exemption of temples and cult institutions from certain dues in produce and labor requisitions is known from a series of royal decrees.

---

[23] H. A. Groenewegen-Frankfort, *Arrest and Movement* (London: Faber & Faber, 1951), pp. 28–44.

These decrees, particularly from the times immediately following the end of Dyn. 6, also deal with the appointment of officials and the ameliorization of grievances.[24]

The impression given by these late decrees is one of a smoothly functioning, centralized government, with local governors appointed by the king to serve as governors of all of Upper Egypt. Yet the loyalty expected by the king from nomarchs of important areas such as Coptos does not disguise a weakness in the state. Just as these officials owed their positions to the king, so the king was increasingly dependent on them, and the exemptions from taxes were dearly bought. The other nomes became more and more independent. Finally a power vacuum developed in Memphis, and the dynasties of the pyramid-builders ended. Anarchy developed in some sections of the country and in the royal residence. The literary sources paint a picture of social upheaval amounting to revolution, with noblemen and noblewomen working in the fields, while their servants enjoyed the property of their former masters. Brothers fought, and men killed their parents. The pyramids and tombs were ransacked, and the files of government officials were thrown in the streets. In the more vivid accounts, the world of nature paralleled this upheaval. The Nile became dry, and men crossed it on foot. The sun was hidden. Crops were diminished, and yet taxes were raised. People fled from the towns to live in the cemeteries.

The Song of Harper, of a later age, harks back to the wisdom literature of the Old Kingdom, the sayings of Imhotep and Hardedef (the sage who served Djoser and the son of Cheops respectively), and the song reflects the sad plight of their tombs: "I have heard the words of Imhotep and Hardedef with whose discourses men speak so much. Where are their tombs now? Their walls are broken apart, and their tombs no longer exist—as if they had neven been."[25] Thus the autocratic Egyptian state, with its administrative and technical skills mirrored in the pyramids, came to an end.[26]

[24] Hans Goedicke, *Königliche Dokumente aus dem Alten Reich* (Weisbaden: Otto Harrassowitz, 1967).

[25] Wilson, *Ancient Near Eastern Texts Relating to the Old Testament*, p. 467.

[26] Adolf Klasens, "A Social Revolution in Ancient Egypt," Études et Travaux, vol. 2, *Travaux du centre d'archéologie mediterranéenne de l'Académie Polonaise des Sciences* 6 (1968):5–13 (Warsaw: Éditions Scientifiques de Pologne). Barbara Bell, "The Dark Ages in Ancient History. I. The First Dark Age in Egypt," *American Journal of Archaeology* 75 (1971):1–26; this article by Bell lays stress on the famines at the end of the Old Kingdom as the primary cause for its collapse. On the question of social mobility in ancient Egypt, see now Pascal Vernus, "Quelques examples du type du "parvenu" dans l'Égypte ancienne," *Bulletin de la Société française d'Égyptologie* 59 (1970):31–47.

FIGURE 36   Djehutynekhte receiving offerings from an attendant. (Dyn. 12.)

[X]

THE DEVELOPMENT
AND DISINTEGRATION OF
THE MIDDLE KINGDOM

[1] DYNASTIES 7 THROUGH 11

The anarchy following the collapse of the Old Kingdom was real, although the literature of the Middle Kingdom doubtlessly overdramatizes the contrast between these disturbed times and the peaceful times that eventually followed.[1] Memphis had ceased to function as the administrative center of the country, and the breakdown of centralized administration caused havoc. Curiously, the districts that played an important role at the end of the Old Kingdom—Elephantine, Coptos, and Abydos—did not fill the power vacuum, nor did the Delta break away to form a separate Kingdom of Lower Egypt. The nomarchs failed to take advantage of their new independence; perhaps their authority had been weakened by the king's administrators and the governors of the south.

The First Intermediate Period has been described as the era of Memphis, Herakleopolis, and Thebes, for these became the areas of historical importance. Information about the Delta is sparse. Memphis at the

[1] On the First Intermediate Period and the Middle Kingdom, see: Wolfgang Schenkel, *Memphis, Herakleopolis, Theben: Die epigraphische Zeugnisse der 7.—11. Dynastie Ägyptens* (Wiesbaden: Otto Harrassowitz, 1965); Jürgen von Beckerath, "Die Dynastie der Herakleopoliten," *Zeitschrift für Ägyptische Sprache und Altertumskunde* 93 (1966):13–20; W. Schenkel, "Zum Feudalismus der ersten Zwischenzeit Ägyptens," *Orientalia* 33 (1964):263–66; William C. Hayes, "The Middle Kingdom in Egypt," fasc. 3, *Cambridge Ancient History*, rev. ed. (Cambridge: Cambridge University Press, 1961); idem, "Egypt: From the Death of Ammenemes III to Seqenenre II," fasc. 6, *Cambridge Ancient History*, rev. ed. (Cambridge: Cambridge University Press, 1962); and J. J. Clère, "Histoire des XIe et XIIe Dynasties Égyptiennes," *Journal of World History* 1 (1954):643–68.

end of Dyn. 6 continued to exert authority over Upper Egypt but became increasingly dependent on the loyalty of local families at Coptos and Abydos. Soon after the final collapse of the Memphite regime the vacuum in the north was filled by Herakleopolis, an area not far south of Memphis in Upper Egyptian Nome 20. It owed its rise to the development of the Fayyum, a basin area west of the Nile fed by the Bahr Yusuf canal. At Herakleopolis there arose the new royal dynasties designated by Manetho as Dyns. 9 and 10. At the same time that the nomarchs of Herakleopolis took over the designation of king (or shortly thereafter), one of the nomarchs of Thebes, in Upper Egyptian Nome 4, did the same. Egypt thus had kings at both the northern and southern ends of Upper Egypt. Neither kingdom recognized the pretensions of the other. The Herakleopolitans knew their enemies as "the southern nomes" or the "head of the south." The Thebans referred to the north as *Per-Khety*, "the house of Khety (Akhtoy)," a name borne by three Herakleopolitan kings. After a period of consolidation and reconstruction, the Herakleopolitan and Theban dynasties confronted each other in a series of skirmishes. The outcome was a Theban victory and the establishment of the Middle Kingdom.

There is a question as to the extent of the First Intermediate Period. Some set its beginning in the last years of the reign of Pepy II, emphasizing the weakened governmental authority at this time. Others set it at the end of Dyn. 8, stressing the continuity of the Memphite rule and the nominal domination of the land throughout Dyn. 8. The Turin Royal Canon shows no break at the end of Dyn. 6. The end of the period is generally fixed at the time of the reunification of the country under Nebhepetre Mentuhotpe, about 2040 b.c., toward the end of Dyn. 11, although a few scholars would date the beginning of the Middle Kingdom as late as the foundation of Dyn. 12.

Dyns. 7 and 8 are best known for the so-called exemption decrees, mainly those addressed to the nomarchs of Coptos with reference to their appointments to the governorship of the south, and the exemption privileges accorded to or renewed for the temple at Coptos.[2] The probable reasons for the collapse of the Memphite rule have been suggested above. In any case, the downfall was real enough. The nomes of the Delta fell prey to incursions of Asiatic Bedouin from the area of Palestine. The nomarch of Herakleopolis succeeded in maintaining order in his nome and in extending his control of the west bank as far as Memphis, where one of his successors built a pyramid. Dyns. 9 and 10 are best considered as a unit, for it is impossible to see the reason for the division made by Manetho; the division is not reflected in the Turin Royal Canon.

---

[2] Hans Goedicke, *Königliche Dokumente aus dem alten Reich* (Wiesbaden: Otto Harrassowitz, 1967).

Literary sources such as *The Story of the Eloquent Peasant*, *The Instruction for Merikare*, the later *Prophecy of Neferti*, and *The Dialogue of the Man and his Soul* yield the best historical background for the period.[3] *The Admonitions of Ipuwer* is a composition that in its present form may belong to the Second Intermediate period. The main historical sources for the Herakleopolitan dynasties themselves are the texts from the tombs of the nomarchs at Siut (U.E. 13), Hermopolis (U.E. 15), and Hebenu (U.E. 16), and *The Instruction for Merikare*. They indicate that the Herakleopolitan kings, whose rule lasted about 120 years (2160–2040 B.C.), managed to regain control of the Delta, its harbors, and trade routes to the north, as well as to exert sovereignty over the northern half of Upper Egypt as far south as Siut and at times as far south as Abydos (U.E. 8). Early in the dynasty the three southernmost nomes were also in their sphere of influence, so that Thebes was checked on both the north and the south. The nomarchs of Siut loyally supported the Herakleopolitan dynasty against its Theban rivals and boasted of their aid in a crucial battle just to the south. A nomarch of Siut named Khety recorded his lifelong association with the king, proudly recalling the days when he learned to swim with the royal princes.

The Instruction for Merikare is a literary composition with advice from a king to his son, various maxims of a general nature, and historical and biographical details. It indicates that there was a period of peaceful coexistence following a Herakleopolitan attack on the Thinite nome (U.E. 8) in the south, and the resulting counterthrust northward by the Thebans, several of whose inscriptions recorded their realm as extending from Elephantine (U.E. 1) in the south to Aphroditopolis (U.E. 10) in the north. The Herakleopolitans later seem to have considered the north the main threat, ignoring the magnitude of the Theban potential.

The Instruction for Merikare illustrates a close personal relationship between man and god. The king advises his son to deal harshly with rebels but to treat his loyal dependents well and reward them. Thus enriched, they will not oppose him or be won over to rebellion. The value of

---

[3] New English translations and commentaries are needed for the literary texts, many of which are not easily accessible in modern editions. In addition to Gustave Lefebvre, *Romans et contes égyptiens de l'époque pharaonique* (Paris: Adrien-Maisonneuve, 1949), and E. Brunner-Traut, *Altägyptische Märchen* (Dusseldorf-Köln: Eugen Diederichs Verlag, 1963), one can consult the excerpts in John A. Wilson, *Ancient Near Eastern Texts Relating to the Old Testament*, ed. James Pritchard (Princeton: Princeton University Press, 1950), and the older versions in Adolf Erman, *The Ancient Egyptians, A Sourcebook of Their Writings*, trans. A. M. Blackman, introduction by William K. Simpson (New York: Harper & Row, 1966). For specific tales, consult: Sir Alan H. Gardiner, trans., "Merikare," *Journal of Egyptian Archaeology* 1 (1914):20–36; R. O. Faulkner, trans., "The Dispute," *Journal of Egyptian Archaeology* 51 (1965): 53–62; and Sir Alan H. Gardiner, trans., "Neferti," *Journal of Egyptian Archaeology* 1 (1914):100–06.

rhetoric is stressed, for "the strength of a man is his tongue, and speech is mightier than fighting." Of the Bedouin it is said:

> The wretched Amu, it is troublesome for the place in which he is, paltry as to water, because of many trees, and the roads are difficult because of the hills.
>
> He has not stayed in a single place, lack of food drives his feet. He has been fighting since the time of Horus. He does not win, nor is he conquered. He does not announce the day of fighting, like as a thief whom strength holds apart from allies.

The king acknowledges some of his errors, an unusual situation in any royal text.

The First Intermediate Period represents a social restructuring of the country as well as a major shift in religious belief, the nature of which is difficult to assess. The royal ritual spells of the pyramids are now revised for the purpose of nonroyal officials and frequently copied on the wooden coffins at the end of the period. (See Figure 36, page 236.) They relate the various "transformations" after death and the journey of the soul in the afterlife and include much magical and cryptic jargon for outsmarting the enemies on the roads. These Coffin Texts represent the same tradition as the Pyramid Texts from which they are derived. Yet there are shifts in emphasis. *The Instruction for Merikare* also presents a picture of the nature of god in these extracts:

> More acceptable is the character of one just of heart than the sacrificial ox of one who does mischief. Act for god that he may do the like for you, with an offering that replenishes the offering altar, and with inscriptions. This perpetuates your name. God is cognizant of him who acts on his behalf. Well provided are men, the cattle of god. He made heaven and earth to please them. He allayed the thirst for water. He made the air that their nostrils may live. They are his images which have proceeded from his limbs. He arises in heaven according to their desire. He made for them agricultural products, cattle, fowl and fish, in order to nourish them. But he slew his enemies, and destroyed his children, because they planned the making of rebellion.

While not the chief subject, an element of concern for the common man is illustrated in *The Story of the Eloquent Peasant*. It is set in the reign of one of the Herakleopolitan kings. An oasis dweller bids farewell to his wife, leaves grain for her and their children, and sets forth, his donkeys laden with various products to trade at the market. A dishonest official who covets his possessions sets his laundry on the narrow path, forcing the peasant to detour into the field. When a donkey eats a wisp of barley, the official seizes the peasant's property as compensation and beats him. The peasant, however, lodges a complaint with the chief steward. He is so eloquent that the king is informed, orders his words copied, and has food sent to his family while the peasant is detained to plead his case. After nine elaborate denunciations of the officialdom, he is freed, hears his pleas read back, and is awarded the property of his antagonist. Although bombastic and repetitious, with frequent allusions to the scales of justice, miscellaneous sayings, and platitudes, his pleas provide insight into the plight of the oppressed. The king, on the other hand, seems more pleased by the eloquence than angered by the wrongdoings of his official. Yet the story is to some extent an entertainment and exhibition of rhetoric, and we can hardly expect the king to have been overly concerned with minor matters.

The times were hard. During the First Intermediate Period there were famines, and nomarchs recorded gifts of their own grain to the people. A certain pride in town and nome is more evident than loyalty to a remote king. The texts include the expressions "my dependents," "my town," and "my nome," and emphasis was placed on building the local temple and local irrigation systems. One of the nomarchs of Siut took pride in the safety of the traveler on his roads. Inscriptions were even dated according to the years of the nome rather than those of the royal dynasty. This loyalty to the nome is a corollary to the decline of the absolute power of the Memphite kingship of the Old Kingdom.

Of the site of Herakleopolis little remains, particularly from its age of prominence in Dyns. 9 and 10. The *Instruction for Merikare* is consequently of special interest. Thebes, on the other hand, was destined to become a world capital, and records of it are better preserved. Although the major Old Kingdom town was Hermonthis, in the southern part of the nome, the collapse of the Old Kingdom laid the ground for the rise of Thebes. There, in a fertile region of the Nile Valley, the Theban nomarchs extended their influence through alliance with and domination of the neighboring nomes. Coptos to the immediate north became an early ally in spite (or because) of its close ties with Dyns. 7 and 8. The hostility of the three first nomes of Upper Egypt and the rest of the south was eventually overcome. A line of nomarchs with the names Inyotef and Mentuhotpe took over a kingship restricted to u.e. 1–10, with the southern seven nomes as the core, and is known to us as Dyn. 11.

Dyn. 11 began soon after the end of Dyn. 8 and particularly in its second part, was contemporaneous with Dyns. 9 and 10. The first major ruler was Wahankh Inyotef II, in whose long reign of fifty-two years fighting with the north was intermittent. From his tomb at Thebes a fragment of a stele indicates that his domination extended to Aphroditopolis (u.e. 10) and that he also subjugated the Thinite nome (u.e. 8) just to its south. He is shown with five of his hunting dogs with their Libyan names and Egyptian translations—"Blacky," "the Oryx," and the like. When a commission examining the robbing of the tombs visited the site some 960 years later in Dyn. 20, the stele was seen and mentioned. His successor, an old man at his accession, ruled for some seven years.

The next important king is Nebhepetre Mentuhotpe, early in whose fifty-one year reign the Herakleopolitans were finally defeated and the country reunited under Thebes. It appears that he changed his Horus name twice and the writing of his prenomen once, so until recently scholars counted him as several kings. The king created an extraordinary funerary monument in the bay of cliffs known as Deir el Bahri in western Thebes.[4] The monument resembles markedly the Old Kingdom pyramid complexes, but there are significant differences. A valley temple and long (nearly three-quarters of a mile) unroofed causeway led to a forecourt, ramp, and platform. On this platform the central space was occupied by a second square platform or giant altar. The mortuary temple was situated to the rear (west) of this element. The two sides of the ramp, with trees on either side, as well as the space on the platform surrounding the altar served as colonnades with pillars, roof, and reliefs. The burial chamber, hewn out of the rock below the cliff, was entered from a concealed place in the pavement of the mortuary temple and reached by a long, underground ramp. The complex includes the tombs and chapels of six royal ladies and the nearby tomb of Queen Nofru.

Looking over the complex in the bay of cliffs are the rock cut tombs of the chief officials of the day, among them the chief treasurer Khety and the chancellor Meketre. In a chamber of the latter's tomb were many models of boats, offering-bearers, workshops, and houses; a master carpenter had created in miniature his master's environment. The practice of rendering some of the relief scenes in three-dimensional sculpture arose during the First Intermediate Period, but these models are of a higher level of achievement than any others. From them we can learn how a private villa, a weaver's shop, a brewery, a granary, and well-rigged boats looked and functioned.[5]

In another of these tombs a cache of letters of the succeeding reign was found. They relate to the affairs of a garrulous farmer, Hekanakht, the Ka-priest of the vizier Ipi. He wrote to his family about seeding, the harvest, and personal matters. He was particularly anxious to rent some land at the right price and to see that his favorite relatives were not treated badly in his absence.[6]

Thus Nebhepetre Mentuhotpe had a court around him in death that paralleled the pyramid and mastaba tomb complexes of the Old Kingdom.

[4] For a description with references, see I. E. S. Edwards, *The Pyramids of Egypt*, rev. ed. (London: Penguin Books, 1961).

[5] H. E. Winlock, *Models of Daily Life in Ancient Egypt* (Cambridge: Harvard University Press, 1955).

[6] T. G. H. James, *The Hekanakhte Papers and Other Early Middle Kingdom Documents* (New York: Metropolitan Museum of Art, 1962).

Later, Queen Hatshepsut built a far larger mortuary temple adjacent to that of Nebhepetre, and Thutmose III added a temple between them. Each with a causeway and way stations on the route from its valley buildings, the three temples form an impressive site at Deir el Bahri.

In a relief from Gebelein, south of Thebes, the king is shown early in his reign smiting first an Egyptian, then a Nubian, an Asiatic, and a Libyan. This is probably a general statement, but his activity in each area is independently attested. He defeated the last of the Herakleopolitan dynasts to bring Egypt again under a single government, administered this time from Thebes. The districts of Nubia appear to have had an independent kingship in the First Intermediate Period, but there is evidence that the agents of Nebhepetre were active there in his reign and that Lower Nubia (Wawat) was at least nominally incorporated into Upper Egypt. From an inscription and other evidence it is clear that the king had to deal with the Asiatic Bedouin. The king is mentioned in a later dedication at Sinai, so he may have attempted to reopen the mines there. No precise details are provided about Libyan campaigns, but it is evident that the Libyans were not a particular threat at the time.

Dyn. 11 ends with Nebhepetre's two successors, Sankhkare Mentuhotpe (twelve years) and Nebtowyre Mentuhotpe (two years). At the end of the latter's reign there is some confusion in the records, possibly due to a lacuna in the annals from which the Turin Canon was compiled. Nebtowyre was not included in the king lists, although he is now generally placed at the end of the dynasty.

Under Sankhkare there is a record of an expedition of three thousand men to the Hammamat during which several large wells or water basins were made. The expedition went as far as Punt, usually identified as an area on the Red Sea's Somali coast, and returned with products of Punt as well as blocks of stone from the Hammamat for royal statues. Under Nebtowyre an even larger expedition, ten thousand men according to the text, quarried in the Hammamat under the vizier Amunemhet for a sarcophagus for the king. The lid for the sarcophagus was chosen from a block on which a gazelle gave birth. A second unusual occurrence recorded was a great rainfall and the discovery of a catch basin filled to the brim with clear water that had not been sullied by gazelles and nomads.[7]

There are several temple reliefs of Sankhkare, executed in a fine, meticulous style, and other evidence for his reign. In the Ramesside king

[7] For the quarrying texts in the Wadi Hammamat, see James Henry Breasted, *Ancient Records of Egypt*, vol. 1 (Chicago: University of Chicago Press, 1906), §§ 427–56. For recent studies on the quarrying in that region and in the Sinai, with references to the main sources, see: Hans Goedicke, "Some Remarks on Stone Quarrying in the Egyptian Middle Kingdom (2060–1786 B.C.)," *Journal of the American Research Center* 3 (1964):43–50, and idem, "The Inscriptions of Hr-w-rʿ (Sinai no. 90)," *Mitteilungen des Deutschen Archäologischen Instituts, Abteilung Kairo* 18 (1962):14–25.

lists at Abydos and Sakkara, he and his predecessor, Nebhepetre, are the only kings of Dyn. 11 mentioned. Whether the confusion in the lists reflects a political upheaval at the end of Dyn. 11 or merely a gap in the sources cannot be determined. The only texts of Nebtowyre recorded his first and second regnal years and were confined to the quarry sites, the Wadi Hammamat and the Wadi el Hudi; he is not attested by building remains. Perhaps he was followed by a succession of pretenders to the throne of the Inyotef-Mentuhotep dynasty, or he may have been succeeded directly by the founder of Dyn. 12.

[2] DYNASTY 12

At the beginning of the second millennium, about 1991 B.C., the kingship of Upper and Lower Egypt was assumed by Amunemhet I, the founder of Dyn. 12. He was of nonroyal birth, very likely the vizier Amunemhet who led the quarrying expedition to the Hammamat in Year 2 of Nebtowyre Mentuhotpe. He was an extraordinary innovator and administrator whose effect upon the Egyptian state was lasting. In his five-name titulary the Horus name "repeating births," or "renaissance," proclaimed a new era.

A literary composition known as *The Prophecy of Neferti* further developed this theme. The scene is set in the reign of Snefru, for whose entertainment and edification a learned man predicts the country's future. He foretells a period of natural disasters and anarchy in the state, the land in lamentation and overrun by Asiatics, at the end of which a king called Ameny was to come from the south, placate the gods, and drive away the Asiatics and Libyans.

At the accession of Amunemhet, Egypt had only recently recovered from the anarchy of the First Intermediate Period, and the borders in the northeast and in the south were not yet really secure. Still, Egypt was recovering stability after her initial period of anarchy and upheaval. The Herakleopolitans had succeeded in pacifying the Delta nomes and the northern part of Upper Egypt. Then, the Thebans had united the south and conquered the Herakleopolitans, profiting from the efforts of the latter. Finally, Amunemhet seized the kingship from the Theban rulers and united Egypt, thereby profiting from both the Herakleopolitans' and the Thebans' efforts.

His first innovation was the shift of the royal residence from Thebes to a new town, just south of Memphis, which he named Itj-towy, "Amunemhet is the one who has taken possession of the two lands."[8] The land

[8] William K. Simpson, "Studies in the Twelfth Egyptian Dynasty: I–II," *Journal of the American Research Center in Egypt* 2 (1963):53–63.

could be more effectively controlled from this point than from Thebes; like Ankara and Washington, D.C., Itj-towy was a "new" town.

His second innovation was the reorganization of the nome structure. The nomarchs' territory was precisely surveyed and marked, and their obligations to the state were defined.[9] The nomarchs of the Middle Kingdom held their offices on an hereditary principle, subject to royal confirmation. They delivered taxes and dues to the various agencies of the state and supplied labor forces for royal projects on a local level as well as for quarrying or military expeditions. Significant of this partial autonomy is the occasional use of year counts according to the era of the nome. Thus Year 25 of the oryx nome (u.e. 16) corresponds to Year 43 of Sesostris I. The tombs of these nomarchs show them attended by their various administrative assistants, servants, and families while inspecting their domains.

Amunemhet's third innovation was the establishment of the coregency system.[10] In his twenty-first regnal year, the king designated his son and heir, Sesostris, as coruler. The two kings thenceforth ruled jointly, and certain documents were dated in terms of the joint reign, Year 30 of Amunemhet I corresponding to Year 10 of Sesostris I. Although such a system had certain inherent problems, it was substantially successful for its purposes. It ensured the succession and minimized the likelihood of a palace rebellion at the death of the king—that is, it made for a smooth transition from one reign to the next. Finally, the new king was given experience and tested. The practice of coregencies may go back to the earliest dynasties, and a form of it was used in the New Kingdom. In Dyn. 12, however, it appears to have been a regular feature of the kingship, with full royal titles accorded to the younger king at his investiture, and the stability thereby achieved was one of the reasons for the success of the dynasty.

In setting out to establish a new era the dynasty took care to root its program in the past. The Memphite pyramid complex was copied, and the plan of the pyramid temple of Sesostris I at el Lisht, south of Dahshur, is

---

[9] The term "feudalism" has been applied to the Egyptian state in the First Intermediate Period and Middle Kingdom, with the nomarchs thought of as roughly equivalent to the barons of the Middle Ages. (W. Schenkel, "Zum Feudalismus der ersten Zwischenzeit Ägyptens.") The analogy is useful but not exact. Feudalism is a highly technical system in the Middle Ages, and our sources for Egyptian society are too scant for valid comparisons. It is best to abandon the term for any period of Egyptian history, with the possible exception of the Third Intermediate Period. In translating Egyptian titles, we constantly face the same danger, for we tend to translate along medieval lines: prince, count, chamberlain, steward, and the like—terms which are meaningful only in respect to their Egyptian equivalent, and have no more validity than governor, representative, secretary of the treasury, or commissar.

[10] William K. Simpson, "The Single-dated Monuments of Sesostris I: An Aspect of the Institution of Coregency in the Twelfth Dynasty," *Journal of Near Eastern Studies* 15 (1956):214–19.

a near facsimile of that of Pepy II of Dyn. 6 at Sakkara. Statues were dedicated to the rulers of the Old Kingdom and Dyn. 11. The cult of Snefru at Dahshur was resumed; and this same king appears as the ruler in *The Prophecy of Neferti*. Art and architecture flourished, continuing the revival made at the court of Nebhepetre in the preceding dynasty.

The nature of the kingship itself changed, however. The inaccessible god-king of the Old Kingdom became the good shepherd or herdsman of his people by the time of the Middle Kingdom.[11] The idealized, youthful, and sometimes bland confidence expressed in royal statuary of the Old Kingdom changes to a brooding, concerned, and even worried strength, sometimes almost brutal, in the portraits of Sesostris III and Amunemhet III. The sphinx was revived as a medium for royal portraiture, since it so forcefully expressed the power of the kingship.

Three literary compositions relate to Amunemhet I. *The Prophecy of Neferti*, discussed above, announces the coming of Amunemhet. *The Instruction of Amunemhet* describes to the king's son the real or attempted assassination of his father and advises the heir on the conduct of the kingship: "Trust not a brother, know not a friend, and make not for yourself intimate companions." The third is *The Story of Sinuhe*. These, and later compositions of the dynasty such as *The Loyalist Instruction* emphasizing the virtue of loyalty to the king, are a literature of propaganda—court compositions in which the king naturally appears in a good light.[12] *The Instruction of Amunemhet* is a sort of apologia, vaunting the achievements of a usurper and citing the ingratitude and disloyalty of his dependents.

The courtier Sinuhe relates how he fled impulsively, as if in a trance, at the death of Amunemhet. Finding a rudderless boat on the west bank of the Nile south of Memphis, he crossed the river, made his way toward Palestine, and, almost dead from thirst, was befriended by Semitic nomads. As an exile, he prospered, married the daughter of a chieftain, and became a chieftain in his own right. Toward the end of his life, he has returned to Egypt, forgiven for his inexplicable flight. There he looks forward to a proper burial instead of interment in a goatskin on Asiatic soil. Among the reasons for the popularity of and interest in *The Story of Sinuhe* are its use of language, the descriptions of the mourning at the death of the king, the adventures of an Egyptian abroad, Sinuhe's fight with a Bedouin chief (prefiguring the David and Goliath episode in I Samuel 17), the description of Palestine, the theme of Sinuhe's homecoming to a proper old age and a traditional burial, the hymn of praise to Sesostris I (stressing the king's wisdom, power, and forgiving qualities), and the figure of Sinuhe as a Bedouin sheikh at the Egyptian court.

Egypt's relations with her neighbors also changed during this period of

[11] Dieter Müller, "Der gute Hirte: Ein Beitrag zur Geschichte ägyptischen Bildrede," *Zeitschrift für Ägyptische Sprache und Altertumskunde* 86 (1961):126–44.
[12] On the literature of propaganda, see Georges Posener, *Littérature et politique dans l'Égypte de la XIIᵉ dynastie* (Paris: Librairie Ancienne Honoré Champion, 1956).

restoration. She exploited the trade to the south for African products, and Nubia itself for gold, copper, semi-precious stones, and quarries. At strategic points, primarily just south of the second cataract in the present Republic of the Sudan, the kings built fortresses to control the movement of the Nubians, and northern Nubia was effectively subjugated. The best preserved of these fortresses, at Buhen, resembles a medieval fortress complete with battlements, slit windows for archers, dry moats, and other defensive elements.[13]

Egypt's general hostility toward her neighbors is illustrated by the execration texts of the time of Sesostris III and later. These imprecations against traditional enemies, found on statuettes and pottery vessels, list the names of rulers and their domains. Over thirty Nubian peoples are mentioned—a large number of names—indicating a familiarity with the lands to the south.

By the reign of Sesostris III (1878–1843 B.C.), when Nubia was firmly under Egyptian control, Palestine and Syria had definitely come under Egyptian influence.[14] Markets for Egyptian exports, many Palestinian and Syrian sites attest to the influence of Egyptian traders. The principalities of Palestine were never actually incorporated into Egypt. On the contrary, the Egyptians were constantly threatened by raids. Amunemhet built the "Walls of the Prince," a line of fortifications to check these incursions, and his successors maintained a balance of power so that Egypt was not seriously threatened. That there was friction is evidenced by references in the execration texts, particularly to the city-states of southern Palestine, and, for the first time the names Jerusalem, Askalon, and Shechem appear in written texts.

After the time of Sinuhe many Egyptians traveled through the Levant, especially to the trade center at Byblos, near modern Beirut. The finds of statues of Egyptian royalty at such sites as Ras Shamra, Qatna, and Megiddo once were thought to suggest Egyptian control over the Levantine area in the Middle Kingdom. At present, few scholars uphold this view, but mention in the execration texts classifies the Levantine neighbors as enemies.

The success of the dynasty in establishing a strong government at home and considerable influence abroad was largely the result of an effective administrative system. A northern department, a southern department, and a department of the "Head of the South" were the three main administrative divisions.[15] In the reign of Sesostris III the local nomarchs were curbed, and the office of Governor of Upper Egypt was temporarily

---

[13] A. W. Lawrence, "Ancient Egyptian Fortifications," *Journal of Egyptian Archaeology* 51 (1965):69–94.

[14] W. A. Ward, "Egypt and the East Mediterranean in the Early Second Millennium B.C.," *Orientalia* 30 (1961):22–45 and 129–55.

[15] William C. Hayes, "Notes on the Government of Egypt in the Late Middle Kingdom," *Journal of Near Eastern Studies* 12 (1953):31–39.

revived.[16] The Fayyum basin provided an opportunity for land reclamation by the control of flow through barrages. These newly won lands contributed to the rising prosperity of the country as a whole and of the royal family in particular. Sesostris II and more so his grandson Amunemhet III devoted their energy to the Fayyum, built their pyramids nearby, and honored its ancient crocodile god, Sobek (Suchos), by erecting temples in his honor. The dynasty of Amunemhet and Sesostris came to an end with a ruling queen, Sobkkare Sobknofru (1789–1786 B.C.), in whose name the god Sobek is honored.

A word has been said about the literary texts that relate to the history of the dynasty. There are many other texts, although few are royal inscriptions. The expeditions sent to the quarries frequently left informative records on the rock quarry faces or on free-standing stelae. In one, an official boasts of overcoming the great hardships of an unusual summer mission; the mountain paths branded his feet and the contours of the land shimmered even in the early morning. Yet he and his crew returned successfully with the prized turquoise. Several stelae set up in the Egyptian temple precinct at Sinai have representations of the brother of the Palestinian prince of Retunu with his donkey.

Among the papyrus documents of the Middle Kingdom, the archive from Illahun is particularly varied. It includes: a text on midwifery; a veterinary manual; hymns to Sesostris III on the occasion of his visit to a southern town; mathematical exercises; announcements of feast days based on star risings; instructions for provisioning various cults; lists of stolen goods; enumerations of households; numerous official letters and model letters used as exercises; and many accounts relating to deliveries and inspections. Among the documents is a conveyance of property from a man to his wife, with many features of a present-day will. The grantor specified that his wife could transmit the property to any one of their children, made provision for his burial, and appointed a friend as his son's guardian. The deed was filed in a local records office along with a copy of the document whereby the grantor originally obtained the property from his older brother.

The Reisner Papyri, a set of accounts found in a tomb on the opposite side of the river from Abydos, provide details of the expenditure of labor on building projects. The accounts include measurements and the cubic content of earthworks and blocks of stone, lists of men arranged by work gangs, and a series of transactions regarding the repairing of copper tools used in the dockyard workshop. There are also administrative orders from the vizier, with directions for the shipment of commodities and the dispatch of men and boats. Through these quarry texts, stelae, inscriptions

---

[16] William K. Simpson, "Provenance and Date of the Stela of Amun-wosre," *Journal of Egyptian Archaeology* 52 (1966):174.

in the rock tombs, and papyri, the life of Dyn. 12 officials becomes vivid and meaningful.

The dynasty prospered through its administrative technology; it was an age of the bureaucrat and the accountant. Nubia was effectively controlled, and Syria and Palestine were not yet under the pressure of Mesopotamian expansion. The dynasty spanned two centuries (1991–1786 B.C.) before its succession failed.

[3] DYNASTIES 13 THROUGH 17

Dyn. 13, founded by King Sobkhotpe I, is designated by the Turin Royal Canon as the dynasty that followed the kings of Itj-towy. The kings were of Theban origin but continued to rule from the north.[17] Although the eight rulers of Dyn. 12 reigned about two hundred years, Dyn. 13, with its fifty to sixty rulers (Turin Canon), lasted but 150 years. The kingship obviously changed hands at a rapid pace. In contrast, the officialdom remained relatively stable and hereditary. The vizierate passed from father to son over a period of several successive reigns. The frequency of change in the kingship is difficult to explain, since political upheaval does not seem to have been very great. Possibly several kings were succeeded by an elder brother rather than by a son, for it is unlikely that the rulers were elected for terms. There is also evidence that the dynasty was made up of several subfamilies, for there are several groups of kings unrelated to their predecessors.

Egypt's prosperity was in decline in Dyn. 13, but monuments and texts of Neferhotpe I and Sobkhotpe III are found throughout the land, thereby indicating their control. Sobkhotpe III is now mainly known from the chance find of fiscal accounts for a month during which he visited Thebes. The accounts of another archive list 215 Asiatic servants attached to the household of an Egyptian official. Among them are the first instances of the names from which Menahem and Sapphira are derived. In the temple of Byblos, the cartouche of his successor, Neferhotpe I, occurs in a relief of the Byblite prince Yantin. Neferhotpe is also known from a stele at Abydos recording his building activities there. The interest of the text lies in its mention of the king's visit to a library to consult the records of the temple of Osiris, Foremost-of-the-Westerners, for the purpose of properly fashioning the cult image of the god.[18]

At some time the western Delta seceded from the control of the rulers of Dyn. 13 and established itself as an independent kingdom based

---

[17] For the major study of the Second Intermediate Period, see Jürgen von Beckerath, *Untersuchungen zur politischen Geschichte der zweiten Zwischenzeit in Ägypten* (Gluckstadt: J. J. Augustin, 1965).

[18] Breasted, *Ancient Records of Egypt*, vol. 1, §§ 753–65.

at Xois and reckoned as Dyn. 14 (1715–1650 b.c.). These seventy-six kings, who ruled 184 years according to one version of Manetho, are almost unknown save for Manetho, the Turin Canon, and isolated monuments. Archeological excavation has not changed the picture appreciably. After the reigns of Neferhotpe and several of his successors, the land became still further divided through the fall of the eastern Delta to a foreign dynasty, the so-called Hyksos.

At this point Egypt entered upon the Second Intermediate Period with a divided kingship. The end of the male line of the kings of Dyn. 12, coupled with the curbing of the nomarchs in the time of Sesostris III, brought the administrative and official class to the fore. Among them were immigrants of Asiatic origin with names belonging to the Amorite (Semitic) language group.[19] The kingship was evidently held by several royal families in a kind of irregular alternation—that is, a short line of kings would be succeeded by an opposing family. Thus, Egypt was splintered— the western Delta a sort of secessionist state at Xois (Dyn. 14), the eastern Delta in the hands of the Hyksos (Dyn. 15) and lesser Asiatic dynasts (Dyn. 16), and the traditional "legal" kingship first in the north at Itj-towy (Dyn. 13) and later restricted to Thebes (Dyn. 17). In addition, Nubian rulers seized this opportunity to become independent and to conduct their own dealings with all or most of the Egyptian powers.

The Hyksos problem is a major theme of history involving opposing interpretations.[20] One tradition is that of Manetho, retold by the Jewish historian Flavius Josephus:

> Tutimaios. In his reign, for what cause I know not, a blast of God smote us; and unexpectedly from the regions of the East invaders of obscure race marched in confidence of victory against our land. By main force they seized it without striking a blow; and having overpowered the rulers of the land, they then burned our cities ruthlessly, razed to the ground the temples of the gods, and treated all the natives with a cruel hostility, massacring some and leading into slavery the wives and children of others. Finally, they appointed as king one of their number whose name was Salitis; he had his seat in Memphis, levying tribute from Upper and Lower Egypt, and always leaving garrisons behind in the most advantageous places.

Scholars have long pondered this description and attempted to identify the invaders of obscure race and the political background in Palestine.

[19] William C. Hayes, *A Papyrus of the Late Middle Kingdom in the Brooklyn Museum* (New York: The Brooklyn Museum, 1955).
[20] Torgny Säve-Söderbergh, "The Hyksos Rule in Egypt," *Journal of Egyptian Archaeology* 37 (1951):53–71; John van Seters, *The Hyksos: A New Investigation* (New Haven: Yale University Press, 1966); von Beckerath, *Untersuchungen zur politischen Geschichte der zweiten Zwischenzeit in Ägypten*; and Donald B. Redford, "The Hyksos Invasion in History and Tradition," *Orientalia* 39 (1970):1–51.

The invasion theory is also supported, it seems, by a text of Queen Hat-shepsut of Dyn. 18 in which she claims to have put in order and rebuilt the temples after kings who ruled "without Re." Another reading of the evidence regards the Josephus account as propagandistic. The Hyksos in-deed used the title "son of Re" and in many cases incorporated the name of Re in their own names. Moreover, there does not seem to be a well-attested razing of the temples at this particular time, and the state seems to have functioned normally.

Noted scholars still attempt to see in the obscure race (on the basis of the names of the rulers) Hurrian or other Indo-European elements. How-ever, most believe that these rulers, although they were indeed of foreign origin and embraced some Hurrian elements, belonged to the Amorite (northwest Semitic) peoples well attested in Syria and in Palestine during the Middle Bronze II Period. The northeast Delta was increasingly infil-trated by Amorites from southern Palestine. At a point in the Second Intermediate Period, one of these magnates assumed control of a large area and, through a kind of *coup d'état*, set himself up as king. In con-temporaneous sources and in the Turin Royal Canon these kings are designated by the term *heqa khoswe* (Hyksos), "chief of foreign lands."

Unlike the kings of Dyns. 13 and 14, the Hyksos rulers maintained relatively long reigns and prospered, soon extending their influence through most of Egypt. It is not clear whether, in dominating the western Delta, the Hyksos supplanted or treated as vassals the rulers of the Xoite Dynasty (Dyn. 14); presumably their increased importance reduced the latter to vassals. The two main rulers were Khyan (whose name some regard as Amorite) and Aauserre Apopi, who ruled for over forty years. In his reign the resurgent power of Thebes became manifest, and the Hyksos were forced to begin a retreat from their Egyptian domain.

The period has recently become better known through systematic excavations by an Austrian expedition at Tell ed Debaa, near the site of Qantir in the eastern Delta.[21] Here a temple and burial site have been brought to light. The main burials consist of bodies of large stature and build unlike the Mediterranean type represented by the Egyptians and the Semites of Palestine and Syria. The non-Egyptian pottery and grave goods are identical to those of the Middle Bronze Age in Palestine. Archeo-logically it is as if the site were actually in Palestine. The characteristic pottery ware is the so-called Tell el Yahudiyeh juglet. In connection with the burials of the men, who frequently have daggers with them, are pairs of small equines, either onagers or donkeys. A level of destruction follows the late Middle Kingdom levels and precedes the Hyksos levels. Thus there is much to support the Josephus account in the discoveries from Tell ed Debaa, if the evidence has been read correctly by the excavators.

[21] Manfred Bietak, "Bericht über die erste Grabungskampagne auf Tell Ed-Dab'a im Ostdelta Ägyptens im Sommer 1966," *Bustan* 1 (1968):20–25; and idem, "Ausgrabun-gen in Ägypten," *Archiv für Orientforschung* 22 (1968):182–85.

The next era is designated as the "wars of liberation," a somewhat propagandistic term in itself, for which our sources are Theban rather than Hyksos.[22] A fragmentary literary tale called the *Contending of Apopi and Seqenenre* suggests that the Theban ruler Seqenenre (Dyn. 17) was taunted by the Hyksos king Apopi about the noise of hippopotami in a canal; the canal may have been at Thebes or in a Theban possession in the Delta.[23] The end of the story is not preserved, but it must have reflected Seqenenre's refusal to obey the Hyksos king. The real "heroes" of the war, however were the brothers Kamose and Ahmose. The account of their deeds is preserved on two stelae set up in the temple of Karnak, the first of which (now in fragments) was copied in part on a writing board.[24] Kamose calls together his court to announce his dissatisfaction with the division of the kingship, and his unwillingness to continue sharing the throne with an Asiatic in the north and a Nubian in the south. His advisers, however, counsel him to refrain since they prefer the *status quo* and fear more is to be lost than gained. They point out that it is still possible to graze their cattle in the north and that the border is firm as far as the first cataract region. Ignoring their advice, Kamose moves northward with his Theban troops and Nubian mercenaries to overthrow Neferusy, a town in U.E. 15, where the local ruler is a vassal of Apopi. After a missing portion of the account Kamose is seen laying siege to the Hyksos residence at Avaris. A Hyksos messenger is captured with Apopi's proposal to the Nubian dynast that they both attack Kamose, one from the north and one from the south. "Then we can divide the towns of this Egypt between us."

Although Kamose returned to Thebes to celebrate his success, it is evident that Avaris did not fall; neither were the Hyksos expelled from Egypt. This task remained for his brother and successor, Ahmose, the first king of Dyn. 18.[25]

[22] "It was in the middle of the sixteenth century B.C. that the Thebans began their revolt against the overlordship of the Hyksos Pharaohs, which because it eventually prospered was not called treason." (Cyril Aldred, *Akhenaten, Pharaoh of Egypt: A New Study* (London: Thames and Hudson, 1968), p. 35.)

[23] Hans Geodicke, "Ein geographisches Unicum," *Zeitschrift für Ägyptische Sprache und Altertumskunde* 88 (1963):83–97.

[24] Sir Alan H. Gardiner, "The Defeat of the Hyksos by Kamōse: The Carnarvon Tablet, No. 1," *Journal of Egyptian Archaeology* 3 (1916):93–110; Mohammed Hammad, "Découverte d'une stèle du roi Kamose," *Chronique d'Égypte* 30 (1955): 198–208; Labib Habachi, "Preliminary Report on Kamose Stela and Other Inscribed Blocks ... at Karnak," *Annales du Service des Antiquités de l'Égypte* 53 (1955): 195–202; and Torgny Säve-Söderbergh," The Nubian Kingdom of the Second Intermediate Period," *Kush* 4 (1956):54–61.

[25] T. G. H. James, "Egypt: From the Expulsion of the Hyksos to Amenophis I," fasc. 34, *Cambridge Ancient History*, rev. ed. (Cambridge: Cambridge University Press, 1965); Hammad, "Découverte d'une stèle du roi Kamose"; and Gardiner, "The Defeat of the Hyksos by Kamōse: The Carnarvon Tablet, No. 1."

FIGURE 37 Detail of the Queen of Punt, from the mortuary temple of Queen Hatshepsut at Dier el Bahri. (Dyn. 18.)

[XI]

THE NEW KINGDOM

With the accession of Ahmose about 1558 B.C., the expulsion of the Hyksos during his reign, and the reunification of the country by the south, Egypt involved herself in the destinies of her neighbors and initiated a radically new era in her history.[1] The northward thrusts of the Theban dynasts continued until the Egyptians crossed the Euphrates River fifty years later. Egyptian armies fought at Megiddo in Palestine and Kadesh on the Syrian Orontes. The same dynasty erected Egyptian temples on a grand scale 1,280 miles south of Memphis, at Gebel Barkal in the Sudan. The vast riches that the state accrued through these foreign expeditions changed the very fabric of Egyptian society. No longer could Egypt function as a Nilotic kingdom in relative isolation. This was an age of intense political and diplomatic activity in which the main protagonists were Egypt, the Mittani state on the Middle Euphrates, the Hittite kingdom in

---

[1] The bibliography on the New Kingdom is so extensive that it is difficult to select a few items for special mention. A comprehensive list of titles could easily exceed several volumes of this length. In addition to the standard histories cited (Breasted, Drioton-Vandier, Gardiner, and Wilson), the following can be recommended for introductory reading: William C. Hayes, "Egypt: Internal Affairs from Tuthmosis I to the Death of Amenophis III," Parts I and II, fasc. 10, *Cambridge Ancient History*, rev. ed. (Cambridge: Cambridge University Press, 1962); Donald B. Redford, *History and Chronology of the Eighteenth Dynasty of Egypt: Seven Studies* (Toronto: University of Toronto Press, 1967); Charles F. Nims, *Thebes of the Pharaohs: Pattern for Every City* (New York: Stein & Day, 1965); Christiane Desroches-Noblecourt, *Tutankhamen: Life and Death of a Pharaoh* (New York: New York Graphic Society, 1963); Cyril Aldred, *Akhenaten, Pharaoh of Egypt: A New Study* (London: Thames and Hudson, 1968); James Henry Breasted, *Ancient Records of Egypt*, vols. 2, 3, and 4 (Chicago: University of Chicago Press, 1906); Arpag Mekhitarian, *Egyptian Painting* (Geneva: Skira, 1954); R. O. Faulkner, "Egypt: From the Inception of the Nineteenth Dynasty to the Death of Ramesses III, fasc. 52, *Cambridge Ancient History*, rev. ed. (1966); and Jaroslav Černý, "Egypt: From the Death of Ramesses III to the End of the Twenty-first Dynasty," fasc. 27, *Cambridge Ancient History*, rev. ed. (1965).

Anatolia, Assyria in northern Mesopotamia, Babylonia in southern Mesopotamia, and a host of principalities in Syria and Palestine. Ethnic movements involving the Amorites, the Canaanites, the Sea Peoples, and the
masses across the Caucasus both changed the political and cultural configuration of the Near East and came to play a part in the early history of
Greece and the Aegean world. (See Figure 38, page 258.) Egypt became a
melting pot, as Amorites entering from the northeast, Nubians from
the south, and Libyans from the west rose to important positions. The
Thutmosid Dynasty of Theban princes, founded by Ahmose, ruled for
about 250 years as Dyn. 18 and was succeeded by the Ramesside dynasties,
installed by Horemheb, which endured for some 220 years as Dyns. 19 and
20. In spite of unremitting destruction and quarrying of the monuments,
robbing of the cemeteries, and continued habitation of the great towns,
the physical remains of the New Kingdom are still wonders of the world,
and the legacy of statuary, painting, literature, and legal and administrative
archives is no less impressive.

[1] DYNASTY 18

Dyn. 18 can be divided into several major subdivisions. The early
Ahmosid stage consists of Ahmose (1558–1533), Amunhotpe I (1533–
1512), Thutmose I (1512–1500), Thutmose II (1500–1490), and Hatshepsut (1490–1469). Although there were some military campaigns after
the expulsion of the Hyksos, the period was basically unmilitaristic in its
outlook. Yet Thutmose I could have boasted that his empire reached from
the third cataract in the south to the Euphrates in the north. As a second
main division we can include the independent reign of Thutmose III
(1469–1436), the reign of Amunhotpe II (1438–1412), and perhaps that
of Thutmose IV (1412–1402). The first two of these reigns, in contrast to
those of the preceding period, were extremely militaristic, with almost
annual campaigns in Syria and Palestine. The third subdivision represents
the last part of the reign of Thutmose IV and the entire reign of Amunhotpe III (1402–1363). It was an age of extreme luxury in the royal court,
unparalleled building schemes for palaces and temples, and intense diplomatic maneuvering abroad. The fourth stage of the dynasty encompasses
the extraordinary reign of Amunhotpe IV (Akhenaten) (1363–1347) and
those of Smenkhkare (1349–1347), Tutankhamun (1347–1338), and Ay
(1337–1333). The fifth and last part of the dynasty, the reign of Horemheb (1333–1303), represents a reaction against the preceding stage. This
chronology of the dynasty, by D. B. Redford,[2] is subject to change.

[2] Donald B. Redford, "On the Chronology of the Egyptian Eighteenth Dynasty, *Journal
of Near Eastern Studies* 25 (1966):113–24.

Although the length of some reigns is known, others have to be estimated. As the overlapping dates show, there are coregencies in which a king began to reign during the lifetime of his predecessor. Events in Syria, Assyria, the Hittite country, and the city-states of Palestine and Syria must be fitted into the chronology of Egypt and considered in estimating the reigns. Some scholars place the end of the dynasty in 1320 and others in 1303 B.C., partly on the basis of the necessity for fitting in the events of western Asia.

The terminology of European historiography is so embedded in the vocabulary of our thought that certain parallels can usefully be drawn to the terms "renaissance," "reformation" and "counterreformation." These terms have lost some of their value, even for European history, as further research has indicated their limitations, and in any case the analogies to Dyn. 18 in Egypt must be drawn with numerous reservations.[3] The first three stages of the dynasty have elements of the Renaissance. Egypt, recently reunified, sought ties with her past. The style of Middle Kingdom statuary and painting was revived but transformed into an art distinctly of the New Kingdom. To some extent the literature of the past was also studied: compositions such as *The Instruction for Merikare* and *The Instructions of Ptahhotpe* were copied. The voyages of discovery of the European Renaissance have parallels in the expedition sent by Hatshepsut to Punt and the Egyptian penetration of Nubia in the south and Syria and Palestine in the northeast. In some respects the age of Akhenaten parallels the Reformation, although it is difficult to imagine more dissimilar characters than the Egyptian king and Martin Luther. In its crucial elements Atenism represented a return to the religion of the sun god, an overt rebellion against the establishment of Amun. The royal defiance was symbolized by the later erasure of the name of Amun from all visible monuments, a shift in the royal residence and capital, the publication on boundary stelae and walls of a new creed, and a return to the autocracy of the pyramid builders. The political, religious, and military policies represented by Horemheb can be seen as a counterreformation.

Each reign can be organized in a traditional history under five headings: first, the length of the reign, the presence or absence of coregencies, and the parentage and family of the king; second, the office-holders of the administration with the names and careers of the viziers, the chief stewards of the temple of Amun, the overseers of the treasury, the overseers of the granary, and so forth; third, the royal building program for the palaces and

---

[3] In a history as long as that of Egypt, terms such as "reform" and "renaissance" can be employed at more than one point. Thus, the term "renaissance" is applied to Dyns. 12 and 26, as well as to the end of Dyn. 20 and beginning of Dyn. 21. Periods of administrative reform are connected with Amunemhet I and Sesostris III of Dyn. 12, Horemheb of Dyn. 18, Seti I of Dyn. 19, the kings of Dyn. 20 at the time of the prosecution of the tomb robbers, and Amasis of Dyn. 26.

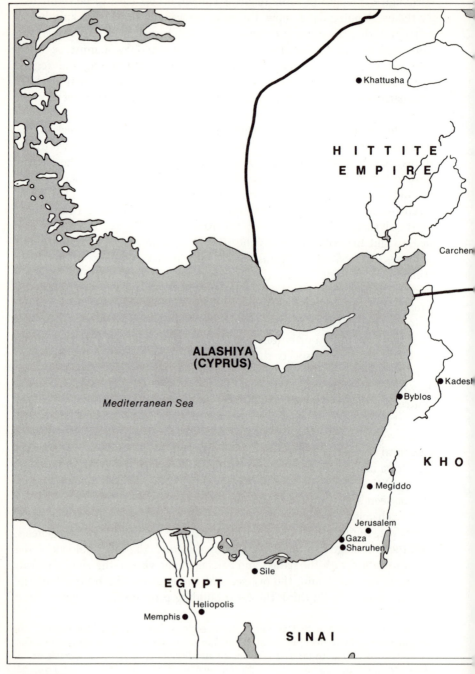

FIGURE 38

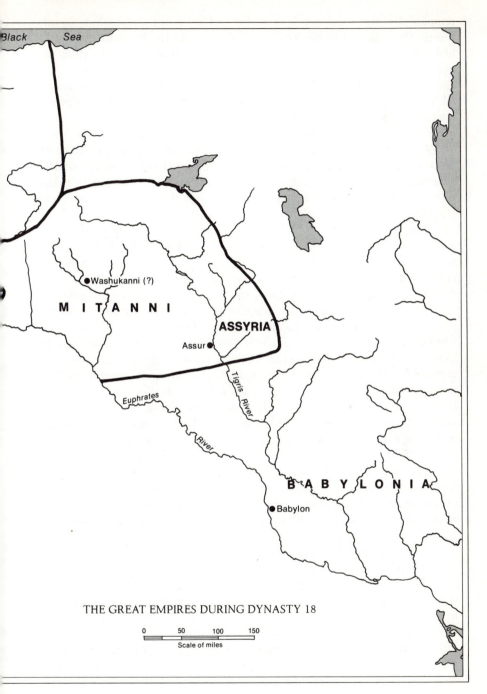

THE GREAT EMPIRES DURING DYNASTY 18

0   50   100   150

Scale of miles

temples, for the royal tomb, and for public works throughout Egypt; fourth, the activities of the kings in Nubia and in the lands to the south; fifth, the Egyptian involvement in western Asia. It is possible to study an office such as the vizierate and follow its holders from the beginning to the end of the dynasty. The history of a dynasty can also be traced through additions to and reconstructions of a temple. It is possible to trace Egypt's relations with a specific foreign area, such as Nubia or western Asia, over a period of years within the dynasty. In terms of the overall administration of Egypt, however, it is still not possible to sort out the precise roles of taxation and distribution assumed by the administrative branches of the government, the temples, and the land-owners and tenants—and this despite the fact that documentation is relatively extensive for the New Kingdom.

The expulsion of the Hyksos was a long, drawn out program. The scant sources for the end of this campaign are the tomb biographies of nobles of el Kab-Nekhen (U.E. 3). In the reign of Ahmose, a noble named Ahmose son of Ebana recounts his campaign in the Delta at the siege of Avaris, in which he served on one of the ships. When the town finally fell he captured a man and three women, and they were given to him as slaves. Sharuhen, a town in southern Palestine, resisted for a number of years, and Ahmose son of Ebana was similarly rewarded when it eventually fell. When the fighting shifted to the southern border, he was there also and received five more slaves and five units of land in his town. Another el Kab noble narrates in his tomb biography his service from the time of Ahmose through the reign of Amunhotpe I, those of Thutmose I and II, and the joint reign of Hatshepsut and Thutmose III. He lists the battle rewards, including bracelets, necklaces, and armlets of gold, he received in each reign. Doubtless he also received slaves and gifts of land. In his old age he was attached to the court of Hatshepsut to rear her daughter and heiress, Nefrure. These warriors were representative of a distinct element of the dynasty, the military who fought in Nubia and Palestine, and against occasional rebels at home, and who were paid in crown lands and the assignment of slaves and booty from the campaigns.

Nubia became increasingly important for its routes to the southern markets and its gold mines in the eastern desert. The Near East had its own gold standard for international exchange, and Egypt, to maintain her status as a prime producer, needed to exploit the available mines in Nubia to supplement those in her own territory. During the Second Intermediate Period, the Nubian chieftains had become entirely independent, as indicated by their rock graffiti along the river and the Kamose stele text with the report of the letter from the Hyksos king to the Nubian king. The resiliency of the Nubians at the beginning of the dynasty is attested by the campaigns that Ahmose, Amunhotpe I, and Thutmose I had to conduct in the south. Later, the Nubians tested Egypt's strength at the accession of a new ruler, Thutmose II. At Tombos, just north of the third cataract, a stele of victory was erected for Thutmose I in which the king boasts of his northern frontier at the Euphrates, "that inverted water which goes downstream in going upstream." This curious designation reflects the Egyptian amazement at a river that, unlike the Nile, flows toward the south.

As early as the reigns of Kamose and Ahmose there were officials designated as (but not actually) kings' sons in charge of Nubia. The title was later expressed as king's son of Kush, equivalent to Viceroy of Nubia. The king's son of Kush became the chief administrative officer for the collection of taxes in Nubia and the conduct of the gold-mining operations; and he served as the overlord of the native Nubian governors. There is a decree, addressed to the king's son Tjuroy, represented by stelae from Kubban in Nubia, near the main road to the gold-mining districts, and at Wadi Halfa at the second cataract. In it Thutmose I announces to the viceroy his accession to the throne and designates his formal, five-part royal name to be used in legal oaths and in the temple offering service. Toward the end of the dynasty the viceroy Huy is shown conducting the procession of tribute-bearers with their Nubian produce before Tutankhamun. Among the colorful elements of the procession are giraffes, monkeys, elephant tusks, varied hides and leather goods, ostrich feather fans, semi-precious stones, and, of course, ingots of gold and bags of gold dust. Egyptian temples were erected in Nubia and the Sudan. The best known are the temple of Amunhotpe III, at Soleb, and the rock temples of Ramses II of Dyn. 19, at Abu Simbel. At the close of Dyn. 20 the viceroy Pinhasy seems to have been powerful enough to secede from Egypt, probably taking the southernmost nome with him.

In the early part of the dynasty a strong matriarchal tendency is observable. The queens and other royal ladies played an important role, and the rise of Hatshepsut to the position of ruler can be explained in part as the natural consequence of this element. Ahmose built a memorial building at Abydos for his grandmother, Queen Tetisheri, and his mother, Queen Ahmose, was remembered in the reliefs at Deir el Bahri. The possible Nubian ancestry of the dynasty may have played a part in this dominant matriarchal element.

Out of the royal burial and mortuary-cult program developed some major new features, foremost of which was the separation of the burial and the cult temples. In the New Kingdom the royal burials were made in the rock tombs of the kings in a distant valley. They featured a series of long corridors ending in a burial chamber. Funerary texts relating to the underworld were inscribed on the walls, with scenes including geographical elements of the afterworld and its guardians; in several instances the constellations in the sky were painted on the ceiling. These tombs were intended to be closed forever, and their entrances were masked for secrecy. On the

Theban plain on the same side of the river, opposite the eastern bank with the great temples of the gods, the kings erected mortuary temples for their cults. These were not connected by any sort of causeway to the tombs of the same kings. Hence the burial and cult functions of the pyramid complex of the Old and Middle Kingdoms were now physically separated. The supervisor of the building works of Thutmose I was Ineni. In addition to recording his work on the pylons, their flagstaves tipped with gold, and on the king's obelisks in front of them at the temple of Karnak, he recounted in his tomb biography his work on the royal tomb. He inspected the excavation "alone, no one seeing, no one hearing." The mortuary temples have greatly suffered through quarrying and the use of their land for cultivation. Few have escaped destruction. However, the temple of Hatshepsut at Deir el Bahri with its terraces was sufficiently removed from the flood plain to escape cultivation, and the temple at Medinet Habu of Ramses III owes its preservation in part to its use as a fortress and then as a Coptic church and colony.

The Thutmosid succession entered an extraordinary phase at the death of Thutmose II. Until recently the picture was most unclear, but it now appears that at the death of the king the throne was assumed by a lesser son, the future Menkheperre Thutmose III, and the sister and queen of Thutmose II, Hatshepsut. In effect, the government was in the hands not of the young king but of his step-mother. She proclaimed herself king, not queen, and was represented in some of her statuary with the royal beard and in some of her inscriptions with the masculine pronouns, for example, His Majesty, not Her Majesty. Hatshepsut was clearly the real power during this joint rule, but she died in about Year 21 of the reign of Thutmose III, and he continued to reign until his own death in Year 54. Toward the end of his reign the memory of Hatshepsut became repugnant.[4] Her statues were destroyed, and the cartouches of the members of the royal family were frequently altered. The names of Thutmose I and Thutmose II were inserted in her cartouches, a situation that led a previous generation of scholars to believe that they had been deposed and returned to the throne after her fall.

Although there is clear evidence of several military campaigns in her reign, Hatshepsut is best remembered for her mortuary temple and its terraces, built north of the mortuary temple of Nebhepetre Montuhotpe of Dyn. 11, which served as its inspiration. A small stone bowl has been discovered with a dedication to Nebhepetre by Hatshepsut.[5] The temple features ramps leading from one level to the next, on either side of which are open courts with retaining walls designed with covered porticos

[4] Charles F. Nims, "The Date of the Dishonoring of Hatshepsut," *Zeitschrift für Ägyptische Sprache und Altertumskunde* 93 (1966):97–100.

[5] B. J. Peterson, "Hatshepsut und Nebhepetre Mentuhotep," *Chronique d'Égypte* 42 (1967):266–68.

fronted by rows of pillars. The reliefs in these porticos are of more interest than the cult scenes on the upper terrace.

On the south side of the colonnade on the middle terrace is a set of reliefs of particular interest, showing an expedition to Punt, an African land, possibly on the shores of the Red Sea, that supplied an aromatic tree gum for the use of the temples.[6] Five large ships under the chancellor Nehsy are shown departing for the distant land. They are received by the prince of Punt named Parehu and his huge, sway-backed wife, Eti, with the donkey that is purported to have carried her. (See Figure 37, page 254.) Their land is shown with round, dome-roofed hut dwellings on stiltlike piles and a fauna and flora including giraffes, hippopotami, apes, dogs, and the valuable myrrh trees. In exchange for Egyptian merchandise, the Puntites provided these incense trees, which were sent with their roots properly gathered for transport, and bags of aromatic gum, ivory, and skins, as well as several Puntites and their offspring. We are told that the expedition was the first to this distant land and was made because of a command given to the queen by an oracle of Amun. Finally, Hatshepsut is shown offering the produce to Amun upon the expedition's return to Thebes. The scenes and their texts must have made a vivid impression on contemporaneous beholders.

On the north side of the same middle terrace is a series of scenes showing the divine birth of the queen, a series of some significance since it stresses her right to the throne. On the lower colonnade, south of the ramp, are reliefs of the transportation of two obelisks. The obelisks lie end to end on a barge towed by three rows of oared barges, twenty-seven in all, with 864 oarsmen. In addition, each row has its own pilot boat, and three more boats accompanying the obelisk barge. North of the ramp the obelisks are shown being dedicated to Amun. The other texts of the lower colonnade refer to the queen's Nubian campaign. Hatshepsut was obviously supported by a court faction, probably led by her chief steward and overseer of works, Senmut, and the high priest of Amun. There is evidence that Senmut was responsible for much of the building in her reign. He was also assigned the management of the estates of the heiress daughter Nefrure, but he apparently fell out of favor later in the reign.[7]

Thutmose III played a minor role during the life of his stepmother, probably in the military activities of their joint reign. The revolt of the Palestinian and Syrian towns in the twenty-second year of the reign coincides with the disappearance of Hatshepsut. The queen is ignored in the

[6] W. S. Smith, "The Land of Punt," *Journal of the American Research Center* 1 (1962):59–61; N. B. Millet, "A Fragment of the Hatshepsut Punt Relief," *Journal of the American Research Center* 1 (1962):55–57; and Breasted, *Ancient Records of Egypt*, vol. 2, 246–68.
[7] B. S. Lesko, "The Senmut Problem," *Journal of the American Research Center* 6 (1967):113–18; and Nims, *Thebes of the Pharaohs*, p. 203, n. 40.

king lists, but it was apparently not until later in the reign of Thutmose III that her inscriptions were covered over or erased. During Thutmose's independent reign of thirty-two years and the twenty-five years of his son and successor, Amunhotpe II, the Egyptian war machine was most efficient and devastating.

The campaigns of Thutmose III appear, in retrospect, to have been well organized as a sequence. In Year 22 the king reached the border fortress of Tjel and led his armies north against the "rebels." He was next at Gaza and departed the following day to Yehem. A consultation took place as to the best route to Megiddo (Armageddon), where an enemy coalition under the prince of Kadesh was gathered to oppose him. The king did not heed the advice of his courtiers, a tradition in these texts, but set forth on the narrow, less favored Aruna road. The battle strategy can be made out in detail from the annals of the campaign.[8] At the end the enemy was forced to pull its allies into the fortress by their clothes, and a vast amount of booty was seized by the Egyptian army. The harvest was taken by the Egyptians and Megiddo was besieged. The annals record its fall with an often repeated phrase, "The capture of Megiddo is the capture of a thousand towns." This was the first of some seventeen campaigns; the other important ones were the fifth, sixth, seventh, and eighth. The ninth, tenth, fourteenth, and seventeenth were merely punitive; the second, third, and thirteenth were probably tours of inspection; the fifteenth and six-teenth are known only from the tribute lists; and the fourth, eleventh, and twelfth are missing from the record.[9]

After the consolidation of his first victory, the king proceeded to gain control of the Syrian ports as preparation for the capture of Kadesh. Boats were built at Byblos for a campaign that took the king as far as the Euphrates. The king recorded setting up a boundary stele on the west bank of the river next to that erected by Thutmose I. Battles were fought at numerous towns that can be identified—for instance, the area of Wan, near Aleppo, and Carchemish. Many details are provided by the annals, the stelae relating to the campaigns, and the tomb biographies of some of the main officers. For example, the prince of Kadesh sent forth a mare in heat into the Egyptian cavalry to render it ineffective, but it was quickly killed by one of the officers. Near Niy a herd of 120 elephants was sighted, and a charging bull nearly killed the king.

The real enemy power appears to have been the Middle Euphrates state of Mitanni, which dominated western Asia at this time. The tribute

[8] R. O. Faulkner, "The Battle of Megiddo," *Journal of Egyptian Archaeology* 28 (1942): 2–15.

[9] For this outline of the campaigns with references, see Étienne Drioton and Jacques Vandier, *L'Égypte*, 4th rev. ed., Clio": Introduction aux études historiques. Les peuples de l'Orient Méditerranéen, vol. 2 (Paris: Presses Universitaires de France, 1962), pp. 398–406.

gathered by the Egyptians, which is specified in great detail, included lapis lazuli from Mitanni's vassals, Assyria and Babylon. The effect of this vast influx of wealth was the creation of major property-holding institutions in the temples to which it was dedicated. In particular the temple of Amun-Re at Thebes became the main land- and capital-owner, as well as the possessor of slaves taken in these campaigns.

The tradition of the military conqueror was maintained by Amun-hotpe II. In his major Asiatic expedition, he crossed the Orontes, taking Syrian towns in the area. The stele in the temple at Amada in Nubia records the sacrifice of seven Syrian princes at Thebes. Six were hung upside down on the walls of Thebes and the body of the seventh was exhibited similarly at Napata, the great town deep in the Sudan just downstream from the fourth cataract. Some seventy-one thousand prisoners were taken. Amunhotpe II exemplifies the tradition of the "sporting king"; his prowess was recorded in several texts. He is said to have shot arrows at metal targets and to have pierced them. These target practices are represented in relief.

With the reign of Thutmose IV the political configuration of the Near East changed. Mitanni had been the major power, with Assyria in the east as its vassal and the Hittite state in Anatolia not yet a threat. The rise of the latter and its interference in north Syrian affairs soon made it clear that a Mitanni-Egyptian alliance was in the interests of both parties. The initiative seems to have come from the Egyptians, for Thutmose IV sent seven letters to Artatama of Mitanni requesting the hand of one of his daughters. (This policy continued under Amunhotpe III, to whose harem came at least two Mitannian princesses.) Possibly Thutmose IV was not the eldest son of his predecessor. His stele placed between the paws of the great sphinx at Giza relates a dream of the young prince Thutmose while on a lion hunt. In his sleep the sun god appears to the prince and promises him the kingship if he frees the sphinx of the sands that have been encumbering it. The stele was set up after he became king and had undertaken the clearing.

Our information about the New Kingdom derives from many sources. There are, for example, royal stelae that provide accounts of a campaign or incident. The dream stele of Thutmose IV cited above is such. Other major examples are the stele, in duplicate, outlining the campaigns and booty of Amunhotpe II's Orontes expedition. Frequently the royal annals on temple walls are supplemented by the stelae accounts, as in the additional information provided about Thutmose III's Syrian campaigns in the stele from Gebel Barkal in the Sudan. An interesting side light on the Syrian expeditions is the series of reliefs in the temple at Karnak that show all sorts of Asiatic plant specimens that were brought home. They are illustrated with their roots, as if in a botanical museum. The tombs of the great officials of the time are a striking source of information about the

duties and activities of the men for whom they were built. One of the most
important is the tomb at Thebes of the vizier of southern Egypt in the
reign of Thutmose III. His name was Rekhmire, and in texts and scenes
his career and duties are outlined in considerable detail.[10] One of the best-
known texts is the address by the king at the installation of the vizier, in
which he says:

> Look to the office of vizier, . . . for it is the basis for the entire land.
> Now as for the office of vizier, it indeed is not sweet, it is as bitter as
> gall! . . . Look at the one whom you know like him whom you do not
> know. . . . Do not hurry with a petitioner whose pleas you have not yet
> attended to.

Another series of texts from the same tomb provides a list of the duties of
the vizier. A long procession shows tax-bearers from towns in Upper Egypt.
Rekhmire is also shown receiving foreign tribute, including a giraffe from
Nubia and horses from Syria, and inspecting the workshops of the temple
of Amun, where, among other things, royal statues were made. Construction, agricultural pursuits, and funeral activities are all illustrated in the
painting on the walls, many of which are exceptionally fine compositions.

Other sources in addition to the royal stelae are the annals and scenes
of battles on temple walls and private tomb reliefs and texts. One of the
comrades-in-arms of the early years of Amunhotpe II, a noble who grew
up at the palace with the future king, was appointed Viceroy of Nubia.
This noble, User-Satet, received a personal letter from the king and recorded it on a stele.[11] In a style unlike the formal business style of the
royal inscriptions, the letter calls to mind their days in Syria and the
women whom User-Satet received as captives from Byblos, Babylon,
Alalakh (north Syria), and Arapkha and then goes on to advise the viceroy
not to be too indulgent toward the Nubians. It also mentions the people
of Takhsy, the same area from which came the seven princes sacrificed to
Amun. User-Satet had an unhappy end. Whether he merely fell out of
political favor or was accused of theft or another crime we do not know.
But for some reason he incurred the enmity of his king, probably after the
death of Amunhotpe II, and his inscriptions in the Aswan region were defaced. His tomb has not been found, and it may have been destroyed.

There are papyrus letters from superiors to subordinates and reports

[10] The tomb representations and texts serve as an excellent introduction to the life
and times of the New Kingdom. See Norman de G. Davies, *The Tomb of Rekh-mi-re
at Thebes*, 2 vols. (New York: Metropolitan Museum of Art, 1943); idem, *Paintings
from the Tomb of Rekh-mi-re at Thebes* (New York: Metropolitan Museum of Art,
1935); R. O. Faulkner, "The Installation of the Vizier," *Journal of Egyptian Archaeology*
41 (1955):18–29; and Wolfgang Helck, *Zur Verwaltung des mittleren und neuen
Reichs* (Leiden-Köln: E. J. Brill, 1958), pp. 29–43.
[11] Wolfgang Helck, "Eine stele des Vize Königs Wśr-śt.t," *Journal of Near Eastern
Studies* 14 (1955):22–31.

from subordinates to their masters. In one such letter the mayor of Thebes in the reign of Amunhotpe II announces to a certain tenant-farmer his imminent arrival in the capital of U.E. 7 north of Thebes.[12] The letter instructs the farmer to pick flowers for offerings, to have new jars of milk made ready, and to cut a quantity of timber. The mayor wrote, "Do not let me find fault with you concerning your post. . . . Now mind, you shall not slack, for I know that you are lazy. . . ." This peremptory letter from a superior to one far below him lacks any greeting or closing and was in fact never delivered; it was found sealed.

Some of the major officials are known to us through a large number of sources. In addition to a man's tomb, there may be statues of him, and his name may appear in rock texts at the quarries, in papyrus letters, and on objects dedicated to the temples.

The reign of Amunhotpe III marks another phase in the destiny of the dynasty. Historians are fond of Amunhotpe III, called "the Magnificent," with his apparent indifference to warlike or athletic endeavors after the first part of the reign. In several reliefs, statues, and statuettes of the king in old age, he appears as a corpulent, almost flabby figure. Aside from leading an important Nubian campaign in his fifth and sixth years, the king probably did not have to contend actively with Egypt's enemies. Through wars, his predecessors had established an empire; it was Amunhotpe's destiny to enjoy its fruits and live off his ancestors' achievements. Throughout Egypt and well into the Sudan there is evidence of his building programs. The temples of Luxor and Karnak attest to his activities there. His vast palace on the other side of the river, however, has vanished. Of his mortuary temple, situated on prime land near the cultivation and flooded during the next dynasty, only two great statues, one of which was known as the Colossus of Memnon, and a reconstructed quarzite stele remain standing. Of other statues, the bases remain, and they bear the names of defeated or tributary countries. Those on the south are of red granite from the south, those on the north of quarzite from the north. Among the suggested identifications of the names of the northern towns are Ashur, Babylon, Damascus, Aleppo, Carchemish, possibly Ilium (Troy), Knossos in Crete, Cythera, Mycene or Mykonos, and Nauplia.[13] On five occasions during the reign a set of commemorative scarabs was issued relating to events in the king's personal history. They were evidently sent as gifts to the great nobles, and several copies of each have been preserved. They record his marriage with Teye, a wild cattle hunt, the total of lions captured (102) in his first ten years, the arrival in his harem of a Mitannian princess, Gilukheba, with her ladies, and the construction of a

---

[12] Ricardo Caminos, "Papyrus Berlin 10463," *Journal of Egyptian Archaeology* 49 (1963):29–37.

[13] Elmar Edel, *Die Ortsnamenlisten aus dem Totentempel Amenophis III*, Bonner Biblische Beiträge 25 (Bonn: Peter Hanslein, 1966).

vast irrigation basin in the Panopolite nome (U.E. 9) on the domains of Queen Teye. The queen, whose parents were not of royal lineage, was an extraordinary personality. She is represented in statuary and is included in many royal inscriptions. The prominence accorded to her and to the later queens in the dynasty, especially Nefertiti, is unparalleled in prior Egyptian history.

The extensive building programs of the reign are associated with a very high level of achievement in the arts. Statuary, both royal and private, flourished. The tombs of the major officials, such as the vizier Ramose and Kheruef, the steward of Queen Teye, who lived into the following reign, are among the finest at Thebes. Among the greatest of the officials was Amunhotpe, the son of Hapu, a loyal citizen of the town of Athribis in the Delta, who was later treated as a god for his works and wisdom. (We should note that few Egyptian sages were deified in this fashion.) He was in charge of many of the more ambitious building projects and became the most respected noble in the reign. For this he was rewarded with his own mortuary temple, of impressive dimensions, in the area of the royal mortuary temples. From his statues and the biographical text on one of them we gain some impression of the man. One of his seated statues shows him at a relatively youthful age (see Figure 39); another depicts him in old age.

The successor of Amunhotpe the Magnificent was his son Amunhotpe IV, of whom more has been written then of any other pharaoh.[14] Although it now seems unlikely, he may have ruled for a time as coregent with his father before assuming sole rule. A more extraordinary ruler could not have been imagined by his ancestors. If many of the facts of his reign are clear, their interpretation is frequently bewildering. Early in his reign he espoused a doctrine centering on the belief in a great god manifested in the sun's disk, a loving creator bringing life to all mankind with his warm rays. The sun god element was not foreign to Egyptian religion—the sun god Re was the dynastic god of the pyramid builders, especially in Dyns. 5 and 6. The huge temple of Karnak was dedicated to Amun-Re as king of the gods, and Re thus continued both as himself and as an element in the compound god Amun-Re. The god that Amunhotpe IV revealed to his people, however, was a more specific aspect of the sun, the Aten, or disk. Although the Aten had figured to some extent in hymns and religious texts of earlier reigns, now a clear dissociation with the past was stressed. The king changed his name from Amunhotpe (Amun is satisfied) to Akhenaten

---

[14] For a stimulating and abundantly illustrated account of the reign, see Aldred, *Akhenaten, Pharaoh of Egypt*. Recent articles of interest are: A. R. Schulman, "Some Observations on the Military Background of the Amarna Period," *Journal of the American Research Center* 3 (1964):51–69; and idem, "The Berlin 'Trauerrelief' (No. 12411) and Some Officials of Tut'ankhamūn and Ay," *Journal of the American Research Center* 4 (1965):55–68.

FIGURE 39   Seated statue of Amunhotpe, son of Hapu, as a scribe.

(the effective spirit of the Aten). Throughout the temples of Egypt and
even in his father's distant temple at Soleb in the Sudan the king later in
his reign had the name of Amun eradicated wherever it appeared as god or
in personal names.

This unparalleled and almost unbelievable program unquestionably
stemmed from a religious fervor of great intensity. To what extent it was
initiated or encouraged by a previous overemphasis on Amun remains a
leading problem. The state religion of Amun-Re, which we must consider
as a whole in its financial and political, as well as religious, configuration,
obviously exerted so great an influence that Akhenaten, for reasons of his
own, sought to check or eliminate it. The reasons may have been entirely
religious: a theological rejection of one major aspect of Egyptian religion,
perhaps because it had become too secular, in favor of the worship of the
supreme creator of man, animals, and all nature. On the other hand, the
reasons may have been intrinsically political: the espousal of the new cause
as a means to reassert the primacy and power of the kingship. The matter
may have started as a growing antagonism between the new king, even
while he was crown prince, and the personalities represented in the Amun
hierarchy of his father's court. Extended and careful study may some day
provide a workable solution to this question. From what we presently

know, however, it seems likely that the so-called Akhenaten revolution or reformation stemmed from basically theological grounds. It would have been difficult or even impossible to reform from within the Amun-Re religion at its center at Thebes. If the king had wished to gain power at the expense of the rising Amun politicians, he probably had the means to do so without resorting to the extremes that he did.

During the first years of his reign Akhenaten built at Karnak a huge structure dedicated to the Aten and stressing the glory of the king and his family. The fate of this temple is curious. After his reign the tens of thousands of small sandstone blocks with reliefs and inscriptions were dismantled and used as builder's fill inside the pylons of the temple of Amun-Re at Karnak. (They have in part been recovered and are being studied.) Akhenaten's structure at Karnak, with its colossal statues (see Figure 40) and reliefs showing a dramatic new departure in art, was a prelude to the next significant move of the reign: the foundation of a new city for the Aten in an area north of the Theban nome on the east side of the river opposite Hermopolis (U.E. 15). The city was named Akhetaten, "the horizon of the Aten," the present Amarna.

The art, our major surviving source for the period, reflects many innovations. The king and his queen, Nefertiti, are constantly depicted together in the temple and tomb reliefs with as many of their six daughters as were born at the time the relief was carved. This emphasis on the royal family as a domestic unit, with the daughters frequently shown in their parents' laps or playing with each other, contrasts strongly with the austere privacy maintained by the families of previous kings. Another innovation is the almost grotesque way in which the king is presented. Heretofore the Egyptian artist represented the king in statuary and relief in so severe a style that it is usually difficult to judge which king is depicted. But Akhenaten is shown with heavy lips, a prominent nose, sallow cheeks, and very heavy hips. Such effeminate characteristics have elicited widely divergent interpretations over the years, each fitting in with the general tenor of the times in which it was proposed. According to one view, the king wished to stress his close connection with the creator god and therefore had himself represented as androgynous, part man part woman. Another view is that he suffered from a physical disability that amounted to an increase in female characteristics and even a gradual change in sex from male to female. There have been several lengthy studies by medical authorities, yielding divergent conclusions, on the characteristics exhibited by these reliefs and statues. A third view lays emphasis on the probable death of the queen near the end of the reign and her possible replacement by a young prince named Smenkhkare, who for a short time was coregent and later king. These matters can properly be studied only in connection with their possible background in Egyptian civilization, and even a short treatment would be out of place in a survey of this brevity.

FIGURE 40 Colossal statue of Amunhotpe IV—Akhenaten—from his temple at Karnak. (Dyn. 18.)

The main residence city of the king shifted at various times in Egyptian history, with Memphis, Herakleopolis, Thebes, Itj-towy, Avaris, Akhetaten, Sais, and other Delta towns each playing a part. The town of Akhetaten represents a startling innovation in itself. It is not a geographical area of any political value, and it did not really serve for longer than the reign of the king who created it. Moreover, it seems to have been built as an anti-city, a capital about halfway between the existing residence towns of Thebes and Memphis, somewhat like the foundation of Washington (away from New York and Philadelphia), Ankara (away from Istanbul), and Brasilia (away from Rio de Janeiro).

Several decades after Akhenaten's death the town was razed, and the remaining building materials were still later transported across the river for the building programs of Ramses II in the next dynasty. Since the town and its structures were conceived with an overall plan at one time and were not repeatedly altered over the centuries, it has been possible to excavate the town and to compare its plan with representations of some of its parts in the nearby tombs. The area of the town, strictly delimited by the important boundary stelae that the king set up, is a semicircular plain marked by the cliffs that retreat from and then return to the Nile. The stelae, of which fourteen are known to have been set up, mark the limits north, south, east, and west, the last on the other side of the river. They were set up in Year 6 of the king and some have a later text of Year 8. In the text the king formally dedicates the town to the Aten and all its lands and people.

A monograph would be required to describe the town itself. Among the features are palaces and temples and a main road over which an enclosed bridge was constructed. This has been identified, but not with complete certainty, as the bridge with the great window of appearances, a feature shown in the reliefs where the king and his family reward the nobles with gifts. (See Figure 41.) Standard temple architecture is characterized by ever-smaller rooms, and a corresponding lessening of light, as one proceeds into the interior, reaching finally the torch-lit, innermost sanctuaries. As befits solar temples, however, the Amarna temples are open to the sun's rays. Even the monumental gateways were designed with an opening in the top of the frame so that the rays cannot be stopped. In reliefs the sun's disk is represented with numerous rays ending in human hands. These hands extend the symbol of life to the royal family or seem to touch the food offerings piled high. In cases they even clasp in a sort of embrace the bodies or crowns of the king and queen.

In the bay of cliffs itself are the tombs of the courtiers of the day, imitating the tombs in the bays at Thebes. The tombs feature prominently the royal family, the temple, other buildings in the plain below, and, to a much smaller extent, the life of the courtier for whom the tomb was constructed. They stress the pomp of the royal court and the intimacy of the royal family. Lines of courtiers are shown bending in a respectful attitude before the king. The king is shown going forth on a royal parade with his scouts and army officers—the parade taking the place of real military campaigns. Frequently, the noble himself is shown being rewarded with collars and necklaces of gold as tokens of royal favor.

The courtiers of the king formed a new group. They clearly did not stem entirely from the old families allied to the Amun bureaucracy and the Theban court. The master sculptor Bak was indeed the son of the master sculptor and builder Men, to whom the Colossus of Memnon and other great projects of Amunhotpe III are generally credited. Yet Bak indicated in an inscription that he was taught by the king himself. To achieve this unusual change in the government the king required the support of the army. This he seems to have been able to control, keeping army officials in the royal service by rewarding them for their loyalty.

The tombs at Amarna include one in which the king was apparently buried. In the tombs of the nobles are copies of the great hymns that form the main source of our knowledge of Amarna religion. In language frequently anticipating some of the Psalms of David, they stress the joy of the earth in the creator, the sun, and the dependence of all mankind on the sun's powers. Short excerpts of a hymn to the sun disk can give a limited idea of its content:

Scale ¼

FIGURE 41   Relief of the king and his family—the Window of Appearances.

When you are risen upon the eastern horizon
You have filled every land with your beauty. . . .
When you set upon the western horizon,
The land is in darkness in the likeness of death.
They sleep in a chamber with heads covered up,
And one eye does not see its mate.
If all their possessions which are beneath their heads are stolen,
They have not perceived it.
Every lion has come out of his den;
And all the creeping creatures bite. . . .
All cattle are content with their herbage;
The trees and plants flourish.
The birds flying from their nests,
Their wings are in praise to your spirit. . . .
Kharu [Syria] and Kush [Nubia] and the land of Egypt,
You put every man in his place.

You provide their needs. . . .
Their tongues are separate in language,
And likewise their nature.
Their skins are distinguished,
For you have distinguished the foreigners. . . .
All faraway foreign lands, you have made their life,
For you have placed a Nile in the sky.
It comes down for them, and it makes a flood on the mountains,
Like the Sea, watering their fields in their towns. . . .
You are in my heart,
And there is no other who knows you,
Except for your son [Akhenaten],
For you have made him skilled in your plans and in your strength.

It is not surprising that military campaigns in Syria and Palestine should have become relatively unimportant to the king in view of his preoccupation with restructuring the state at home. The period was an age of intense competition for the trade and domination of the Levant. It was a complex age that saw the fall of the Mitannian kingdom and the rise of the Hittites, under their conquering king Shuppiluliuma, to a level of power sufficient to challenge Egypt's overall domination. By rare good fortune a sizable portion of the period's diplomatic correspondence in Akkadian has been preserved on the cuneiform tablets found at Amarna. These consist mainly of correspondence between the Egyptian king and the rulers of the great powers of the time: the Hittites, Assyrians, Mitannians, Kassites, Cypriotes (Alasians), and the peoples of the numerous city-states of the Levant, including Byblos, Jerusalem, Gezer, Askalon, Kadesh, Amurru, Sidon, Tyre, and Ugarit. Some of these letters are confirmed, and the overall situation is made clearer, by the archives at the Hittite capital, Boghazkoy, and in the cuneiform texts from Ugarit. The general picture is of a host of city-states acting as nominal, tribute-yielding vassals to the Egyptian king but actually in conflict with one another and constantly threatened by the major Hittite power. Rib-Adda of Byblos complained unceasingly to the Egyptian king and requested troops to support his struggle with neighboring Amurru. The king of Assyria complained that Babylon, as his vassal, should not undertake direct communication with Egypt.

Akhenaten ruled with the support of the army for some seventeen years. Although not a participant in campaigns, he affected military dress, and the reliefs of his reign abound in scenes of military parades. He was succeeded by his favorite, Smenkhkare, who already had served for a short time as coregent. The latter was apparently soon ousted in favor of Tutankhaten, a young prince whose claim to the throne was established through his marriage to Ankhesenpaaten, one of the daughters of Akhenaten and Nefertiti. The king changed his name from Tutankhaten to

Tutankhamun and soon abandoned Amarna for the traditional capital at Thebes. Here, upon his death, he was provided with a tomb that, by a near miracle, survived almost intact until its discovery in 1922. The richness of the tomb equipment, now on exhibit in the Egyptian Museum in Cairo, is difficult to believe, but modern color photography has made its treasures available to those unable to see it in person.[15] With the death of Tutankhamun the power of the military was reasserted. Ay (who had constructed his tomb at Amarna in the reign of Akhenaten, the tomb from which the best-preserved example of the great Aten hymn comes) held the throne jointly with Tutankhamun at the end of the latter's reign. It is Ay who appears in the painted scenes in the tomb of Tutankhamun as his successor.

A curious episode took place at this time. The Egyptian queen, evidently Ankhesenamun, wrote to Shuppiluliuma, King of the Hittites, saying that her husband had died and that there was no one among the Egyptian princes or nobles whom she deigned to marry. She therefore earnestly requested him to send one of his sons to become her consort and serve as king of Egypt. The request amazed the Hittite, but he eventually sent Prince Zannanza to marry the widow. On the way the prince was slain on the orders of an Egyptian officer, and the Hittite lamented his son's death and the new attacks on the Hittite borders. The sources for this episode come from the Hittite archives as part of the *Deeds of Suppiluliumas* as related by his son Mursilis II. Some scholars maintain that the letter and events refer to the time after the death of Akhenaten himself, in which case the queen might have been Nefertiti, if she survived her husband.[16]

The renewed military activity and the lack of a smooth dynastic succession resulted in the rise to power of Horemheb, a military officer who assumed the kingship after the death of the already old Ay. During his reign, which was of uncertain duration, Amarna was ignored. Horemheb instituted a number of administrative reforms. The tomb he prepared at Memphis has yielded an interesting series of reliefs; they were altered to indicate the royal uraeus on his brow after he assumed the kingship. As king he also built a traditional tomb in the valley of the kings of Thebes. The building activity at the temple of Amun at Karnak and the temple of Luxor, which had been resumed under Tutankhamun, was continued with major expenditures, as if to make up for the neglect under the Amarna heretics. It was during this reign that the huge sandstone temple set up at Karnak in the early years of Akhenaten was dismantled. An inscription dated in Year 59 of the king indicates that at some stage in the reign he may have dated his monuments from the death of Amunhotpe

---

[15] Desroches-Noblecourt, *Tutankhamen.*
[16] Redford, *History and Chronology of the Eighteenth Dynasty of Egypt*, pp. 158–62, p 162, n. 311.

III, tacitly ignoring the reigns of the tainted Amarna group: Akhenaten, Smenkhkare, Tutankhamun, and Ay. Likewise the Ramesside king lists pass directly from Amunhotpe III to Horemheb, omitting these same kings.

[2] DYNASTY 19

Ramses I, founder of Dyn. 19 and originator of the Ramesside Era (Dyns. 19 and 20), was a military commander and probably the vizier in the last years of Horemheb. Horemheb had certainly selected him as his successor, and it is likely that Horemheb early in his career had had considerable influence on the succession to the throne before he himself assumed the kingship. The Ramesside dynasty was of Lower Egyptian origin, and its patron deity was the god Seth of Avaris. The important role played by Re, attested by the name Ramses (Re-mes-su), may in part reflect the working out of the Aten element; the renewal of a major role for Re was one of the few aftereffects of the days of Amarna.

Several currents of change are clear. Although the cult center of Amun at Thebes continued to play a major role and the Ramesside kings and queens were buried on the western side of Thebes as were their predecessors, the real seat of the government was in the north. The Ramessides built palaces at Memphis near those of the kings of the previous dynasty. A great residence town named Pi-Ramessu was founded and richly ornamented at a site near modern Qantir, in the Delta. Schoolboy exercises included several hymns of praise and admiration for the town, and many items, among them colorful glazed tiles with representations of prisoners, attest to its magnificence.[17] Another current of change was the rising importance in the government of foreign-born or foreign-named officials and courtiers, mostly from the Semitic populations of Palestine and Syria. These adventurers settled in the Delta and prospered. Libyans and Mediterranean peoples also appeared, first as enemies and as pirates, then as settlers. Although the trend parallels the situation in the latter part of Dyn. 12 and in Dyn. 13, this time the stage was set for a really cosmopolitan element in Egypt, one that characterizes her history to the middle of the present century. The diplomatic interchanges attested by the Amarna letters, the existence of Egyptian cult centers for Asiatic gods, such as Baal and Reshef, the statues of Egyptian gods exported to Asia, and the universalist sun religion of Akhenaten—all reflect this cosmopolitanism.

A change at this point in the decoration of the Theban tombs indi-

[17] Ricardo Caminos, *Late-Egyptian Miscellanies* (London: Oxford University Press, 1954); E. P. Uphill, "Pithom and Raamses: Their Location & Significance," *Journal of Near Eastern Studies* 28 (1969):15–39.

cates an important religious development. The scenes of the official busy upon his own or his master's business on inspection tours or in the field gave way to scenes of the funeral, the judgment in the afterworld, the rituals conducted by the various classes of funerary priests, and the soul as a bird flying or alighting. When agricultural scenes occur, they usually represent the man and his family reaping grain in the fields of the after-life, not those of this world. Gone is a cheerfulness and commitment to the daily activities of this world that the courtier of earlier times, perhaps naively, hoped would continue magically in the next. A cleavage between the state and temple religion, with its host of priest-officials, and the pietistic religion of the private person is particularly marked. An eminent Egyptologist has observed that the official or bureaucrat served as the model for the society of the Middle Kingdom, the military adventurer as the model for Dyn. 18, and the priest and temple official as the model for the Ramesside period. The law courts, susceptible to bribery as they must have been, once decided cases, but now the temple oracle began to take over this role. The culmination of this scheme came with the "god's state of Amun" in Dyn. 21, at which time the kingship underwent a basic change.

At various stages in Egyptian history a feeling for the past comes to the fore, and it is probably no coincidence that the majority of the king lists date to the Ramesside era. This feeling for the past is evidenced on several levels. The prince Khaemwese, son of Ramses II, restored monuments that had fallen into decay, a traditional boast of many kings who actually did little in this respect. Even the pyramids of the Old Kingdom were restored in part. Seti I restored many of the inscriptions defaced during the reign of Akhenaten. In a tomb chapel at Sakkara a relief represents many famous men of the past, including Imhotep of the time of Djoser as well as the authors of books of instruction. In the Ramesside scriptoria the traditional compositions of the past were recopied by students and teachers, frequently on ostraka and writing boards, which have in some cases survived better than papyrus. *The Story of Sinuhe, The Instruction of Amunemhet, The Hymn to the Nile, The Satire on the Professions,* and *The Prophecy of Neferti* are among literary works of the past represented in numerous copies. New compositions are also represented, sometimes by a single papyrus. Such are *The Story of the Two Brothers* and *The Enchanted Prince.*[18] A series of papyri, generally referred to as the *Late Egyptian Miscellanies,* consists of short selections of advice to the idle schoolboy, hymns of praise to the Ramesside residence, model let-

---

18 For the literature of the New Kingdom and the copies of earlier texts, see Adolf Erman, *The Ancient Egyptians: A Sourcebook of their Writings,* trans. A. M. Blackman, introduction by William K. Simpson (New York: Harper & Row, 1966); and Gustave Lefebvre, *Romans et contes égyptiens de l'époque pharaonique* (Paris: Adrien-Maisonneuve, 1949).

ters, lists of chariot parts, and the like, and occasionally one of the standard compositions. The Ramesside age was one of introspection about the past, as befits a new era seeking its roots and reassessing its history.

Ramses I ruled a short two years before he was succeeded by his son Seti I. The latter is known for his campaigns in Palestine and Syria as recorded in the great battle reliefs on the outer walls of the hypostyle court at the temple of Amun at Karnak. The style of these reliefs, with the king on a large scale in his chariot storming his enemy's forts, set a new pattern copied by Seti's successors, but without the same verve and originality.[19] Egyptian authority was established again in the Levant, and a peace treaty with the Hittite king Muwatallis was concluded. In addition to his great tomb in the Valley of the Tombs of the Kings at western Thebes and the mortuary temple in the Theban plain, Seti I built an extraordinary cenotaph complex at Abydos. This, still relatively well preserved or restored, consists of a large temple dedicated to the gods of its seven chapels—Osiris, Isis, Horus, Amun, Ptah, Re-Horakhty, and Seti I (as a god)—and, to its rear, a monumental subterranean complex originally reached by a long ramp from the north. Similarities have been pointed out between the function of the temple and subterranean complex and that of the pyramid complex of the Old Kingdom, which featured a tomb complex reached from the north by a ramp and a cult temple on the eastern side.[20] The bas reliefs relating to the cult of the temple of Seti I are of the finest execution but appear somewhat devoid of life and energy. At Nauri, near the third cataract, a copy of the decree relating to the temple and its staff was inscribed. Part of the wealth with which the temple was built derived from the gold-mining operations in the south, and a small temple built in the Wadi Mia east of Edfu has inscriptions referring to the king's construction of a well for the thirsty mine workers.

After a reign of only fourteen years Seti I was succeeded by his son Ramses II, in whose sixty-seven-year reign a final settlement was reached with the Hittites. The building program of Ramses II has left traces throughout Egypt, the best known being the rock-cut temples at Abu Simbel in Nubia. (In the 1960's, just before the Aswan High Dam caused flooding, these temples were cut into blocks, moved by a rare feat of engineering to a plateau above the original site and thus preserved for future generations.) At Abu Simbel, Karnak, Abydos, and the Ramesseum (the king's mortuary temple) at Thebes, the great campaign against the Hittites at Kadesh in Year 5 is described in some detail in the literary record, a composition sometimes called the Poem; and the pictorial record provides a second account of the same battle, with legends identifying the action and the

[19] H. A. Gronewegen-Frankfort, *Arrest and Movement* (London: Faber and Faber, 1951), pp. 114–41.
[20] Paul Barguet, "Note sur le complexe architectural de Séti 1er à Abydos," *Kêmi* 16 (1962):21–27.

FIGURE 42   The storming of Askalon.

numerous participants.[21] In the latter record are many features: the town
of Kadesh surrounded by the Orontes River, the Egyptian camp at rest
and in readiness, the countless chariots of the two armies, the beating of
two Hittite scouts to make them reveal the enemy's presence, the coming
of reinforcements, Ramses in the midst of battle shooting at his enemies
from his chariot, the prince of Aleppo held upside down to empty him of
water he swallowed when cast into the river, Hittite and other com-
manders by name, the king's horse and its name, and the foreign warriors
in league with the Hittites. The four divisions of the Egyptian army were
named after the gods of their towns: Amun, Pre, Ptah, and Seth. At one
point Ramses was surrounded and all but captured. He addressed Amun to
remind the god of all that he had done for him in the building of temples
and the assignment of endowments. The Hittite confederacy failed to
win, but the Egyptians, for their part, could not hold northern Syria. Six-
teen years later a formal treaty was concluded between Ramses and the
then king of the Hittites, Khattusilis. One version was inscribed in Egyp-

---

[21] Sir Alan H. Gardiner, *The Kadesh Inscriptions of Ramesses* II (Oxford: Oxford
University Press, 1960).

tian on the walls of the temples; a second was preserved in the Hittite archives.[22] The gods of both countries are invoked to witness provisions for fugitives to be treated on a reciprocal basis and for joint defense measures to be taken. Nowhere is a border specified between the two areas of interest; this must have been settled otherwise. The Hittite archives have revealed further correspondence between the kings, including the arrangements of a marriage between a Hittite princess and Ramses himself. As in the case of Egypt and Mitanni several generations earlier, Hittite-Egyptian hostility gave way to alliance in the face of common enemies.

The thirteen(?)-year reign of Merneptah followed that of his father Ramses II. (Ramses had outlived his first twelve sons among some one hundred offspring.) Merneptah's fifth regnal year, like his father's, proved to be of considerable importance. A Libyan prince led a coalition of Libyan tribes (the Libu, Meshwesh, and Kehek) and Mediterraneans against the towns of the Delta. They were roundly defeated, and six thousand captives were taken. Among the allies of the Libyans were the Sherdan, Shekelesh, Lukka, Tursha, and Akawasha. These "peoples of the sea" represent wandering groups of pirates and soldiers who had previously turned up in Egyptian or hostile forces. It is thought by some that the Sherdan, easily recognizable by their headdress in the Kadesh battle reliefs and elsewhere, eventually settled in Sardinia and gave that island their name. Some scholars identify the Tursha in Egyptian inscriptions as the ancestors of the Etruscans.

The dynasty ended in a period not noted for its monuments at home or prowess abroad. Merneptah was succeeded by Amunmose, Seti II, Siptah, and Queen Tawosre, the last perhaps, like Hatshepsut, assuming the kingship itself. The chancellor Bay, who may be Irsu, an Asiatic cited in an account of the confusion of the land at the end of Dyn. 19, obviously played an important role at this time. His inscriptions appear in prominent places in several temples. The same account of the plundering and confusion in the land ends with praise of Sethnakhte, the king who brought order out of confusion and reestablished peace.

[3] DYNASTY 20

Around the year 1200 B.C., Sethnakhte founded Dyn. 20, the second of the two Ramesside dynasties. Like the founder of Dyn. 19 his reign lasted only two years, and he was succeeded by an unbroken line of kings, all assuming the name Ramses (Ramses III through Ramses XI), who ruled from 1198 to 1085 B.C.

[22] John A. Wilson and Albrecht Goetze, *Ancient Near Eastern Texts Relating to the Old Testament*, ed. James Pritchard (Princeton: Princeton University Press, 1950), pp. 199–203.

Ramses III reigned for thirty-two years, the longest reign of the dynasty, and combined careers as a builder and as a warrior. His great funerary temple at Medinet Habu at Thebes has survived remarkably, in part because of its use first as a fortress and later as a Coptic church and settlement. From the reliefs and texts on its walls, as well as from other indications in Papyrus Harris (see below, page 282), the historical picture can be pieced together. Some of the administrative troubles in the land are well attested by ostraka and papyri from later in the reign. In Year 5 the Libyan menace again became a reality, but Ramses III, like Merneptah before him, managed to defeat these hordes intent upon settling in the rich farmland of the Delta. A Libyan incursion which occurred in Year 11 was likewise repelled.

In Year 8, between these Libyan attacks, one of the worst crises befell the Egyptian state. For many decades the roving Mediterranean tribes had been seeking a foothold on the coast. Certainly their activity, difficult to document in view of their mobility, played a part in pushing the Libyans toward Egypt. Many of them became mercenaries in the great armies of the time, the Egyptian and the Hittite. Some settled in Egypt and many more in Palestine and Syria. At the same time conditions in western Asia produced major movements of peoples seeking land. As the texts relate, a virtual storm broke in Year 8 of Ramses III, and the Sherdan, Shekelesh, Denen, Peleset, Tjekker, and Weshesh, with ox-carts and all their baggage, overran the Levant. The great Hittite empire collapsed, but Ramses checked the enemy army before it reached Egypt. The reliefs from Medinet Habu show in some detail the Egyptian naval victory. Egypt was consequently spared the full brunt of the attack by the Sea Peoples. Many Sherdan and Kehek settled in Egypt, however, as mercenaries and then as farmers. The Peleset, who settled in part on the southern strip of the Levant, gave the land the name Palestine.

Although the middle years of Ramses III were peaceful and saw a large scale expedition to Punt as well as the building of the king's great mortuary temple and palace at Medinet Habu, troubles of various sorts plagued the end of the reign. Documents from Year 29 of Ramses relate workers striking on the building projects of the king's and princes' tombs.[23] They complained that they had not been paid their rations and sought redress from the authorities. Another set of papyri records the trial of conspirators in the harem who attempted to assassinate the king.[24] The

[23] William F. Edgerton, "The Strikes in Ramses III's Twenty-ninth Year," *Journal of Near Eastern Studies* 10 (1951):137–45.
[24] On the harem conspiracy, see: Breasted, *Ancient Records of Egypt*, vol. 4, §§ 416–56; A. de Buck, "The Judicial Papyrus of Turin," *Journal of Egyptian Archaeology* 23 (1937):152–64; Hans Goedicke, "Was Magic Used in the Harem Conspiracy Against Ramses III?" *Journal of Egyptian Archaeology* 49 (1963):71–92; K. Baer, "The Oath sdf3-tryt in Papyrus Lee, 1, 1," *Journal of Egyptian Archaeology* 50 (1964):179–80; and Wilson, *Ancient Near Eastern Texts Relating to the Old Testament*, ed. James Pritchard, pp. 214–16.

harem-conspiracy documents throw light on some of the legal practices of the times. There are also major accounts of the robbing of tombs and the trials of the thieves.[25]

One of the most important documents for our knowledge of the administration and land tenure is Papyrus Harris, a roll some 133 feet long with 117 columns of text. It records Ramses's donations of land and material to the temples of Egypt.[26] The document was prepared under the orders of Ramses IV for inclusion with the tomb equipment of his father. Its purpose was to show that Ramses III had done so much for the gods that he and his son deserved constant attention. The property of the three main temples of Egypt—that of the temples of Amun of Thebes, Re of Heliopolis, and Ptah of Memphis—is listed along with the annual gifts and income. An analysis of the document provides considerable information about the temple land holdings and their relative importance. Even a cursory glance shows the extraordinary preeminence of Amun of Thebes, a concentration of wealth that had major effects on the historical development of the dynasty.

Ramses IV claimed in an address to Osiris, "More numerous are the excellent things which I have done . . . in these four years than that which King [Ramses II] did for you during his sixty-seven years." The reign was difficult to emulate, and the six years credited to Ramses IV continued to be troubled. Building activity was extensive, and several large expeditions to the greywacke quarries in the Wadi Hammamat are attested. A map of these quarries, dating from this time, is one of the earliest known charts. A well-executed plan of the tomb of Ramses IV at Thebes is also extant. It is curious that such rich documentation survives of the reigns of Ramses III, IV, and V. The document known as Papyrus Harris has been mentioned above. Papyrus Wilbour, in the Brooklyn Museum, is a rich record of field surveying and taxation in the area south of Memphis during the reign of Ramses V. The owner and tenant of each field and its predicted yield are listed in such a way that, from the data, we know the pharaoh and the temples owned the greater part of land. From the reigns of Ramses IV and V there is an archive relating to the criminal activities, including thefts and embezzlements of cattle, cloth, and grain by priest-officials of the temple of Khnum at Aswan.

The dramatic increase in documentation at this time and our careful study of the papyri and ostraka, as well as of the temple scenes and dedications, have made the reigns of the lesser kings at the end of Dyn. 20 better known than the reigns of the great pyramid-builders. Many officials also are well known through their activities in building projects and administrative matters, such as the delivery of rations or supplies. In partic-

[25] For a short account of the tomb robberies, see Nims, *Thebes of the Pharaohs*, pp. 133–37.
[26] Breasted, *Ancient Records of Egypt*, vol. 4, §§ 151–412.

ular an official named Ramsesnakhte became extremely important; he held a variety of posts, including that of High Priest of Amun, from the reign of Ramses IV through the reign of Ramses VI. His son, Usermarenakhte, was appointed Steward of Amun, and father and son in effect controlled the administration of the wealth of both the pharaoh and the temple of Amun. Another son, the High Priest Amunhotpe, served under Ramses IX and X. His power was so great under the former that he is shown in a relief on an almost equal footing.

Toward the end of the dynasty the king shared power with the High Priest of Amun and another major official, the Viceroy of Nubia. A complex series of actions resulted in considerable civil strife with the three powers in conflict. The Viceroy Pinhasy not only controlled Nubia but also was a military commander and overseer of the royal granaries. It seems that he in effect challenged the power of the high priest and suppressed him. His success was not long standing, however, and he must have returned to his base of power in Nubia. The High Priest of Amun, in the person of Hrihor, appears as the real force in the reign of Ramses XI. He probably arose as a military officer rather than as a temple official. By the end of his tenure he dedicated buildings and used the royal cartouches in them for his name, both prerogatives of the pharaoh alone. He also annexed in name the office of Viceroy of Nubia. The temple of Khonsu at Karnak illustrates stages in his rise to power. In the earlier portions he is shown as high priest with Ramses XI; in the last reliefs he has the full royal titulary and is shown alone. Although Ramses XI continued to rule, Hrihor adopted the fiction that he himself was king. Certainly he controlled Thebes and the south, although still nominally under Ramses XI. After the death of Ramses XI, the north was in the hands of a Delta dynast, possibly of a family from Mendes that actually ruled from Tanis. Egypt was effectively divided. Nubia, if not still under Pinhasy, was in any case not under Egyptian domination. Information about the Delta dynasts is sparse, but Nesubanebded (Smendes) of Tanis claimed the kingship and probably asserted control over the rest of the Delta.

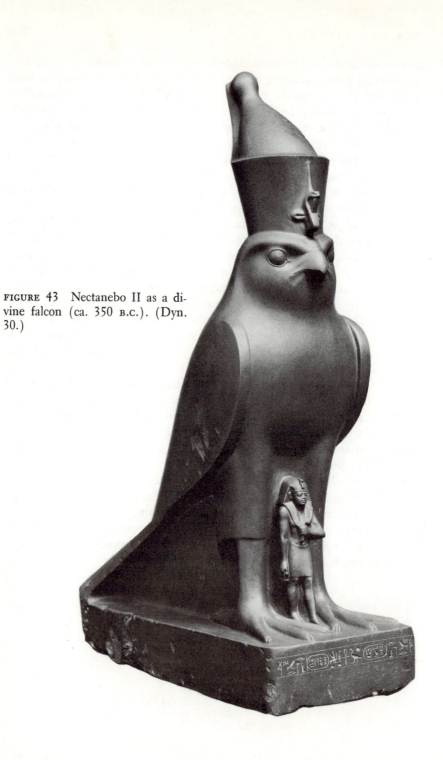

FIGURE 43 Nectanebo II as a divine falcon (ca. 350 B.C.). (Dyn. 30.)

[XII]

THE THIRD INTERMEDIATE PERIOD, THE SAITE DYNASTY, THE LATE PERIOD, AND THE CONQUEST OF ALEXANDER

From the beginning of Dyn. 21 to the end of Dyn. 25 (1085–664 B.C.), Egypt developed along very different lines. The Third Intermediate Period embraced the diverse dynasties between the Ramesside and Saite periods. Several salient features can be noted. The political dominance of Upper Egypt and its traditions, already seriously questioned in the Ramesside era, gave way to the rise of the prosperous Delta cities, with their farmlands and trade centers. True cities, in the modern sense, first developed at this time. The Libyan incursions, so frequently attested in the Ramesside era, grew into a massive settlement comparable to the Amorite-Semitic settlement at the end of the Middle Kingdom. Finally, events in Asia and Africa resulted in the extraordinary confrontation of Sudanese and Assyrian armies on Egyptian soil.

[1] DYNASTY 21

Dyn. 21 comprised a line of kings at Tanis, ruling from 1085 to 945 B.C.: Smendes, Amunemnisu, Psusennes I, Amunemope, Siamun, and Psusennes II. Several of their tombs, in which much of the equipment was still present, were excavated at Tanis in the northeast Delta. At Thebes a parallel line of high priests, the descendants of Hrihor, ruled on behalf of Amun. The two states were usually at peace, and there were ties of marriage between them.[1] The loss of Nubia reduced the income of Amun appreciably, and an inability to exploit the Levant through successful campaigns and a vassal system similarly checked the Tanite rulers. When King David of Israel marched against Edom, its prince, Hadad, sought asylum in Egypt, thereby developing ties between the Egyptian dynasty and the house of Edom. It is thought that Siamun gave his daughter, with the town of Gezer as her dowry, to Solomon.

The relationship between Egypt and the Levant and the internal situation in Egypt at the beginning of the dynasty are illustrated in an extraordinary way in the report known as *The Misadventures of Wenamun.*[2] This narrative of a messenger of Hrihor has long been regarded as a literary composition, but its factual style, its use of colloquial Late Egyptian, and the method in which it is written suggest rather that the papyrus was a real report. It tells of Wenamun being sent to Syria to buy cedar for the processional barque of Amun-Re by the god and his high priest, Hrihor. On the way he presents his credentials at Tanis to the Delta dynasts, Smendes and his wife Tentamun, who aid him. One mishap after another befalls him; he is robbed of his money, robs one of the thieves' confederates in turn, sends to Smendes and Tentamun for a loan, and as the papyrus abruptly breaks off, is hounded by the residents of Cyprus and appeals for justice to Hatiba, queen of that island kingdom. At one point, he waits on the shore for an audience with the ruler of Byblos, while the ruler daily orders him to leave. The ruler of Byblos is uncertain of Wenamun's right to represent Egypt since his credentials are lost, and

[1] On the chronology of Dyns. 21 and 22, see: Jaroslav Černý, "Egypt: From the Death of Ramesses III to the End of the Twenty-first Dynasty," fasc. 27, *Cambridge Ancient History*, rev. ed. (Cambridge: Cambridge University Press, 1965); Eric Young, "Some Notes on the Chronology and Genealogy of the Twenty-first Dynasty," *Journal of the American Research Center* 2 (1963):99–112; E. P. Uphill, "The Egyptian Sed-Festival Rites," *Journal of Near Eastern Studies* 24 (1965):365–83; idem, "The Date of Osorkon II's Sed Festival," *Journal of Near Eastern Studies* 26 (1967):61–62; and Helen K. Jacquet-Gordon, "The Illusory Year 36 of Osorkon I," *Journal of Egyptian Archaeology* 53 (1967):63–68.

[2] Sir Alan H. Gardiner, *Egypt of the Pharaohs* (Oxford: Oxford University Press, 1961), pp. 305–14; John A. Wilson, *Ancient Near Eastern Texts Relating to the Old Testament*, ed. James Pritchard (Princeton: Princeton University Press, 1950), pp. 25–29; and Jaroslav Černý, *Paper and Books in Ancient Egypt* [An inaugural lecture delivered at University College, London, 29 May 1947] (London: H. K. Lewis, 1947), p. 22.

is fearful of the Tjekker, one of the Sea Peoples with whom Wenamun has picked a quarrel and with whom the Byblites have constant commercial relations. The interest of the tale is manifold. His reception by the rulers of Dor, Byblos, and other towns contrasts in many ways with Sinuhe's reception almost a thousand years earlier. Egypt was then a rising power beginning to make her influence felt; Egypt is now a memory, without credit and friends in court. Sinuhe is a self-assured, successful man, able to survive the desert and create a life abroad on the basis of his cunning and personality. Wenamun is a pitiable figure, shattered by the discrepancy he finds: his ingrained belief in the superiority of Egypt and in Amun as the owner of the world opposed to the reality of a commercial world in which Egypt is treated as a second-class, has-been state.

The configuration of political and religious strength that existed at Thebes survived for many centuries, but from Dyn. 21 on it was less dependent on royal favor. The central figure continued to be the first priest of Amun, who was frequently allied with the royal family by blood or marriage. Another important office was that of the wife of the god Amun, called the Divine Adoratress. This office was passed on by adoption; when a new dynasty succeeded an old, the new king imposed upon the adoratress or her already designated heiress one of his own daughters as next heiress.[3] A sort of theocratic state, with Amun as the king, existed at Thebes in the shadow of the dynasties of the Delta. Law cases were tried by Amun, who was treated as an oracle. The alternatives were presented to an image of the god which the temple officials manipulated, moving a part of the statue to indicate Amun's decision. As this state religion became increasingly the property of the vested interests of the Amun priesthood, popular, pietistic religion began to grow separately from the religion of the temples. Prayers and pleas were addressed more often directly to the deity himself than through a priest, and a chasm developed between temple religion and personal piety.

[2] DYNASTIES 22 THROUGH 25

Dyns. 22 and 23 are generally designated as the Libyan dynasties, for during the latter part of the New Kingdom the peoples west of Egypt began to play an increasingly important role. Although repelled on various occasions, they eventually managed to settle in the western Delta and the Fayyum. Their leaders bore titles such as Great Prince of the Libu, Mek,

---

[3] A new publication of the Nitocris adoption stele serves as a model of the Egyptologist's craft and indicates the methods and problems in the field of text analysis. See Ricardo Caminos, "The Nitocris Adoption Stela," *Journal of Egyptian Archaeology* 50 (1964): 71–101.

and Prince of the Meshwesh. As far as can be seen they became thoroughly Egyptianized, betraying their Libyan origins only through their un-Egyptian names—Sheshonq, Osorkon, and Takelot—which are assumed to belong to one of the tribal languages west of the Nile. The founder of the Libyan dynasties, Sheshonq I, first appeared as a petitioner before the last ruler of Dyn. 21, of whom he requested permission to set up a mortuary cult at Abydos on behalf of his father. The appeal was entertained by Amun at Thebes during the high-priesthood and generalship of Pinedjem II, and Sheshonq was both accorded his wish and confirmed in the offices previously held by his father. It is clear that Sheshonq's family had been very prosperous residents of Herakleopolis for some five generations before his accession to the family leadership. The funerary endowment set up at Abydos was considerable. It is therefore not surprising that, when the influence of the kings of Dyn. 21 had run its natural course, Sheshonq should have acquired the kingship through his astute policies, which evidently included excellent relations with the god's state of Amun at Thebes.

The historical record is surprisingly silent about the appreciable span of time covered by the two Libyan dynasties—some 220 years (950–730 B.C.)—but some of the reasons and the background can be set forth. The shift of power to the Delta resulted in the survival of fewer texts and building inscriptions. Manetho records the seat of Dyn. 22 as Bubastis and the seat of Dyn. 23 as Tanis, both in the eastern Delta. Although the two dynasties originated at Herakleopolis, the main seat of both was evidently Bubastis. The dynasties partly overlapped. For the most part our records reveal only the relations of these dynasts with their Theban contemporaries, the high priests of Amun, and with their neighbors in Palestine during the rule of Solomon and the divided monarchy of Israel and Judah. The complicated details of the relationship between the Theban high priests and the Sheshonqids need not detain us. The annals of the high priest Osorkon at Karnak indicate that there was a civil war during the reign of Takelot II. There is also a record of a major flood in the reign of Osorkon III of Dyn. 23. At the end of the dynasty Egypt was obviously divided, with several of the Delta city-states relatively independent. One of these city-states, Sais, was ruled by Tefnakht and Bakenrenef (Bochchoris), the dynasts who comprised Dyn. 24 (ca. 720–715 B.C.).

At this point in the development of Egyptian history a most extraordinary and dramatic event interrupted the apparently somnolent rule of the Sheshonqids: the invasion of Piankhy (Pi) of Napata. Subsequent to the loss of Nubia and the Sudan at the end of Dyn. 20, a line of Sudanese kings developed an African kingdom, its capital at Napata, downstream from the fourth cataract. The gods of this Meroitic kingdom included Amun-Re and others from the Egyptian pantheon, and its African language was later written in Egyptian hieroglyphs and a cursive variant. During Dyn. 23 a Sudanese king named Kashta extended his influence to

FIGURE 44   Detail of the triumphal stele of King Piankhy showing the submission of four dynasts. (Dyn. 25.)

the southern boundaries of Egypt and claimed her kingship. His son, Piankhy, conducted an extraordinary campaign farther north, about 730 B.C., and confronted the Delta dynasts. The record of the campaign is preserved on a great triumphal stele set up in the Gebel Barkal temple in the Sudan and now in the Egyptian Museum in Cairo. It is one of the major texts of Egyptian history, manifesting a new sense of annalistic, straightforward narrative. No clearer picture of the fragmentation of Egypt can be afforded than in the scene at the top of the stele. Here Piankhy faces Amun-Re and the goddess Mut, and four kings are shown: Nemrot leading his horse and Osorkon, Iuwapet, and Peftuabast on their knees kissing the ground. (See Figure 44.) The text of the Piankhy stele, eked out with the evidence of donation stelae and other documents of the time, describes the "Libyan anarchy" of the Third Intermediate Period. The evidence has only recently been assembled in a major study by the scholar Jean Yoyotte.[4]

The rule of the Napatan family in Egypt is reckoned as Dyn. 25. At about the time of Piankhy's campaign in his twenty-first year of reign (730 B.C.), the land of Egypt was controlled in large part by an aristocracy of Libyan tribal chieftains of the Meshwesh and, to a lesser extent, of the Libu. The Meshwesh are depicted with a slanting feather on their head-dress, the Libu with an upright feather. The Meshwesh domination of

[4] Jean Yoyotte, "Les principautés du Delta au temps de l'anarchie libyenne," fasc. 4, *Mélanges Maspero* 1 (Cairo: Institut français d'archéologie orientale, 1961), 121–81.

Egypt brought the Sheshonqid dynasties to power. However, although they were recognized as the heirs to the line of divine kings, the Sheshonqids had limited territory because major sections of the country were actually controlled by a series of local princes of the same tribal background. These princes or dynasts were frequently the sons of the reigning Sheshonqid monarch, but they in time developed their own local dynasties, and at no time were all the local dynasts sons of the reigning king. In Upper Egypt the regions of Thebes, Hermopolis (where Amarna was situated), and Herakleopolis were indepedent entities. Thebes was later governed for a long span by Montuemhat, the fourth prophet of Amun and the heir to the god's state of Amun. The most powerful of the dynasts at the time of Piankhy was Tefnakht, whose territory was the Great Kingdom of the West in the Delta. On his western borders were the Libu tribes, and he called himself a chief of the Libu as well as of the Meshwesh. Other states were those of Sebennytos, ruled by Akanosh, Athribis in the southern Delta, ruled by Petisis, Leontopolis to the east, under Iuwapet, and the city-states of Mendes, Hermopolis parva, and Pisapti in the eastern Delta, as well as Busiris in the central Delta. The "real" kings ruled at Bubastis and Tanis. A tribal chieftain ruled at Memphis until the area was taken over by the Great Kingdom of the West. In 730 B.C. there were at least four dynasts between Siut and the Mediterranean coast who regarded themselves as kings. At the end of the Kushite-Ethiopian domination of Kashta, Piankhy, and their successors, the Assyrian annals used the Akkadian term *shar*, "king," to designate as many as twenty dynasts. Relations among the dynasts were necessarily complex, as were their transactions with the god's state of Amun at Thebes. The Sheshonqids succeeded in naming many of their family to the high-priesthoods as well as to the office of Divine Adoratress. Their societal structure has been called feudalistic, since many of the dynasts were allied to the royal houses through military associations. Moreover, the family and tribal relationships at this time parallel those of medieval Europe, leading historians to apply such terms as count, baron, and vassal.

The occasion, provocation, or excuse for Piankhy's campaign, as recorded in the Gebel Barkal stele, was the announcement made to the king that the Prince of the West, Tefnakht, had incorporated several adjacent areas and was advancing south. The text states that "the princes and rulers of walled towns are as dogs at his heels." The king of Hermopolis fell before Tefnakht, and only Herakleopolis held out. In his northern advance Piankhy besieged Hermopolis successfully, and the queen begged mercy from the ladies of Piankhy's harem. When Piankhy visited the stables he became alarmed at the mistreatment of the horses during the siege. Town after town fell to him. Even Memphis was taken in an attack from the river side. Eventually all the dynasts came with their submission and tribute, except for the wily Tefnakht. He finally surrendered in absentia and took an oath of fealty. The text abounds in detailed description. For example, at the submission of four of the dynasts only one was allowed to enter the palace, since he alone had not eaten fish. Piankhy is shown as a strong, zealously pious ruler, disdaining the women of Egypt and devoted to his family. After the campaign, the king returned to Napata and, as is characteristic of the period and the years immediately following, ruled through his vassal dynasts.

Piankhy's brother, Shabaka, succeeded him, reconquered Egypt, and was followed by Shabataka and then Taharqa. As a token of the Kushite domination of Egypt and the Sudan, the kings of Dyn. 25 wore on their crowns a double cobra device. They were buried in their homeland in a series of very sharp-angled pyramids. Perhaps through a desire to assert their claims to the true kingship of Amun and to root their program in the past, they adopted various practices that linked them to the great ages of the past, such as the revival of the pyramid burials. In addition, the kings took for one of their names that of a great king of the past, a practice already attempted by the Ramessides. Piankhy used the prenomen of Ramses II, Shabaka the prenomen of Pepy II, and Shabataka the prenomen of Djedkare of Dyn. 5. Monuments of the past were copied again—such as the famous Memphite Theology (and perhaps also the Palermo Stone Annals) under Shabaka. Taharqa's artisans copied the scene of Libyan tribute at Kawa in the Sudan from the pyramid temples of the Old Kingdom at Sakkara and Abu Sir.

Events in Asia, however, prevented a long Kushite hegemony. Assyria had intervened in Palestine and Syria, and the war machines of the Sudanese and Asian rulers were destined to clash on the banks of the Nile before both powers were forced to return to pressing matters in their respective homelands. The campaigns in Syria and Palestine of the Assyrian kings Tiglath-pileser III (744–727 B.C.), Shalmaneser V (726–722 B.C.), Sargon II (721–705 B.C.), and Sennaherib (705–681 B.C.) culminated in direct and intense conflict between Kushite Egypt and the Assyrians under Esarhaddon (680–669 B.C.) and Assurbanipal (668–627 B.C.). Esarhaddon claims that he utterly destroyed Memphis, routed Taharqa and the Kushites, and appointed new dynasts and administrative officers. Although Taharqa later reoccupied Memphis, Assurbanipal routed him again and drove him to the Sudan. Statues of Taharqa were taken to Nineveh on the Tigris for the Assyrian palace. Thebes itself was sacked by Assurbanipal in 663 B.C. Taharqa's son, Tanutamun, who succeeded his father in 664 B.C. before the sack of Thebes, was unable to regain much of the empire controlled by his ancestors, although he boasted of success in his so-called Dream Stele. In the dream he sees two serpents, and this is interpreted to mean that he will rule both Upper and Lower Egypt. But with Tanutamun the extraordinary Kushite venture came to an end. Assurbanipal appointed vassals loyal to the Assyrian cause as dynasts in

the Delta. Neko, an Egyptian who had been carried off to Nineveh, was
sent back to Sais in the Great Kingdom of the West, and his son was
made dynast in adjacent Athribis. Nevertheless, troubles in the Assyrian
capital soon made it impossible for the Assyrians to control their vassals
in Egypt, and once again Egypt became independent.

[3] DYNASTY 26—THE SAITES

The dynasty of the Saites, so called after its capital city of Sais in the
western Delta, lasted a not inconsiderable span of 139 years, from 664 to
525 B.C.[5] It saw a return to a single kingship over the entire land and an
end of specifically foreign rule. Its rulers were native Egyptians in the
same sense that their Libyan predecessors were. Their names belong to a
Libyan or Napatan rather than Egyptian language group. The Saite Renaissance, as it has frequently been designated, incorporated several salient
features of interest discussed more fully later: the beginning of mercenary
armies and fleets manned by Greek and Aegean peoples, the appearance
of Greek merchants as a class and the foundation of their colony at Naucratis, the development of the system of property divestment exemplified
by the donation decrees, and the appearance in art of archaism—a conscious return to older models. All these elements were present to some extent in the Third Intermediate Period, but it is in the Saite Period that
they found their characteristic expression.

The independence achieved by Egypt seemed at first destined to be
merely a reversion to the times before the Napatans and Assyrians. Each
dynast installed by the Assyrians controlled only a piece of the land, and
many belonged to the same Libyan tribal families. Herodotus relates that
the land was ruled by twelve princes, each under oath not to transgress
against this dodekarchy and establish a single state. Yet an oracle an-
nounced that the one who made a temple offering with a bronze vessel
would become king and rule the others. Psamtik, ruler of Athribis and
later of his father's territory at Sais, entered the temple one day with his
eleven co-dynasts. The attendant brought only eleven offering vessels, and
Psamtik unconsciously used his bronze helmet as his own. He was then
exiled by the others to the Delta rim. A second oracle foretold that he
would succeed when bronze men came from the sea. This prophecy was
fulfilled when Ionian and Carian mercenaries and pirates landed near his
place of exile in the Delta. With their help he seized the kingship.

[5] For an outline with references of the Saite Period, the reader is referred to Étienne
Drioton and Jacques Vandier, L'Égypte, 4th rev. ed., "Clio": Introduction aux études
historiques. Les peuples de l'Orient Méditerranéen, vol. 2 (Paris: Presses Universitaires
de France, 1962).

Although evidently apocryphal, these tales reflect quite accurately the general situation of the times. The Assyrians were unable to control their vassals, and Gyges of Lydia, among others, aided the Egyptians in their resistance. Although the Assyrians were able to crush Gyges, Egypt henceforth remained out of their reach. Psamtik's father, Neko I, had played the Napatans against the Assyrians, had been taken to Nineveh by Assurbanipal, and then had been installed by the latter as ruler of Sais. His son learned the rules of this diplomacy of self-interest and was soon free to develop it in subjugating all of Egypt.

Having firm control of the Delta, he proceeded to take mastery of Upper Egypt from the powers loyal to Napata. Foremost of these was the extraordinary Montuemhat, fourth priest of Amun of Thebes, but in effect the ruler of the southern nomes. Montuemhat had managed to see Thebes through the Napatan domination and the Assyrian sack, and he prospered in the Saite era. To mitigate his power Psamtik used the services of two great officials, the new fleet master and nomarch of Herakleopolis, Smatowytefnakht, whose sphere of influence lay generally in the northern part of Upper Egypt, and the new nomarch of the south, Nesnawiau. The former escorted a daughter of Psamtik, Nitocris, to Thebes to become adopted by the Divine Adoratress Shepenwepet II, daughter of Piankhy, as her successor, even though the office would first pass to Amunirdis II, daughter of Taharqa. Montuemhat and Shepenwepet, unable to resist the authority of the new ruler, evidently still managed to retain most of their own prerogatives. Montuemhat's tomb at Thebes is more impressive than many a king's, and it is known for fine statues and reliefs. The objects inscribed with his name have traveled to museums the world over.

In the north Psamtik laid siege at Ashdod in Palestine and succeeded in capturing it after twenty-nine years. The troubles of Assyria were legion. Within the reign of Psamtik, and despite his attempt to help, Nineveh fell to the Babylonians. It was a different political world, dominated by the Medes, the Scyths, and the Babylonians, that Psamtik left to his son and successor, Neko II.

Neko II (609–594 B.C.) must be counted as one of the most ambitious of the extraordinary Saite kings, if not one to whom lasting success was granted. Having at his disposition the army created during his father's fifty-five-year rule, Neko attempted to revive the Egyptian empire of the New Kingdom in the face of Babylonian competition. During the first part of his reign he managed to control most of Palestine and Syria, intervening enough in the kingdoms of Judah and Israel to depose one of the kings of Judah, Jehoahaz, and replace him with an older brother, Jehoiakim, more favorable to the Egyptian cause. From the garrison at Carchemish on the Euphrates he seconded the attempts of Assyria to survive the power of Babylon. But in the spring of 605 B.C. the new Babylonian king, Nebukanezzar, utterly defeated the Egyptian army and sent the sorry remnant hurrying home. In 601 B.C. Nebukanezzar nearly succeeded in invading Egypt. Yet the armies of Neko laid the groundwork for the Saite domination of the southern part of Syro-Palestine. Neko's grandiose schemes also included an attempt, which may have been successful, to link the Mediterranean and the Red Sea by a canal from the latter to the Nile. This achievement is credited to Darius in the following dynasty, but the texts relating to his works suggest that Darius was reopening the route. Less doubtful is Herodotus's statement that Neko sent a successful mission from the Red Sea to circumnavigate Africa. The sailors reported that the sun, which usually rose on their left, one day began to rise on their right, thus confirming the success of their three years' journey.

Psamtik II (594–588 B.C.) had to abandon a vigorous policy in Asia to secure the southern borders neglected by his father. He sent Egyptians under the general Amasis and a mercenary army of Greeks, Phoenicians, and Jews under the general Potasimto. The army reached Pnubs, south of the third cataract, and returned by Abu Simbel, where the soldiers left graffiti in their own languages. Very likely the fourth cataract was also reached in this attempt to check a Napatan invasion in the making. It seems unlikely that the king played an active part in Palestine, previous writers to the contrary. The stelae at Karnak and Shellal (Aswan) record the Nubian campaign in Year 3 of Psamtik and indicate that he brought back 4,200 captives.

Apries (588–568 B.C.) came to the throne at a time when Palestine was still dominated largely by Babylon. Nebukanezzar had punished a Judean revolt by sacking Jerusalem and taking into captivity many of its inhabitants (the Babylonian captivity). An Egyptian siege of Tyre lasted some thirteen years. But the circumstances which cost Apries his throne lay west in Libya. The Libyans sought his aid against the Greek colonists there, and Apries sent Amasis with an Egyptian army to combat them. Amasis profited from this commission to seize the kingship for himself, forcing Apries to retire for the last two years of his life.

Amasis (568–526 B.C.) ruled this kingdom of Egyptians and mercenary and merchant Greeks for a span of forty-two peaceful yet not uneventful years. To curb internal race and class dissensions, a problem that was to become intense later under the Ptolemies, he founded the Greek merchant colony at Naucratis near the future Alexandria. Yet the rise of the Achaemenians in Persia boded ill for the Egyptian state. Croesus of Lydia fell to Cyrus in spite of his alliance with Egypt, Sparta, and Babylon. Similarly, Polycrates of Samos fell to Cambyses, the son of Cyrus, before he could aid Amasis. And it was perhaps one of Amasis's own Greek generals who led the Persian army of Cambyses to a decisive victory over the Egyptians at Pelusium. The last ruler of the Saite Dynasty, Psamtik III, ruled for six months (526–525 B.C.) before the kingship was seized by Cambyses.

Our sources for this brief sketch of the Saites are clearly of a new type—in many cases properly "historical." Although royal stelae and Egyptian inscriptions provide details, the major source is Herodotus. At times his information can be faulted, as in his account of the suffocation of Apries by Amasis. Yet we might wish we had such a history for the preceding twenty-five dynasties.

The Saites are credited with a revival of older forms in art and architecture. However, this archaism is well attested in the Libyan period of Dyns. 22 and 23 and especially in Dyn. 25, the Napatan pharaohs even going to the extremes of copying reliefs of Pepy II of Dyn. 6 and using for some of their cartouches the names of past rulers. Montuemhat of Thebes actually copied scenes from Dyn. 18 tombs in his own.

The Saite Renaissance also represents a turning point in Egypt's relationship with the Aegean world, a process starting with the invasion of the Sea Peoples in Dyn. 20, continuing with the merchants and mercenaries in the Third Intermediate Period, and culminating in the conquest by Alexander the Great and the later subjugation of Egypt by the Romans. Greek and Demotic now become the languages of business documents. Contacts with the kingdoms of Israel and Judah also gave rise to Jewish colonies in Egypt. (The Aramaic records of the Jewish colony at Elephantine are a major source for Judaic research.) At the same time the country prospered. The king, however, controlled the growing fortunes of the landed nobility by forcing them to make donations of land and capital to temples, from which they derived income or offices.

Our view of the Saites would be incomparably fuller if their great city of Sais had been preserved with the remains of the temple of Neith and the royal necropolis. Unfortunately, these have long since vanished, and our history is derived from Herodotus, temple reliefs elsewhere in Egypt, biographies on stelae and statuary of officials, and the business and account documents of a prospering age.

[4] DYNASTY 27

Where the Assyrians had failed, Cambyses succeeded. Like the Hyksos before him, and Alexander, the Ptolemies, and the Romans after him, he assumed the kingship of Egypt in his own name. Hieroglyphic inscriptions show the names of Cambyses, Darius, and Xerxes in cartouches. This policy was evidently suggested by Persian collaborators among the Egyptian nobility.[6] An extraordinary text of some length on a statue now in the

---

[6] For the main treatment of the period, see Georges Posener, *La première domination Perse en Égypte*. Bibliothèque d'Étude, vol. 11 (Cairo: Institut français d'archéologie orientale, 1936). In the field of art, see, for example, J. D. Cooney, "The Portrait of an Egyptian Collaborator," *Bulletin of the Brooklyn Museum* 15 (1953):1–16.

Vatican Museum provides the biography of Udjahorresne, the chief of the Egyptian navy under Psamtik III at the time of Cambyses' invasion and a medical practitioner and citizen of Sais. Udjahorresne details his service under Cambyses and states that he formulated the king's Egyptian titulary and cartouches. The official claims that he swayed the Persian to respect the Egyptian gods and particularly Sais and its temple. Throughout the dynasty statues of these Persian sympathizers show details of dress, ornament, and jewelry of Achaemenian origin or inspiration. With the Achaemenian genius for governing subject countries under a Persian satrap, the country was ably administered. In the region of Darius a rebellious satrap, who coined money with his own image, was executed after an abortive Libyan campaign.

During the Persian domination of Dyn. 27 Aramaic became an important language in the land, as it was the diplomatic and business vehicle for the Persian empire.[7] The Egyptian legal system was codified by Persian decree, and the Egyptians were governed mainly under their own laws. Quarries were reopened and temples built. The temple of Khargeh in the western oasis, a work of Darius, is still standing. The canal between the Red Sea and the Nile was completed or reopened. But Egypt did not permit this domination to last without interruption. The Greek victory over the Persians at Marathon in 490 B.C. pointed the way to an unsuccessful revolt in the Delta against Xerxes in 484 B.C. and another rebellion against his successor, Artaxerxes, in 460 B.C. In the latter year Amyrteus of Sais and Inaros, a Libyan dynast, with the crucial aid of three hundred Athenian triremes, defeated the Persians, the great battle taking place at Papremis in the Delta. The victory was not lasting, however, for the Persians retired to Memphis and held it. Inaros was killed, and a second Athenian fleet was destroyed by a Phoenician fleet of the Persians. Persia, like Assyria before, lost hold of Egypt through problems at home in the Persian capital.

[5] DYNASTIES 28 THROUGH 30

Manetho's Dyn. 28 consists solely of one Amyrtaeus (404–398 B.C.), through whose rebellion against the Persians (410–404 B.C.) Egypt again became independent. In 401 B.C. an outbreak of xenophobic sentiment led to the destruction of the Jewish temple at Elephantine, but the Jewish community survived. Another dynasty arose in Mendes, Manetho's Dyn. 29, from 398 to 378 B.C. The major rulers were Nepherites I and Achoris, and their policy abroad consisted of an alliance with Sparta against the Persians and then with Athens. Rivalry among the Greek states benefited

---

[7] Bezalel Porten, *Archives from Elephantine: The Life of an Ancient Jewish Colony* (Berkeley and Los Angeles: University of California Press, 1968).

Persia. The internal situation in Egypt was obviously unsatisfactory, and yet there are traces of major buildings constructed under these kings.

Dyn. 30 (378–341 B.C.) brings to a close Manetho's canonical list with three important kings: Nectanebo I, Teos, and Nectanebo II. In 373 B.C. a Persian army nearly seized Egypt but was prevented by faulty strategy and the Nile flood. The kings of Egypt became increasingly dependent upon the aid of Greek mercenaries, and the cost of this aid was high for their means. Teos, hoping to reconquer Syria and Palestine with a large army, imposed major financial burdens upon his subjects and the temples. He was betrayed by his brother, who offered the kingship to Teos's son, Nectanebo II. The latter won over Agesilaus of Sparta, and Chabrias of Athens, then in Egypt, was sent home. Under Nectanebo II a considerable amount of building took place, and many gateways, sphinxes, and blocks of his temples survive. (See Figure 43, page 284.) Yet the political situation at home, with a rebellion in the Mendesian nomes, and the advent once again of a forceful policy on the part of Persia spelled the end of the long succession of dynasties. Artaxerxes III Ochus sacked the Delta with a large army, installed a new satrap, and forced Nectanebo to retreat for his final two years to the south. The so-called Second Persian Domination, designated by some as Dyn. 31, was fated to be brief (341–333 B.C.)—Alexander the Great of Macedon was well on his way to the conquest of the world.

In 332 B.C. Alexander arrived in Egypt as its newest lord, paid homage to the Egyptian temples, visited the great oracle of Amun in the Siwa Oasis, and was recognized as a savior. The central sanctuary of the temple of Luxor shows a king in the ritual acts appropriate for the structure, and in the cartouches are the names of Alexander. The central sanctuary at Karnak is similarly inscribed, in traditional Egyptian style, with the name of his successor, Philip Arrhidaeus (323–316 B.C.).

The conquest of Alexander marks a turning point in Egyptian history. In the incredibly troubled affairs of his successors, the Ptolemies, we see constant intrigue and the outbreak of increasing animosity among classes and ethnic elements in a complex society. Egyptians, Greeks, and Jews lived in a turbulent world in which learning and technology far outran any semblance of social equilibrium. The Greek papyri detailing the business life of the large estates, the contracts, the sales of land, and all the major and minor affairs of a commercial nation, are one of the most rewarding legacies of the time. Yet they belong to the Hellenistic world more than to the continuum of ancient Egypt. Throughout the Ptolemaic and the succeeding Roman period the kings erected Egyptian temples on a large scale, inscribed with traditional, hieroglyphic formulas, endowed with considerable properties, and staffed by an active priesthood performing the great rituals of the religious calendar. The best-preserved temples standing today, those at Edfu, Dendereh, and Philae, belong to these later periods, but the absentee Roman emperors in whose names they were erected could not read hieroglyphs and frequently never saw the temples in which they are represented in the act of offering to strange gods in a distant land. Although it is difficult to mark a break in the continuum of Egyptian history, particularly since the Ptolemaic dynasty continued many of the earlier traditions, the conquest of Alexander marks a convenient point. Henceforth the rulers of Egypt will vie with the kingdoms that rose from the shattered empire of Alexander. The major sources will be in Greek, and Egypt will be on a new course.

[6] CONCLUSION

Today, dynastic Egypt seems to many a chapter in the tale of oriental despotism, one of the dead and fossilized precursors of the more exciting and pertinent Greek adventure in fifth-century Athens. Its heritage does not form an immediately recognizable stratum in Western civilization. The hieroglyphs and art have something of the quality of a dumb show or exotic pantomime. And there is romance in the ruins among the palms and, in the desert, the fallen granite body of the pharaoh Ozymandias. On the stage or screen the triumphal processions in *Aida*, the sets for Mozart's *The Magic Flute*, Shakespeare's *Antony and Cleopatra*, Shaw's *Caesar and Cleopatra*, are among the little that renews our somewhat ambivalent, tenuous relations with the Egyptian past. The pyramid and obelisk, the pylon and the axial temple plan are the main stimuli across the ages. Greece and Rome are represented not only by temples, statues, and vase painting, but also by drama, philosophy, and epic poetry. They have come to us through the Middle Ages and the Renaissance and have entered into our national consciousness. Visually they are reflected in our public buildings from the colonial period on—the America of Thomas Jefferson was imprinted with classical forms. Neither Egypt nor Mesopotamia have fared well in this respect. Egyptian literature, art, and history were virtually unknown until Bonaparte's campaigns, and their visual aspects were utilized mainly in decorative media such as furniture and design of an admittedly bizarre and exotic character. Thus Egypt, which contributed so much to the classical world, is connected in our minds with the Napoleonic empire, an era not particularly agreeable to the student concerned with civil rights, the computer, outer space exploration, and competing technologies reminiscent in fact of Ptolemaic Alexandria, as well as the rival ideologies of socialism and communism.

Yet the Egyptian experience is a significant legacy, representing the formulation of a system of norms over a not inconsiderable time span. The analysis of its history, its processual models of experience, its natural and adaptive factors of development, and its societal configuration have only recently been undertaken. The analytic study of Egypt provides a fertile discipline for today's student and scholar.

APPENDIX

PROTODYNASTIC

Kings of Upper Egypt, Kings of Lower Egypt, and Kings of Upper and Lower Egypt, as inferred from the Old Kingdom Annals. Of the last, the following are known only from their own monuments: Ka-Sekhen and Rosette-Scorpion (Scorpion).

EARLY DYNASTIC

DYNASTY 1
ca. 3100–2890 B.C.

Narmer (Menes?)
Aha
Djer
Djet (Wadji)
Den (Wedimu, Dewen)
Anedjib
Semerkhet
Qa

DYNASTY 2
ca. 2890–2686 B.C.

Hotepsekhemwy
Re-neb (Nebre)
Nyneter
Peribsen (Seth name)
Khasekhem
Khasekhemwy (Horus and Seth name)

OLD KINGDOM

DYNASTY 3
ca. 2686–2613 B.C.

Sanakhte
Neterirykhet (Djoser)
Sekhemkhet
Khaba
Huni (Nisuteh)

DYNASTY 4
ca. 2613–2494 B.C.

Snefru
Khufu (Cheops)
Redjedef (Djedefre)
Khafre (Chephren)
Menkaure (Mycerinus)
Shepseskaf

DYNASTY 5
ca. 2494–2345 B.C.

Userkaf
Sahure
Neferirkare Kakai
Shepseskare Isi
Neferefre
Neuserre
Menkauhor Akauhor
Djedkare Isesi
Unis

DYNASTY 6
ca. 2345–2181 B.C.

Main kings:
Teti
Userkare
Meryre Pepy I
Merenre Antiemsaf
Neferkare Pepy II
Netjerykare
Queen Nitocris

DYNASTY 7
ca. 2181–2173 B.C.

About nine kings

DYNASTY 8
ca. 2173–2160 B.C.

About six kings

FIRST INTERMEDIATE PERIOD

DYNASTIES 9 AND 10
ca. 2160–2040 B.C.

Main kings:
Meryibre Akhtoy I
Nebkaure Akhtoy II
Wahkare Akhtoy III
Merykare

PRECONQUEST DYNASTY 11
ca. 2133–2040 B.C.

Mentuhotpe I
Inyotef I
Wahankh Inyotef II
Nakhtnebtepnefer Inyotef III
Nebhepetre Mentuhotpe II

MIDDLE KINGDOM

POSTCONQUEST DYNASTY 11
ca. 2040–1991 B.C.

Nebhepetre Mentuhotpe II
Sankhkare Mentuhotpe III
Nebtowyre Mentuhotpe IV

DYNASTY 12
ca. 1991–1786 B.C.
Amunemhet I 1991–1962
Sesostris I 1971–1928
Amunemhet II 1929–1895
Sesostris II 1897–1878
Sesostris III 1878–1843
Amunemhet III 1842–1797
Amunemhet IV 1798–1790
Queen Sobkkare Sobknofru
    1789–1786

DYNASTY 13
ca. 1786–1633 B.C.

Main kings:
Sobkhotpe I
Auibre Hor
Sobkemsaf I
Sobkhotpe III
Neferhotpe I
Sobkhotpe IV
Dudimose (Tutimaios)

SECOND INTERMEDIATE PERIOD

DYNASTY 14
ca. 1786–1603 B.C.
Seventy-six kings of Xois

DYNASTIES 15 AND 16
The Hyksos
ca. 1674–1558 B.C.

Main kings:
Khyan
Aauserre Apopi

DYNASTY 17
ca. 1650–1558 B.C.

Main kings:
Seqenenre Tao I
Seqenenre Tao II
Kamose

NEW KINGDOM

DYNASTY 18
Thutmosid
ca. 1558–1303 B.C.

Ahmose 1558–1533
Amunhotpe I 1533–1512
Thutmose I 1512–1500
Thutmose II 1500–1490
Queen Hatshepsut 1490–1469
Thutmose III 1490–1436
Amunhotpe II 1438–1412
Thutmose IV 1412–1402
Amunhotpe III 1402–1363
Akhenaten 1363–1347
Smenkhkare 1349–1347
Tutankhamun 1347–1338
Ay 1337–1333
Horemheb 1333–1303

DYNASTY 19
First Ramesside Dynasty
ca. 1303–1200 B.C.

Ramses I 2 years
Seti I 14 years
Ramses II 67 years
Merneptah 10–13 years

Amunmose
Seti II
Siptah
Queen Tawosre

DYNASTY 20
Second Ramesside Dynasty
        ca. 1200–1085 B.C.

Sethnakhte 1200–1198
Ramses III 1198–1166
Ramses IV through
    Ramses XI 1166–1085

THIRD INTERMEDIATE
PERIOD

DYNASTY 21
        ca. 1085–945 B.C.

Smendes
Amunemnisu
Psusennes I
Amunemope
Siamun
Psusennes II

DYNASTY 22
Libyan
        ca. 940–717 B.C.

Sheshonq I 940–919
Osorkon I 919–883*
Takelot I 883–860
Osorkon II 860–831
Takelot II 837–812
Sheshonq III 812–760
Pami 760–754
Shesonq V 754–717
    * only 15 years are definite

DYNASTY 23
Libyan
        ca. 817–730 B.C.

Pedubast
Sheshonq IV
Osorkon III
Takelot III
Amunrud
Osorkon IV

DYNASTY 24
        ca. 730–715 B.C.

Tefnakht
Bakenrenef

DYNASTY 25
Napatan
        ca. 760–656 B.C.

Kashta
Piankhy (Pi) 751–716
Shabaka 716–701
Shabataka 701–689
Taharqa 689–664
Tanatumun 664–656

SAITE RENAISSANCE

DYNASTY 26
        664–525 B.C.
Psamtik I 664–609
Neko II 609–594
Psamtik II 594–588
Apries 588–568
Amasis 568–526
Psamtik III 526–525

LATE DYNASTIC

DYNASTY 27
First Persian Domination
        525–404 B.C.

Cambyses 525–522
Darius I 522–485
Xerxes 485–464
Artaxerxes 464–424
Darius II 424–404

DYNASTY 28
        404–398 B.C.

Amyrtaeus

DYNASTY 29
        398–378 B.C.

Nepherites I 398–393
Muthis 392–391
Psammuthis 391–390
Achoris 390–378
Nepherites II 378

302 APPENDIX

DYNASTY 30
378–341 B.C.

Nectanebo I (Nakhtnebef) 378–360
Teos 361–359
Nectanebo II (Nakhthorhebe) 359–341

DYNASTY 31
Second Persian Domination
341–330 B.C.

Artaxerxes II Ochos 341–338
Arses 338–335
Darius III Codoman 335–330

CONQUEST OF ALEXANDER
332 B.C.

MACEDONIAN DOMINATION
332–304 B.C.

Alexander 332–323
Philip Arrhidaeus 323–316
Alexander IV 316–304

PTOLEMAIC DYNASTY
304–30 B.C.

Ptolemy I through
Ptolemy XII and
Cleopatra VII

ROMAN CONQUEST
30 B.C.

BIBLIOGRAPHY

[1] MESOPOTAMIA AND THE ASIATIC NEAR EAST

GENERAL HISTORIES

Cambridge Ancient History, rev. ed. Cambridge: Cambridge University Press, 1961–. Now being reedited by numerous scholars and preissued in fascicles, this is the standard history of the preclassical world in English.

Bottéro, Jean, et al. *The Near East: The Early Civilizations*. 3 vols. Translated by R. F. Tannenbaum. London: Weidenfeld and Nicholson, 1967–. A shorter survey of the field, written by a smaller number of specialists, than the *Cambridge Ancient History*, it gains in unity what it loses in detail.

Kramer, Samuel Noah. *The Sumerians: Their History, Culture, and Character*. Chicago: University of Chicago Press, 1964. Oppenheim, A. Leo. *Ancient Mesopotamia*. Chicago: University of Chicago Press, 1964. These two volumes cover the major components of cuneiform culture. The second includes a chronological list by John A. Brinkman of all major Mesopotamian rulers.

Roux, Georges. *Ancient Iraq*. Harmondsworth: Penguin Books, 1966. Saggs, H. W. F. *The Greatness that was Babylon*. London: Sidgwick and Jackson, 1962. Readable surveys, less authoritative but at times more objective than the preceding.

Pallis, S. A. *The Antiquity of Iraq: A Handbook of Assyriology*. Copenhagen: E. Munksgaard, 1956. Includes a detailed history of Assyriology and of exploration and excavation in Mesopotamia.

Hawkes, Jacquetta, and Woolley, Sir Leonard. *Prehistory and the Beginnings of Civilization*. Vol. 1. Pareti, Luigi; Brezzi, Paolo; and Petech, Luciano. *The Ancient World*. Vol. 2. History of Mankind: Cultural and Scientific Development. New York: Harper & Row, 1963–65. These are confined to nonpolitical history, but seen from a global viewpoint.

THE NEIGHBORS OF MESOPOTAMIA

Bibby, Geoffrey. *Looking for Dilmun*. New York: Knopf, 1969. Exploration of the Persian Gulf area.

Hinz, Walter. *Das Reich Elam*. Stuttgart: W. Kohlhammer, 1964. An up-to-date survey of pre-Achaemenid Persia.

Gurney, Oliver. *The Hittites*. Baltimore: Penguin Books, 1952. The standard survey in English of Anatolian culture.

Bright, John. *History of Israel*. Philadelphia: Westminster Press, 1959. de Vaux, Roland. *Ancient Israel: Its Life and Institutions*. Translated by

John McHugh. New York: McGraw-Hill, 1961. Biblical history and
institutions reconstructed from textual and archeological evidence.

Pfeiffer, Charles F., ed. *The Biblical World: A Dictionary of Biblical Archeology*. Grand Rapids, Mich.: Baker Book House, 1966. A useful, though
uneven, survey of archeological sites and discoveries, organized alphabetically.

MONOGRAPHIC TREATMENTS OF SPECIFIC TOPICS OR PERIODS

Ehrich, Robert W., ed. *Chronologies in Old World Archaeology*. Chicago: University of Chicago Press, 1965.

Beek, Martinus Adrianus. *Atlas of Mesopotamia: A Survey of the History and
Civilizations of Mesopotamia from the Stone Age to the Fall of Babylon*.
Translated by D. R. Welsh. New York: Nelson, 1962.

Parrot, André. *Sumer, the Dawn of Art*. Translated by Stuart Gilbert and
James Emmons. New York: Golden Press, 1961. Parrot, André. *The Arts
of Assyria*. Translated by Stuart Gilbert and James Emmons. New York:
Golden Press, 1961. Superbly illustrated surveys of Mesopotamian art.

Forbes, Robert J. *Studies in Ancient Technology*, 2nd ed. 9 vols. Leiden:
E. J. Brill, 1964–.

van der Waerden, F. *Science Awakening*. Translated by Arnold Dresden. New
York: Oxford University Press, 1961.

Yadin, Yigael. *The Art of Warfare in Biblical Lands in the Light of Archeological Study*. 2 vols. Translated by M. Pearlman. New York: McGraw-
Hill, 1963.

Pritchard, J. B., ed. *Ancient Near Eastern Texts*, 3rd ed. Princeton: Princeton
University Press, 1969. The standard anthology of ancient Near Eastern
literature in translation, fully annotated and indexed.

Oates, David. *Studies in the Ancient History of Northern Iraq*. Oxford: Oxford
University Press, 1968.

Orlin, Louis. *Assyrian Colonies in Cappadocia*. The Hague: Mouton & Co.,
1970.

Laessøe, Jørgen. *People of Ancient Assyria, Their Inscriptions and Correspondence*. Translated by F. S. Leigh-Browne. London: Routledge and Kegan
Paul, 1963.

Brinkman, John A. *A Political History of Post-Kassite Babylonia, 1158–722
B.C*. Rome: Pontificium Institutum Biblicum, 1968.

Diakonoff, I. M., ed. *Ancient Mesopotamia*. Moscow: USSR Academy of Sciences, Institute of the Peoples of Asia, Central Department of Oriental
Literature, 1969. A concise introduction, in English, to the extensive Rus-
sian literature in the field of Near Eastern social and economic history.

MONOGRAPHIC SERIES ESPECIALLY DEVOTED TO
THE ANCIENT NEAR EAST

David, M., et al., eds. *Studia et Documenta ad Iura Orientis Antiqui Pertinentia*. Leiden: E. J. Brill, 1936–.

Albright, W. F., and De Buck, A., eds. *Documenta et Monumenta Orientis
Antiqui*. Leiden: E. J. Brill, 1947–.

Analecta Orientalia. Commentationes Scientificae de Rebus Orientis Antiqui. Rome: Pontifico Instituto Biblico, 1931–.

The Oriental Institute of the University of Chicago. *Assyriological Studies.* Chicago: University of Chicago Press, 1931–.

Oppenheim, A. Leo, ed. *Texts from Cuneiform Sources.* Locust Valley, N.Y.: J. J. Augustin, 1966–.

Hallo, William W.; Finkelstein, Jacob J.; and Simpson, William K., eds. *Yale Near Eastern Researches.* New Haven: Yale University Press, 1967–.

Studia Pohl: Dissertationes Scientificae de Rebus Orientis Antiqui. Rome: Pontificium Institutum Biblicum, 1969–.

Council of the British Academy. *The Schweich Lectures.* Oxford: Oxford University Press, 1909–.

PERIODICALS

The footnotes in the text provide a representative sampling of the many periodicals in which current research is presented in short articles. The following periodicals, listed with the place of publication and date of the first volume, are particularly important sources. Unless otherwise noted, they are issued annually.

Anatolian Studies, London, 1951.

Iraq. London, 1934 (semiannual).

Journal of Cuneiform Studies. New Haven, 1947 (quarterly).

Journal of Near Eastern Studies. Chicago, 1942 (quarterly).

Journal of the American Oriental Society. Boston, 1849 (quarterly).

Orientalia. Rome, 1920 (quarterly).

Revue d'assyriologie et d'archéologie orientale. Paris, 1884 (semiannual).

Zeitschrift für Assyriologie und Vorderasiatische Archäologie. Leipzig, 1886.

ANNIVERSARY VOLUMES

Important articles are often compiled or reissued in anniversary volumes in honor or in memory of a scholar. Note especially the following.

Cihar, V.; Klima, J.; Matouš, L., eds. *Symbolae ad Studia Orientis Pertinentes, Frederico Hrozny Dedicatae.* 5 vols. Prague: Orientální Ústav, 1949–1950.

Mallowan, M. E. L., and Wiseman, D. J., eds. *Ur in Retrospect, in Memory of Sir C. Leonard Woolley.* London: British School of Archaeology in Iraq, 1960.

Wright, G. Ernest, ed. *The Bible and the Ancient Near East, Essays in Honor of William Foxwell Albright.* Garden City, N.Y.: Doubleday and Company, 1961.

Biggs, R. D., and Brinkman, John A., eds. *Studies Presented to A. Leo Oppenheim.* Chicago: The Oriental Institute of the University of Chicago, 1964.

Güterbock, Hans G., and Jacobsen, Thorkild, eds. *Studies in Honor of Benno Landsberger on his Seventy-fifth Birthday.* Chicago: University of Chicago Press, 1965.

Sachs, A., ed. *Special Volume Honoring Professor Albrecht Goetze.* Cambridge: American Schools of Oriental Research, 1969.

Hallo, William W., ed. *Essays in Memory of E. A. Speiser.* New Haven: American Oriental Society, 1968.

Mallowan, M. E. L., and Wiseman, D. J., eds. *Volume in Honour of the Seventy-fifth Birthday of Professor C. J. Gadd.* London: British School of Archaeology in Iraq, 1969.

Sanders, James A., ed. *Near Eastern Archaeology in the Twentieth Century, Essays in Honor of Nelson Glueck.* Garden City, N.Y.: Doubleday and Company, 1970.

COLLECTIONS

Articles of enduring interest from a single journal or by a single author are occasionally reissued as a collection, which facilitates retrieval and reference. Note especially the following.

The Biblical Archaeologist Reader. 3 vols. Vol. 1, Wright, G. Ernest, and Freedman, David Noel, eds. Chicago: Quadrangle Books, 1961. Vols. 2 and 3, Campbell, Edward F., Jr., and Freedman, David Noel, eds. Garden City, N.Y.: Doubleday and Company, Anchor Original, 1964–70.

Jacobsen, Thorkild. *Toward the Image of Tammuz and Other Essays on Mesopotamian History and Culture.* Edited by William L. Moran. Harvard Semitic Series, vol. 21. Cambridge: Harvard University Press, 1970.

Dhorme, Edouard Paul. *Recueil Édouard Dhorme: Études bibliques et Orientales.* Paris: Imprimerie Nationale, 1951.

Speiser, Ephraim Avigdor. *Oriental and Biblical Studies, Collected Writings of E. A. Speiser.* Edited and introduced by J. J. Finkelstein and Moshe Greenberg. Philadelphia: University of Pennsylvania Press, 1967.

Boyer, Georges. *Mélanges II, d'histoire du droit oriental.* Recueil de l'Académie de Législation, 6e série, tome III, 115e année. Paris: Sirey, 1965.

Boehl, Franz Marius Theodor. *Opera Minora.* Groningen: J. B. Wolters, 1953.

[2] EGYPT

BASIC BIBLIOGRAPHICAL AIDS

Pratt, Ida A., comp. *Ancient Egypt: Sources of Information in the New York Public Library.* New York: New York Public Library, 1925. A list of volumes and articles published prior to 1925, arranged under subject headings but without annotations or abstracts.

Ancient Egypt 1925–1941. A Supplement to Ancient Egypt: Sources of Information in the New York Public Library, New York, 1925. New York: New York Public Library, 1942. A continuation of the above.

Federn, W., comp. "Egyptian Bibliography (January 1, 1939–December 31, 1947)." *Orientalia* 17 (1948):467–89; 18 (1949):73–99, 206–15, 325–35, 443–72; 19 (1950):40–52, 175–86, 279–94. This bibliography, without abstracts, bridges the gap between the preceding and following references.

Janssen, Josef M. A., and Heerma Van Voss, M. S. H. G., comps. *Annual*

Egyptological Bibliography/Bibliographie Egyptologique Annuelle 1947.
Leiden: International Association of Egyptologists, 1948. Subsequent
volumes have been issued for 1948 through 1965. The entries, made
alphabetically according to author, include abstracts. (Sometimes indexed under International Association of Egyptologists.) *Annual Egyptological Bibliography. Indexes 1947–56.* Leiden: International Association
of Egyptologists, 1960. This includes subject and lexical indexes, without
abstracts, to the first ten annual bibliographies.

Porter, Bertha, and Moss, Rosalind L. B., comps. Topographical Bibliography
of Ancient Egyptian Hieroglyphic Texts, Reliefs, and Paintings. Oxford:
Oxford University Press. Vol. 1, *The Theban Necropolis* (1927); Vol. 2,
Theban Temples (1929); Vol. 3, *Memphis (Abû Rawâsh to Dahshûr)*
(1931); Vol. 4, *Lower and Middle Egypt (Delta and Cairo to Asyût)*
(1934); Vol. 5, *Upper Egypt: Sites (Deir Rîfa to Aswan, excluding Thebes
and the Temples of Abydos, Dendera, Esna, Edfu, Kôm Ombo, and
Philae)* (1937); Vol. 6, *Upper Egypt: Chief Temples (excluding Thebes),
Abydos, Dendera, Esna, Edfu, Kôm Ombo, and Philae* (1939); Vol. 7,
Nubia, the Deserts, and Outside Egypt (1951). Second edition. Oxford:
Oxford University Press. Vol. 1, *The Theban Necropolis*, Part 1, "Private
Tombs" (1960); Part 2, "Royal Tombs and Smaller Cemeteries" (1964).

Leclant, Jean. Articles in recent issues of *Orientalia* on excavations in progress
in Egypt and the Sudan. Particularly valuable and interesting accounts
with complete bibliographical references.

Council on Old World Archaeology. *Surveys and Bibliographies*. "Northeast
Africa, Area 9," No. 1 (1959), edited by W. K. Simpson, No. 2 (1962),
edited by W. K. Simpson and T. H. Carter. Surveys of archeological
activity and abstracts of recent articles on archeology, arranged according
to period.

Wedge, Eleanor F., comp. *Acquisitions List*. Brooklyn: Wilbour Library of
Egyptology, Department of Ancient Art, The Brooklyn Museum. Issued
semiannually.

GENERAL WORKS

Gardiner, Sir Alan H. *Egypt of the Pharaohs*. Oxford: Oxford University Press,
1961. (Also available in a paperbound edition.) A detailed and rewarding
view.

Wilson, John A. *The Culture of Ancient Egypt*. Chicago: University of
Chicago Press, 1951. A modern, anthropology-oriented view.

Breasted, James Henry. A *History of Egypt*. New York: Scribner, 1905. Well
written, but out of date in specific details.

Hayes, William C. The Scepter of Egypt. New York: Metropolitan Museum
of Art. Vol. 1, *From the Earliest Times to the End of the Middle Kingdom* (1953); Vol. 2, *The Hyksos Period and the New Kingdom* (1959).
With an historical background and abundant illustrations, this is an
introduction to the Egyptian collections in the Metropolitan Museum of
Art.

Smith, William Stevenson. *Ancient Egypt as Represented in the Museum of*

Fine Arts, Boston, 4th rev. ed. Boston: Museum of Fine Arts, 1961. An introduction with illustrations drawn from the Boston collection.

Edwards, I. E. S., James, T. G. H., and Shore, A. F. *A General Introductory Guide to the Egyptian Collections in the British Museum*. London: British Museum, 1964. A guide to the collection with text on a number of subjects, a list of kings, and other useful material. Both the hardbound and paperbound editions are reasonably priced. Highly recommended.

Breasted, James Henry. *Ancient Records of Egypt*, 5 vols. Chicago: University of Chicago Press, 1906–07. Although most of these translations can be improved to a large extent, this collection of texts has yet to be replaced by a modern version and remains a source of considerable value to the beginner and to the advanced scholar.

Černy, Jaroslav. *Paper and Books in Ancient Egypt*. [An inaugural lecture delivered at University College, London, 29 May 1947.] London: H. K. Lewis, 1947.

Drioton, Étienne, and Vandier, Jacques. *L'Égypte*, 4th rev. ed. Paris: Presses Universitaires de France, 1962. In the series "Clio": Introduction aux études historiques. Les peuples de l'Orient Mediterranéen II. An extremely useful history with copious notes and references.

PERIODICALS

Many of the major advances in the study of ancient Egypt are reported in a variety of annuals relating to Egyptology itself or to Egyptology as part of a wider field. Only the main periodicals are cited here, and those that have been discontinued are omitted. The place of publication and date of the first volume are given. Unless otherwise noted, these periodicals are issued annually. In addition to these journals, there are many series of monographs.

Annales du Service des Antiquités de l'Égypte. Cairo, 1900.

Kush, Journal of the Sudan Antiquities Service. Khartoum, 1953.

Journal of Egyptian Archaeology, London, 1914.

Journal of the American Research Center in Egypt. Boston and Princeton, 1962.

Journal of Near Eastern Studies. Chicago, 1942 (quarterly).

Journal of the American Oriental Society. Boston, 1849 (quarterly).

Journal of the Economic and Social History of the Orient. Leiden, 1957.

Orientalia. Rome, 1920 (quarterly).

Revue d'Égyptologie. Paris, 1933.

Kêmi, Revue de Philologie et d'archéologie égyptiennes et coptes. Paris, 1928.

Bulletin de l'Institut français d'archéologie orientale. Cairo, 1901.

Zeitschrift für ägyptische Sprache und Altertumskunde. Berlin and Leipzig, 1863 (semiannually).

Mitteilungen des Deutschen Archäologischen Instituts. Cairo, 1930.

Bulletin of the Metropolitan Museum of Art. New York, 1906 (ten issues per year).

Bulletin of the Museum of Fine Arts. Boston, 1903 (quarterly).

Annual of the Brooklyn Museum. Brooklyn, 1959/1960.

Chronique l'Égypte. Brussels, 1925.
Wiener Zeitschrift für die Kunde des Morgenlandes. Vienna, 1886.

PREDYNASTIC AND EARLY DYNASTIC EGYPT

Baumgartel, Elise J. "Predynastic Egypt." *Cambridge Ancient History,* rev. ed., fasc. 38. Cambridge: Cambridge University Press, 1965.

Trigger, Bruce G. *Beyond History: The Methods of Prehistory.* Studies in Anthropological Method Series. New York: Holt, Rinehart & Winston, 1968.

Arkell, A. J., and Ucko, P. J. "Review of Predynastic Development in the Nile Valley." *Current Anthropology* 6 (1965):145–66.

Frankfort, Henri. *The Birth of Civilisation in the Near East.* London: Benn, 1951.

Childe, V. Gordon. *New Light on the Most Ancient East,* 4th ed. London: Routledge & Kegan Paul, 1953.

Edwards, I. E. S. "The Early Dynastic Period in Egypt." *Cambridge Ancient History,* rev. ed., fasc. 25. Cambridge: Cambridge University Press, 1964.

Emery, Walter Bryan. *Archaic Egypt.* Baltimore: Penguin Books, 1961 (Pelican Book A 462).

Kemp, Barry J. "The Egyptian 1st Dynasty Royal Cemetery." *Antiquity* 41 (1967):22–32. An explanation of the Abydos/Sakkara controversy in which the author suggests that the royal burials took place at Abydos.

THE OLD KINGDOM

Smith, William Stevenson. "The Old Kingdom in Egypt and the Beginning of the First Intermediate Period." *Cambridge Ancient History,* rev. ed., fasc. 5. Cambridge: Cambridge University Press, 1962.

Edwards, I. E. S. *The Pyramids of Egypt,* rev. ed. London: Penguin Books, 1961.

Aldred, Cyril. *Egypt to the End of the Old Kingdom.* London: Thames and Hudson, 1965.

THE MIDDLE KINGDOM

Hayes, William C. "The Middle Kingdom in Egypt: Internal History from The Rise of the Heracleopolitans to the Death of Ammenemes III." *Cambridge Ancient History,* rev. ed., fasc. 3. Cambridge: Cambridge University Press, 1961.

Hayes, William C. "Egypt: From the Death of Ammenemes III to Seqenenre II." *Cambridge Ancient History,* rev. ed., fasc. 6. Cambridge: Cambridge University Press, 1962.

Clère, J. J. "Histoire des XIe et XIIe Dynasties Égyptiennes." *Journal of World History* 1 (1954):643–68.

Badawy, Alexander. A *History of Egyptian Architecture: The First Intermediate Period, the Middle Kingdom, and the Second Intermediate Period.* Berkeley and Los Angeles: University of California Press, 1966.

Van Seters, John. *The Hyksos: A New Investigation.* New Haven: Yale University Press, 1966.

THE NEW KINGDOM

Hayes, William C. "Egypt: Internal Affairs from Tuthmosis I to the Death of Amenophis III." *Cambridge Ancient History*, rev. ed., fasc. 10. Cambridge: Cambridge University Press, 1962.

Redford, Donald B. *History and Chronology of the Eighteenth Dynasty of Egypt: Seven Studies*. Toronto: University of Toronto Press, 1967.

Nims, Charles F. *Thebes of the Pharaohs: Pattern for Every City*. New York: Stein & Day, 1965.

Mekhitarian, Arpag. *Egyptian Painting*. Geneva: Skira, 1954.

Aldred, Cyril. *Akhenaten, Pharaoh of Egypt: A New Study*. London: Thames and Hudson, 1968.

Desroches-Noblecourt, Christiane. *Tutankhamen: Life and Death of a Pharaoh*. New York: New York Graphic Society, 1963.

Faulkner, R. O. "Egypt: From the Inception of the Nineteenth Dynasty to the Death of Ramesses III." *Cambridge Ancient History*, rev. ed., fasc. 52. Cambridge: Cambridge University Press, 1966.

Černy, Jaroslav. "Egypt: From the Death of Ramesses III to the End of the Twenty-first Dynasty." *Cambridge Ancient History*, rev. ed., fasc. 27. Cambridge: Cambridge University Press, 1965.

Gardiner, Sir Alan H. *The Kadesh Inscriptions of Ramesses II*. Oxford: Oxford University Press, 1960.

Caminos, Ricardo. *Late-Egyptian Miscellanies*. London: Oxford University Press, 1954.

Wente, Edward F. *Late Ramesside Letters*. Chicago: University of Chicago Press, 1967.

Peet, T. Eric. *The Great Tomb-robberies of the Twentieth Egyptian Dynasty*, 2 vols. Oxford: Clarendon Press, 1930.

Badawy, Alexander. *A History of Egyptian Architecture: The Empire (the New Kingdom)*. Berkeley and Los Angeles: University of California Press, 1968.

THE LATER DYNASTIES

von Zeissl, H. *Äthiopen und Assyrer in Ägypten*. Glückstadt: J. J. Augustin, 1955.

Kienitz, Frederich Karl. *Die Politische Geschichte Ägyptens vom 7 bis zum 4. Jahrhundert vor der Zeitwende*. Berlin: Akademie-Verlag, 1953.

Elgood, Percival George. *Later Dynasties of Egypt*. Oxford: Blackwell, 1951.

Gyles, Mary Francis. *Pharaonic Policies and Administration, 663 to 323 B.C.* Chapel Hill: University of North Carolina Press, 1959.

Bothmer, Bernard V., comp. *Egyptian Sculpture of the Late Period, 700 B.C. to A.D. 100*. Brooklyn: The Brooklyn Museum, 1960.

INDEX

Abu Simbel, 261, 278
Abydos, 194, 206, 208, 211f., 237, 249, 278
Acheulian assemblage, 7
Adab, 51, 62f.
Adad-guppi, 128, 147–49
Adad-nirari III, 129f.
Admonitions of Ipuwer, The, 239
agriculture, 19, 28, 43, 188; agricultural revolution, 11–15, 28
Ahab, 126–28
Ahaz, 136f., 140, 144
Ahmose of Thebes, 192f., 252; expulsion of Hyksos, 192, 252–55, 260; reunification of Egypt, 255
Ahmose, son of Ebana, 191, 260
Aka, 45f.
Akhenaten, 268ff., 276; religious and political policies of, 257; religious revolution of, 268ff.
Akhetaten (now Amarna), 270–73
Akkad, 24, 60ff., 77f., 114f., 174, 215; arts of, 62f.; collapse of, 66; culture of, 24, 54; literature of, 48, 62, 155, 165f.
Akkadian language, 17, 24, 62, 108, 152–54, 178
Alexander the Great, 190, 297f.
alphabet, 112, 157
Amarna heretics, 194f., 275f.
Amasis, 294f.
Amorites, 24, 36, 71ff., 79, 81, 84, 86, 88–92, 97, 153, 251, 256
amphictyonic league, 39
Amun, cult of, 269, 276, 293; "god's state of Amun," 277, 288f.; priesthood of, 283, 286f., 289
Amunemhet I, 192, 244ff.; innovations in regency and in state structure, 245

Amunhotpe III, called "the Magnificent," 267f.
Amunhotpe IV, *see* Akhenaten
Amunhotpe, son of Hapu, 268f.
Amurru, 24, 45, 56, 71f., 274
Amyrtaeus, 296
An (god), 44, 59, 170f.
animals, domestication of, 11, 14f.
Anatolia, 15, 17, 34, 54, 56, 94, 110, 130, 182, 229; Cappadocia, *see* Cappadocia; Hittite kingdom in, 96, 105f., 229, 255f., 274f., 278ff.
Anitta, 95f., 105
Anshan, 87, 93
Arabian Nights, The, 167
Aramaeans, 120, 124, 129, 141, 144
Aramaic language, 124, 131, 152, 178
Aramaic script, 144, 154, 178, 296
architecture: niched, 189, 207, 209; of solar temples, 272; ziggurats, 78f., 108, 114, 147; *see also* pyramids
archival texts, 48, 155; *see also* cuneiform texts
archives: Egyptian, 248, 256; Hittite, 110–12, 169, 274f., 280
Arsacids (Parthians), 143, 154
Assur (god), 115, 171
Assur (city), 87, 93, 96, 113ff., 143, 171, 181
Assurbanipal, 141–43, 291–93; library of, at Nineveh, 141, 147, 181; sack of Thebes, 291
Assyria, 56, 93, 95, 113–17, 124–45, 174, 179–83, 256, 291–93; ascendancy of, 124ff.; and Babylonia, 93, 101, 108, 114f., 116f., 129f., 137, 139, 141–45, 293f.; collapse of, 143; consolidation of Neo-Assyrian empire, 131ff.; emergence of, 113ff.; Great Revolt in, 129; literature of,

311

city-state, 173; institutional patterns of, 174; king and, 174ff.; priesthood and, 175, 177f.; religious organization and, 175; *see also* kingship

government officials and administration (Egyptian), 229f., 234, 237, 247f., 261, 277, 282f; *see also* nomes and nomarchs, viziers and vizierate

Great Kingdom of the West, 289ff.

Greece and Greek culture, 34, 110, 117ff., 144, 154, 190

Gudea, 68, 72, 79

guilds, 167, 177

Gulkishar, 106

Gutian Period, 66–68

Gutians, 63, 66, 72, 77

Hamath, 127, 136, 138f.

Hammurapi, 38, 57, 100ff., 116n., 174, 182; foreign policies of, 101f.; reunification of Mesopotamia, 101f.; and rise of Babylon, 101

Harkhuf, 191, 231f.

Harran, 143, 147ff.

"Harrow," 40

Hathor (goddess), 204, 206

Hatshepsut, 194, 243, 251, 254, 257, 261–64

Hattic culture, 94, 96, 105

Hattina, 120, 127

Hazael, 128f., 132

Hebrews, 55n., 74f., 113; *see also* Bible, Israel, Judah, Palestine

Herakleopolis, 206, 237f.; struggle with Thebes, 192, 238f., 241–44

"heretic" rulers of Amarna, 194f., 275f.

Herodotus, 147, 224, 292, 294f.

Hezekiah, 140–42

Hierakonpolis, 203, 206, 212

hieroglyphics, Egyptian, 189f., 196f., 288; Hittite, 111, 124

Hittites, 94, 109ff., 120, 123, 281; kingdom of, in Anatolia, 96, 105f., 229, 255f., 274, 278ff.; language of, 17, 124; writing of, 111, 124

homo sapiens, 8f.

Horemheb, 256, 275f.

horses, 111

Horus (god), 193, 202–04, 206, 211f., 217

Hrihor, 283, 286

Hurrians, 66, 74, 109ff., 120; *see also* Cilicia, Mitanni

Hyksos, 250ff.; domination of Egypt, 251; expulsion of, by Thebes, 192, 251f., 255, 260

Hymn to the Nile, The, 277

Iakini, house of, 145f.

Ibbi-Sin, 57, 75, 84–87, 95, 165

Ice Age, 5, 7

Ilushuma, 93

Imhotep, 218, 220, 229, 235

Inanna (goddess), 44f., 55, 59, 78, 164, 171f.

Instruction for Merikare, The, 239–41, 257

Instruction of Amunemhet, The, 246, 277

Instructions of Ptahhotpe, The, 257

Iran, 44, 50f., 54, 180

Iraq, 35, 183

iron, 123

Iron Age, 123ff.

irrigation, 28, 78, 92f., 187, 209, 243, 268

Ishbi-Irra, 86–88

Ishtar (goddess), 55, 60, 114, 163, 171

Isin, 86–93, 100, 102, 120

Israel, 120, 123–43, 175; conflicts with Assyria, 127f., 130, 132f., 136f.

Jemdet Nasr, 28n., 29, 35

Jericho, 15f., 18n., 34

Josiah, 140, 143

Jotham, 132, 136f.

Judah, 127–30, 132–40, 142f., 178; Assyria and, 133, 136, 139f., 142f., Babylonian conquest of, 147; religious reforms in, 140, 143

Kadesh, Battle of, 196, 255, 264, 278f.

Kalah, 125, 130, 132, 143, 181

Urukagina, 50, 53, 57, 80
Utu-hegal, 77f., 165

viziers and vizierate, 41, 229–31, 249,
  266; *see also* sages

Weny, 191, 229; biography of, 228,
  231
Window of Appearances, 272f.
wisdom literature, 83, 166f., 170, 197,
  217
Wooing of Inanna, The, 164
writing: Aramaic, 144, 154, 178, 296;

Egyptian, 189f., 196f., 288; Hittite
hieroglyphics, 111, 124; invention
of, 5, 23f., 27, 29, 33f., 151; West
Semitic, 154; *see also* cuneiform
writing

Xoite dynasty, 249–51

Yamhad, 100
Yaubidi, 138f.

ziggurats, 78f., 108, 114, 147